לחנן גרינפילד,

בהערכה רבה על הסיוע
בתרגום והוצאת ספרי באנגלית.
מקווה שקריאת הספר, תועיל
למדינת ישראל ועם ישראל.

בברכה,

מ. יעלון

The Longer, Shorter Path

Moshe "Bogie" Ya'alon

Translated by

Jessica Setbon

Jerusalem 2020/5780

Cover Design: Benjie Herskowitz
Typesetting: Optume Technologies
ISBN: 978-965-7023-00-6
1 3 5 7 9 8 6 4 2

Gefen Publishing House Ltd.
6 Hatzvi Street
Jerusalem 9438614,
Israel
972-2-538-0247
orders@gefenpublishing.com

Gefen Books
C/o 3PL Center
3003 Woodbridge Ave.
Edison, NJ 08837
516-593-1234
orders@gefenpublishing.com

www.gefenpublishing.com
Printed in Israel

Library of Congress Control Number:12019914262

To my comrades in arms, my soldiers and my commanders – those who are with us, and those who have fallen along the way –
may we be worthy of their sacrifice!

CONTENTS

Foreword
By Amotz Asa-El

Moshe "Bogie" Ya'alon did not dream of a military career. In fact, as a young paratrooper he even turned down his commander's request that he attend the IDF Officer Training School, choosing instead to complete his regular service as a sergeant and become a pioneering farmer.

Ya'alon therefore proceeded to Kibbutz Grofit in the arid Arava Valley north of the Red Sea, where he was operating bulldozers and helping build a farm when an external event changed the course of his life.

The event was the 1973 Yom Kippur War, whose shock to Israeli society made the twenty-three-year-old kibbutznik change his mind about a military career, not because he felt he needed one, but because his conclusion from the war – in which he fought on both banks of the Suez Canal – was that the IDF needed him.

Ya'alon's military career thus started off very differently from those of most other generals, whose long decades in uniform were not interrupted by civilian years. In this regard, Ya'alon's spontaneous career change brings to mind Roman general Cincinnatus, who emerged from his farm to lead the defeat of a foreign invasion, and also the biblical Saul and Gideon, farmers who were called to lead ancient Israel's wars, one while herding his cattle, the other while beating his freshly harvested wheat.

Ya'alon's successive promotions in the military – rising within less than two decades from lieutenant to general through key positions such as commander of the elite Sayeret Matkal (General Staff Reconnaissance Unit) and commander of the Paratroopers Brigade – were remarkable enough, but this is the résumé that in Israel is expected from every senior military commander.

Likewise expected is the mettle Ya'alon displayed throughout his military decades, most famously when he led the operation on Palestinian arch-terrorist Khalil el-Wazir, better known as "Abu Jihad," in a Tunisian villa fourteen hundred miles (2,300 km) from Israel. The courage Ya'alon displayed in this operation is obviously impressive, but he would be the first to insist that his colleagues, in that operation as in many others, were equally brave.

The same is true of the operational complexity that such a raid involved, deploying simultaneously – in that case – missile frigates, a submarine, airborne electronic warfare, a team of Mossad spies, and of course the commando warriors whom Ya'alon, then a colonel, led from enemy shores to their target and back. Such complicated planning and meticulous execution have been demonstrated repeatedly throughout the IDF's history, involving over the decades hundreds of IDF commanders.

What sets Ya'laon apart from other generals, not only in Israel but in all of military history, is the daunting task he faced when he assumed command of the IDF in 2002, at the height of that decade's Palestinian assault on the Israeli home front, and the role he played in its defeat.

By sheer coincidence, Ya'alon became deputy chief of General Staff in September 2000, twelve days before the outbreak of the Second Intifada. By the time of his appointment as chief of General Staff two years later, the raging confrontation that was underscored by 150 suicide attacks as well as hundreds of bombings, stabbings, and drive-by shootings throughout Israel was at its peak.

By the time Ya'alon left the IDF in 2005, Israel had won the war.

The war that cost 1,056 Israeli lives posed a challenge no modern army had previously faced: namely, the targeting of the civilian population by terrorists emerging from within and hiding behind their own population. The soft-spoken Ya'alon was the unsung hero at the heart of Israel's victory.

Displaying poise, originality, and resilience while civilians were killed week in and week out in buses, malls, restaurants, and cafés, Ya'alon inspired the IDF's increasingly innovative and systematic counterattack, which demanded new weaponry, undercover units, and inventive methods, such as the targeted killing, which brought together for the first time in military history the combat pilot and the secret agent.

Ruling that conventional war was making way for what came to be called low-intensity warfare, Ya'alon rearranged the IDF's resources, shrinking its armored and artillery corps, adding special units that the new battlefield demanded, and building from scratch military schools for anti-terror warfare, all of which is now being studied and copied by dozens of armies worldwide.

Ya'alon will therefore go down in history not only as the general who led Israel to victory in what Israelis now call the War of the Suicides, but also as a shaper of the post–conventional warfare that this century's Islamist terrorism demands.

The unconventional way in which Ya'alon's military career began and culminated was replayed in his transition to civilian life.

In a country where newly discharged generals commonly sign fat consultancy contracts, Ya'alon made the unusual move of joining a Judaic studies think tank in Jerusalem, Beit Morasha, as its chairman.

For the secularly raised Ya'alon, it was a fitting prelude to the political career he would launch three years later. Coupled with fellowships at the Washington Institute for Near East Policy and the Shalem Center in

Jerusalem, where he expanded his expertise in strategic affairs, Ya'alon prepared for his second career by studying Israel's civilian challenges, an effort that, nearly fifteen years on, has yet to abate.

During seven years as a lawmaker and minister, and another three as leader of his own movement and co-leader of the Blue and White Party, Ya'alon has studied Israel's social, economic, and cultural problems more thoroughly than most politicians, not to mention most retired generals.

The consequent systemic approach to Israel's historic problems was reflected in Ya'alon's treatment, as defense minister, of Israel's military spending. Taking stock of the annual cockfights between the Treasury and Defense Ministry over the military's share in the national budget, and realizing the wrangling was harmful not only for the military, but also for the national interest, Ya'alon devised with the Treasury a multi-annual budgeting formula that prevented the fiscal time bomb's annual explosion.

Ya'alon has since expanded this systemic thinking to other fields, devising long-term plans for overhauling Israel's health services, public school network, and mass transit systems.

Judging by the imprint he has left on Israel's security in particular, and on military history in general, it would be wise to follow Moshe Ya'alon as he sets out to tackle Israel's domestic challenges. Like his military stamp, his civilian impact might emerge undetected, only to later prove impossible to erase.

Preface

After I resigned from the government and the Knesset, I decided to run for national leadership. I traveled around the country to speak to different cross-sections of the public: right- and left-wing voters, religious and secular Israelis, new immigrants and long-time citizens, young and old alike. One of the responses that I often hear at the end of a meeting is, "Wow, we never really knew you before." Often, people seeing me for the first time in person, say, "You're thinner and taller." I tell them that the television screen makes me look shorter and fatter. With all due respect, that's not the only distortion that the media creates.

I learned from these meetings that people don't always understand my outlook and opinions. I met people who thought I was a right-wing extremist, even a fanatic. Others who met me after my resignation thought I was a left-winger. This kind of black-and-white classification is problematic. People are influenced by image, but my viewpoints are complex and multifaceted. In politics I am a hawk, Mr. Security. In the economic realm I believe in a free market economy and competition, but from a compassionate worldview.

My main issue of disagreement with the prime minister and some coalition members is the ideological basis of the State of Israel as a Jewish and democratic state. Unfortunately, people tend to split politicians into two groups. Either they are right-wing, violent extremists from the dark side, or they are left-wing troublemakers, traitorous bleeding hearts. This makes it hard to understand the real me.

After a ninety-minute meeting with me, people understand that I'm not what they thought I was. But that's not enough. Ninety minutes is not enough time to touch upon all the important issues and the challenges that the State of Israel will face in the visible future. I also cannot convey the experience that I have accumulated over many years in military service, whether in uniform or plainclothes.

The Israeli political system is based on three hubs of power: wealth, the ruling regime, and the press. I am at a disadvantage because I've never owned my own newspaper or television station. While I served as minister, I was limited in the use of the social networks, which requires funding. This has made it even more difficult to present my views and protect myself from attacks by politicians and their underlings, who try to harm my political status by various methods.

These are my reasons for writing this book, which is targeted to anyone who cares about the State of Israel. I feel that it is my privilege and obligation to convey my experiences to the readers. When I wrote the first edition of this book in 2008, I learned that the very act of committing ideas to writing sharpens and clarifies the content. That is why I persevered.

I wrote the first edition of this book after completing my IDF service. It was important to me to put my thoughts down on paper, and especially my conclusions.

The course of my life, from my IDF service in 1968 until I completed my position as chief of GENERAL STAFF (COGS) in 2005, led me to situations and events that influenced the State of Israel in the past and will continue to do so in the future. Throughout this period, I found myself in close proximity to the decision-making junctures of the state. This experience began when I served as Judea-Samaria division commander in 1992–1993. It was followed by participation in cabinet meetings after I was appointed chief of the Military Intelligence Directorate (Aman) in June 1995, and it ended with my stint as COGS in June 2005. All these positions offered me a unique perspective on extremely significant processes, mainly on the Israeli-Palestinian track. Military service also provided a rare perspective on the Jewish nation, especially the younger generation as they are drafted into the IDF and cope with the challenges of regular military service and reserve duty.

I was troubled by the insights I accumulated over the years. I felt that it was incumbent on me to share them with the Jewish people or, to be more precise, with those who value the Zionist enterprise and appreciate the importance of a Jewish national home. I was uneasy to discover, in my recent years of service, that my perceptions have not been properly expressed in the Israeli public discourse. This discourse has been greatly affected by interests of elites and pressure groups, a culture of ratings and spin, and in recent years, the "likes" and "trolls" that have fanned the flames.

This is also how I felt after my years as minister, cabinet member, and Knesset member in the State of Israel. In the seven years that I was closely involved in security issues, I accumulated additional experience and insights in the diplomatic, defense, and political realms, as well as in other spheres. This gave me the opportunity to update the previous chapters in my book and add new ones.

My book is not the result of historical research. Rather, this is my personal, subjective vantage point on events and processes as they were taking place. The book reflects my interpretation of these events, sometimes after the fact. My main goal is to convince the reader that my interpretation explains the events that we experienced, mainly since the beginning of the 1990s, in a more convincing, complete way than other interpretations.

I believe in the importance of the Jewish national home – the State of Israel. I am concerned about the future of this home, yet I believe that the Jewish people still have the ability to guard and strengthen it.

In this book I share my perspective with the citizens of Israel, as public opinion has great importance in a democratic state. I have learned that diplomatic and military leadership cannot function without the nation's support, and that is for the good. I hope that my book will inspire deep thinking in the entire Israeli public, with its wide spectrum of opinions, and contribute to serious discussion on the issues involved.

The Second Lebanon War was fought while I was writing the introductory chapters of the first edition of this book. This was the first war in Israel in which I did not participate, since becoming an adult. However, I was involved in the IDF's preparations for this war, and I was well informed about the challenge posed to us on the Lebanese front in the summer of 2006, so I added my analysis of that war to my book.

I never thought of writing an autobiography that would include stories of battles and heroism. It is not in my nature to write about myself; instead, I have always preferred that my actions speak for themselves. However, Rami Tal, editor of the first edition of the book, and Dov Eichenwald, CEO of Yedioth Books, convinced me to spice up my analyses with personal vignettes. This was to reveal more of myself to the reader, as well as to include examples that demonstrate the development of my analyses and assessments.

By the time I finished writing, I felt that my book had more stories than I had intended. Nevertheless, it is not an autobiography. I did not mention all the wars, battles, and military actions in which I participated, nor all the experiences I accumulated in my life. However, I hope that despite the personal stories, I have not deviated from one of my most important principles: "Walk humbly."

At every intersection in my life, I've chosen to assume responsibility. I did so when I decided to live in the Arava in southern Israel after my mandatory military service and when I decided to return to permanent army service following the Yom Kippur War. I did so when I joined the officers' training course and as I continued in the military up to the role of COGS. Finally, I did so when I entered the world of politics, where the truly crucial decisions are made. Even after I concluded that I must resign from the government and the Knesset, I knew that I would not shirk my responsibility. Ironically, the crisis that led me to resign was the reason I decided to continue to assume responsibility and aspire to national leadership.

The crisis that developed may appear to be one of personal relationships and a personal settling of accounts. Clearly, that is how my opponents try to present it. But the truth is that this crisis developed gradually over the years and resulted from what I believe is the crossing of red lines: by the government, by certain elements in the coalition and the Likud Party under Prime Minister Benjamin Netanyahu, who bears overall responsibility. The crisis developed gradually because the Likud after the 2013 elections was very different than the Likud I had joined in 2009. This was even more pronounced following the 2015 elections. To me, this difference of vision was a matter of principle, based on my view of the Likud and how it should operate. It also stemmed from my concept of the role of Israel's leadership in molding a future in which Israel maintains its values and becomes the model society to which its founders aspired.

The crisis developed gradually. I was a Knesset member and a minister, member of the Likud Party and of the coalition government. My dilemma was how to address what I saw as a crisis. Should I do it from inside the system, or from outside? Even when the negative incidents multiplied, I continued to handle them from inside the system. Many people ask me why I didn't resign immediately. I knew that politics always involves compromises – until the moment when red lines were crossed, and I understood that I could be more influential by resigning than by remaining a minister.

The crisis that raised red flags for me was the naval vessels deal in February 2016. Even then, after I averted the deal, I still did not have the entire picture regarding the involvement of the prime minister and his entourage. I only found out about that later. I sensed that something was amiss, but I had no proof. I continued my work as minister out of my desire to continue to protect national values and interests as I viewed them. I followed this worldview in preventing the naval vessel deal and in the debate surrounding the actions of soldier Elor Azaria, who shot an incapacitated terrorist in Hebron. I continued this course during the debate surrounding the rule of law. I thought that my contribution would be greater if I continued to serve as defense minister than if I would resign from the government.

But in the final days of my tenure, when I realized that others wanted to oust me, I decided to beat them to it and resign. I felt strongly that the prime minister's trajectory was inappropriate, for numerous reasons: issues of integrity and morality, crossing red lines on ethical issues, and his maneuverings against those he called "elites that don't allow [me] to rule." In fact, Netanyahu was threatening the checks and balances system vital to Israel's democracy. It is difficult to explain these subjects to the public, particularly due to the manipulations of the prime minister and his supporters in response to my harsh criticism of the government's functioning.

This book is not about revenge or payback, as my opponents claim. I am not a person who settles scores. But I could not avoid personal criticism of certain individuals, sometimes even severe criticism. Everything I have written is designed to help us learn from successes and failures, from correct and incorrect behavior of people around me. I am doing this is for the future of the State of Israel, and I hope that my readers will view my criticism through this lens.

I thank the administration of the Shalem Center for encouraging me to write the first edition of this book and then supporting me in my efforts. I received much help and advice from the center, especially from its president, Dr. Daniel Polisar, who also read my draft and gave me excellent advice and comments. The writing of the new edition of the book was made possible by the Institute for National Security Studies (INSS) and its head, Major General (Ret.) Amos Yadlin.

My thanks to Ari Shavit, whose discussions contributed significantly to the writing of the first edition; Anat Shinkman Ben-Ze'ev, who was of great help to me in writing this book; and to Yoav Keren, editor of this edition, whose wise comments were very helpful.

I thank my anonymous friends who agreed to read the draft and write comments. Of course, the responsibility for the final version is mine alone.

I express my gratitude to the team at Yedioth Books for their work on the original Hebrew edition of this book: CEO Dov Eichenwald, who orchestrated the project, dispensed wise advice from his vast experience, and gave me excellent staff. I thank Rami Tal, editor of the Hebrew version, who convinced me to describe my motives behind my actions, so as to convince the reader (and himself first). Tal's knowledge and experience contributed a great deal. Kudos to Kuti Tepper and the members of his production team, and especially Keren Sitbon-Hamou.

I would also like to thank the entire staff of Gefen Publishing House of Jerusalem for their tireless and professional work preparing the manuscript for publication in English. Particularly, CEO Ilan Greenfield identified the value of my words for the English-speaking world and encouraged me to publish an English edition. Translator Jessica Setbon took on the challenge of transforming the Hebrew into smooth English and adapting the manuscript to a non-Israeli audience. Project Manager Daphne Abrahams orchestrated the production of a worthy finished product that I can proudly present as my book.

And last but not least, I thank my lovely wife Ada, who supported the writing of the book with her comments on style and content. We walk together, hand in hand, the whole way.

PART I
Origins

CHAPTER 1

EARLY LIFE

While I was serving as deputy chief of general staff (DCOGS), I participated in a meeting with Ehud Barak, who was then prime minister and defense minister. I looked around me and suddenly realized that except for the prime minister, all the participants in the discussion had grown up in Kiryat Haim: chief of Military Intelligence Major General Amos Malka; GOC Central Command Major General Yitzchak (Itzik) Eitan; Coordinator of Government Activities in the Territories Major General Amos Gilad; Defense Ministry director Major General (Ret.) Ilan Biran; and myself, deputy chief of general staff. All of us hail from Kiryat Haim. At that moment I asked myself, what was so special about Kiryat Haim that inspired us all to become such take-charge adults? What led us to understand that we were faced with a major mission and that we had to assume responsibility for it?

I was born in 1950 in Kiryat Haim. My mother was a Holocaust survivor, my father a production laborer in the Shemen oil factory. We lived in a typical apartment complex for veterans of Mapai (center-left precursor of the Labor Party): tile roof, small courtyard, vegetable plot.

Everyone wore simple clothing, everyone read *Davar* newspaper. A good life, but modest. Very modest.

My father David immigrated to Israel in 1925 from Kremenchuk in the Ukraine. He was fifteen when his parents decided to make aliyah after one of his brothers was murdered on the Dnieper, on his way home from the Politechnikum where he had registered for college. My Uncle Yosef was murdered at age eighteen because he was a Jew. At first, the family lived in Jerusalem. Then they moved to the Chalisa neighborhood in Haifa and from there to Kiryat Motzkin, where they were among the first to settle. My father never had the opportunity to attend high school, but he was an autodidact who accumulated broad knowledge. He served in the Haganah and then in the Jewish Brigade of the British military. When I was a child, he worked shifts at the Shemen factory. I remember that he would leave home on the first bus from the neighborhood at ten to five in the morning so that he would arrive to work by six a.m. In the summer, he always wore short khaki pants and an undershirt at home. Father was an admirer of Ben-Gurion and a faithful supporter of Haifa's mayor, Abba Chushi. During his leisure time he would sit beside the radio, read a book, or solve crossword puzzles with great expertise.

My mother Batya grew up in Zolkiew in Galicia (then part of Poland). In 1939, when she was eighteen, her parents realized that the situation would get very bad, and they encouraged her to run away and escape. She listened to them and spent the war years on her own. To this day I don't know exactly where she went or what she did. I do know that she was never in the concentration camps because she joined the partisans in the forests. After the war ended, she found herself alone. Her parents and sisters had all perished. Not one remained; everything was wiped out. In 1946 she arrived in the Land of Israel (Palestine) despite the British ban on immigration, and a short time later she married Father, who was ten years older than her. At first, they lived in my grandfather's home in Kiryat Motzkin. Later they bought a house in Kiryat Haim, where they raised their three children: my older sister Yaffa (Yafik), who was born during the War of Independence; myself, born two years later; and my younger brother, Tzviki, of blessed memory, who was born two years after me.

It never occurred to me at the time that we were poor, but Mother would send me to the store to buy black bread instead of white because the white bread cost a penny more. We ate zucchini salad, mock chopped liver made from zucchini, zucchini compote, and even zucchini jam, because that was the cheapest vegetable. We bathed only once a week. Our clothes were passed down from one child to the other. Shoes had to serve us for several years, so they were always too big or too small. Nothing was wasted in Mother's thrifty household; nothing was thrown away. Mother would sew clothing for us from sugar sacks, for example. Everything was used for maximum efficiency.

Mother did not talk about the Holocaust. There was only silence about the past, but somehow, we understood. Mother and Father always tried to convey the message that we should be good children, and study hard and help build the state. After everything that had happened, we must work to build the State of Israel. But it was mainly Mother who pushed us to get an education. She wanted us to get ahead, so we should become engineers or scientists. We must take advantage of the opportunities that she never had. So even though I was a mischievous kid, I was also a very good pupil. Education was valued above everything, and my parents never stinted on education.

Kiryat Haim was a politically homogeneous neighborhood. Almost everyone around me voted for the same party (Mapai) and were members of the same labor union (Histadrut). Even my childhood interest in music was colored by the political atmosphere. In second grade, I played the recorder, at nine I joined an orchestra as a piccolo player and soon switched to the clarinet. As a teenager I played the clarinet in the Haifa youth orchestra, and we performed in the First of May parades, waving red flags and playing the Soviet "Internationale" anthem. On Israel's Independence Day, I accompanied the marches organized by Mayor Abba Chushi on Herzl Street. Our family was an inseparable part of "Red" Haifa and the Krayot, the workers' neighborhoods outside Haifa – a diehard socialist community. Our lives were very modest and disciplined, but also full of joy and infused with great hope.

The first military event of my life was the 1956 Sinai War. I was six years old, and suddenly we had to dig a shelter in the small yard, darken the windows, and fill sacks with sand. Everyone was worried about a possible enemy assault, by air or by sea. Fear dominated the atmosphere. It was the first time I understood that Israel was constantly threatened by war and enemies who endangered my world. But after the Sinai campaign, the first victory album appeared on the shelf with photographs of paratroopers entrenched at Mitla Pass, and life was relatively quiet. True, the 1960s saw reprisals and conflict with the Syrians over water and the demilitarized territories in the north. My friends and I knew the time would come when we would be recruited to fight for the state. But our direction for mobilization was the settlement enterprise rather than the army. The youth movement hammered us into shape and prepared us for serious challenges, but our leaders spoke about going to work on kibbutz, not joining the military.

Nevertheless, I prepared myself for the draft. Until eleventh grade I was a chunky kid and a slow runner, but then I understood that I had to take myself in hand. I started to train and run simply out of self-discipline, and within a year I was the first in my class to cross the finish line. I think the values I absorbed in the Krayot instilled in me this self-discipline and ability to overcome weaknesses.

Those of us from Kiryat Haim were on the same page. We shared the sense of immense commitment to a great dream. Something very special was taking place, and we were all part of it. It was in the air, in the sand, in the people, though no one talked about it directly. In the equilibrium between the needs of our society and the needs of the individual, the emphasis was definitely on Israeli society. That is how we grew up. It was taken for granted. The silent but threatening background of the Holocaust and the Labor movement's legacy of pioneering spirit merged together into a tight, strong network of values. This network did not prevent us from being happy and living a very rich life, or even acting like rowdy teenagers sometimes. It didn't stop us from watching films, going to concerts, and spending entire summers on the beach. But it placed our lives in a very clear context: we were here to build a state. True, the state already existed, but we were still helping to form it. Each and every one of us had a role to play, a mission to undertake. Our private lives could not be completely disconnected from Israeli society as a whole. If the society as a whole faced a conflict, then we all had to join forces in that struggle. We all would do whatever was necessary to win.

I was at the end of eleventh grade when the Six-Day War broke out. Again, we dug shelters, filled sacks with sand, and darkened our windows. We did agricultural work for Kfar Bialik farmers who were called up for reserve duty. But we felt that we were missing out – if only we'd been two years older, we would have been drafted, too, and we could have contributed far more to the war effort. That was the atmosphere in Kiryat Haim. The emphasis was not on militarism, but on sacrificing ourselves for the general public; we aimed to serve not the individual, but the entire society. I learned this at home, in kindergarten and school, and in the youth movement. We were here for a reason. We were here because after everything that had happened, we were building the state.

My parents, but especially my mother, were disappointed when I chose kibbutz life. She had hoped that I would be an engineer or a doctor, not a kibbutznik. My parents sympathized with the settlement project and the movement's values, but only up to a point. The main thing for the children of a Jewish mother was to get an education and achieve. After the Yom Kippur War, when I decided to remain in the regular military, I was afraid to tell my mother. I was sure she'd tell me, "That's not the way to do it. If you're going to leave the kibbutz, you should go study and advance." But to my surprise, she congratulated me! She had wanted me to study and become a professional, but she accepted the fact that I wanted to join the army because that was what the state needed. Even though she was a Holocaust survivor who had lost her entire family, then raised a daughter and two sons with enormous effort, she could not turn her back on the state if her children were needed. Like it or not, you do what you have to do. That was the message from my home and from Kiryat Haim.

And that is where I come from.

CHAPTER 2

WHAT WENT WRONG?

I grew up in a home that supported the Haganah (precursor to the IDF) and the Labor movement. Even before I was born, my father had been part of the central stream of the Labor movement, which accepted the partition proposals of 1937 and 1947 and believed in territorial compromise. The worldview on which I was raised was that no piece of land was so holy that it could not be given up. If it was to the benefit of the Jewish people to relinquish some parcel of land, we'd give it up, but we'd never renounce the need to establish a Jewish national home in the Land of Israel. We were willing to fight for that ideal.

There was no fanaticism in my background, only realism. When I grew up, I never negated the rights of anyone to live in Israel – not the rights of the Palestinians nor the rights of others. The Palestinians are human beings, just like us. They also have aspirations, and should their aspirations collide with mine, I must make certain that these do not prevent me from living in my land. No more than that. I grew up in a home and environment in which human life took precedence over land on our scale of values.

After the Six-Day War, and the Yom Kippur War as well, I found the Allon Plan very attractive. This program was formulated by political leader Yigal Allon after the Six-Day War. It offered the Judea and Samaria Arabs an independent entity or one connected to Jordan, while maintaining Israeli sovereignty in the Jordan Valley and the eastern mountain ridge (where the Arab population is sparse), as well as in areas surrounding Jerusalem. I was in IDF uniform, so I didn't share my opinions or dabble in politics. But it was clear to me that in order to return to the 1967 lines, we would have to be reassured that the other side had no intention of continuing the conflict. The '67 borders are very attractive to Israel's enemies; they invite an attack on Israel. Therefore, a hypothetical return to them can only be accomplished when it is completely clear that the conflict is behind us. But I never negated a return to the '67 lines in principle, and therefore I did not oppose the Oslo process. At first, I saw Oslo as an opportunity, but then I sobered up. If I am ever convinced that the current Arab (mainly Palestinian) agenda has changed to one of peace, joint economic development, and coexistence, I would be ready to retreat – even to these most difficult lines. But I believe that we've never been in that situation, and I see no chance that we'll reach it in the near future.

These viewpoints were dominant in the public discourse waged in the Jewish Yishuv before the establishment of the state, and also after its establishment. But the public discourse in the 1990s was defeatist in nature; to a certain extent, it was post-Zionist discourse. The salient argument in this discourse, which still rules today in large swathes of the Israeli public, asserts that "It is possible to put an end to wars." This argument assumes that the State of Israel is the entity that determines whether a war will break out, and that the reason for the wars is Israel's control of Judea and Samaria and other territories that were conquered in the Six-Day War.

But the Iranian hatred for the State of Israel is completely unrelated to Judea and Samaria. The same is true for Hezbollah. Hamas doesn't talk about the '67 borders but about a Palestinian state "from the river to the sea." Yasser Arafat, despite his endless manipulations, never accepted the right of the State of Israel to exist as the nation-state of the Jewish people. So, it is clear as day that the arguments and assumptions of the defeatist discourse are not based on reality. Instead, they are a result of feeling fed up with the conflict, sick and tired of the wars. This weariness leads to an illusion, and the illusion spreads in all directions, because no leadership has dared to call it by name. This illusion has ruled the public atmosphere in previous decades because someone had a vested interest in leading a "no more wars" agenda. Someone wanted to prove that salvation was just around the corner. Israel will just make another few territorial concessions, and everything will be okay. One more capitulation to pressure, and we'll have peace and quiet.

This illusion views 1967 as the most important year in the history of the conflict in the Middle East, and the Israeli-Palestinian conflict as the source of instability in the region. It views resolution of the conflict as the means for stabilizing the entire region. I, on the other hand, view 1979 as the critical year. That was the year when Israel and Egypt signed a peace agreement. Egypt is the largest of the Arab countries, and previously it had led the Pan-Arab ideal (diplomatic, social, and economic unity among the Arab nations and states in the region). The peace agreement dealt a death blow to the Pan-Arab concept, which had begun to fade with the Arab defeat in the Six-Day War. Simultaneously, but in an unrelated development, the Islamic Revolution took place that year in Iran. It gradually changed the conflict in the Middle East from a national conflict to a religious conflict. Since that revolution, we have witnessed the strengthening of Islamic powers that refuse to accept Israel's existence. They view the destruction of Israel as a vital stage toward defeating the West.

Between 1948 and 1979, we enjoyed an upward swing. Israel's victories in the War of Independence, the Sinai campaign, and the Six-Day War convinced the neighboring countries that no military might could defeat us. King Hussein bin Talal of Jordan was the first to realize this, so he became a covert ally of Israel from 1970. President Anwar Sadat understood this soon afterward and tried to reach an agreement with Israel's Prime Minister Golda Meir in 1972, but he was turned down. Following the Yom Kippur War, Sadat made his historic visit to Jerusalem in 1977, which led to the signing of the peace treaty between Israel and Egypt in March 1979. Meanwhile, the Khomeini Revolution in Iran took place in parallel, and began to create an opposing trend, although its significance was only understood twenty years later.

Hezbollah's presence in Lebanon in the early 1980s was not a result of the First Lebanon War as many people think, but a result of the Iranian revolution. Israel did not understand this new threat. It continued to act within the Israeli-Arab and Israeli-Palestinian contexts, which became increasingly less relevant.

The beginning of the internal change in Israeli society was in 1983, when the Israeli public started hitting the streets to demonstrate against the First Lebanon War. Multitudes expressed public anger over the number of Israeli soldiers killed in Lebanon. This was the first crack in Israel's public image as a powerful, cohesive society, and our neighbors began to reassess our resoluteness and staying power. Whether or not that war was justified is an entirely separate question that I will not address here. But clearly, the overall mood that the war created within Israel led us to a significant turning point, a change that continues to affect our security situation and the way we are viewed by the parties in the region. The internal Israeli protests and body counts from the war led to Israel's withdrawal from Lebanon, which in turn was perceived as a sign of weakness. Israel was now viewed as a divided society lacking endurance. Thus, the withdrawal from Lebanon and the Jibril prisoner exchange deal of 1985 led to the First Intifada of 1987. (In the Jibril Agreement, the Israeli government under Shimon Peres released 1,150 security prisoners in exchange for three Israeli prisoners captured during the First Lebanon War.) The First Intifada ultimately led to the Oslo Accord of 1993, which was also viewed as a sign of weakness. Then the Oslo failure, together with the one-sided retreat from Lebanon in May 2000, led to Arafat's terror attacks in September 2000. When the barrier constructed against those attacks fell due to the one-sided withdrawal from Gaza in 2005, the path was paved for the Hamas victory and the Second Lebanon War.

Israel did not understand the significance of the rise of radical Islam, and thus it failed to develop an overarching strategy to address it. Instead of responding with counterattack that would reach outside Israel and involve nonmilitary scenarios, Israel developed a pattern of repetitive withdrawals which fed on the defeatist discourse. This destructive pattern served the short-term interests of the three sources of power in Israeli society: a leadership that does not lead, a media that does not report the truth, and a group of very wealthy people who want quiet, even deceptive quiet, to ensure their maximum profits.

These withdrawals were ostensibly supposed to satisfy the territorial demands of the Arabs, while ignoring the fact that the problem is not territorial but ideological in nature. In fact, Israel was conducting a battle of postponement and retreat from the Zionist endeavor. This is a battle that is very difficult to win, and it continues to endanger the future of the State of Israel.

The Yom Kippur War was the last war in which we were attacked by Arab military forces. Since the peace agreement with Egypt was signed, Israel has not had to face the nationalist, multistate threat of the first thirty years of its existence. But simultaneously with the downfall of the old threat, the new Islamic extremist hazard emerged. Israel is not alone in this battlefield, but it definitely stands on the front lines. Radical Islam has very ambitious goals: to defeat the West and its culture. It plans to defeat the West in stages, and one of the initial stages is to destroy Israel. If, in the past, the Palestinian and nationalist Arabs had a plan in stages for Israel's destruction, today the Israel destruction goal is part of a larger Islamic stages plan, with the goal of imposing radical Islam on the entire world.

The West, and unfortunately certain groups in Israel as well, find it difficult to understand the new threat. They refuse to see how ambitious and how dangerous it really is. For example, people say that Iran is not part of the Arab world and that within Iran itself, the extremists are not the majority. All that is true, yet radical Islam has continued to gather strength over the last four decades. Even though most of the Arab world is Sunni, and murderous Sunni organizations like ISIS (Islamic State) hate Iran no less than they hate the West and Israel, the extremism rooted in the Iranian Revolution is what sets the tone throughout the region. Arab regimes fear Iran, but they lack the power to bring it down.

Many of our neighbors want moderate government policies, perhaps even democracy, but the agenda of the Arab-Muslim world is dictated by radicals. Egypt underwent a revolution and then a counterrevolution, yet its regime is still fighting the Muslim Brotherhood and Islamic State. Syria suffers in the throes of a bloody eight-year civil war that has killed more than half a million human beings. In Iraq, the Shi'ites and Sunnis are still fighting each other, while the Kurds are fighting for their autonomy. Yemen's Sunnis are fighting the Shi'ite Houthis. The problem is not the Israeli-Palestinian conflict, nor the 1967 "occupation." Instead, it is rooted in that strain of radical Islam that has been growing gradually stronger since the winter of 1979.

Today's Middle East is witness to a struggle for hegemony among the three strains of Islamic extremism: Shi'ite Islam led by the Iranian regime, which hopes to "export" the revolution and enlarge its control in

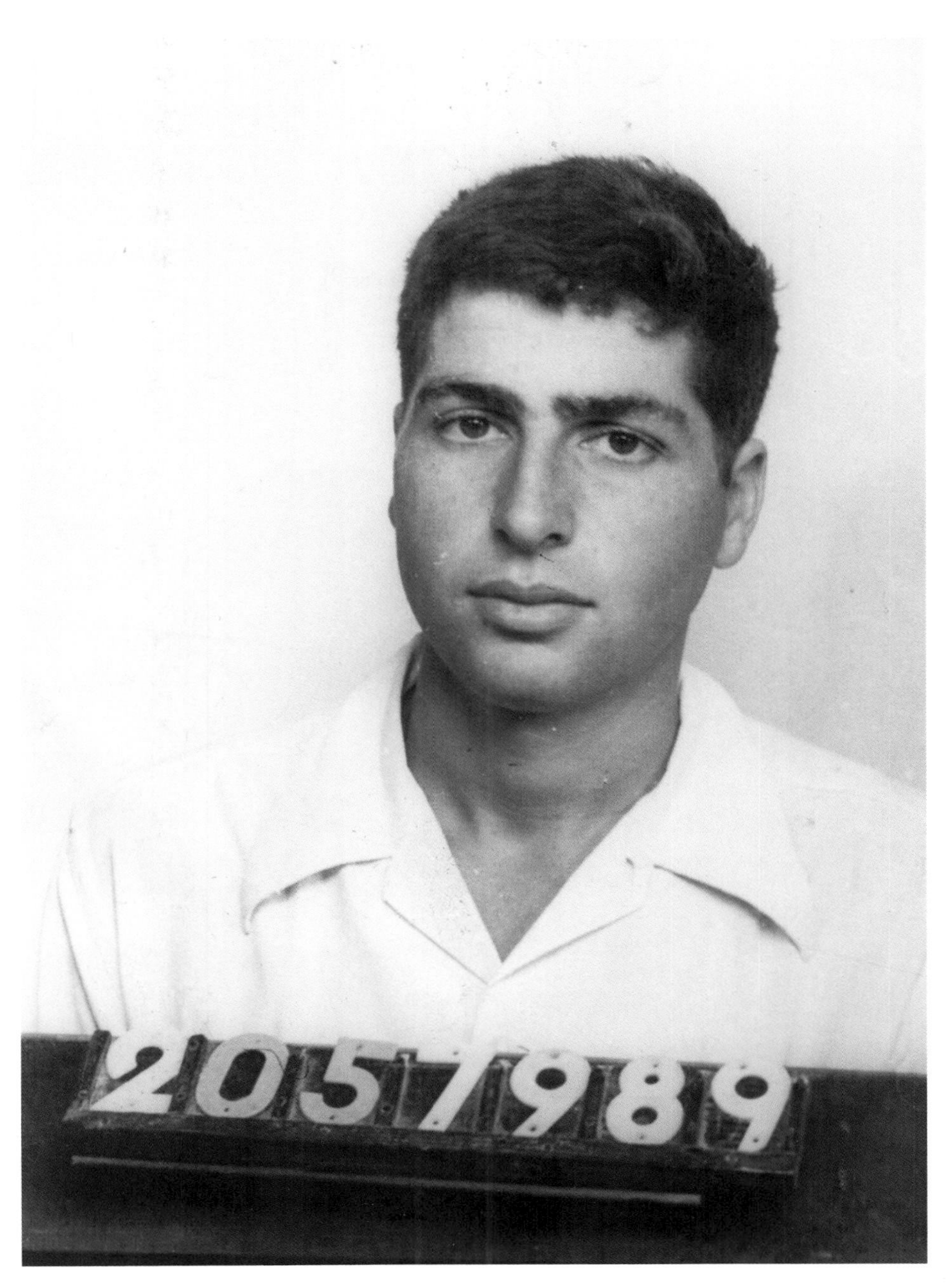

My IDF draft photo with identity number 2057989

Origins – Kiryat Chaim

Top right: my father as a soldier in the Jewish Brigade
Top left: my father
Center (left to right): myself, my brother, and my sister
Bottom right: my mother
Bottom left (top to bottom): my mother, myself, and my sister (wearing clothes made from sugarcane sacks)

Top right: with my father on a trip to Jerusalem
Top left: on a trip to the Negev
Center right: in a class at high school in Kiryat Chaim
Center left: in agriculture class
Bottom left: my uncle as a guard in Kiryat Motzkin

Beginnings in the Nachal

Top left: basic training – waiting to be released for Shabbat
Top right: pre-military service at Kibbutz Grofit
Center right: basic training exercises
Center left: ceremony for completion of squad commanders' course

Bottom left: meeting of my Garin managing committee at Camp 80 base (I am first on the left)

Top: ceremony for completion of officers' training course (I am leading, with the beard)
Center row, right: platoon commander in Battalion 50
Center row, left: with Brigadier General Dan Shomron (left, as chief paratroop and infantry officer) as he affixes rank at completion of officers' training course
Bottom: company commander in Battalion 50

Dad Kibbutznik – Kibbutz Grofit

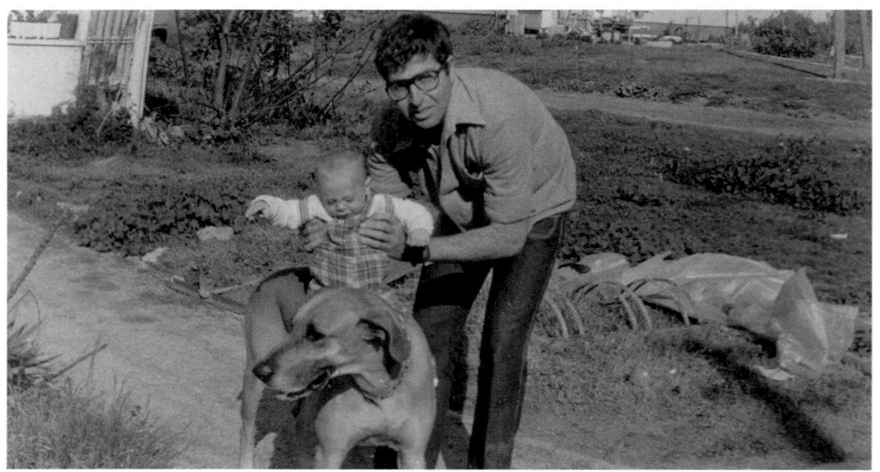

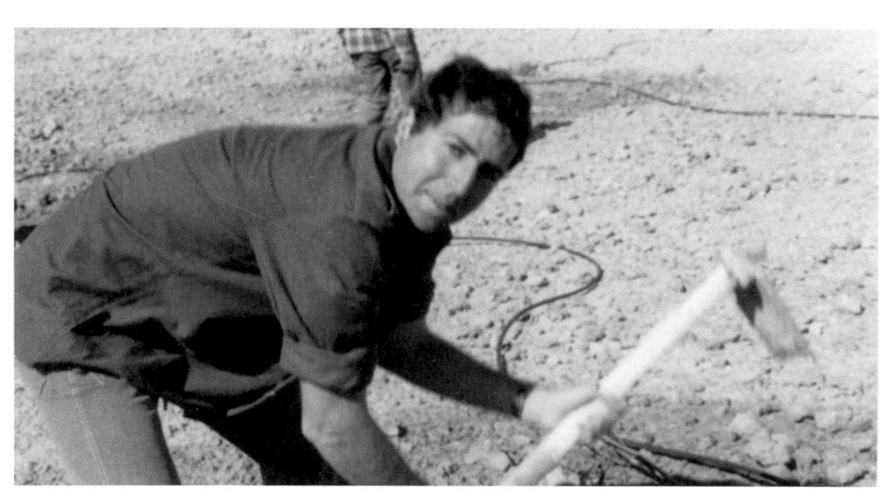

'94 7 6

With Friends

the region and beyond; Sunni radical Islam represented by Islamic State and Al Qaida, that aspire to found an Islamic state (caliphate) in the region and beyond; and the Muslim Brotherhood movement, led by Turkish president Erdogan.

The Iranian regime acts from a religious-messianic and apocalyptic stance, and from a deep sense of religious obligation. The leader, considered God's emissary, will be the one to bring back the Hidden Imam (the Mahdi) in our time. Iran's spiritual leaders, headed by Ali Khamenei, speak seriously about the messianic transformation that will take place soon. But for this transformation to take place, the entire world must be Muslim according to Shi'ite Islam's definition of the term. The precondition for this is that Israel must be wiped off the map. The reason that Iran wants Israel's destruction has nothing to do with Judea and Samaria, checkpoints or settlements, or even with the Palestinians. It is because that is what is needed to bring about the arrival of the Hidden Imam. This is not passive messianism, it is active messianism.

The Iranian regime does not only operate out of religious fanaticism. It also operates in the real world, in which it tries to identify opportunities. The "dry tree" allegory used by former Iranian president Mahmoud Ahmadinejad expresses identification of this opportunity: "Israel is a dry, rotten tree that will be destroyed in one storm." This is the Iranian version of Hezbollah leader Hassan Nasrallah's speech after Israel's withdrawal from Lebanon, in which he compared Israel to a spider web.

Since 1983, when Israel began to retreat from certain territories and publicly count its military casualties, its enemies in the region began to feel that they had found the Zionist entity's weak spot. They realized that they could not defeat Israel and the IDF in face-to-face conventional warfare on the battlefield, but perhaps they could do so using nonconventional methods, deliberately targeting civilians with terror, guerrilla warfare, rockets, and missiles. Those agents interested in Israel's elimination, especially the Islamic extremists, felt that they could break the spirit of

Israeli society. Thus, Nasrallah and his cohorts have advocated a war of attrition against Israel that would create civilian victims on an ongoing basis. Their goal is to erode Israel's endurance over time, blow after blow, especially its insistence on maintaining a Jewish national home in Israel.

This is the point where the perspectives of Khamenei and Nasrallah overlap. Both view Israel as an affluent Western society that is unwilling to continue to fight. Both believe that it is a society reluctant to sacrifice human life to realize its goals, and so it will be defeated. According to Khamenei, Nasrallah and their ilk, the Muslims will win because they are willing to commit suicide for their beliefs, while the Westerners, who are not willing to do so, will die. They are certain that the steadfast spirit of Islam will be victorious.

I do not accept their assessments, but I strongly urge that we take them seriously. The "spider web" challenge is real; the "dry tree" comparison is a real threat. Until Operation Defensive Shield in 2002, the Islamists identified Israel as internally weak, just as hungry animals in the forest target on a weak animal. The same was true after the disengagement from the Gaza Strip in 2005. I have always believed that they are wrong, but I understand how they reached their conclusions. They saw how they banished the Americans and the multinational force from Beirut in 1983–1984 by subjecting them to gruesome terror attacks. They saw how they pushed Israel out of Lebanon in 1983 and 1985 with guerilla fighting. They chased us out of Lebanon in 2000 because we were unwilling to pay the price of twenty casualties a year. They saw how they drove us out of Gaza because we could not withstand the ongoing terror attacks, and how we failed to inflict a stinging defeat in the Second Lebanon War. They also witness the United States' indecision and hesitancy about fighting them in the Middle East, and how Europe submits to waves of Islamic immigration that bring terror to cities such as London, Paris, Berlin, and Barcelona.

Their conclusion? They believe that they are on an upward spiral, on the path to victory. All they have to do is continue to pressure us, to kill us one by one, and they think they will break our spirits. That is why I believe that the illusion created by the post-Zionist defeatist worldview is so dangerous, and why I attribute so much importance to the correct diagnosis of the problem. This is why we must tell the correct story. The defeatist illusion prevented us from seeing the dangerous challenges presented by the Iranian regime, Hezbollah, radical Islam, Muslim Brotherhood elements, and last but not least – Hamas. It caused us to live in a fictitious world of self-deception, which weakened us and played into the hands of our most dangerous enemies. Because of our illusions, we were unable to muster all our strength to fight the good fight and defend our very existence.

Often, an illusion goes hand in hand with a preconceptions, each of them feeding into the other. This is a well-known psychological phenomenon, and sometimes we cannot discern which came first, the illusion or the preconception. One example from military history is the preconception that held sway over Stalin and the Soviet leadership prior to the German surprise attack on the Soviet Union on June 22, 1941. According to this preconception, Hitler would not attack the Soviet Union until Germany defeated Great Britain, so that Hitler would not have to fight on two fronts simultaneously. The Soviet leadership lived under this illusion and when the Germans did attack, the Soviet Union was completely unprepared. As a result, it suffered severe defeats that almost led to its collapse.

When I assumed the position of director of the Military Intelligence Directorate in 1995, the Yom Kippur War trauma was on my mind. To be more precise, I was concerned about the preconception that led to the prewar intelligence failure. I felt that the greatest danger facing the intelligence system was to blindly follow a false perception. For example, information may be filtered and altered to follow the set perception, which for whatever reason is convenient to uphold. Therefore, when I put on the hat of the "national evaluator" (as the Intelligence Directorate head is nicknamed) I began to systematically learn about the conflict between us and the Palestinians. I was very careful not to let accepted, preconceived notions and "truths" affect my view of reality. I went to great efforts not to look at the world through an ideological lens of any sort, but to look at it directly and dispassionately to see things as they are.

I am well aware that it is impossible to investigate and verify, or negate, any kind of hypothesis without first making certain kinds of basic assumptions. This is true in any scientific research, and it is also true in intelligence work. Without basic assumptions, the intel person can never gain insights from the almost infinite amount of data collected. But the intelligence system, like scientific research, must occasionally put these assumptions to the test. For example, we must cross-check data and pieces of information to verify the basic assumptions. No assessment should be negated only because it does not fit a premise. Always, always beware of following certain conceptions blindly, despite their seeming charm.

When I took over the position of Aman director, it took only a few months for me to realize that the military and diplomatic system in which I functioned was bogged down by preconceptions. Here I must clarify: in my perspective, the Oslo Accord was and remains an honest attempt to reach a solution to the conflict on the basis of dividing the land. As opposed to disengagement, I did not view the Oslo Accords as "spin," nor did I identify the Oslo process as fundamentally destructive. I viewed the agreement process as a political act made in good faith by the Israeli leaders, out of good intentions and true hope that we had a partner with whom we could formulate a solution of two states for two peoples. I thought that if our leadership suggested giving up land for peace and quiet, then anyone desiring peace should support it – and I wanted peace as much as anyone. But when I took over as head of the Intelligence Directorate, almost two years after the Oslo Accords were formulated and less than a year after the start of implementation, I realized that the reality was very different from the hope that was behind the agreements. Although Arafat was clearly ridiculing us, when Shimon Peres replaced Yitzchak Rabin (who understood the issue), the Israeli public was betrayed by its leadership, which preferred self-deception. At a certain stage, I came to view the Oslo process as an existential threat to the State of Israel. Unfortunately, I was right: land for peace became land for terror, with over one thousand dead and thousands of wounded.

Although years passed before I reached the definitive conclusion that Arafat was not a partner, I realized at an early stage that his behavior in particular, and the Palestinians' behavior in general, did not fit the expectations of the Israeli leadership, which chose the Oslo path. Still, the Oslo concept ruled supreme, and it was impossible to question it. Anyone who came out in public against the Oslo concept was marked in the Israeli public discourse as "extreme," "deluded," "illegitimate." The information that contradicted it was suppressed. Any voice criticizing it was silenced. In the IDF, however, debate on the issue was out in the open (although it goes without saying that in implementing the agreements, anyone who questioned the Oslo concept still carried out the political echelon's orders carefully and faithfully).

Criticism of Oslo from within the IDF was heard from the heads of the Intelligence Directorate research divisions: Brigadier General Yaakov Amidror (today major general, Ret.); his successor, Brigadier General Amos Gilad (today major general, Ret.); and Colonel Yossi Kuperwasser (today brigadier general, Ret.), who was deputy head of the research division for analysis, then intelligence officer at Central Command under my command, and eventually head of the research division.

As if we'd forgotten all that we'd experienced in the Yom Kippur War, again we preferred an a priori dogmatic view instead of empirical, realistic evaluation. Incredibly, this conception was dominant for a long period, as demonstrated at the conferences at Annapolis (November 2007) and Paris (December 2007). It was evident in the attempts of then US president Barak Obama, at the beginning of his term in 2009, to reach a final settlement between Israel and the Palestinians within one year. It was also behind the efforts of former US Secretary of State John Kerry to reach an agreement at the end of a nine-month diplomatic process that began in July 2013 and ended in failure in April 2014.

On September 15, 2000, I began my term as deputy chief of general staff. Two weeks later a Palestinian war of terror broke out ("the Second Intifada"). Although I and my colleagues at the general staff anticipated this war and understood exactly what it would be like, in our dialogue with the political echelon, we found ourselves again facing a certain preconception. This time, the presumption was that the violent incidents were not a deliberate Palestinian attack, but rather "street incidents that spiraled out of control." In this view, Arafat was not the initiator, but a helpless figure who was accidentally dragged into the eye of the storm. Further, this preconception asserted that the violence would dissipate within a short time, and so we could not "break the rules" but rather we had to act carefully and with restraint in order to return to the Oslo path as soon as possible. Terror should not undermine Oslo or cast doubt on its basic assumptions.

For eighteen months, the IDF senior command had to fight this conception. Because of it, the IDF fought the Palestinians for a long time with one hand tied behind its back. The facts were clear as the light of day, but the politicians, media and leading groups in the Israeli public did not want to see them as they were. It was only in March 2002 that the transformation began, after things reached a head. After hundreds of Israelis paid with their lives, the preconception finally collapsed. But even then, after the murderous terror attack on Passover eve at the Park Hotel in Netanya, in which thirty Israelis were killed, and after beginning Operation Defensive Shield, the remains of this preconception did not completely fade. Influential sectors of Israeli society continued their need to believe in a false picture of reality and waited for the next opportunity.

In early 2004, in the middle of my term as chief of general staff, the concept of disengagement arose. Just a few weeks after Prime Minister Ariel Sharon threw that new term into the global conversation, it became the new golden calf, the new fashionable consensus of the Israeli elites.

From the outset, it was clear that disengagement was a half-baked idea – an immature concept. Both the right and the left considered it an illogical idea. It led nowhere. Still, reflexes went into action. A new presumption was constructed around the idea of unilateral retreat from Gaza, and no criticism of it was permitted. The previous cycle of behavior repeated itself – information that contradicted the presumption was suppressed. Any legitimate voice that criticized it was silenced. From early 2004 to early 2006, when eyes began to open following the Hamas victory, only the right-wingers warned that the king was wearing no clothes, while their legitimacy was questioned. When I acted in a professional manner within the limitations placed on me as a military man and presented the possible consequences of the disengagement in closed forums, I was treated like a thorn in the side of the politicians. As a result, certain elements undermined my authority and sullied my good name. In the end, this led to the end of my term as chief of general staff.

I identify four false assumptions that hindered the State of Israel in the last decade of the twentieth century and the early decades of the twenty-first, and they are intimately related. All four are part of one thought paradigm that for a long period dominated public discourse in the State of Israel and the rest of the world regarding the Israeli-Palestinian conflict.

The first false assumption is that the Land of Israel west of the Jordan River can be divided between two states – Israel and Palestine – based on the borders of June 4, 1967. This assumption determines that the two-state solution can be stable and grant security to Israelis and national satisfaction to the Palestinians. The various ideological barriers raised by extremists on each side will be removed, and we will achieve a state in which a secure Israel and a viable Palestine live side by side in peace and prosperity. Israel will have sovereignty over some 78 percent of the Land of Israel between the Jordan River and the Mediterranean Sea, and Palestine will have sovereignty over the remaining 22 percent.

The second false assumption is that Israel has a partner in peace. This assumption asserts that there is a Palestinian leadership that accepts the solution of two states on the basis of the 1967 lines. Despite the rise of Hamas and the conflicting statements also made occasionally by senior Fatah officials, this assumption states that a central political entity that still leads the Palestinians has accepted the existence of the State of Israel, and is truly and honestly willing to live alongside it, if we only allow it to establish the Palestinian national state in Judea, Samaria and the Gaza Strip.

The third false assumption is that we must have peace now. The "occupation" is intolerable, the situation is not sustainable, the demographic clock is ticking, and Israel's legitimacy is in danger. Therefore, we must act to end the conflict immediately. Not only must we end the conflict now, but it is possible to end it now. We cannot continue to live with the bloody, never-ending conflict, and there is no need to do so. We do not have the patience, forbearance, or willingness to wait for long-term processes to ripen. Peace – now! A permanent arrangement – immediately! It's not possible that there is no solution. According to the urgent timeline of the "Now"-sayers, there must be a solution that can be implemented.

The fourth false assumption is that the Israeli-Palestinian conflict is the main source of instability in the Middle East. In its extreme version, this assumption asserts that the "Israeli occupation" of Judea and Samaria is the root of all evil in the region. Because of the "Israeli occupation," the Palestinians hate Israel, because of it the extremists in the region hate the United States, and because of it, fundamentalism is increasing and moderate forces are threatened. In its milder version, this assumption admits that although there are other problems in the Middle East – radical Islam, the legitimacy of Arab regimes, and more – but the "Israeli occupation" causes these problems to intensify and creates a situation that precludes a solution.

These four assumptions join the thought paradigm that in the past two decades has become dogma, in an almost religious sense of the term. This dogma cannot be questioned or criticized. Each one of these conceptions became a kind of golden calf that was the object of irrational worship, and combined to form the overall paradigm, a gigantic golden calf that the public was asked to idolize and accept unquestioningly.

I permit myself to question the four assumptions of the reigning paradigm. First of all, I think that in the present generation, perhaps even the present century, it will not be possible to divide the Land of Israel on the western side of the Jordan River into two nation-states – Jewish and Palestinian – that live side by side in peace on opposite sides of the border lines from June 4, 1967. If such a division takes place, and I doubt whether it can happen, this will lead to the establishment of a Palestinian state that is not economically viable and is not nationally fulfilled. This tiny, divided, bitter nation will certainly be aggressive and subversive (irredentist) in relation to its neighbors – Egypt, Jordan, and mainly, Israel. Sooner or later, this aggression will lead to war.

Second, it is crystal clear to me that Israel has no partner for solution by division of this type, even if the solution were possible. The truth is bitter, but it must be stated out loud: no Palestinian leadership exists today that has true intentions for a two-state solution. Rather, their leadership desires the establishment of an Arab entity instead of and on the ruins of the State of Israel. There is no such leadership – certainly not within Hamas, but not within Fatah either. Unfortunately, I believe that in the foreseeable future as well, no Palestinian leadership will view the arrangement with Israel as a permanent solution. They view it as a stage on the way to the next round, in which Israel will finally be defeated.

Third, as a consequence of the two previous statements, I truly believe that there is no possibility of reaching a true solution to the conflict in this decade or in the coming decades. Instead of expecting an immediate solution, which will be false and dangerous, we must say to ourselves with honesty and courage that the process of peacemaking between Israelis and Palestinians has not reached maturity. In several aspects, the process has even slid backwards. Therefore, we must not try to bring the conclusion forward in time. We must not believe in futile, hopeless solutions. A nation that aspires to longevity must have patience and determination. We must be willing to accept that we will have to wait many years, even generations, until an acceptable solution is found for the conflict between us and the Palestinians.

Fourth, it is not true that Israeli sovereignty in Judea and Samaria is the source of regional instability. The Israeli-Palestinian conflict is not what lies at the root of instability in the Middle East. The struggle of radical Islam against the West is much more dominant, and threatens to spiral downward into a third world war. The clash between Islamic fanaticism and Western culture, Western powers and Western power is what has led to the great upheaval in the region. In addition, we can name other conflicts that do not result from the Israeli-Palestinian conflict and are unrelated to it: the struggle between Sunnis and Shi'ites, between Persians and Arabs, between nationalists and Islamists (in Iraq, Syria, Lebanon, Egypt, Jordan, Yemen, the Palestinian Authority, and elsewhere). Most of these conflicts began before the establishment of the State of Israel, and would still exist today, even if the State of Israel had never existed. To these we may add instability in the Arab world that derives from the vast gap and resulting tension between the mega-rich (mainly from oil) and the desperately poor. This is also unrelated to the

Israeli-Palestinian conflict. What is the connection between the popular uprising against the regime in Tunisia and the Israeli-Palestinian conflict? There is none. What's the link between the civil war and bloodbath in Syria and the Israeli-Palestinian conflict? There is none! The same is true for the ethnic-religious wars in Iraq, Lebanon, Yemen, and Bahrain, as well as the revolution and counterrevolution in Egypt.

These conceptions are faulty at best – or to be more exact, at their worst! Some argue that Palestinian violence toward us is the result of despair. But I assert that the source of their violence is hope – the hope of destroying the State of Israel. How I wish they would despair of this.

I have never discounted those who believe in the right to the entire Land of Israel. As a military commander, in my contact with settlers in Judea, Samaria, and the Gaza Strip, I made every effort to maintain a relationship of mutual respect and cooperation with them. Mainly, my goal was to protect them from Palestinian terror, and I believe I succeeded in this mission. Still, I am not a territorial ideologue. As a point of departure, I believed that it was right to reach stable peace agreements based on territorial compromise. I supported the view that assumed that if we submit certain concessions to the Palestinians, and if we allow them to live comfortably and develop economically, they will be a responsible and rational partner with whom we can share the land. But during the decade when I served as head of Military Intelligence, head of Central Command, deputy chief of general staff, and chief of general staff, the reality that I came to recognize made me open my eyes. I concluded that the Palestinian partner wants to live instead of us, not beside us. In this situation, concessions do not increase stability, but rather undermine it. I concluded that fundamentally, we do not have a partner for the two-state solution.

Israel has great power to positively influence the complex reality in which it finds itself. But when leadership suffers from a misunderstanding of reality, or when it ignores reality and makes irrelevant decisions based on an unfounded conception – as was the case in the 1990s and the first decade of 2000 – Israel's powers are not fully expressed, while its weaknesses are intensified. As a result, today our enemies are on the offense, while we are waging a battle of retreat and delay.

The paradigm of "land for peace" was created from a position of strength and sense of power following the victory of the Six-Day War, and through Israeli desire to end the conflict with our neighbors. After Oslo, it was transformed into a strategy of retreat based on a sense of Israel's weakness – in my opinion, a false sense. The image of Israel in retreat is the direct result of our pattern of behavior during those years, and our disregard for the consequences of this behavior on our geostrategic position. On every one of the fronts we faced, Israeli withdrawals only served to strengthen the image of Israel as a weak state in a historical process of retreat. As a result, each front saw developments that were worrisome and sometimes even dangerous.

The damage that Israel has caused itself due to enslavement to a mistaken paradigm affects much more than our dealings with the Palestinians. Egypt has provoked us and ignored smuggling of weapons to the Gaza Strip. Syria has used aggressive, threatening language. Iran has threatened to destroy us and continues to do so. Finally, the discourse in a significant part of the Arab and Muslim world negates the existence of Israel and fans anti-Israel sentiment. These facts may seem unrelated on the surface, but they share a common denominator – beyond being considered a foreign transplant and illegitimate entity, Israel is also considered by many of its neighbors as a state that can be beaten, one that does not defend its national interests firmly. To them, Israel is a temporary phenomenon that is in retreat and can be forced to disappear.

CHAPTER 3

The Long Way

The very first person on the Defense Ministry's list of terror victims is Avraham Zalman Shlomo Zoref, who was murdered in Jerusalem by Arabs in 1851. "How long?!"—is the question that many people ask me. How long will we suffer endless victims and live with bereavement? How long will we have to fight? How long must we wait for peace? How long must we live by our swords? I quote the words of Ze'ev Jabotinsky and of Dr. Moshe Beilinson: "Until the last of our enemies understands that we are here to stay – forever."

In 1923, Jabotinsky wrote a well-known article entitled "The Iron Wall (We and the Arabs)." He asserted, "Zionist settlement [in the Land of Israel] must either stop, or else proceed against the will [of the Arab population]. Therefore, it can continue to develop only under the protection of a guardian power that is independent of the local population [the Arabs – MY] – an iron wall that the local population cannot breach."

Another formulation, somewhat clearer, was developed by Dr. Beilinson, deputy editor of Davar (the Labor movement daily), in an article published on June 23, 1936, at the start of the Arab riots. He responded to the question, "How long will we have to fight?" or in its biblical wording, "Must we wield our swords forever?" Beilinson wrote:

> Till the fiercest and most zealous of our enemies, in all enemy camps wherever they may be, know with certainty that there is no means with which to crush the power of the Jewish people in its land. It bears the obligation of life and the truth of existence, and there is no other alternative but to come to terms with it. That is the reason for our struggles.

These thinkers understood that the longest path is actually the shortest.

To a certain extent, we are building Jabotinsky's "iron wall." We are no longer under the threat of armies that can destroy the State of Israel. We have a peace agreement with our most important neighbor, Egypt. We have a peace agreement with Jordan, and even before that we had strategic agreements with that neighbor. We have joint interests with Arab Sunni countries with which we share a common enemy.

The road to resolving the conflict with our Palestinian neighbors is still long. From the very dawn of Zionism, there has never been an Arab leadership that has recognized the rights of the Jewish people to an independent Jewish state in the Land of Israel, with its own borders. In other words, no leadership was willing to share the land with us. From the origin of Zionism in general, and specifically from 1967, no Palestinian leadership has been willing to limit itself to a Palestinian state in the 1967 borders, or any other suggested partition of the territory, in an agreement that would constitute the "end of the conflict" and "finality of claims."

Consequently, for the foreseeable future there is no chance of stabilizing a reality of security and peace on the basis of a "two-state solution." Thus we do not talk about "solving" the Israeli-Palestinian conflict, but rather "managing the conflict." Therefore, we must propose a strategy for managing the conflict. The strategy must do so while preserving and strengthening our interests, and preparing the ground to stabilize the situation in the distant future. I am convinced that we must cease searching for a "solution" and release ourselves from this failed outlook. Instead, we must encourage new thinking patterns in new directions.

Every so often, someone attempts to market a golden calf: Peace Now, disengagement, convergence plan – in order to generate hope. But before these golden calves shatter, they exact a very high price, and they do not resolve the conflict. I am a realist and pragmatist. I oppose all the various "peace processes" so long as the time is not right, but my objection does not stem from a fanatic world view. I do not ignore the existence of Palestinian society. On the contrary, I want them to live next to us with dignity and wellbeing. Thus an appropriate modus vivendi must be created for the two entities so that they both can conduct their lives with security. (Modus vivendi means "way of life" – both sides share arrangements that ensure their way of life, despite the conflict and without solving it at this stage.) How long? Until they become convinced of our right to live here as the nation-state of the Jewish people.

To those who ask, why not make this demand of other countries as well, I say, that's a good question. When Egyptian president Anwar Sadat came to Israel, he promised, "No more war, no more bloodshed, no more attacks." Egypt never provoked us. Jordan did not argue about territory with us. The vegetable patch of Kibbutz Grofit, where I lived as a young man, was located beyond the Jordanian border, and the Jordanians willingly gave us the territory in exchange for dunes somewhere else. We came to an agreement with them and they did not use terror. The debate about our right to live here in Israel was not relevant when it came to Egypt and Jordan, because those countries never claimed rights to Akko, Haifa, Jaffa, Ramat Aviv (Al-Shaykh Muwannis), or Ashkelon (Majdal) – nor do they make these claims today. By contrast, the PLO, for example, still lays claim to "Palestine from the [Jordan] River to the [Mediterranean] Sea, and from Ras-A-Nakura (Rosh Hanikra) until Umm Al-Rashrash (Eilat)."

Arafat violated the agreement he signed with us, on the very first day. Instead of fighting terror, he used it against us. He proved that he never really intended to end the conflict. The Oslo accords did not bring an end to the bloodshed, even though Arafat agreed to stop the violence and signed on the dotted line. The reverse is true: Arafat viewed the Oslo agreement as part of the Islamic stages doctrine. He violated his commitment to change the Palestinian covenant to include the rights of the Jewish people to live on its land. In fact, no Palestinian leadership has been willing to share the territory with us. Thus, the recognition issue is the key and the very heart of the conflict.

If we have no partner who recognizes our rights to live in Tel Aviv, why should we begin every discussion with evacuation of the settlements? The settlements are not the source of the conflict and are not obstacles to peace. The conflict between the two sides existed long before 1967. Every negotiation for a permanent agreement must begin with their recognition of our right to live here. In every research institute I have visited, whether in Israel or the US, I have asked my research assistants to search for quotes of Palestinian leaders who said that by the end of the diplomatic process we will live side by side, that the '67 lines marked the end of the conflict and the end of their demands and claims. So far, no one has found such a quote. I know this is disappointing to hear, especially among those who supported the Oslo accords, but better to suffer disappointment than to ignore reality and truth.

The Fatah policy is to pressure us into uprooting Jews and withdrawing from Judea and Samaria. They view this as the end of Zionism, and perhaps there is some truth to this. People on our side talk easily about uprooting a hundred thousand Jews, which could lead to an internal split or rift and perhaps even civil war. All this is unnecessary. In the disengagement, we uprooted eight thousand Jews from the Gaza Strip. None of the Jews lived on private Palestinian land – they lived on state-owned land. What did we gain from this? The destruction and uprooting caused economic distress for many of them. It also caused a credibility crisis regarding the State of Israel and its leaders. The disengagement harmed not only us, but the Palestinians as well. For years, 3,700 Palestinian families benefited from working in Gush Katif. Another 4,500 families benefitted from work in the Erez industrial zone. After we left Gaza, many of them were left destitute.

Even the more moderate elements in the Palestinian leadership have a different priority list that does not stop at Gaza or Judea and Samaria. To them, the biggest "settlement" is Tel Aviv. They impose deliberate diplomatic pressure for evacuation of settlements and partitioning of Jerusalem, because they hope that this will cause such a major crisis in Israeli society that Zionism will simply collapse. Abbas Zaki, a Fatah ideologist and member of the movement's Central committee, makes statements like these. He says things that Arafat never dared to say, and Abu Mazen (Mahmoud Abbas) doesn't dare to say them either.

Take the following statements made by Zaki in an Al Jazeera interview on September 23, 2011: "We understand, and all of us know, that we can't achieve the big goal [all of Palestine – MY] all at once. But if Israel retreats from Jerusalem, if Israel uproots the settlements, what will happen to Israel? Israel will come to an end!" In an interview with Assyrian National Broadcasting (ANB) television channel on May 11, 2012, he said:

> Regarding the two-state solution, in my opinion Israel will fall apart. Because if they leave Jerusalem, what will happen with all their talk of the Promised Land and the Chosen People? What about all the sacrifices they've made – only to tell them to leave? They think that Jerusalem has a spiritual status. The Jews think that Judea and Samaria are the cradle of their history. If the Jews leave these areas, the Zionist enterprise will start to collapse – it will collapse on its own. Then we will begin to advance!

Even Palestinian sources such as Marwan Barghouti, who have met with Israelis and were viewed as moderates, praise statements such as these. Later Barghouti was responsible for the murder of thirty-five Israelis during the Second Intifada (also known as the Al-Aqsa Intifada).

We should stop playing this dangerous game. Instead, we must help create a reality in which the Palestinian leadership understands that a Jewish homeland exists here and will continue to do so forever. Meanwhile, our side also needs to accept the fact that the Palestinians won't disappear either. Therefore, I oppose annexation of unpopulated Area C territories (as per the Oslo II definition), and I am against construction on every hill and valley.

Anyone aspiring for peace should not be talking about uprooting people, whether Arabs or Jews. The same holds true about the concept of "transfer." You can't be working toward peace if you want to transfer people. I can sketch a map in which the two populations could live peacefully with one another, without uprooting or transferring one single Jew or Arab. But the first stage of the process must be educational reform in which the younger Palestinian generation is taught to accept our existence here. Then, in the negotiations process, we can offer unsettled territories in Area C to the Palestinians. Ultimately there would be territorial continuity, certainly transportation continuity, for Palestinian and Jewish residents of Judea and Samaria. An Arab from Jenin would be able to travel to Hebron without encountering an Israeli soldier, except if the security situation necessitates it. A Jew from Tel Aviv would be able to travel to Itamar or Elon Moreh without encountering the Palestinian police.

The new strategy will also have to address the problem of refugees. For various reasons, the Palestinian refugees have received unprecedented attention and importance in the world. This is the only case in modern history in which people who left, abandoned, escaped, or were expelled from their homes during a war remained "refugees" after seventy years. They retain this status without a solution in sight, not even a partial one, although refugee problems on much larger scales were resolved successfully in the past.

Here are some examples:

Following the Greco-Turkish war (1919–1921), more than a million Greeks were transferred from the region under Turkish rule to Greek territory. Simultaneously, some seven hundred thousand Turks were transferred from areas under Greek rule to Turkey. The League of Nations placed Norwegian North Pole explorer Fridtjof Nansen in charge of caring for these refugees, and he received the Nobel Peace Prize in 1922 for his contribution toward their resettlement.

After World War II, there were at least eight million refugees in Europe who had lost their homes or were expelled from them. All of them, without exception, were resettled within a short time.

Due to three wars between India and Pakistan (in 1947, 1965, 1971), millions of people escaped or were driven away from their homes. They, too, were resettled within a few years.

Only the Arab refugees of 1948 and their descendants (second, third, and fourth generations!) continue to live in refugee camps to this very day. The UN has two refugee agencies. One, the United Nations Relief and Works Agency for Palestine Refugees (UNRWA), is in charge of the Palestinian refugees alone. The other, United Nations High Commissioner for Refugees (UNHCR), is in charge of all the other refugees around the globe, estimated at more than twenty million. This number includes hundreds of thousands who fled the wars in Syria, Iraq and Libya.

Why this distorted treatment? Mainly because various agents (mainly Arab entities) have a vested interest in preserving and intensifying this situation. They use it as a weapon against the State of Israel's legitimacy and against the very existence of a Jewish state, by insisting on realization of the Palestinians' "right of return."

Israel's interest is parallel to the private interests of most of the refugees: to provide humanitarian aid to every refugee as an individual, as early as possible. This is reasonable, and the problem must be treated as part of a new strategy for managing the conflict. Israel must not allow even one refugee into the State of Israel.

One of the Oslo assumptions was that a diplomatic solution and economic development would bring peace, and peace would bring security. I call this viewpoint a "top-down" approach, and it also prevailed at the Annapolis Conference (November 2007) and at the Paris Donors Conference (December 2007). President Obama and Secretary of State Hillary Clinton felt the same way when they went through the motions of restarting the diplomatic process in 2009, as did Secretary of State John Kerry in 2013–2014 when he tried to reach an agreement within nine months.

But my approach is the opposite. The first question we must ask is, how can a discussion on a final settlement be made with those who do not believe in the legitimacy of an independent Jewish state? The second question is, how can we negotiate with a party that has not proved that is it willing and/or able to rule responsibly? In my view, any new strategy must be carried out through the "bottom-up" approach, to allow the Palestinians to prove to us that they are willing and able to rule responsibly. It is not in the Israeli interest to rule the Palestinians or manage their lives. Therefore, we should strengthen the political separation between us, which has been in place since implementation of the Oslo agreement. We must also continue to cooperate in the spheres of economics, infrastructure, and security.

It is in our best interests that any independent political entity existing alongside us function properly and responsibly. Actually, there are two such Palestinian entities, with almost no connection between them: Hamastan in Gaza and the Palestinian Authority in Judea and Samaria. We can live with this situation, so long as there is an address in Gaza.

Today it is Hamas, and we must learn how to get along with it – with carrots and sticks. Even though we physically left the territory, the Gaza residents remain very dependent on us. Merchandise enters via Israel, and we provide their water and electricity. This is even truer with regard to Judea and Samaria. The relationship is like Siamese twins, for better and for worse.

The Palestinian economy is overwhelmingly dependent on the Israeli economy and on working in Israel. That is why I felt compelled to raise the number of work permits to allow Palestinians to work in Israel. When the wave of stabbing attacks began in September 2015, there were sixty thousand Palestinians with permits. As I write these words, the maximum number has risen to one hundred thousand. Work is an existential need. If we do not allow the simple fellow living in Jenin or Nablus to make a decent living, he may be pushed into violence. I realize that many Israelis feel uncomfortable about employing more Palestinian workers when Palestinians are trying to stab us. But although this policy won't receive Facebook "likes," the facts speak for themselves. During the wave of stabbings and vehicular assaults in 2015, out of the sixty thousand licensed Palestinians working in Israel, only one attacked, by raising a hammer to a Jew in a building site in Modi'in. None of these workers stabbed or murdered Jews.

Tens of thousands of Palestinians are employed by Jews in Judea and Samaria and make a good living. The Palestinian production manager of a plant in the Barkan Industrial Park can earn 17,000 NIS per month, while the cost of living in the PA is much lower than in Israel – families in Ramallah or Nablus can live on 2,000 or 3,000 NIS a month. I once spoke to a Palestinian manager who told me that he supports 120 people on his salary. BDS supporters forced the SodaStream plant to relocate from the Mishor Adumim Industrial Park to Rahat, thus harming the livelihood of some one thousand Palestinians. Thousands of Palestinians work as subcontractors for the Israeli industry, for example in garment factories. More than 70 percent of Palestinian exports are targeted at the Israeli market. It is not a coincidence that their currency is the shekel. The tax system is joint: Israel collects the value added tax (VAT) on imports and the excise tax (plus VAT) on fuel, and transfers the money to the PA. I don't see any way of disconnecting completely from the PA regarding these issues.

Dependence of the PA on Israel also extends to infrastructure. Israel continues to supply electricity to Judea and Samaria and Gaza. Israel supplies water to Judea and Samaria and also to Jordan. Who else will provide them with gas? Our neighbors, mainly the Palestinians, enjoy our resources.

Israel and the Palestinian Authority enjoy security cooperation, and this is absolutely necessary because we share common interests. Hamas, Islamic Jihad, and Islamic State (ISIS) are enemies of Israel as well as of the PA. We have freedom of action in the security realm thanks to Operation Defensive Shield in 2002. This operation instigated a major change that halted a massive terror wave. We do most of the security work involved, for ourselves but also for the Palestinians. If we have information on a terrorist who is about to leave Jenin, we can arrest him within hours. We cannot afford to lose our freedom of operation in Judea and Samaria, as former US Secretary of State Kerry wanted. The first to suffer would be PA president Abbas, because Hamas would gain control of Judea and Samaria as it did in Gaza. Thus, when Abbas threatens to discontinue the security cooperation, as he sometimes does, we know this is an empty threat. He understands it would be suicide to do such a thing.

Despite our successful cooperation with the PA in the spheres outlined above, one important issue still remains: we have been unable to force the Palestinians to reform their educational system. They still teach their children to hate us and blow themselves up to kill us. This is not just incitement; it is deeply rooted in their education system. As minister of strategic affairs in 2009–2013, I initiated the "incitement index," which examines the messages targeting Palestinian children in the PA. We check the Palestinian media, social networks, and television, mainly children's programs. We examine school textbooks, leadership rhetoric, educational programs on the official television station, and the Palestinian Authority website, and we look for evidence of positive change. Every three months the Ministry of Strategic Affairs presents a report on the subject which is distributed to the government and used in diplomacy.

This report demonstrates the severity of the situation, and how the Palestinian territory is woefully unprepared for real peace. Tel Aviv does not appear on the map in Palestinian textbooks, because to them it is an illegal settlement. The poems they learn in language classes negate any possible connection of the Jews to this country. Three-year-old children practice wearing explosive belts in kindergarten. Classroom walls are adorned with pictures of suicide terrorists holding rifles. These are supposed to be exemplary figures for the children to model! When the wave of stabbing attacks began following the Temple Mount crisis, the official Palestinian media fanned the fires by claiming that the Al-Aqsa Mosque was in danger. This is hardly education toward peace.

On our part, we must activate diplomatic pressure on those who donate to the Palestinians. We must demand that the donors condition their largesse on the cessation of incitement and preparation of the people for peace with us. Of course, we must also insist that they cease funding the families of terrorist prisoners in Israeli jails. The Palestinians pay the prisoners on a sliding scale according to how much Israeli blood they spill. A Palestinian given a life sentence receives a higher "salary" than one who receives only three years because he was unsuccessful in murdering Israelis. The family of a suicide killer (who is called *shahid* or "martyr") receives a lifelong stipend from the PA.

Western nations have important tools that could improve the situation. Sadly, they do not do enough, but only come to us with their complaints. Sometimes, however, I do see improvement and some of the governments have acquiesced to our demands. For example, the British government under Theresa May stopped transferring cash to the Palestinians and, instead, allocates budgets for specific projects. Another example is the Taylor Force Act, which was passed by the US Senate in 2018. Taylor Force was an American citizen who was murdered by a Palestinian terrorist in Jaffa in 2015. Under the law, the US will give taxpayer money to the Palestinian Authority only if the PA stops its funding of terrorist prisoners and their families. I add to this list a demand for reform of the educational system, as this is a crucial issue. As far back as 1995, I showed several Palestinian schoolbooks to Rabin prove to him that Arafat was not seeking peace, but jihad instead.

Since then I have been waiting for the moment when we will see real change, for the Palestinians to prove that they seek peace. I am not certain that this moment will ever arrive. But without the necessary changes, there is no chance at all.

My paternal grandparents, Avraham and Sarah Smolainsky, did not move to the Land of Israel in 1925 to evict Arabs from their lands or to kill them. The founders of Zionism purchased land and caused the desert to bloom. They understood that they had no choice but to hope and pray for a state, to realize the dream of generations to establish a Jewish national home in the Land of Israel, and to protect themselves. Since then, our situation has only improved. We have no reason for despondency. We no longer face the existential threat of armies – not from Egypt, nor from Jordan or Syria. Instead, our enemies choose to attack us with rockets and use terror against our civilians. This is because they feel that the weak link in our security chain is the staying power of our society. They want to undercut our resilience and staying power, and our desire for a Jewish home. They have not succeeded.

If we had searched for an immediate solution for the conflict, we would no longer be here. So long as our enemies preserve their nefarious intentions, we must maintain relations based on the stick as well as the carrot. We must continue to develop our relationship until a leadership on the other side arises that understands one thing: we are here for good, period. Perhaps it will happen in another generation or two, or it may never happen at all. But we are strong enough to deal with the situation.

Meanwhile, we will live side by side with two independent Palestinian entities – because I do not envision a reconciliation between Hamas and the Palestinian Authority in the near future. This is, in fact, a situation of autonomy. We could call it "the New Palestinian Empire" – the name isn't important. It is autonomy, and not an independent state, because it must be demilitarized. We must supervise what enters and what leaves it, since we can't rely on or trust them. The Oslo Accords created a reality of land in exchange for terror, and the disengagement led to land in exchange for rockets.

I would like the Arab states that created the Palestinian problem as a weapon against us to become partners in a regional agreement to stabilize the situation. We have tried numerous times to convince regional players to become partners in the process, but they evaded us (even in the governments that ruled after 2009). I understand this. Egypt is busy with internal problems. Saudi Arabia and other countries are busy dealing with the challenges posed by the Iranians and others. They see Iran taking advantage of the vacuum left by the Americans and becoming a dominant, if not hegemonic, player. Iraq is headed by a Shi'ite government. Syria is under Assad's regime, Hezbollah runs Lebanon, and the Houthis dominate Yemen. For the moderate Arab regimes, this is a nightmare constellation because of the Shi'ite-Sunni conflict. These days, the Palestinians do not bother them. To some extent, we are in the same boat with Saudi Arabia and Egypt because we have common enemies.

The Arab countries are in no hurry to resolve the Palestinian problem. Perhaps the opposite is true: they created the problem as a weapon against us, but now that we are in the same situation, they are in no rush to use this weapon. For example, Saudi Arabia has significantly cut back its investments and donations on the Palestinian front. It was only due to contacts with the Trump administration that it decided to renew its monetary assistance. The Qataris are the only ones who are still investing significant funds in the Palestinians, and they are doing so mainly in Gaza, less in Judea and Samaria. In fact, the Palestinian issue does not even appear on the agenda of the Arab League. Even when we fought against the Gaza Palestinians in Operation Protective Edge (2014), none of the other Arab states or entities pressured us.

Our political separation from the Palestinians was completed under the Oslo Accords. Economic relations were regulated in the Paris Agreement. We must continue to cooperate based on common interests that will benefit both sides. True, Israel's prime minister has not met President Abbas at the negotiating table, but cooperation on the ground continue daily. This includes contact with Hamas through mediators. As for the diplomatic "peace" issue: we tried unsuccessfully, we got the picture, and now it's time to move on. If a leadership arises that is willing to compromise on the dream of "Palestine from the [Jordan] River to the [Mediterranean] Sea," then it would be appropriate to discuss additional territory with them.

What makes it hard on us is the demand from the public – both right and left – for an immediate solution, and politicians' attempts to sell hope, which then becomes an illusion. It is difficult to explain complex issues in such a reality, but I insist on speaking the truth consistently. I have never tried to evade the issue with comments such as "we see things that you don't." I never promised to eliminate Hamas or issued irrelevant ultimatums to Ismail Haniyeh, as others have done. These are empty slogans that erode our credibility. Politicians use them because they count on the public's short memory.

Clearly, this process is sometimes frustrating. It is much easier to promise to liquidate Hamas or bring peace than to talk about managing the conflict wisely until conditions are ready to discuss peace. But I mean what I say, and I don't try to fool the public or build them a golden calf.

In this reality, I believe in taking the long way.

CHAPTER 4

A Life-Changing Decision

My life and education in Kiryat Haim and my involvement in the youth movement formed a natural progression that led me to choose the Nahal unit for my military service, along with the other members of my youth group. Nahal emphasized the Zionist ideal of settlement of peripheral regions of the country, and we had been educated through the youth movement to put this ideal into practice.

Service in Nahal permitted me to train in a combat parachute unit, and also to realize the goal of my education and the focus of my beliefs: settling Israel's borders, culminating in establishing a new kibbutz with a vibrant communal life. The decision of our group to move as a unit to Kibbutz Grofit was practically a given. The challenge of developing a newborn kibbutz beckoned to me, and we moved far away from home to the Arava Valley, an arid region south of the Dead Sea and near Eilat.

Before I was drafted and even during my mandatory service, I never intended to make the army a career. I didn't even consider becoming an officer. I didn't think military security was the highest priority. Instead, like most Israelis at the time, I believed that the Six-Day War had been the war to end all wars. I shared the overall sense of complacence and self-confidence that pervaded Israel until the Yom Kippur War broke out six years later. I, too, thought that the glowing Israeli victory had convinced (or would convince) the Arabs that it was worth their while to make peace with us. I, too, accepted the "land for peace" formula that was articulated after the 1967 war and expressed in the government's decision not to annex the territories (except for East Jerusalem). Instead, the territories were viewed as a kind of guarantee until a peace agreement would be finalized.

I was drafted into the Israel Defense Forces (IDF) in September 1968 and did my mandatory service as required, but no more. I think that if someone would have told me then that I'd remain in the military for another thirty-plus years, I would have laughed at them. That life was not for me. True, there were aspects about military service that I truly enjoyed and that gave me much satisfaction, such as working with people and being part of the IDF spirit and value system. On the other hand, I remember how hard it was for me on Sunday mornings to return to the regiment after spending Shabbat at home. That is usually not characteristic of people who love the military and its lifestyle.

Ironically, however, I proved to be a good soldier, starting from basic training. After completing basic training, my commanding officers wanted me to attend the squad commanders' course. My friends in the Nahal group preferred that I remain with them, as I was group secretary. We reached a compromise: I'd attend the squad commanders' course, but only in another year.

During my mandatory service, many of us began to emerge from the sweet illusion of peace that was ostensibly achieved in the Six-Day War. We fought Palestinian terror along the border with Jordan. Our group lost Shlomo Svirsky when terrorists shelled Kfar Ruppin, and Dudik Kimmelfeld while pursuing terrorists deep inside Jordan. Our incursion into Jordan was payback for the Jordanians who bombarded Moshav Ein Yahav with powerful 82 mm mortars. (We also lost Simcha Sapir, platoon leader in Battalion 50, in a training accident.) We participated in the War of Attrition at the Suez Canal. Still, these experiences had no effect on my personal priorities.

Toward the end of the squad commanders' course, Nehemiah Tamari summoned me for an interview. Tamari was commander of the squad commanders' company of Battalion 50, the Nahal Paratroopers Battalion that was part of the regular Paratroopers Brigade (the 35th Brigade). He asked me to serve as squad commander, but only for a short time, as afterwards he wanted me to attend an officers' training course. I had suspected that he was going to ask me something of the sort, so I made up my mind in advance to turn him down firmly. I knew that participants in the officers' training course must sign on to serve for another year in the regular army, and in my mind, I rejected that notion completely. What I wanted was to join the young Grofit kibbutz as soon as possible. My group was the third to join it, and I felt responsibility toward its members as well as toward the kibbutz. After all, the group had already allowed me to continue the command track in Battalion 50 instead of joining them at the kibbutz for an unpaid period of service.

But despite my determination to leave military service, and the fact that I didn't have the least desire to become an officer, it was not easy to turn Nehemiah down. I held him in high esteem.

Years later, when Nehemiah was commander of Central Command, he was killed in a helicopter accident. I was asked to eulogize him, and said, "I was well acquainted with Nehemiah's back – even more than his wife Hannah." I followed him as a soldier in his company. In the first cross-border operation I participated in, Nehemiah led the way. When I returned to regular military service, my military trajectory was very similar to his: platoon leader and then company commander in the paratroopers of the Nahal Infantry Brigade, commander of the Paratroopers Brigade Reconnaissance Company, commander of Battalion 890, commander of General Staff Reconnaissance Unit (Sayeret Matkal), Paratroopers

Brigade commander, and commander of Central Command. I returned to serve under him, even as his deputy, and always held him in high esteem. Throughout my entire army career, Nehemiah set a high standard and model for me.

The members of our group had their first real taste of kibbutz life when we met at Kibbutz Grofit following our final high school matriculation exams in mid-July 1968. The kibbutz was less than two years old, and it was named after the first settlement group, which was called Grofit. The main source of employment and livelihood for kibbutz members was the vegetable garden. I will always remember my first day of work. Due to the oppressive heat, we preferred to start work early in the morning. But since we didn't have enough work tools for all the members, we had to divide into two shifts. I was assigned to the second shift, which began in the afternoon. Mid-July temperatures in the Arava region can reach 50°C (122°F) in the shade – this was our welcome reception. Our job was staking tomato vines. We used a blazing hot pile driver to drive metal stakes into the ground, and then we hung the tomato vines onto wires stretched between the stakes. This method exposed the vines and the fruit to the sun, which encouraged early ripening. Everything was scorching: the tin water tank, the tractor, the cart. Yet our enthusiasm outweighed the discomfort. It was easy to fall in love with kibbutz life and the stunning Arava scenery.

Military service took us far away from Grofit. The women returned to the kibbutz after eighteen months while the men continued their service in the Nahal paratrooper unit. I divided my weekend breaks between my parents' home and my girlfriend Ada, who was at Grofit. Toward the end of my mandatory service, Ada and I decided to get married after my discharge. This decision came naturally, as did our decision to set up our home in Grofit.

Kibbutz life appealed to me, as it implemented the values I had been raised with at home in Kiryat Haim. Even as a youth, I searched for a life with meaning beyond fulfilling everyday material needs. I was drawn to ideals such as equality, social justice, and mutual responsibility. Our group often discussed ethical issues. We even instituted an "open cash-box" system – everyone contributed money according to their ability and received according to their needs.

When Ada and I decided to Hebraicize my family name of Smolainsky, we chose the name of our settlement group, Ya'alon (after a mountain and stream located north of Grofit).

Life on kibbutz was physically exhausting, but gratifying. Ada worked in agriculture and in caring for the newborn babies. I started in agriculture but soon found myself operating a power shovel (backhoe loader), which put me in the heavy mechanical equipment branch. We mostly worked on building Etzion Airport, near Eilat (the airport was ultimately transferred to Egypt in 1979 after the peace treaty was signed).

As members of a small, young kibbutz, we spent much of our after-work hours in various committee meetings and enjoying the cultural life of Grofit. Of course, we also worked hard, all of us. The following joke about life on kibbutz does not describe Grofit. A child asks his grandfather, member of a veteran kibbutz, "They say that in the early years on the kibbutz, you worked hard every day and danced all night. How did you have the energy?" The grandfather replies, "What do you mean? There were those who worked, and those who danced." Not on Grofit!

On the eve of Rosh Hashanah (the Jewish New Year) in late September 1973, about two years after finishing my mandatory military service, I was elected secretary of the kibbutz. Only ten days later, the Yom Kippur War erupted. It is not an exaggeration to state that the war changed the course of my life. It remains an indelible part of me.

It was the middle of the solemn fast day of Yom Kippur, October 6, 1973, slightly after two o'clock in the afternoon. A kibbutz member named Meir Ramon knocked on the door of our small apartment. In those days we had no telephones of our own, but Ramon told me that he'd walked past the kibbutz office and heard someone on a two-way radio calling from regional military headquarters in Eilat. When he answered, he was told that a war had broken out and he should operate the sirens. He came to me because I was the kibbutz security coordinator, in addition to my other duties.

I was unsure at first, because Meir was well known for his practical jokes. Was Israel really in a war, or was this just another gag? My doubt reflects the feeling of the entire State of Israel: this war took us all by complete surprise. But that night, I was ordered to report to my reserve unit in the center of the country. Buses from Eilat collected reservists like me from the area. I was a young reservist in the well-known 55th Paratroopers Brigade. This brigade had liberated Jerusalem in the Six-Day War under Motta Gur, who later became IDF chief of general staff. In the Yom Kippur War, Colonel Danny Matt (later major general) was commander of the brigade.

Israel was forced to make an abrupt transition from the complacency and cocky self-confidence of the post-1967 period to a feeling of existential threat. (The term "destruction of the Third Temple" is attributed to Moshe Dayan, then defense minister.) A sense of imminent danger permeated the public from the very beginning. This intensified over time, as reports arrived of the Egyptian capture of Israeli fortifications on the Suez Canal and Syrian capture of the Golan Heights. The news of large numbers of Israeli soldiers killed and wounded in battle, and mainly those taken captive, intensified the sense of threat and danger.

Those days of tense waiting in the brigade camp were the hardest of all. We heard disturbing reports from the battlefront while we sat and waited with our equipment. They explained to us that our destination still wasn't clear – Sinai or the Golan Heights. Finally, our brigade was sent to the Egyptian front in Sinai. On the night between October 15 and 16, 1973, we were the first brigade to cross the Suez Canal. Later on, this emerged as the strategy that tipped the military scales in our direction and led to a cease-fire under reasonable conditions. The brigade battled to cross the Canal and established a bridgehead on the western bank. We then continued toward the city of Suez, thus encircling Egypt's Third Army.

I don't remember exactly at what moment I decided that if I survived the war, I would sign on to serve in Israel's regular army. In fact, I'm not sure that such an exact moment truly existed. But as soon as the war ended, I realized that I had to make the change. There were several factors involved, though I don't know which of them tipped the scales. One was the sense of powerlessness and existential threat in the tense days of waiting at the beginning of the war. There was the fact that the Nahal Paratroopers Battalion 50, in which I did my mandatory service, had suffered many casualties during the Syrian offensive in the southern Golan Heights, and was forced to retreat on foot to the Sea of Galilee. Perhaps I lost a bit of my faith in Israel's political and military leadership. I knew that I returned to the kibbutz after the war without contributing something to the rehabilitation of the IDF, I'd suffer pangs of conscience.

During the war and afterwards, my wife and I corresponded about the changes I was considering. Then, on my first leave after the war, we reached our decision. On my way back to my unit in Suez, I stopped by the headquarters of Battalion 50, located at Gidi Pass, a strategic location in Sinai. I reported to Battalion Commander Yoram Yair ("Yaya," later a major general) and informed him of my intentions. I had my eye on the position of platoon leader, and I wasn't thinking about a long period of army service.

But life and fate led me elsewhere.

In talks with officers, military cadets, and youth after the 2006 Second Lebanon War, I noted in them the same sense of crisis and distrust vis-à-vis the leadership that I felt after the Yom Kippur War. Israel's top political and military leadership failed in both these wars. In the Yom

Kippur War, the tactical units saved the situation because the goal was clear: to risk our lives to defend the state. The issues surrounding the Second Lebanon War were more ambiguous. No clear goal was defined for the tactical land units, so they operated in an improvised manner and with frequent changes of mission. I believe that the tactical units of the Second Lebanon War were severely hampered by the high-level political and military echelons.

My decision to return to regular army service, if only for a short time period, was made after much agonizing on my part. I felt great commitment to the kibbutz, especially after I was elected as secretary. The kibbutz needed me, but the army needed me more. Meanwhile, Ada began her academic studies. Together we considered our options, and finally we decided that under the circumstances there was no point to living in Grofit. It would be better for us to leave until Ada finished her degree and I completed my army service. Then, afterwards, we would decide where to continue to build our home.

During my service in Battalion 50, I served as platoon leader, deputy company commander, and battalion operations officer, and in 1975 I was appointed company commander. It was not easy for a married family man to assume these positions. Even when I had to remain on base, Ada and I tried to spend our weekends together. She would come to wherever I was posted from Har Dov in the north to Mitla Pass in Sinai, in her green Simka 1000 car that became part of battalion folklore. For about three years we left Grofit and lived in Kiryat Tivon, until Ada completed her studies. Then we returned to Grofit, where Ada fully returned to kibbutz life and I visited on the weekends.

By the time we returned to the kibbutz, I was a company commander in Battalion 50, yet I still viewed my military service as temporary. I was sent for four months to serve as an instructor at Bahad 1 training base while I waited to take command of the paratrooper reconnaissance unit. I imagine that had they asked me to continue in such training positions, I would have concluded my army career and returned to kibbutz life. But when my commanders asked me to assume command over a paratrooper commando unit, I couldn't turn them down. This pattern was to return in later years as well, and I imagine that other officers had similar experiences when they considered leaving the army for civilian life. They received very tempting offers from the military – offers too fascinating and challenging to turn down.

Thus, my army service continued, from one interesting challenge to the next. Meanwhile Ada would remind me every once in a while that the man she'd married had been a mere sergeant in the reserves!

In 1978–1979, I served as commander of the Paratroopers Brigade Reconnaissance Company. Toward the end of my course of duty, it was again Nehemiah Tamari who called me in for a talk. This time, he offered me a position in the Sayeret Matkal commando unit (General Staff Reconnaissance Unit). Everyone who has ever served in that unit has a very simple nickname for it: "the Unit." As always, Nehemiah's offer took my breath away. He skillfully explained to me the great challenge involved in such a position, and I agreed to take it. My first period of service in the Unit was 1979–1981, at first as squadron leader and afterwards as a deputy commander under Uzi Dayan and Shai Avital. The demands placed on a combatant and commander in the Unit are very complex. On the one hand he must be able to resolve problems on his own and make decisions in real time. On the other hand, he must know how to work as part of a team, in harmony with the other combatants. That is not as easy as it may seem, because most soldiers tend to excel at one or the other (working alone or in a team), but not both. Thus, very few of those who want to serve in the Unit pass the rigorous selection process and its tests.

At the end of 1981, after I completed my term as deputy commander of Sayeret Matkal, I decided to take a leave of absence from the military.

I felt that I needed to be home with Ada and our growing family: our son Imri born in 1978 and our daughter Eshchar, born in 1980, and a third child was on the way (daughter Eshbal, born in 1981). I also wanted to return to kibbutz life, at least for a while. I returned to my family and kibbutz life while leaving my options open regarding military service. I worked in the dairy and was also fully involved in committees and cultural life on Grofit.

After seven months' leave of absence, I was summoned urgently to the Unit for a mission, and then the First Lebanon War broke out (June 1982). My leave came to an abrupt end, as did my life as a full-time kibbutznik. Ada remained an active kibbutznik. She was in charge of the irrigation system and the palm grove, was involved in the local educational system, and also served as regional manager for attracting new members. I, on the other hand, became a weekend father and kibbutznik.

Our status on the kibbutz was to change years later, in 1996. At that point, our children had grown up and I had a desk job in the army for the first time (head of the Military Intelligence Directorate at the Kiryah headquarters in Tel Aviv). Ada and I made a special arrangement with the kibbutz. We moved to central Israel, but we still try to visit Grofit, our true home, on occasional weekends.

I observed the crisis in the kibbutz movement with regret, if only as a bystander. I believe that the kibbutz movement itself, and especially its leaders, bear responsibility for the predicament. I have observed that societies, organizations, and countries must be prepared to reinvent themselves when necessary. In a world in which all spheres of life are changing at a constantly accelerating pace, we have to keep asking ourselves, "What has changed?" Otherwise, we become irrelevant. The kibbutz movement, and certain kibbutzim in particular, ignored changes that were affecting the world and Israel. They were blind to vicissitudes in the economy and society, until they reached the crisis point.

I believe that the communal lifestyle will continue to attract certain kinds of people, even in a world that has chosen capitalist rules for its economic game. A communal society still must follow capitalistic rules of the game in its relationship with the outside world, and it can enjoy the benefits involved. But regarding its internal life, it must maintain collective values. This is not easy, but I believe that it is possible.

In addition, the kibbutz movement must make a statement in the social justice sphere, even within a capitalistic country and society. For example, it should aspire toward an "enlightened social welfare capitalist society" and not a "capitalist pig" society.

Today, some kibbutzim, moshavim, and urban communes have given up community life and chosen different lifestyle rules. By contrast, others have preferred privatization, which completely changed the essence of kibbutz. I'm not one to eulogize the kibbutz movement. In my opinion it still has a future, but that depends on its members, and mainly its leadership.

The current crisis is caused by the failure of the movement's leadership in recent decades to present an updated version of its vision, an ideology relevant to the changes that have taken place in the world and Israel, and to Israel's future challenges. Instead, the energies of the kibbutz movement and its youth movement have focused on an internal debate regarding "resolving the conflict with our neighbors," under the slogan of the Peace Now concept. This is another reason behind the crisis. Following the failure of the Oslo Accords, the Peace Now movement became an "anti" movement, mainly focused on battling the settlements. The kibbutz movement was dragged along, together with its youth movements.

There can be no revival for a movement based solely on opposition to something else. A renewal plan must present a vision that aspires for something, instead of only opposing something else. The national religious movement succeeded in creating such a vision after the Six-Day War, and that is the secret of its success.

Kibbutz Grofit offered a warm, friendly environment for our children. For me, it was a weekend refuge, disconnected from the hustle and bustle of military life. Our children's positive view of Grofit strengthened our appreciation of it. During one of our weekends, we watched a television program about Ein Chatzeva, another desert community, far off in the northern Arava. The subject seemed interesting, so we all sat down to watch, including our children. The program showed Palestinian laborers from the southern Hebron hills on a wagon hitched to a tractor, on their way to pick melons. Our eldest was in kindergarten at the time and had never before seen a Palestinian. He commented, "Their volunteers don't look bad at all." (Volunteers from all over the world had worked on Grofit, but it was against the law to employ Palestinians in our region.) When I asked him what he meant, he said, "At least they don't have earrings in their ears." Ada and I realized that our kids lived in a "greenhouse," isolated from the rest of Israel.

In another incident, on a trip from Grofit to visit family in Haifa, our two-year-old boy fell asleep on the back bench of the military Renault 4 vehicle. He woke up when we approached the Carmel Mountains, lifted his head, stared incredulously at a mountain, and said, "Look what happened to this mountain! It's green!" It was the first time he'd seen a mountain that wasn't brown and desolate, like in the Arava.

In the Arava you can be isolated from the entire world. In Grofit, you can hear the quiet. The silence, the distance, the view, and of course, the members, made Grofit a hothouse for the children and a refuge for the adults. This was the reason we loved the place.

CHAPTER 5

Moving Up the Ranks

When the First Lebanon War (Operation Peace for Galilee) broke out in June 1982, I came to an agreement with Sayeret Matkal commander Shai Avital that during this operation, I would command an independent force of the Unit. My first mission was to "mop up" the Lebanese villages at the foot of Mount Dov, from Shuba to Al-Mari. Then my force and I joined another force that had begun to open the Wadi Sheba'a artery, and this led to a battle at a site known as the Meyu'eret ("forested hill").

The Meyu'eret controlled the northern entrance route to Wadi Sheba'a (Lebanon's easternmost artery, on the border of the Syrian side of Mt. Hermon) and the villages in the Ain Aata region. Control of this territory was vital for opening a route to the Beirut-Damascus road. Thus, a Unit team under Ilan Dvir secretly infiltrated the Meyu'eret at night.

The Syrians detected the advance of Unit infantry and mechanized forces on the wadi route and thought that the Meyu'eret was empty. They sent a company-size force there. When I heard the report about the Syrian force climbing toward the Meyu'eret, I advanced rapidly with my force on foot, to reinforce Ilan Dvir's team in anticipation of battle. Later, Commander Shai Avital joined us.

When I reached the heights of the Meyu'eret, I met Ilan, who already had set up shooting positions under cover of the rocky terrain. I spotted trucks transporting the Syrian force, one tank, and two BMP APCs (armored personnel carriers), which accompanied the force and provided cover as it climbed toward us.

We surprised the Syrians with initiated fire that harmed most of their force. The tank and the BMP started to shoot in our direction, but since we had no effective anti-tank weapons, we used armor-piercing artillery that knocked out two of the three vehicles. Meanwhile, the third one retreated and cut off contact. Within a short time, we had destroyed most of the Syrian force and won the battle, and we had zero casualties.

The division commander, Brigadier General (later major general) Emmanuel Sakal, justifiably wanted to exploit our success, so he backed up this effort with armored forces. He placed the deputy division commander, Colonel (later brigadier general) Menashe Inbar, in charge.

From this point on, our advance on the route was by armored vehicle, instead of by foot as earlier. We also advanced by day, not night, despite disagreement on this between me and Shai. The next morning, the armored force that tried to lead the attack was hit by exploding mines and antitank missiles. The battle became a rescue operation. The Unit lost Sergeant Nir Yeshua, who was killed when his APC was hit by an anti-tank missile.

Once again, we learned what Yaya's paratrooper brigade had proved in the First Lebanon War: "Sometimes the longer way is shorter, while the shorter route is longer." We learned that walking on mountainous territory is faster than travel in armored vehicles.

At the end of this stage of the operation, our forces were on the outskirts of Beirut. Most of the Unit's soldiers returned to the base. Shai agreed that I would remain with a limited staff at the headquarters of the Northern Command, in Aalay close to Beirut. The idea was to remain close to the arena and try to plan missions that would give the Unit a relative advantage.

I conducted patrols on the outskirts of the Lebanese capital, aiming to locate deployments of terrorists and the Syrian army, and so we would be ready to conquer the city if necessary. On one of these patrols, in the vicinity of the Lebanese government offices, I almost paid with my life. I looked out the window of the office of the Lebanese Health Ministry toward a group of terrorists stationed in the row of buildings in front of us. I moved my head from the corner of the window, and a fraction of a second later, a bullet hit the spot where my head had been.

Next I was given the mission of locating Arafat, but I was unable to accomplish this.

During those days of tense waiting for the command to conquer Beirut, an incident led me to decide to leave army service. One Saturday between the end of the first stage of the Lebanon War and our invasion of Beirut, I received orders to appear early Sunday morning at Northern Command headquarters in Aalay. When I reached the office, the intelligence officer and the Northern Command Operations officer filled me in on the latest news. It seemed that Defense Minister Ariel Sharon had put pressure on Chief of General Staff Raphael (Raful) Eitan, and on GOC Northern Command Amir Drori, to send a Sayeret Matkal team to approach the Syrian-controlled area at the northern edge of Beirut's international airport. I was clearly told that Raful, Drori, and headquarters officers saw no point in such an operation, as it would endanger the force and would not provide any new information. They tried to convince Sharon to back down from his plan. However, I was also told that during that Shabbat, Sharon had called Raful and expressed his fury that the operation had not been carried out. Sharon ordered Raful to impose the task on the Unit, to be carried out on Sunday night.

Amir Drori personally gave the order, and I could easily sense that he did not agree with the operation. After I received the order and the briefing, I said that I'd study the mission and return by the afternoon with a plan.

I went out to tour the area, and very quickly it became clear to me that Raful's and Drori's impressions were correct: the task was risky, and there was little benefit to be gained. There was another way to solve the problem, and at far less risk. Considering the complex situation and the indecision involved, I called Unit commander Shai Avital to join us. I was certain that I wouldn't risk soldiers for a mission I didn't believe in, but I was very disappointed at the way the chief of general staff and the GOC had responded to the defense minister. I felt that it was inappropriate for a defense minister to intervene on the tactical level to determine how a mission should be carried out, just as it was inappropriate for a COGS and GOC to forward the order for execution instead of halting the entire process.

When Shai reached Aalay, we met with the GOC. We had agreed between us that under the circumstances, it would be inappropriate to carry out the mission as planned. Simultaneously a force was prepared, in the hope that the mission would be changed in such a way that we could execute it.

Ultimately, Major General Drori became convinced that there was no point in carrying out the mission in the original format. He instructed us to do something minimal, so that he could report to the defense minister that the mission had been performed.

After the mission was over, I announced to Shai that I had no desire to serve in such an army. "I will continue my service until I finish my missions in Beirut, and then I will request a discharge," I said. I was angry over Sharon's behavior as defense minister, as well as the behavior of the COS and GOC toward Sharon and toward us, the soldiers in the field.

Shai spoke to me several times, trying to convince me to change my mind. The events of Sabra and Shatila and the appointment of the Kahan Commission (Commission of Inquiry into the Events at the Refugee Camps in Beirut) offered me an escape. After the commission was appointed, I was willing to wait and make my final decision based on its findings. Indeed, its conclusions – mainly regarding the defense minister, the COS and the GOC Northern Command – did permit me to change my mind. I thought that the system had proved that it was able to deal with unworthy behavior, even of its top brass.

After the murder of Lebanese president-elect Bashir Gemayel, we took control of Beirut. The Unit, under my command, participated in this mission without any complications. When the battles died down, we focused on efforts to locate Arafat, but again we were unsuccessful. The only time that Arafat was seen up close was when he boarded a ship that took him away from Beirut along with his PLO supporters, as part of their surrender agreement. We had him in the sights of a sniper rifle at only six hundred feet (180 m) away – the odds were almost 100 percent that we could have killed him. However, at that point we no longer had authorization to shoot him.

After the PLO evacuated Beirut, my role in Lebanon came to an end. I decided to take a command and staff officers' course, in the hopes of receiving the post of battalion commander in the Paratroopers Brigade, and afterwards compete for the position of Sayeret Matkal commander.

About nine weeks after beginning the course, I was urgently asked to assume command over Battalion 890. The battalion's commander was dismissed after a series of operational and safety-related mishaps that took place during Operation Peace for Galilee and afterwards.

Battalion 890 was in crisis. Some soldiers were wounded, others had died because of the mishaps, and now there was the additional trauma of the commander's dismissal. When I assumed command, I heard voices saying, "What bad luck, to get a battalion in crisis." By the way, I heard similar expressions after assuming three other positions during my military service. But when I finished these same roles, people told me, "What luck you had to assume this position during such a good period!"

I began to understand Napoleon Bonaparte's famous expression, "I don't need generals with brains – I prefer generals with luck." In other words, to have "luck" you need to have "brains."

Actually, this expression can have another meaning, similar to a statement made by Lieutenant General Yigael Yadin, archeologist and former chief of general staff. Some say that after he found the hidden scrolls in the Judean Desert, he was asked to explain the source of his luck. Yadin answered, "I learned from my service in the IDF that to have 'luck,' you need a very good battle procedure." In other words, you must plan meticulously and execute those plans precisely.

I learned that command and war are arts. Precisely because war is the very essence of uncertainty, the only guarantee for success, or "luck," is prior thinking and planning, attention to detail without losing the big picture, modesty, and experience – the key to wise action. When I concluded my role as commander of Battalion 890, I sensed that I had that luck. The same was true regarding the other three functions when I heard comments about "bad luck" at first. These three roles were commander of Sayeret Matkal, commander of the Judea-Samaria division, and COGS.

Three weeks after I received command of Battalion 890, the first and last training accident took place during my watch as commander. Soldier Aryeh Kroll was killed when a grenade blew up during training in a populated area in the Golan Heights. Even when it came to accidents, I learned that "luck" has a lot to do with preparation and performance in battle. I succeeded in lowering the percentage of accidents of all types, in the units I commanded, and as chief of general staff, throughout the IDF.

I commanded Battalion 890 for about two years beginning in December 1982. During this period, the battalion successfully handled terror attacks by Hezbollah and other organizations in the Ain Zhalta region, Tyre, and Sidon. I also worked to instill law and order in the tension between Druze and Christians in the Shouf Mountains of Lebanon. The battalion thwarted many attempted attacks and killed many terrorists.

Several soldiers on our side were wounded, but not one was killed. Our success was the result of creative thinking, high operational tension, and discipline, avoiding routine so as not to reveal weak spots in operational and administrative activity. As I had learned, in the art of command and the art of war, success – or "luck" – is in the details.

In 1984, I finished my stint as Battalion 890 commander and was appointed deputy commander of the 35th Paratrooper Brigade. Toward the end of my service, on May 27, 1985, I was wounded in the foot while leading pursuit of a band of Hezbollah terrorists in Lebanon. After two weeks in the hospital, I returned to duty and hobbled around on crutches until the end of my term of service.

In late 1985, I took a sabbatical to study at the British Army's Camberley Staff College. After a long and extended process, I had finally realized that army service was my life's mission. It was not a sudden bolt of lightning. But you don't take your family to study in England, at the IDF's expense, in order to quit the army when you return to Israel.

In May 1986, in the middle of the school year, I received a phone call from Amnon Lipkin-Shahak, head of the Military Intelligence Directorate. He asked to meet with me urgently, following a series of failures in Sayeret Matkal. So one weekend, I flew to Switzerland and met Amnon in the airport. He was returning to Israel from the US and stopped in Switzerland specifically to meet me.

Amnon told me about problems in the Unit. He asked me to leave my studies in England shortly before the official end of the year and return to the Unit, which was in crisis. The British were adamant that I could not interrupt my studies, so I was able to complete the academic program. At the beginning of 1987, I was appointed commander of the Unit.

Many people view my period as Sayeret Matkal commander as the height of my career, for many reasons. In my term, the Unit carried out a plethora of operations, particularly compared to its activity in earlier periods. When I served as chief of general staff, the number of Sayeret Matkal operations also rose significantly. Part of the reason for this was that as a former Unit commander, I could push for certain activities and stubbornly insist to the prime minister about certain missions, even when others opposed or expressed their doubts. Of course, I took full authority for my perseverance and for the results of the operations. There were at least several operations that the prime minister would probably have refused to authorize, had I not insisted as COGS and a former Unit commander. I commanded the Unit during its difficult period, but I related to the crisis situation as an opportunity for change. My point of departure was the understanding that failures in operations over the border start here in Israel, on the base, in the norms of daily behavior.

When I look back on the past, I think that one of the reasons that I was successful in my Unit command period was that I brought something new to the unit, something that past commanders lacked – outside experience. I came to Sayeret Matkal after having served in other units, as paratrooper platoon leader and company commander, commander of the paratrooper reconnaissance unit, battalion commander, and deputy brigade commander.

By contrast, most of the Unit's previous officers and commanders were trained, educated, and grew within the Unit, without any experience in other units. The tradition in Sayeret Matkal was that a commander of an excellent team would be picked as the next Unit commander. Their experience was in planning reconnaissance operations. Most of the Unit commanders stubbornly refused to deal with administrative work, a sphere that was viewed as especially repulsive. As far as they were concerned, the only important thing was to hold "a knife between the teeth." This model became entrenched in the Unit for years.

On the other hand, I felt that attention to detail in kitchen, the backyard, and the armament department were also important, no less than planning the next operation. For example, the armament department might be responsible for providing that "one little nail" that proved vital to the operation's success.

Over the years, the Unit's soldiers and officers were taught to view themselves as the best, and that was indeed correct. However, many of them went one step too far. They decided that everything was permissible to them, and this led to inappropriate behavior. For example, the general IDF directives specify that the beret belongs on the shoulder. Yet some commanders said to their soldiers, "You can walk around with the beret in your pocket. Just be ready to whip it out, and heaven help you if a military policeman catches you!" I viewed such statements as extremely problematic. This is how a criminal subculture develops, and I refused to condone it.

The battle against such practices was not easy. Coming from the rank-and-file military, I realized that such behavior was at the root of the problem. In such an atmosphere, a soldier does not know the difference between permitted and forbidden, or how far he can stretch the disciplinary boundaries. It was not hard to see the direct connection between everyday discipline issues, training safety issues, and operational discipline. When there is dissonance between how a soldier is supposed to behave and what the soldier actually does, this creates a serious problem. Of course, it's good to be creative, daring, and proactive – but soldiers must also be disciplined. I led the Unit to its achievements according to this worldview.

From the beginning, I was meticulous in transmitting messages that were clear and unambiguous. Of course, the operational sphere is the heart of the Sayeret's activity, but my assumption always was that the strength of a unit is the strength of its weakest link. Therefore, I emphasized subjects such as the importance of safety in training, strict observance of procedures, and proper handling of equipment and armaments.

I learned in the Unit that elitism and individualism breed a tendency toward the "soloist" phenomenon, in which each soldier sees himself as the best. He forgets that the best soloist in the world cannot play a concerto without an orchestra. So, for example, I insisted that when there was an operational success worthy of citation, the decoration would be bestowed on the entire unit. Success results from the actions of all soldiers, from commanders to those in the lowest-ranking administrative positions. Indeed, in the course of my period as commander of the Sayeret we received a record number of citations. Elitism and individualism can easily lead to arrogance, which is a recipe for failure. I believe that individual modesty and the channeling of high-level personal abilities into harmonious teamwork raises the chances of success. I attribute my successes to this form of cooperative leadership.

I also feel that it is important for officers to occasionally leave their units for positions outside the unit. These officers offer their new units important operational experience and strong personal qualities. In addition, they acquire experience in commanding other types of missions and coping with varied time schedules, subordinates, and environments. This is important for improving the command abilities of the officers in anticipation of their return to the Sayeret. It also widens their horizons to other service tracks in the military. I was pleased that numerous officers rose to the challenge, and some of them still serve in senior IDF positions today.

During my service in Sayeret Matkal, my problem-solving skills were perfected. Sometimes I had to deal with problems that seemed, at first glance, to be lacking solutions, and obstacles that seemed insurmountable. It's as if someone places an obstacle opposite you and tells you that you must find a way to penetrate it to get to the other side. Your instinctive response is, that's impossible. Yet in the Unit, you realize that it is possible. You think about the obstacle, you collect data about it, you think creatively, and you find out-of-the-box solutions. If there's enough time – and usually there is – the impossible becomes possible. From a philosophical perspective, if a human being in this world has created something, then someone else can create something to destroy it. For every protection system created by a human, another human can break into it. The only unknown is which resources must be allocated toward the objective. Sayeret Matkal has almost unlimited time at its disposal. It also has the most advanced intelligence capacities available to the State of Israel (and that's a great deal), and it also has financial means beyond all other army units. Most importantly, it has outstanding people. In this framework it is possible to develop operational tools on the highest level.

When I began my term as Sayeret Matkal commander, I understood that the Unit would have to use its top operational abilities to attempt to release captured navigator Ron Arad. This involved intensive, covert operational activity and efforts to locate where he was held. In addition, I instructed the Sayeret intelligence officer, Major Eyal Regunis, to track down Hezbollah operatives and others whom we could use as bargaining chips for Ron's release.

The first target that was identified as a bargaining chip – someone we could find and bring to our territory – was Jawad al-Qazfi Hasin, a mid-level Hezbollah commander in the Tibnit region of southern Lebanon. He was mentioned as being responsible for an attack on the IDF and South Lebanese Army (SLA) convoys in the Beit Yahoun region. Yosef Fink and Rahamim Levi Alsheikh were both killed in this attack. Al-Qazfi was also cited as being responsible for additional terror attacks against IDF and SLA forces in South Lebanon's security zone.

Regunis and his staff conducted painstaking intelligence work for a few months on al-Qazfi to discern his pattern of activity in the area where he lived. They discovered, for example, that almost every morning he went to visit a greenhouse that he owned.

At first, a daylight operation in Lebanese territory seemed impossible. But in line with Unit tradition, we succeeded in planning an operation that would exploit the enemy's weak spots, which always exist. On the morning of the operation, we waited close to the border. I was at the command post. Beside me was division commander Brigadier General Nehemiah Tamari, in case of any complication and need for assistance. To avoid leaks, the regular IDF forces on the border knew nothing of what was happening right under their noses.

Around seven-thirty a.m., intelligence sources spotted al-Qazfi driving his car toward the greenhouse. With perfect timing, the camouflaged force was dispatched, and they caught him. Al-Qazfi was heavy, and he tried to resist without knowing who he faced. He was loaded onto the force's vehicle as planned and taken to our territory. I reported to Chief of General Staff Dan Shomron and to Head of Intelligence Amnon Lipkin-Shahak that "the package is in our hands."

Aware that only one card in our bargaining deck was hardly sufficient, we continued to search for additional targets. The Unit succeeded in bringing two more significant bargaining chips from Lebanon: Sheikh Abdel Karim Obeid (an operation that I started to plan, which was carried out a few months after I left the Unit) and Mustafa Dirani.

Unfortunately, we didn't succeed in locating Ron Arad.

Another operation from the same period that eventually became public, was Operation Presentation of Purpose – the elimination of master terrorist Khalil al-Wazir, known as Abu Jihad, in his home in Tunis. Abu Jihad had been responsible for a series of terror attacks and the murders of dozens of Israelis.

Military Intelligence Head General Amnon Lipkin-Shahak told me in a meeting that the task of eliminating Abu Jihad had originally been imposed on the Mossad. When the Mossad found the task to be too difficult, it was given to the Unit.

I began examining the feasibility of the operation by instructing Regunis, the Unit's intelligence officer, to collect and present all the intelligence material he had about Abu Jihad. After analyzing the material, we understood that it might be feasible to carry out the mission in Tunis, where he lived and operated. I appointed Nachum Lev as commander of the operation, and we plunged into advanced planning. We chose the fighting force and conducted operational preparations and training – in other words, battle procedure.

The operation presented many challenges due to the large distance involved. We also were uncertain about our ability to keep close tabs on our target and bring in the force exactly on time, when Abu Jihad was in his house. This meant that we required the cooperation of the Air Force, the Navy, Military Intelligence units, and the Mossad.

In most operations, the Unit commander oversees the operation from the tactical headquarters, as that is the where one can get the most exact picture of the situation for decision-making purposes. But in this case, due to various developments that could feasibly take place during the operation, I realized that I should join the force in the field. Such a decision requires authorization from the head of the Military Intelligence Directorate as well as from the COGS, and I received the requisite authorizations.

After meticulous preparations within a relatively short timetable, the operation was carried out successfully.

When people ask me which function I enjoyed the most in my military service, I answer without hesitation, "commander of the Unit." In that unit I was exposed to unique operational challenges that the commander must address. I also had access to the best of our youths and the best resources, and independence in my job. I never had such independence in any other position, not even as chief of general staff. The Unit commander position enables the expression of creativity, the ability to plan and to implement, and above all – daring. This is reflected in the slogan of the Sayeret Matkal: "He who dares, wins."

The Unit is like an orchestra in which the commander is both composer and conductor. The challenge of the commander is to compose a melody that soldiers will be able to carry out perfectly. Most importantly, the commander-conductor knows how to produce the best from his subordinates. To do that, command and headquarters positions must be occupied by excellent officers.

When I commanded the Unit, I was privileged to work with an excellent group of staff officers and commanders, very few of whom are familiar to the public. One example was my deputy Pinchas Buchris, who was a brigadier general at discharge, after commanding Unit 8200 of the intelligence corps and serving as Defense Ministry director. Others were Nachum Lev (who was killed in a motorcycle accident in the Arava after he was discharged from the IDF as colonel); Ran Shachor (who also replaced me as commander of the Unit, and was discharged as brigadier general), Tal Russo (discharged as major general, after serving as head of the Operations Directorate and GOC Southern Command), and Yossi Baidatz (discharged as major general, after he had served as head of the research department in Military Intelligence and commander of the military colleges). Team commanders who were known to the public included Nitzan Alon (who also commanded the Unit, advanced to the rank of major general and served as head of the Operations Directorate), Hagai Peleg Fadida (commander of Yamam, the special counterterrorism unit of the border police, director of the Ministry of Internal Security and the Ministry of Strategic Affairs), and Dror Weinberg (who was killed in a battle with terrorists in Hebron, when he served as commander of the Judea Brigade).

One of the officers who served under my command in the Unit was Captain (Ret.) Benjamin Netanyahu. During that period, he was Israel's ambassador to the UN, and thus was not required to serve in the reserves. Nevertheless, he did reserve duty every year, mainly to take command of a special training course series. Our paths crossed again when he was elected prime minister in 1996. At that time, I was head of the Military Intelligence Directorate. In my joint work with Netanyahu as prime minister, I witnessed his inexperience at the beginning of his term, but also the way he bridged the initial gaps through intensive study, and mainly through his consolidated strategic vision, broad knowledge, and deep understanding of history.

Among the officers in headquarters, intelligence officer Eyal Regunis stood out (he died from an illness after he was discharged). To me, Eyal was the ultimate intelligence officer, a true model for the other intelligence officers. I first met him as a noncommissioned intelligence officer (NCO) in the Paratroopers Reconnaissance Company. He was with me in the same APC during the Litani operation. I took note of his abilities and sent him to the officers' training course. We went our separate ways when he became intelligence officer of Battalion 890 and then of the Paratroopers Brigade. When I was informed of my appointment to commander of the Unit, I decided that I wanted Eyal as my intel officer. By then, he had been discharged and had returned to his civilian work as architect, but I contacted him and urged him to accept the position. After "wooing" him intensively and spending many long hours in his home, he finally agreed.

Eyal was a man of integrity and was also very thorough, diligent, and creative. Last but not least, he had strong opinions, which he shared with me even when they disagreed with my own. He also didn't hesitate to share them with people of higher rank. Eyal might have been shunted aside had he served under commanders who prefer yes-men, but under me he flourished. As noted, the success of the Unit during my command was based on good officers, and Eyal stood out for his unique contribution. May his memory be a blessing to us all.

I've often been asked to pinpoint the first time that I thought I might be appointed chief of general staff. I don't have an exact answer, but I do know that it happened in parallel to the realization that military service was my mission. Once I understood this, I wanted to do the maximum – as always – and in the army, the "maximum" is the position of COGS. The awareness that I might reach that position ripened when I was a commander of Sayeret Matkal. Toward the end of that period, my commanders advised me to consider long-term service in the IDF.

At this point I would like to note that throughout my military service, I was careful not to push myself forward while stepping on others along the way. I did not try to sell myself. I didn't make connections with politicians or ingratiate myself with reporters. Some people tried to explain to me that I was making a tactical mistake. They insisted that I'd need to adopt these methods in order to make my way up the ladder. I answered by saying that the army is not a beauty pageant. Even if my approach was wrong, I would not participate in such a game because I'm simply not built for it. I truly believed that my actions would speak for themselves, and that I didn't need to promote myself.

I also emphasize that I never set the rank of lieutenant general as a goal for myself, not even when I assumed the position of deputy chief of general staff. The opposite is true: I viewed every position, and invested in every position, as if it were my last stint in the army, and not as a stepping-stone to the next role.

CHAPTER 6

Fighting Terror

I was troubled by the way the IDF conducted itself in Judea and Samaria, beginning in my years as Sayeret Matkal commander (1987–1989) when I sent teams of young soldiers there for occasional operations. Then, as Paratroopers Brigade commander (1990–1991), I accompanied the brigade's units in their regular security activities in Judea and Samaria. I was dissatisfied by what I saw, and I felt that the IDF could be more effective in dealing with the Palestinian terror threat.

I expressed my criticism in various settings: to Chief of General Staff Dan Shomron, and then to his deputy Ehud Barak (who eventually replaced Shomron). I also expressed my criticism to Military Intelligence head Amnon Lipkin-Shahak and GOC central commanders from Amram Mitzna onward. Finally, in 1991, newly appointed GOC Central Command Danny Yatom asked me to test my use of force concept for the IDF in Judea and Samaria, and then to offer my recommendations.

In 1991, I went out to the field with brigade officers headed by operations branch officer Major (later colonel) Chaim (Ras) Avital, and intelligence officer Major (later colonel) Yoram Moyal. After a few weeks,

I sent a report in which I dissected the situation and the existing views, and offered a new perspective.

Evidently it was this report that led to my appointment as commander of the Judea and Samaria division in January 1992, instead of traveling to the United States for studies. I never regretted this move, because it was one of the most challenging positions I have occupied. In 1991, after the Gulf War was over, I made an important observation that I brought to this position. At that time, the IDF was acting as if the Intifada was still going on, when in truth, the Gulf War drastically changed the nature of the confrontation. The IDF had amassed much experience in dealing with the intifada phenomenon, especially large-scale riots, but it failed to notice that things had changed drastically. Basically, the IDF was prepared for and handling the previous conflict – but after it was already over. By the summer of 1991, I discerned a drop in the major demonstrations and a rise in terror activities: from throwing stones on passing cars to shooting and killing Israeli citizens, or killing Arabs suspected of being Israeli collaborators.

The "wanted persons" (terrorists) phenomenon became the main threat, and we dealt with it through arrests and preventive activities. The situation improved over the years as we established new units: the Mista'arvim units of Duvdevan and Yamas of the Border Police (counterterrorism units that operate undercover in Arab towns), and the unit for Operations Observations in the Judea-Samaria division. Nevertheless, the number of wanted terrorists continued to rise every month, and the IDF was not able to resolve the problem.

The problem was that certain neighborhoods in Jenin, the casbah (Arab market) and refugee camps in Nablus, and certain towns (like Qabatiya, Arrabe and others) were controlled by organizations and gangs like the Black Panther and Red Eagle. Entering these places involved a military operation on the scale of a battalion or even an entire brigade.

What I sensed, and even heard, in the IDF was the statement, "There is no military solution." This was accompanied by a shrug of the shoulders that said, "There's nothing we can do about it." This statement was uttered by high-ranking IDF commanders when the Intifada broke out in 1987 and throughout its course. I did not like this at all.

I did not agree with this statement at the time, and I still do not approve of it, just as I do not like the oversimplified statement "Let the IDF win." Philosopher Carl von Clausewitz famously uttered that "War is the continuation of policy by other means" (*Principles of War* [London: John Lane, 1943], 11). In my opinion, this statement remains true and will remain true forever; what it means is that military activity does not stand alone. Instead, war has always served political goals, and will always do so. Thus, the applications of military force should be viewed only as one means among others to achieve diplomatic goals. The additional methods are, of course, political, diplomatic, economic, and social, plus "the battle for hearts and minds" (public relations).

To clarify, the army is certainly expected to strive to overpower the threats that it faces, and each echelon should strive for victory on its level. However, the different echelons do not stand by themselves. Multiple victories on the tactical level are not enough to achieve victory, especially when the operative and/or strategic management is weak. Sometimes, military victory is even followed by diplomatic surrender (one example was Israel's disengagement from Gaza in 2005 after the Defensive Shield military campaign in 2002). Such situations are generally complex and should not be addressed on a superficial level.

The victory over terror in Gaza in 1970–1972 is an example of victory on the tactical and operative level. But it did not result in strategic defeat of the Palestinian threat or resolve the conflict that erupted again in 1987 (the First Intifada). I learned that military power can defeat terror on the tactical and operative level, but strategic defeat is only achieved by undercutting the enemy's motivation to use terror tactics. Thus, military victory over terror (tactical and operative) is a necessary, but not sufficient, condition for achieving strategic victory. Strategic victory necessitates additional components, in the realms of politics (and I do not mean "giving in" to terror), diplomacy, and public relations (to convince others that you are right and have them agree to your narrative as the accepted one). In addition, victory involves shoring up the country's inner stability by strengthening the resilience of the society under attack, their belief in the legitimacy of their path, and their determination not to surrender to terror. Another important component of a strategy to defeat terror is the battle over hearts and minds, in the international political and public arena as well as on the enemy side.

I believed that the Judea-Samaria division could and should do more (and do it better) to defeat terror on the tactical and operative levels, within its operational district.

Below is a summary of the steps that I adopted:

1. I abolished irrelevant activities designed to handle mass riots, since that threat no longer existed (these included on-call readiness for dispersing Palestinian crowds emerging from mosques on Fridays; reinforcing forces to deal with strike days; and allotting aerial means to locate mass riots, among others).
2. Enhanced the special operations capabilities for imprisonment of "wanted" individuals, both methods and means, while personally training the commanders and units involved in this sphere.
3. Enlarged the scope of special operations by delegating authority to brigade commanders. (When each operation demanded authorization of the division commander, only about five operations were carried out a week. When the brigade commanders were authorized to do so, the number rose to about fifty operations per week.)

4. Raised the level and capabilities of the intelligence officers in the six regional brigades (Hebron, Bethlehem, Ramallah, Nablus, Jenin, and Qalqilya).
5. Classified stone throwing as an act of terror and declared war on anyone involved in the circle of violence, "from the stone thrower and up."
6. Encouraged normalization in the lives of Arab residents by abolishing the nightly curfews, making only minimal use of curfews in general, and abolishing many of the checkpoints. Finally, we encouraged economic development in coordination with local entities and the head of the civil administration, Brigadier General Gadi Zohar.
7. Abolished many guard duty tasks. Instead, the force is used for flexible preemptive activities.

Beyond the change in policy regarding the use of the forces, I felt that it was important to infuse a fighting spirit in the soldiers. Officers who shrug their shoulders and explain that "there is no military solution" discourage the fighting spirit of their soldiers.

I decided to involve the commanders in a sphere that became problematic during my watch: the issue of Metzach investigations (Military Police Criminal Investigation Division or MPCID) and the involvement of the state prosecutor who used penal tools for military operations. I took action to strengthen the responsibility of the commanders for problematic actions of their soldiers and to avoid the military courts, for as many cases as possible. (At first the commanders resisted my policy, but eventually I was able to coordinate with the Military Advocate General). That is why I was so angered by the political attacks on me as defense minister and claims that I had abandoned the soldier Elor Azaria. I explain this in detail later in this book.

I also fought against several absurd issues that I had discovered back when I was a brigade commander. For example, I demanded certain changes in the open-fire directives. I changed the definition of "risk to life," which enables and requires shooting to harm or kill any individual who throws a Molotov cocktail (incendiary bomb) or improvised bomb.

(At the beginning of the discussions on the subject, some attorneys tried to make a distinction between an "improvised" bomb and a "standard" bomb – as if soldiers can distinguish between the two when something is hurled at them, and especially at night!)

In one incident, a soldier fatally harmed someone, even though he only intended to injure the victim, during implementation of a suspect arrest. I demanded that when Metzach investigate the case, they begin the process by investigating the highest commander of the sector – at least the level of brigade commander. Ultimately, this issue was concluded in discussions with the chief of general staff, to my satisfaction and that of the military attorney general, Brigadier General Ilan Schiff.

I ascribe special importance to these issues. We must give our fighters practical tools with which to handle the enemy and back them up when they follow the rules. This includes cases when something goes wrong, but not because of premeditated intent or malice.

In discussions on these issues, I discovered that the commanders had developed a habit of blaming the prosecutors for meddling and misunderstanding the territory and conditions. However, I discovered that these commanders had only themselves to blame. They tended to leave their soldiers to the mercy of the prosecutors, who then took advantage of the situation when prosecuting the soldiers.

The changes I initiated in the division became evident within a short time. In my second month of duty in February 1992, we performed a sequence of successful arrest operations, as well as a series of skirmishes which ended with dead terrorists. This created the impression that the Israelis were "going nuts." At that point, people on the wanted list preferred to surrender themselves rather than risk being killed.

One of the first operations that led to accelerating the extradition process for wanted individuals took place during that second month of duty. An undercover Mista'arvim force, which was on alert regarding a certain operation in the Tulkarm region, received information from the Shin Bet on a Hamas wanted man. The target would be participating in a public soccer game in the town of Shuweika. According to the report, he would be playing left wingback and wearing a red shirt with the number eleven. Based on this description, the experienced force quickly planned their operation for arresting the terrorist before the game ended.

The six-man force approached the soccer field in a vehicle and split up into two cells, advancing on foot to surround the playing field on both sides. The cell that entered from the east planned to make the arrest. They identified the wanted man in the northwest corner of the field and circled the field innocently in his direction. When they got to the corner, the target smelled a rat. He began to run to the northern fence, toward an opening that he evidently knew about.

The Mista'arvim cell pulled out their weapons, donned police hats for identification, and shouted for the suspect to stop. Then they fired into the air. The man kept running, so they shot toward his feet. The fugitive slid on a muddy patch of ground near the break in the fence, took a bullet in his lower back, and died.

Although this was an accident, about three hundred people sitting in the stadium balcony viewed the assassination in the light of day. The next day, eight wanted terrorists from the same town surrendered at the Civil Administration offices.

During another arrest attempt in the Jenin refugee camp, a wanted terrorist pulled out a gun while trying to escape from the window of a house. Our forces shot and killed him. That led Faisal Husseini to hold a press conference in which he attacked the IDF's "execution policy." Head of Central Command Danny Yatom and I came under attack in the Israeli media by several Knesset members and reporters for the "change in policy," and were asked to explain ourselves.

I held that we should not explain the rules of engagement in detail, as we wanted to preserve the sense of threat and fear among the wanted individuals. To calm the wave of criticism, I suggested that we invite the Knesset members who criticized our policies to visit the division, especially the Mista'arvim undercover units. That way they could view the activity from up close and see with their own eyes the commanders and soldiers they were criticizing. So, for example, Knesset Member Shulamit Aloni of the Meretz Party visited the Duvdevan unit, where she discovered fighters who have values similar to her own and who operate according to orders. After the visit, she toned down her critique – at least for a short time period.

Within a few months, about 180 wanted terrorists gave themselves up.

The multiplicity of the special operations also led to several snafus. In one, Duvdevan fighter Sergeant Eli Isha was killed in a friendly fire incident. Due to this tragic event, I dismissed the commander of Duvdevan unit. However, I did not change my decision regarding the decentralization process: brigade commanders were still authorized to conduct operations. I emphasize this because I have seen that after an operational mishap, commanders tend to want to raise the rank for authorizing operations. I learned that the higher the rank needed to authorize operational activity, the fewer the number of operations authorized. Further, raising the authorization level does nothing to resolve or prevent accidents. Therefore, we must aspire to reduce authorization levels to the lowest possible ranks, even when we experience mishaps.

An additional change was expressed in the activities of the regular battalions and the reserve regiments in the division. The numerous guard missions meant that company and battalion commanders became mere

Once a Paratrooper…

Top: Commander of Battalion 890 before parachuting in an exercise

Center: Chief of General Staff, at the parting parachute drop

Bottom right: deputy commander of Brigade 35, after I was wounded

Bottom left: Commander of the Unit

Commander of the Unit

Change of command ceremony in the unit. *From left:* Giora Zore'a, Nehemiah Tamari, Giora Inbar, Amnon Lipkin-Shahak, Moshe Ya'alon, Moshe Levi, Yiftach Atir (Reicher).

Visit of Prime Minister Yitzchak Shamir. *From left:* Moshe Ya'alon, Yitzchak Shamir, Dan Shomron, Ehud Barak.

With combat soldier Avi Dichter

Change of command ceremony in the Unit. *From left:* Moshe Ya'alon, Amnon Lipkin-Shahak, Yiftach Atir (Reicher), Omer Bar-Lev, Chaim Bar-Lev.

Tel Aviv half marathon

With Unit officers in the field

Commander of Judea and Samaria Division

Receiving rank of brigadier general and position of division commander; with COGS Ehud Barak, Ada, and the kids

With Defense Minister Moshe Arens on a visit to Judea and Samaria

Major General Nehemiah Tamari, GOC Central Command (fourth from right), visits Judea and Samaria Division during a training exercise (I am third from right with back to camera)

Visitors to Judea and Samaria

MK Shulamit Aloni visits Duvdevan Unit, with GOC Central Command Danny Yatom *(right)*

Deputy Minister of Defense Mordechai (Motta) Gur *(right)*

With president of Israel Ezer Weizman. *From left:* Ram Rotberg, Weizman, Ya'alon, Zvi Kan-Tor, Ehud Barak.

Visits by COGS

COGS Moshe Levi visits Battalion 890. *From left:* COGS Moshe Levi, chief paratroop and infantry officer, Brigadier General Yitzchak Mordechai and company commander- Captain Michael Cohen.

COGS Ehud Barak visits Brigade 35 during a training exercise. Standing from left to right: Brigadier General Shmulik Arad- chief paratroop and infantry, COGS Ehud Barak, GOC Central Command Danny Yatom. (I am sitting on the ground in the center)

Head of Military Intelligence Directorate

With participants in Arabic course, before beginning as head of Military Intelligence Directorate (I am third from right)

Receiving the rank of Major General and position of head of Military Intelligence Directorate. *From left:* Yitzchak Rabin, Amnon Lipkin-Shahak, and the Ya'alon family.

Change of command ceremony for head of Military Intelligence Directorate. *From left:* Brigadier General Chaim Yifrach (chief intelligence officer), Ya'alon (incoming), and Uri Sagi (outgoing).

Visitors to Military Intelligence Directorate

President of Israel Ezer Weizman visiting Ya'alon

Prime Minister Benjamin Netanyahu *(second from left)* and Minister of Defense Yitzhak Mordechai *(far left)* visiting MID

coordinators for these scheduled missions. They were left with little energy to initiate activities based on their own assessments. Once permanent routine security tasks were abolished, though, more forces were available for initiated activities, requiring assessment of the situation on company and battalion level for planning and implementation. For many young commanders, this was a significant change for the better as compared to their earlier tasks as mere coordinators. The change led to positive operational results, as well as much personal satisfaction.

The Shin Bet was also of great help to us. They sent us intelligence material that was relevant to our regular security activities, but of course nothing connected to their clandestine counterterrorist activities. This led to important operational results in encountering and detaining terrorists during our routine activities.

I used to tell the commanders of the units that a neighborhood, village, or town that was too risky to enter with six of our combatants was an area where we weren't in control. Our goal was to ensure full control of the field, so that we wouldn't need entire battalions or brigades to enter a specific location.

When I first assumed my position on January 3, 1992, there were 434 wanted terrorists in our division. When I finished my position in August 1993, there were only fifty-six wanted terrorists on the list. There was not a village, town, or neighborhood that we could not enter with a foot patrol of six combatants or in two vehicles. True, the territory was not completely calm; the Israeli-Palestinian conflict had hardly ended. But the IDF had fulfilled its role and mission in its war against terror.

No longer did soldiers shrug their shoulders and say, "There is no military solution."

Before I conclude this chapter, I must mention someone who served as defense minister in the first period of my command over the

Judea-Samaria division – Moshe (Misha) Arens. He served in the defense establishment for many years, and made significant contributions, even though he had no prior experience in the military world. As opposed to Defense Minister Yitzchak Rabin, who preceded him, Arens knew little about military tactics and had no awareness of the minute details of the territory. Instead, Arens held a distinctly civilian outlook and handled military thinking admirably. I was very impressed by his well-formed worldviews, and his knowledgeability about many different topics. I was also impressed by his awareness that there were issues about which he knew very little. For these issues, he would ask complex and incisive questions, and these put us, the army people, to the test. We officers were challenged to explain and convince him of our stance. I called our encounters with him "fruitful friction" because every discussion with him was challenging. Yet we gained new insights from these talks, which also deepened our own understanding of the issues involved.

PART II

The Dream and the Awakening

CHAPTER 7

Tunnel Vision

When the Oslo Accords were signed, I was serving as the commander of a tank division. I remember that two weeks after the signing, while completing a division exercise, one of my senior reserve officers asked, "Why are we still practicing? We've just made peace." This comment reflected the atmosphere and euphoria among the public. I stood up and said, "Let's take this slowly. The rifts are deep. It could be that there is a chance for peace. But we are the army, and we must be prepared for any possibility."

Even so, deep down inside, I had no doubt: I wanted the Oslo Accords to succeed. I really, really wanted the Oslo Accords to succeed. On the one hand, I was concerned because I saw "the holes in the Swiss cheese" – I identified many loopholes that had not been closed. I was not acquainted with Arafat at that time, but I did not have much trust in him. On the other hand, I felt the hope, and I strongly identified with Yitzchak Rabin. I believed that if Rabin reached this decision, he probably knew what it was all about. I trusted that Rabin could not be "fooled into something." I even identified with Rabin's qualms, so that despite my ambivalence and all the problems, I thought this was worth a try. If the Oslo Accords succeeded – we succeeded. If the Oslo Accords didn't succeed – at least we'd know where we stood. We wouldn't continue with the internal disagreement within Israeli society, which was worrying me already back then, and concerns me much more today.

When I arrived home for my first vacation as commander of the Judea and Samaria region, my fourteen-year-old son asked me: "Abba, how do you cope with the *mitnachablim* ["settler-terrorists"]?" He had heard this derogatory slang term at the kibbutz school from a radical left teacher. I had to give him a vital lesson in the need to avoid generalizing and invalidating entire sectors of society. A short while later, as part of my position, I visited the town of Ofra in the northern West Bank. A sixteen-year-old girl who heard I was a kibbutznik began hurling similar insults at "those kibbutzniks who eat non-kosher animals, those parasites who do nothing for our country." These two incidents strengthened my belief that we suffer from demonic polarization – both extremes demonize and delegitimize each other. This worried me deeply. Clearly, our national resilience was more important to our security than the number of jet planes in our air force. To ensure our existence, we had to establish internal solidarity and basic agreement. Therefore, when the Oslo Accords were brokered, I told myself that maybe this was our chance to reach a joint national agreement on the critical issue of land, settlements, and the Israeli-Palestinian dispute. I hoped that, whatever would be, we would never again disagree on this matter.

I learned the real ins and outs of the Oslo Accords only two years later, when I was appointed as director of Military Intelligence. In the three months leading up to the start of this position, I studied the various arenas, the Arabic language, and the Oslo Accords and the new reality they had created.

Before beginning my position as head of intelligence, I also decided to learn about the intelligence failure during the Yom Kippur War. I read the Agranat Commission Report and set up meetings with those who were responsible for the intelligence warnings before the war, mainly the director of Military Intelligence at that time, Major General Eli Ze'ira, and research assistant to the Military Intelligence director, Brigadier General Aryeh Shalev.

I was very impressed with the people who were involved in the failed warning process. These were excellent and intelligent people, experts in their field. These meetings did nothing to placate me. It would have been easier if I had concluded that these people who failed to sound the warning were incompetent. But at the end of my research on this matter, I concluded that the failure that preceded the Yom Kippur War could happen to both incompetent and competent people – the former due to lack of ability, the latter due to an exaggerated self-confidence. It was Major General Eli Ze'ira's excellent skills that instilled in him too much self-confidence. In retrospect, this was understood by those around him as intellectual tyranny. People around him did not dare to dispute his decisions, even if he never intended this.

I had learned this lesson in the concluding section of my bar mitzvah haftarah reading (Micah 6:8): "Walk humbly." I then learned it firsthand from someone who had made the mistake of being too arrogant. I took this lesson with me to every position I took upon myself, and it continues to guide me to this day.

During my term as director of military intelligence, I always encouraged those around me to question and raise doubts about my opinions and evaluations. I encouraged intelligence analysts to refer to a document entitled "Another Opinion," recommended by the Agranat Commission for use by analysts at all levels who dispute the opinions of their superiors. Analysts are permitted to use this document to write directly to the prime minister, minister of defense, and chief of general staff, with a copy to the head of intelligence. The use of this document is very rare. During my term as head of Military Intelligence, only two junior analysts ever used it. They were both wrong, but I praised their courage and integrity.

I held open discussions, not necessarily according to the accepted rank levels – by which the lowest-level soldier present speaks first and the highest level, last. These were open discussions, where anyone who believed that he had something to contribute was entitled to speak, regardless of his rank.

As head of intelligence, I was asked often, "Could the failure to read the warning signs happen again, as in the Yom Kippur War?" One of these times was at a meeting of the Knesset Foreign Affairs and Defense Committee. I responded in the affirmative and gave my reasons. The next day I read a newspaper report in which the MK who had asked that question attacked me, for saying that military intelligence had not learned its lesson from the Yom Kippur War and might fail again in sounding the warning. There was no connection between my response to the MK and the news item. The MK had not even heard my reply, because he had fallen asleep straight after asking the question... But of course, he, his spokesman, or parliamentary assistant saw no reason to refrain from sending this item to the newspaper.

In my response, I explained that the failure to recognize the warning signs before the Yom Kippur War might repeat itself, because Military Intelligence assessments are based on the best possible human judgment, and humans could always make mistakes. We must teach, and more importantly, educate those involved in making top decisions in the army to be humble in their evaluations. They must doubt and avoid excessive self-confidence, be curious, and always be willing to learn. No process, procedure, or organizational structure will help if people are not humble. Even in Intelligence, arrogance is the mother of failure.

I believe that in this respect there is also some similarity between the Yom Kippur War and the Second Lebanon War. In the latter, there was no failure in intelligence. But the senior military staff and political leadership were guilty of the sin of arrogance. This arrogance led to self-confidence and complacence in the year before the war, and it caused intellectual tyranny before and during the war. This time as well, it affected people with high personal abilities.

Following the Second Lebanon War, the Winograd Commission recommended a structural and procedural change in the government to facilitate the decision-making process. I agreed with its recommendations. The Agranat Commission also submitted recommendations in this area. I always felt the need for a strong administrative body to operate alongside the prime minister and therefore claimed that we must implement the recommendations, mainly in regard to the role and status of the National Security Council (NSC). Indeed, several steps were taken to strengthen that body. Despite all this, even today it does not function in the necessary and appropriate manner. In my view, the strength and status of the NSC depend on the prime minister's attitude toward it and the level of the people serving on it. These two factors are connected strongly.

From my experience I have learned that excellent people, in every sense of the word, make correct decisions even without organizational and procedural changes. But these changes are insufficient without excellent people in the key decision-making positions.

One of my most important conclusions from studying the Agranat Commission Report and from conversations with the main representatives of Military Intelligence during the Yom Kippur War was that the failure of that war could happen again. Our systems might have improved, but, in the end, everything depends on human beings, and human beings make mistakes. In addition, in any hierarchical system, people tend to develop intellectual tyranny, self-indoctrination, and shared thinking. To prevent the repetition of such a failure, we must ensure that our organizational culture encourages openness, self-criticism, and skepticism. This also applies from the lower ranks upwards. The leadership of Military Intelligence must be based on teamwork, not tyranny.

Based on this awareness, I began to reevaluate the reality of our life with the Palestinians in the years following the Oslo Accords. I discerned that we were dealing with a wild beast – as long as we fed it, it remained calm. But this beast was never satiated, and when crisis struck, hunger would cause it to pounce. So, in the meantime, we would throw it another tidbit, and another. But what if in the end we had no more to give? What would we do then?

One of the first things I did was to examine Arafat's rhetoric toward the Palestinians. What was he teaching the next generation? To make peace or to go to war? I quickly realized that the Palestinians were receiving no education for making peace. I identified a major difference between Hafez al-Assad, who wished to achieve a peace agreement and prepared the Syrian public and army officers of his time for the possibility, and Arafat, who never prepared the Palestinian people for peace. Arafat continued to use jihad rhetoric, the rhetoric of war. In English he spoke of "the peace of the brave," an ambiguous term, and in Arabic he called to continue the jihad battle. One year after Arafat entered Israel, the Palestinian education system denied any connection between the Jewish people and the Land of Israel. The Palestinian education system ignored the existence of the State of Israel. It treated Haifa as a Palestinian city and Tel Aviv as a settlement, just as it spoke of the settlements in Elon Moreh and Beit El. The State of Israel did not appear on their school maps. Neither did it appear on the maps in the offices of the Palestinian officials that I visited. Thus, I slowly discovered that we were dealing with a leader who made no efforts to prepare his people to make peace with the State of Israel or to recognize its right to exist as an independent Jewish state.

In one of my first appearances before the Foreign Affairs and Defense Committee as Military Intelligence director, MK Benny Begin took out his personal laptop and read a quote from a speech Arafat had made at a mosque in Johannesburg, South Africa, after the signing of the Oslo

Accords and the beginning of their implementation. Arafat specifically spoke of a jihad against the State of Israel. I was embarrassed to admit that I had not heard this quote. Accordingly, I "shook up" the Intelligence Division, as I believed that one of the responsibilities of the research and information units was to find such statements, analyze, and distribute them. At the time, I had many question marks regarding Arafat's behavior, and mainly his intentions. MK Benny Begin already had many exclamation marks. Retrospectively, he was right.

Other than the issue of education, we had to face terrorism. During that time, Yahya Ayyash (known as "the Engineer") carried out attacks, but Arafat did not treat him as if he were fighting terrorism – instead, he took a symbiotic approach. After several months in my role as director of Military Intelligence, I realized that Arafat was not upholding his principal commitment in the Oslo Accords: no more violence. This refined the question of whether Arafat had any true intention of stopping the violence, or whether he had no control at all. Shimon Peres, for example, claimed that it was a process and that Arafat would slowly lead his people toward peace; he was not able to start using peace rhetoric right from the beginning. I saw things differently – the problem was not Arafat's ability, but his desire. Proof of this is that when Hamas threatened him, he didn't hesitate in instructing the Palestinian police and security forces to take the most aggressive stance against the Hamas protestors. On November 18, 1994, this led to the toll of thirteen dead and over 150 injured in clashes between them and Hamas and the Palestinian Jihad Islamists near the Palestine Mosque in Gaza. Only six months after entering Gaza, Arafat was not afraid of dealing with his opponents with a firm hand, and proved that he was, indeed, able to do so. In July 1995, Arafat instructed his men to arrest four senior Hamas leaders (including Dr. Mahmoud al-Zahar) and shave off half their beards and moustaches – an extremely humiliating act that proved his ability to confront his opponents. When Israelis were killed in terrorist attacks, Arafat did nothing. Only when a gun was put to his head would he order the arrest of the terrorist who murdered or planned to murder Israelis, and put them on trial. The terrorist would be sentenced for the crime of harming Palestinian interests or causing civil disorder, incarcerated in five-star accommodation, and informed by Arafat's men that he had been arrested to protect his life from the Israeli security forces. Both punishment and imprisonment were for public display only, to the extent that this phenomenon was described as a "revolving door." All this occurred at the height of the Oslo Accords, in 1995, long before anyone could claim that the process was deteriorating because of the murder of Yitzchak Rabin and its aftermath.

One of the most prominent events occurred in August 1995, in connection to a terrorist named Awad Silmi. We received intelligence information showing that a Hamas cell headed by Silmi was planning to bring a car bomb from Gaza and blow it up somewhere in central Israel. This information required the immediate closure of the Gaza Strip. The head of the Israeli Security Agency (ISA or Shin Bet), Carmi Gilon, was instructed by Prime Minister Rabin to call Arafat and notify him about the information and the circumstances under which Israel was forced to impose the closure. Gilon also demanded that Arafat arrest the terror cell, as a condition for calling off the closure.

That night Awad Silmi was arrested by the Palestinian general intelligence forces, headed by Amin al-Hindi. During the operation other Hamas activists were also arrested, but because Israel demanded only the arrest of Silmi, they released the others.

Arafat ordered Silmi's trial, and the Palestinians reported a sentence of fifteen years of hard labor for "harming Palestinian interests." Silmi was "jailed" in a building near the government offices (Saraya) in Gaza City. His jailers explained to him that this was a "protective arrest" to guard him from the long arm of the Israeli military. Accordingly, he was permitted to hold a gun and a hand grenade and to leave the building during daytime hours.

In February and March 1996, fifty-eight Israelis were murdered in four suicide attacks. Arafat ordered widespread arrests of Hamas militants. His decision was the result of an ultimatum made by the US ambassador to Israel, Martin Indyk, who warned Arafat that if he did not take stricter measures, the political process would be halted. About twelve hundred Hamas activists were arrested. To show Israel and mainly the US that Arafat was in fact conducting these arrests, some were covered by the media. So, we watched news reports on the Palestinian television channel showing the Palestinian security forces arresting no other than Awad Silmi, the prisoner who had supposedly already been sentenced to fifteen years in jail. This was brought to the attention of the Israeli government, which queried representatives of the Palestinian Authority, but they avoided providing any substantial response.

This event reflects the situation that led to a growing lack of trust between IDF officers, the Shin Bet, and the Israel Police, and their Palestinian counterparts. Clearly, because the Palestinians were not upholding their commitments, we were unable to fulfill all of ours, which only underscored the lack of mutual trust.

The transfer of civil and security responsibility over Area A to the Palestinian Authority meant that the security of Israeli citizens was dependent on the willingness and ability of the Palestinian Authority's security leadership and forces, and required cooperation between them and the IDF, Shin Bet, and Israel Police. When the Authority's forces entered Area A in May 1994, rules were set regarding coordination between the security forces on both sides, including joint patrols in certain areas.

The implementation of the Oslo Accords began with great hopes. But difficulties developed and suspicion grew after it became clear that the Palestinian Authority was not ensuring security as the Israeli side had hoped ("without the High Court of Justice and without B'Tzelem" – to echo Prime Minister Rabin's definition of Israeli expectations). The lack of trust began to eat away at the process as it became clear that the Palestinians were not thwarting terrorist attacks. In many cases, information given to them to prevent an attack was used to try and expose our sources of intelligence. Arrests were made with limited interests, and not out of a strategy of annihilating terrorist organizations. The most severe attacks were in 1994–1995, mainly suicide bombings on buses, planned by the "Engineer," Yahya Ayyash, who operated freely from the Gaza Strip and directed terrorist attacks in Judea and Samaria. This exacerbated the sense of distrust.

In June 1995, I began my term as director of military intelligence. Two months later, in August 1995, I took my new insights to Yitzchak Rabin, then prime minister and minister of defense. I told him: "Mr. Prime Minister, I am sorry, but I do not identify any signs of conciliation on the Palestinian side, not in education and ending the incitement and not in fighting against terrorism. It could be that the process will blow up in the end, because Arafat does not really intend on reaching a permanent agreement based on a two-state solution."

I suggested that the prime minister put the situation to a test. Rabin asked what we could do – what kind of leverage did we have? I responded that we had to set several conditions for continuing the peace process: Arafat had to arrest all terrorists known to us; stop incitement against Israel in the official Palestinian media, which was under his control; and initiate a total change in his education system with regard to its attitudes toward Israel. Rabin agreed with me but claimed that it would be better to wait for Arafat to be elected in the official Palestinian elections, which were due to be held on January 20, 1996. Rabin thought that it would be difficult for Arafat to confront the terrorist organizations. But after he was elected, chances would be greater that he would accept our demands. Elections would grant him support and legitimacy. For the time being, Rabin instructed me to initiate a meeting with Arafat, during which

Carmi Gilon, head of the Shin Bet, and I would present our demands regarding the fight against terrorism.

The meeting was held on October 7, 1995, in the coordination and liaison office at the Erez Crossing. Minister of Foreign Affairs Shimon Peres headed the Israeli mission. During this meeting Arafat denied the existence of terrorism in the Palestinian Authority areas. He claimed that there were terrorists only in Iran, Syria, Lebanon, the extreme right wing in Israel, and areas where Israel was responsible for security (one of the understandings between Arafat's men and the terror organizations was that the organizations had to make sure not to select terrorists from Area A, where full control had been given to the Palestinians. They were only to choose terrorists who came from Areas B and C, where Israel still controlled security, in order not to leave any Palestinian Authority fingerprints there. At the same time, the dispatchers of suicide terrorists even tore out the tags from their shirts, to prevent any evidence of their place of manufacture or purchase within the Authority areas).

The meeting changed nothing in Arafat's behavior.

At the same time, meetings were held between Arafat's representatives and Hamas leaders to bring about some quiet in terrorist attacks before the Palestinian elections in January 1996. This arrangement ended in "understandings" that were achieved between the sides in Cairo in November 1995, according to which Hamas would freeze terrorist attacks until the elections. In other words, the two sides agreed that Hamas would renew the attacks after the elections.

On November 4, 1995, Rabin was assassinated.

I received news of the prime minister's assassination while in my home on Saturday night. Two of my children participated in the peace rally at Malchei Yisrael Plaza (today known as the Yitzchak Rabin Plaza) in Tel Aviv. The COGS, Lieutenant General Amnon Lipkin-Shahak, was the one who told me the bitter news of Yitzchak Rabin's death, and throughout that night I received updates from the head of his bureau.

I had known Yitzchak Rabin for many years. He had served as minister of defense while I headed Sayeret Matkal. The head of the Unit maintains contact with the minister of defense, sometimes directly. I had the opportunity to get to know him more closely when I became commander of the Judea and Samaria division.

In the summer of 1992, the Labor Party won the Knesset elections. Yitzchak Rabin was appointed prime minister and minister of defense, and a short while later visited the division. It was his first visit to the Israel Defense Forces after convening the new government.

Throughout his visit Rabin impressed me with his ability to learn the details, investigate, and ask the most intricate tactical particulars, as well as to see the overall strategic picture. After receiving reviews at division headquarters, we went on a reconnaissance patrol. He asked me to travel with him in his armored vehicle, and specified that Chief of General Staff Ehud Barak, his deputy Amnon Lipkin-Shahak, and General Officer Commander Danny Yatom would follow us or remain at headquarters. We drove through Ramallah. On the way we spoke about various issues, from rules of engagement in different scenarios to my recommendations for changes in military and civil policies in the area.

Throughout my military service, I met politicians who preferred not to deal with the details. This was so that they could claim that they knew nothing, thus avoiding responsibility and the provision of backup. Rabin was radically different. He both took responsibility and gave backup. I won't forget how he stood up to the cameras and microphones after the failed rescue of Sergeant Nachshon Wachsman, of blessed memory. In that military action, we also lost First Lieutenant Nir Poraz, of blessed memory, a Sayeret Matkal team commander. Rabin did not send officers to give explanations. Instead, he stood up there himself and said, "I am responsible!"

During my period as COGS, as well as during the Second Lebanon War, I witnessed a different culture – politicians instead of statesmen. The politicians spoke like lawyers in front of the media, but used a different tone when they were not being recorded. Mainly, they avoided taking responsibility or giving support when this was required. They made unrealistic statements, such as "We give the IDF full freedom of action," or "The IDF has no limitations" – woe to us if that were the real situation! This extended to avoiding responsibility for the failure of the Second Lebanon War, placing the blame on others, and failing to back up the IDF when the IDF needed support.

Under Rabin, discussions on Judea and Samaria demonstrated his great strategic understanding and tactical knowledge. I learned to appreciate him for his tendency to focus on the details, in order to ensure that his policy was implemented and that he was responsible for it. All this was done in a practical and open atmosphere, where even the most low-ranking soldiers dared to express their opinions.

I got to know Rabin more deeply after my appointment as director of Military Intelligence in June 1995. I saw him up close, mainly in personal meetings between the director of Military Intelligence and the prime minister (and, in this case, also minister of defense). The more I got to know him, the greater my appreciation for this man.

The despicable murder was unexpected. I had become acquainted with the extreme margins of society while serving as the commander of the Judea and Samaria division – the dangerous extremist rabbis who claimed to represent Judaism and held racist and fascist attitudes, and the marginal groups who followed them. I felt that they needed to be handled through legal measures. I supported moves such as delegitimizing the extreme right-wing Kach Party because of its racist platform, and taking strong enforcement steps against groups who used violence against Arabs and challenged the law enforcement system.

I discovered that these extreme marginal groups were denounced by the vast majority of residents in Judea and Samaria, but the general Israeli public used them to delegitimize all Jewish residents of these areas. I regarded this process as a dangerous way of backing hundreds of thousands of people into a corner. This form of conduct was repeated after the assassination of Yitzchak Rabin. The attempts to put blame for the murder on an entire sector only intensified the polarization, and in most cases, thwarted any attempts to reach reconciliation and introspection in all camps.

Some took advantage of Rabin's assassination to strengthen the claim that the murder cut short the peace process that started in Oslo. I don't accept this. Others rewrote Rabin's heritage and presented it as one of unconditional territorial surrender. Rabin's speeches and policies before his death contradict this.

The personal and national introspection that was required after this despicable murder was conducted here and there, but not necessarily in the places where it was most needed. I believe that the most important lesson to be learned from the assassination is the vital nature of the rule of law. In certain situations, a democratic regime is obliged to take legal steps that might be considered antidemocratic in order to protect itself. In this case, this means taking measures against elements who voiced opinions and acted in ways that endangered democracy. To use a farming metaphor, weeds grow near sources of water, like a dripping faucet in the field. Here the water was a small group of extremist rabbis, while their followers were the weeds. The failure to deal with these "weeds" through legal procedures, in the name of freedom of speech, neglecting to limit their actions before it was too late, prepared the ground for the assassination of the prime minister.

Tilting the balance on the question of personal rights in favor of the criminals – in this case, individuals who endangered the public or democracy – was to our detriment, and this remains the case in additional areas.

Shimon Peres took over from Rabin as prime minister and minister of defense. Ehud Barak took over from Peres as foreign minister. About three months after this appointment, Peres called for new elections for the Knesset and prime minister, which were set for May 1996.

On January 5, 1996, Yahya Ayyash, the same arch-terrorist whom Arafat denied was in Gaza, was killed in a targeted attack in Beit Lahiya in the Gaza Strip.

I met with Prime Minister Peres in January 1996 and reminded him of the ultimatum that we were supposed to give Arafat immediately after the elections. This had become extremely urgent, as we had accumulated intelligence information that Hamas's military wing, headed by Muhammad Deif and the Islamic Jihad, were planning five major terrorist attacks in retaliation for the killing of Yahya Ayyash. I thought that with his international status, Peres would be the most suitable person to submit the ultimatum in which Rabin had sincerely believed.

Arafat was elected as Ra'is ("ruler"), and on January 24 we held a meeting with him at Erez Crossing. Representing Israel were Shimon Peres, Avi Dichter as head of the Southern Command of the Shin Bet, and myself as director of Military Intelligence. I was requested to give a review and state our security demands, including the list of wanted terrorists for arrest. First on the list was Muhammad Deif, the most senior wanted terrorist in those days. When I mentioned his name, Arafat naively asked the head of his security services (parallel to the Israeli Shin Bet), Muhammad Dahlan: "Muhammad *shu*?" (Muhammad who?) – as if he had no idea who Deif was! I believe that this was a very significant moment, as we knew very well that Arafat knew who Deif was. It was clear that he was lying straight to our faces. All our suspicions about him since he had arrived in Gaza were verified. Arafat's advocates on the Israeli side were led by the late Yossi Ginossar, former senior Shin Bet representative, who served as a personal emissary for Rabin and Peres to Arafat. They claimed that Arafat wasn't deceiving us, but that Arafat's men were deceiving him. But here we had clear-cut proof that exposed Arafat's tricks and lies.

I realized that if we did not portray a determined position, demanding that he arrest the terrorists as a prerequisite to continuing the process, the situation would only deteriorate. Arafat had heard from us that this specific group was about to attack us. He knew that we knew he was tricking us! If we knew and did nothing, that meant we were too weak and scared to act. This weakness indicated to him that we feared any confrontation with him. He abused this situation until the bitter end, and continued deceiving us for another four and a half years. From that day on, I understood that Arafat was not the only problem. The Israeli leadership was no less responsible. I realized that our leadership did not want to challenge the truth, because that would be admitting the failure of its path. I started to understand where this weakness was leading us, and I understood that Arafat identified the weakness and would take it very far.

In addition to this, Arafat avoided amending the Palestinian National Covenant. In the Oslo Accords, Arafat had committed to amending this document in a manner that would annul the sections negating the State of Israel's right to exist as a Jewish state. This would mean de facto recognition of this right by the PLO. The amendment of the document required the convening of the Palestinian National Council (PNC), which included the resistance organizations (Palestinian terrorist organizations that opposed the Oslo Accords). For this, the Government of Israel approved the entry of the leaders of these organizations and their representatives into the Gaza Strip.

The PNC convention ended on Yom Ha'atzma'ut (Israel's Independence Day) 1996. The intelligence experts (military intelligence and the Shin Bet) realized that Arafat had deceived us in the wording of the decision, which enabled him to avoid making the required amendment:

1. The wording in the English version stated that the amendment (demanded by Israel) would be implemented immediately, while the Arabic version stated that it would be implemented in the future. Members of the PNC who objected to the amendment were told that the Arabic version was the binding document.
2. The decision stated that the amendment would be made by a legal committee that would convene within six months. To date, the committee has never convened.

Knowledge of the PNC's decision reached Prime Minister and Minister of Defense Peres on the afternoon of Yom Ha'atzma'ut, and I heard from his military secretary that he planned to offer his congratulations on the nonexistent amendment that evening, at the festive reception to be held at the Defense Ministry Rose Garden (an event traditionally held on the evening following Yom Ha'atzma'ut). As director of Military Intelligence, I clarified the deceit in the PNC's decision to the military secretary. I demanded to meet with Peres urgently, in order to convince him not to go public with any congratulations for the fictitious amendment. I was called to meet with Peres before he left for the reception. He did not accept my opinion. In front of the many media representatives present at the event, he ceremoniously announced the "amendment," and congratulated Arafat for his "decision."

Not only was Arafat deceiving us – we were deceiving ourselves.

Throughout my service as director of Military Intelligence, I never used exclamation marks in my statements. Unfortunately, I cannot say that I was decisive enough. I never defined Arafat in unequivocal terms.

All I did throughout those years was to add another question mark for myself, and yet another question mark. Due to my view of my position and following the lessons from the failed intelligence reports during the Yom Kippur War, I refused to brush things under the carpet. While others cut corners and found excuses, trying to adapt the intelligence reports to the leaders' moods and spirit of the times, I insisted that we remain on track, that we see things as they truly are. Even so, I could not deny the claims of those who believed that we had the strength to push Arafat into a corner, in a way that would force him – out of realpolitik considerations – to accept a two-state solution, which he did not want. I knew that he would not accept such a solution, but I still believed that we could force this on him.

To this day I believe that if Rabin had not been assassinated, things would have been managed differently on the Israeli side. Rabin had suffered bitterly from Arafat and did not trust him at all. When Arafat lied to us, Rabin would say it: Arafat is lying. He did not ignore reality like others did. He evaluated the political scene as he saw it, both internally and internationally, and this led him to prefer to defer the moment of conflict. As I see it, if Rabin had been alive, he would have entered conflict with Arafat in early 1996. But Peres was a different person, and he acted otherwise. He wasn't interested in the details. He didn't want to be confused with the facts. He followed his vision and did not let reality derail that plan. He believed that by fulfilling his dream, he would change reality. How I wish that he had been successful.

Benjamin Netanyahu's election to the post of prime minister in May 1996 gave Arafat the chance to start a new game, one he knew how to play successfully, both on the international arena and within Israel. According to the rules of this game, which Arafat himself set, he could have made "the peace of the brave" with Rabin, but some insane right-wing Israeli extremist assassinated him, and, instead of Rabin, we got someone who wanted to put a spoke in the wheel of peace, someone who didn't want peace. Between 1996 and 1998, Arafat manipulated public opinion in this way, and to a large extent, he succeeded.

Justifiably, Netanyahu demanded mutual recognition. In other words, he demanded that in order for Israel to continue implementing the Oslo Accords, the Palestinians must abide by the agreement. He refused to close his eyes and would not brush things under the carpet, but Arafat presented him as an obstacle to peace. The international community and a significant sector of Israeli society went along with Arafat on this matter. They accepted Arafat's manipulations, especially when influential factors in the Israeli media systematically delegitimized Prime Minister Netanyahu. Therefore, when Arafat met with Netanyahu's insistence, he initiated the Western Wall Tunnel riots in September 1996 and continued leading everyone astray throughout the ensuing years.

Sadly, the intelligence services in Israel were not vigilant enough to prevent this trickery. Shin Bet head Ami Ayalon did not bring to the table the sober estimates of his research unit and other divisions. He relied only on his own opinion and that of his external advisor, Dr. Mati Steinberg, who claimed, throughout the years, that the Palestinians had accepted the historical decision and were heading for a solution. Ayalon and Steinberg claimed that when push came to shove, the Palestinians would also waive the right of return. At a later stage, when Ehud Barak was preparing for the Camp David summit, individuals such as Amos Gilad in the intelligence unit warned him that the rift between Israel and the Palestinians was too large. But Ayalon brought Steinberg to the prime minister and promised him that the issue of the right of return could be solved. They assumed that Arafat would waive the right of return, in exchange for an Israeli waiver over Jerusalem. But during the Tunnel riots, the dispute continued between Ayalon, as head of the Shin Bet, and myself, as director of Military Intelligence. Ayalon was systematically lenient in interpreting Palestinian behavior. He claimed that Palestinian violence was not a result of Arafat's orders, but because he had lost control. This approach shocked me. It did not fit the facts or the intelligence information that I had witnessed.

In October 1996, a summit was held in Washington, with Netanyahu, Arafat, King Hussein of Jordan, and US president Bill Clinton. At the height of the preparations in the Israel intelligence community, Ami Ayalon received a phone call from his subordinates: "Information has been received from the heads of the Palestinian security forces in Judea and Samaria that the Palestinians are threatening to blow up Bethlehem and Ramallah if Netanyahu does not accept Arafat's demands." Ayalon said that he had to call the prime minister to notify him and warn him of the impending danger. I said that if he talked to the prime minister, I would too. Ayalon told Netanyahu that if he did not agree to the proposals made in Washington, things would blow up on the ground. I took the telephone from him and said: "The sources are such and such, and this is a Palestinian manipulation. This is an attempt to scare you, to force you into reaching a decision under pressure."

In the end, the Americans exerted pressure and Netanyahu signed the Hebron Protocol. I am not getting into a discussion of whether this agreement was right. But from the Palestinian perspective, they used violence – and won. They initiated the Western Wall Tunnel riots. They were not stopped by a reinforced wall of Israeli public opinion or of global entities headed by the United States. As a result, they achieved the Hebron Protocol. From their viewpoint, they had broken the prime minister of Israel. Once again, they learned that violence gets them what they want. Violence makes the Israelis retreat. Violence pays off.

In March 1997, the same argument erupted. After a hiatus of about one year in suicide bombings, Arafat convened the head of the terrorist organizations for a long discussion, during which he spoke in jihad terms. He initiated the conference in response to Netanyahu's insistence on mutual recognition, and after the construction permit was issued for the new neighborhood of Har Homa in Jerusalem. Arafat did not issue a direct order for a terrorist attack, but he spoke along those lines. Later, intelligence derived from this meeting that the terrorist leaders there understood from Arafat that he expected attacks, including suicide bombings. The Hamas leaders debated his true intention, fearing this might be Arafat's scheme to use an attack by them as a pretext for an offensive against their organization, as he had done in March–April 1996.

On March 11, at the request of Hamas and following a night of talks, Arafat released Ibrahim al-Makadmeh, a major terror activist who was arrested at President Clinton's demand. The Hamas request for his release was given to Arafat as a "test," to see how serious he was in requesting that they renew intensive terrorist attacks. Hamas perceived this release as Arafat's "green light" for mass attacks. On March 21, 1997, they attacked the Apropos Café in Tel Aviv, murdering three women and injuring forty-seven. On April 1, 1997, Islamic Jihad attacked the access road to Kfar Darom. At this time, we also discovered that Ghazi Jabali, the Palestinian police commissioner, had instructed two senior police officers, Commander Jihad Masimi of Nablus and Commander Munir Abboushi of Tulkarm, to carry out terrorist attacks. They understood that the order had come from Arafat. A squad of Palestinian policemen from the Nablus area shot at the car of the rabbi of Elon Moreh, at Askarim Junction at the eastern exit from Nablus. The event ended without injuries, and the squad was arrested en route to carrying out another attack in the Har Bracha area. So, it seems that not only the Hamas understood Arafat's intention during that late-night meeting.

To me, the picture was clear: the terrorist attacks were a result of the "green light" that Arafat had given to the terrorist organizations. But the head of the Shin Bet claimed that we had no proof. This drove me mad. It is true that there was no specific order in writing, but it was totally clear that the rhetoric was to attack. Possibly, we did not have sufficient evidence to place Arafat on trial. But in terms of intelligence and circumstances, the situation was crystal clear. In any case, there are still those among us who refuse to see the clear picture.

During that period of the late 1990s, I was increasingly considered as the one who opposed everything. Politicians and journalists have an easy time adopting the comfortable approach, and my opinions were not comfortable. I was not working based on some ideological world view. I was not motivated by any ideological or political consideration, but by an organized and methodic reading of the facts. As time went on, my question marks about the Oslo Accords and Arafat only intensified. I felt that there was a growing rift between the reality that I was seeing and the picture that was being presented to the Israeli public at that time. I realized that Arafat wanted violence in order to push Netanyahu into giving up the principle of mutual recognition.

In 1998, I ended my term as director of Military Intelligence and was appointed GOC Central Command. Just as when entering any new position, I believed that it was important to learn about the situation in the region directly from the ground. Two meetings left their impression on me. First, in the office of the Palestinian governor of Nablus, I saw a map of all Palestine without the State of Israel, as if our existence had changed nothing. Second, during a visit to the industrial zone of Ramallah, I saw fewer factories than during the pre-Oslo era. As commander of the Judea and Samaria region in the early 1990s, I had made every effort, together with Brigadier General Gadi Zohar, head of the civil administration, to strengthen the Palestinian economy. Now, after the Oslo Accords, I found that in this vital area, matters had declined. Reports in the Israeli and world media of affluent businessmen from Saudi Arabia and the Persian Gulf who had invested in the Palestinian Authority were true for only a short period.

I conducted the tour of the industrial zone in the car of the governor of Ramallah, Abu Firas Liftawi. I asked him to drive there because I considered economic development to be an extremely important element in improving the security and political situation. I also regarded the improved economic situation as an important moral dimension. When I showed my surprise and asked my host about the decline in the economic situation in comparison to the time when the IDF controlled Ramallah, he smiled sarcastically. He told me that it was true that many investors, mainly from the petroleum exporting countries, had visited the city immediately after the Palestinian Authority took control, to investigate investment opportunities. When they discovered that in order to do business in Ramallah, they would be required to pay "this guy, that guy, and the other guy" – they fled. I asked, "So what did you say to them?" He responded, again with a smile, "Pay only me!" The investors disappeared because they encountered serious corruption and a rotten government culture.

Unfortunately, we discovered other cases of corruption in their contacts with the Israelis on central issues, such as the energy and petroleum markets. Both Palestinian and Israeli corruption damaged the Palestinian economy and Israeli strategic interests. But above all, I was shocked by the indifference of the Palestinian leadership toward their people's economic situation. As I had been commander of Judea and Samaria in 1992–1993, I had a basis for comparison. I found that I cared more about the Palestinians than their leaders themselves.

Only later did I discover that I was one of what David Ben-Gurion defined as the "naive Zionists." Only later did I realize that I was part of the same incorrect perception that I described in the first chapters of this book.

CHAPTER 8

Squeezing the Israeli Lemon

In June 1999, I completed my first year as GOC Central Command. Several weeks earlier Ehud Barak had been elected as prime minister. Following his victory, he announced that he would strive to get the IDF out of Lebanon within one year and reach a permanent agreement with Syria and the Palestinians within fifteen months. This period was due to end in September 2000, seven years after the signing of the Oslo Accords.

I believed that Barak's decision to force Arafat's hand was correct, and that clarifications were in order. As I had told Rabin back in 1995, I believed that we were in a "salami" process – we were being forced to slice off more and more (i.e., land) to satiate Arafat, but he was leading us to a point where there would be nothing left to feed him. What would we give in the end? Haifa? Tel Aviv? For many years we gave substantial assets, and in return got nothing but words. We didn't get security. We definitely didn't get peace. We only had the hope that in the future Arafat might change. Possibly, if we gave him more, he might reach a point where he would truly agree to a solution. But after all the experience we had accumulated, I doubted whether Arafat would ever agree to a solution. For that reason, I agreed with Barak's statement, which basically pushed for clarification. We would no longer be leading ourselves astray. Instead, we would be informing ourselves about where we stood and what we were facing.

Even though I fully agreed with Barak's statement, I soon realized that we were heading for an escalation of the situation, instead of calming down. I followed the response of Arafat and the Palestinian Authority to Barak's statement regarding his intention to reach an agreement within fifteen months. I understood that September 2000 was due to be a pivotal date. Indeed, discussions on evaluating the situation within the senior planning forum of the Central Command led me to the conclusion that Arafat was planning for war around that date. This war could have two different logical approaches. The first could be termed "optimistic": Arafat would not want to receive a state by agreement only. Rather, he wanted a battle that would be the "final battle" before the permanent agreement, so that he would go down in history not only as the one who received a state from Israel, but also as the one who fought in battle on behalf of this state. The second approach was "pessimistic": Arafat would launch a war to avoid a permanent agreement that would be based on the principle of "two states for two peoples." He would continue his military battle on the assumption that opening fire would push all sides to strive for a cease-fire. This would be achieved at the expense of a significant Israeli price, or a unilateral retreat from Gaza and Judea and Samaria, or parts of these regions, but without reaching a permanent agreement.

Following intense meetings with Central Command staff and command officers and with officers at the Judea and Samaria Division, in July 1999 I issued the first document resulting from this situation, titled "Preparing for September," in which I gave my assessment of what would happen in September 2000. I shared my insights with Chief of General Staff Shaul Mofaz and with the General Staff, and this led to the COGS situation assessments. The result was that the IDF under Mofaz, particularly the Southern Command under Major General Yom Tov

Samiya and the Central Command under myself, began preparing for the war of terror, which indeed broke out in September 2000.

The intelligence warnings before September 2000 were translated into a correct assessment of the situation, and this enabled the IDF to prepare for this war. This contrasted with the failure in 2006 (the Second Lebanon War). The IDF leadership had not made sensible use of the intelligence warnings that had been given in late 2005 and early 2006, regarding possible escalation in the north and south. The IDF failed to use these warnings to prepare for war in Lebanon and the Gaza Strip.

In November 1999, I estimated that Arafat would maintain quiet in early 2000, to use the millennium celebrations and the visit of Pope John Paul II to gain global legitimacy for the Palestinian Authority. I anticipated that immediately after the celebrations died down, the situation would escalate, peaking in a violent eruption leading up to September. And this is exactly what happened. The Pope left at the end of March 2000, and two weeks later, my predictions came true: on April 13 a roadside explosive (IED) was blown up near an IDF-secured convoy of civilian cars on the entrance route to Netzarim. The parties responsible were Fatah members, who were subject to Muhammad Dahlan's Preventive Security Force. This was the first of five terrorist attacks that this group carried out, even before Ariel Sharon visited the Temple Mount. The last of the five attacks took place on September 27, 2000, one day before the visit to the Temple Mount. In this attack, Givati combat soldier, Staff Sergeant David Biri was killed.

But the most prominent sign of what was due to happen in September 2000 were the events of Nakba Day – May 15, 2000.

Elections for secretary general of the Fatah in the West Bank were also held that year. Arafat wanted Marwan Barghouti, the central figure in the Tanzim (the Fatah's military wing), to win. Apparently, Arafat regarded

Barghouti as a leader who would be able to lead the war that Arafat was scheming. But Barghouti's political competitor, Hussein al-Sheikh, won the elections and Arafat was supposed to confirm this appointment. He delayed signing, and despite Barghouti's loss in the elections, he appointed his preference as secretary general of Fatah on May 1, 2000. From my point of view, this was an ominous sign leading up to Nakba Day. Intelligence was accumulating on the intentions of the Tanzim, led by Barghouti, to initiate severe clashes with IDF soldiers on that day.

Together with my staff officers at Central Command, who were partners in the deliberation process as part of situation assessment, we concluded that Arafat regarded Nakba Day as an opportunity to raise Palestinian awareness of the struggle in preparation for war in September 2000, because the ordinary Palestinians were not yet considering war. Who was better than Barghouti for this mission?

On May 8, several days before Nakba Day, Barak, and Arafat met in Ramallah. This meeting was most definitely not intended to warn of impending clashes, especially considering the prime minister's intention to reach a permanent agreement that year. But Arafat thought differently. Immediately after the meeting, Arafat sent a message to Barghouti: "Heat it up." Three days after this very personal summit, on May 11, the ground began to burn.

Clashes peaked on Nakba Day, May 15. This was the day when the Tanzim armed forces under Barghouti opened fire on IDF soldiers at all possible "flashpoints": in Jenin at the junction of the road leading to the settlements of Ganim and Kadim; in Tulkarm at Mesilla Junction; in Qalqilya on the "seam"; in Ramallah at Ayosh Junction; and in Bethlehem near Rachel's Tomb.

Following the situation assessment leading up to Nakba Day, the Judea and Samaria Division under Brigadier General Shlomo Oren prepared for this unique threat. IDF forces were deployed at the flashpoints in ways that avoided exposure to fire by Tanzim snipers, who were set up behind the protesters, waiting for opportunities to fire on IDF soldiers. IDF lookouts and snipers stood on the other side, waiting to identify and shoot at the Tanzim. I emphasized that at the end of the day, the result of the clashes should be decisive: as many Tanzim snipers as possible dead, and minimum injuries on our side. As opposed to the goal that Arafat had set – "raise awareness of the Palestinian struggle" – we had to make clear to the Palestinians that violence does not pay off.

After identifying the Ayosh Junction as the most significant site of clashes, I arrived at division headquarters in Beit El, close to the junction, early in the morning. I conducted a final evaluation of the situation and verified that the division was ready. At some stage, when clashes erupted, I went to the junction to observe preparations and events from close by. The City Inn Hotel, constructed after the Oslo Accords in the hope that the peace would bring tourists to the area, is located near the junction. This hotel's location was suitable for us to use as observation and sniping positions, and so we took control of some of the rooms. (The hotel operated until the outbreak of terrorism in September 2000. The last tourist who left the hotel was British, and local legend relates that when asked why he was leaving, he replied, "It's too noisy here.")

When shooting began on the Palestinian side, we took cover. Our sharpshooters located the Tanzim snipers, responded with fire and hit several of them. I instructed the head of the Coordination and Liaison Headquarters (responsible for communication with the Palestinian security forces), Brigadier General Dov ("Fufi") Zedaka, to contact General Haj Ismail, head of the national security forces in the West Bank, to demand that he come to the junction and stop the clashes immediately. I also requested that a similar message be sent through the Shin Bet channels to the heads of the Palestinian security systems, Jibril Rajoub and Tawfik Tirawi.

We found out that the Palestinian officers and military were meeting with Arafat at his headquarters, the Mukat'a in Ramallah, just half a mile (800 m) from the clashes, where they were holding consultations. We received evasive responses such as "We'll get there soon," "We're coming soon," "We're just finishing a consultation with the Ra'is and then we'll come."

In the meantime, we received reports on clashes in other areas. Most events began in the afternoon hours, a phenomenon that repeated itself in the first days of the terror war in September 2000. At first, I thought that it was because of the school hours. School and university students were transported in organized buses to the protests by the Fatah Tanzim. But after the outbreak of clashes in September 2000, *New York Times* journalist Tom Friedman gave me another perspective on the timing of the clashes.

During one of my meetings with him after the outbreak of the September 2000 clashes, Friedman described a journalist's tour that he had arranged in Ramallah a short while earlier, which had been coordinated with Barghouti's men. He told me that when he wanted to set a time for the tour, the Palestinian liaison arranged to meet him at 1 p.m. at a certain spot. On his way to the meeting, Friedman was surprised to see a vibrant city, while he had thought that he had come to a city at war. After some light refreshments and a briefing, they ventured out to the Palestinian side of Ayosh Junction. There Friedman was witness to the Palestinian preparations for the daily battle at the junction. He saw Tanzim militants armed with Kalashnikovs, dressed in leather jackets and donning sunglasses, preparing the scene as if it were "choreographed," in his words. They received the students who arrived by bus and prepared them for the demonstration. They arranged the line of ambulances that would add to the drama by driving over to the demonstration to rescue the injured, while sounding loud sirens. They placed the television teams in position.

Just before two p.m., Friedman noticed that the armed Tanzim militants had shifted into the adjacent houses and taken up sniper positions.

At two p.m. on the dot, the battle began.

"Why two p.m.?" Friedman asked rhetorically. He went on to explain, "Because two p.m. in Ramallah is seven a.m. on the East Coast." Exactly at this time of the day, the American channels are broadcasting their morning news shows, which have the highest viewing percentages. So, US residents woke up every morning to scenes broadcasted directly from Ayosh Junction.

Immediately after Friedman left Ayosh Junction, he was invited to a meeting with Barghouti at a fancy restaurant in Ramallah, where he was served a five-star meal. "On my way back to Jerusalem," said the renowned journalist, "I told myself that I had just witnessed a 'deluxe war,' that was being managed for the television screen. This war was being conducted at specific times and in specific places, with the sole intention of filling the screen and creating the impression of a constant war going on everywhere."

To return to Nakba Day, when I found out that the Palestinian officers were stalling, I spoke to Chief of General Staff Mofaz and recommended that he send attack helicopters, while sending Arafat and his men a message: if they did not leave the Mukat'a and come to Ayosh Junction to stop the shooting, he had better get into the bomb shelter in the Mukat'a, because we were going to attack them.

The message was delivered simultaneously in several methods. Prime Minister Barak called Arafat, division head Oren called General Ismail, and the Shin Bet informed the heads of the military wings, while attack helicopters circled up above. Within minutes we received a response that General Ismail and Jibril Rajoub were heading out to the junction. Our forces did, in fact, see them show up at the site and stop the fire. Then taxis came to pick up the snipers. The day of battle ended at close to seven p.m., with ten Tanzim snipers dead and several injured among our forces.

The day after Nakba Day, Barghouti boasted in a television interview that his men had shot six thousand bullets at IDF soldiers. Arafat later reprimanded him for this claim. As the one who initiated the clashes, Arafat wanted to characterize them as a popular uprising – Intifada – and most definitely did not want to give proof that he had lit the fire and was responsible for the conflagration.

Nakba Day was just one example out of many that documented Arafat's control over the clashes. In the Western Wall Tunnel clashes in September 1996, I defined his control as follows: "He lit the match; he is able to put out the fire. But he does not control the height of the flames."

On Nakba Day it became clear that Marwan Barghouti was Arafat's right-hand man, even his "alter ego," in instigating the violence. Matters concluded in private between the two of them led to the violent outbreak in September 2000, while exploiting MK Ariel Sharon's visit to the Temple Mount as the excuse.

One of the Palestinian leadership's lessons from the Western Wall Tunnel clashes in September 1996 was that they had to have greater control over the violent attacks. Therefore, it was important for the Fatah to operate and lead the violence without the other organizations. The PA achieved this by arming the Tanzim as proxies. The Tanzim did not outwardly represent the Palestinian Authority and Barghouti as its head – instead, it was presented as a reflection of the atmosphere among the Palestinian public.

The violent clashes that Arafat initiated even before Camp David were not in line with the accepted conception regarding Arafat's intentions. Here was an Israeli prime minister who was talking about a permanent agreement, a two-state solution and an end to the conflict this year. Why instigate violent clashes? Why mark Nakba Day of the year 2000 specifically as a day of violence?

The rationale guiding Arafat was exactly the same as what I described in a document that I wrote in November 1999. He had to go to war in

order to avoid a final settlement that would mean the "two states for two peoples" solution. Arafat did not want the two-state solution, which would leave the Palestinians with 22 percent of Israel's territory and give Israelis 78 percent. He would not be satisfied with the 1967 lines. That is why he never took off his uniform. That is also why he never saw himself ruling a state within the 1967 lines. From a strategic approach, he did not recognize the State of Israel and its right to exist as an independent Jewish state. But the new Israeli position adopted by Barak, the Israeli majority that was ready to agree to a far-reaching compromise, Clinton's international leadership, and European pressure – these created a tunnel that led all participants toward a two-state solution. When Arafat understood this, he decided to bomb the tunnel.

Arafat believed that each of the possible results of this explosion would be positive for him. If the Israelis continued to hold on to the illusion, if they kept up their pattern of behavior, they would try to placate him by giving him another slice of the salami. They would "go the extra mile for him," and give up even more. (The American term "go the extra mile" toward Arafat was common language in the negotiations held between the outbreak of terror in September 2000 and the end of the Taba talks in December.) But if the Israelis insisted, they would receive an explosion that would prevent the very agreement that Arafat wanted to avoid, and would cause the entire world to condemn Israel for its stubbornness. Arafat thought he was resilient, because either way nobody would blame him. Would the world admit to its mistake? After they all promised peace, would they retract this promise? Would they take his Nobel Peace Prize away from him? Would they blame him? No matter the outcome, Arafat, would not have to rule a country within the 1967 lines, but would be able to continue his battle against Israel – and this is exactly what he wanted.

In November 1999, when I served as GOC Central Command (a position I held until August 2000), I realized that I had to prepare the forces and train them for a new kind of war. For this purpose, I instructed them to build a mock Palestinian village in Beit Guvrin, for training all battalions – regular army and reserve soldiers – who were due to operate in these areas. In May 2000, I convened officers at the rank of battalion commander and higher in the hall at Ammunition Hill and informed them that we were going to war. I explained what this war would look like and why we had to prepare. I told them that we would be operating in a civilian environment and prepared them for the possibility of retaking control over the Palestinian cities and occupying them.

Some officers thought that my preparations seemed strange. We were nearly at Camp David. Peace was at hand – why prepare for war?

In July 2000, I met with a group of Americans from the Washington Institute for Near East Policy (which I joined as a research fellow for a time after completing my military service). I spoke in a similar line, and I noticed that they were shifting uncomfortably in their seats. I later found out that when talking among themselves about my claims of an expected clash in the near future initiated by Arafat, some had said they considered my statements deluded.

The Israeli leadership, however, understood my approach. Barak said that he was going for a move that would "bring peace or expose Arafat's true face." And if he exposed Arafat's true face, there would be war. The captain of the ship himself shared the assessment that we had to prepare for war. He believed that going to Camp David was a way of recruiting the Israeli people to war, so that the public would know that Israel had turned over every stone in its path toward compromise and peace, and that the war was imposed on it. This would be a "no choice" war. This is how I saw the situation.

But the public atmosphere in Israel was totally different during that year. Israel was enjoying a euphoric sense that the conflict had ended and peace was just around the corner. This created a major gap between the general atmosphere within civilian Israel and the IDF's preparations in general, particularly at the Central and Southern Commands. Later, some accused us of responsibility for the war, saying it broke out because we prepared for it, like a self-fulfilling prophecy. This is nonsense. The army's responsibility is to prepare for war, and even more so when the prediction is that war is close. This does not mean that the army wants war, and definitely not the army that I know. The IDF is not an army that looks for wars. But during 2000, I found myself planning a war and preparing for war, while a large part of the public was preparing for peace.

Even before the war broke out, I explained to everyone around me, both within and out of the IDF, that this would be a war like no other since the War of Independence. It was easy to say this within the IDF. The Central Command and General Staff also came to this conclusion. But our contacts with the civilian society and with politicians were not easy. The warning signs were all there, we could see where this process was leading, but we couldn't make everyone else see what we could see. I remember speaking to a group of soldiers' parents. When I finished one mother got up and said, "If you are right, then the education I gave my children is irrelevant. I taught them that peace was near, but you are telling us that we must continue to fight." I told her that if this is what she took away from my talk, then I did not talk in vain. This is exactly what I meant.

I also remember a meeting with the members of the Knesset Foreign Affairs and Defense Committee, held several days after the outbreak of clashes in September 2000. One MK asked me if the worst of the clashes was already behind us. In the most dramatic manner, I held my head in my hands. I asked rhetorically, "Where is this MK, and where am I in understanding the situation we're in?" I had known for more than a year that this conflict would erupt, and I knew that, when it did, it would last for months or years. Yet here, opposite me, sat a person who was part of the Israeli leadership, and he had failed to grasp the reality toward which we were heading, the reality in which we live.

During 2000, before setting off for Camp David, Prime Minister Barak held organized discussions on the possibility of reaching a peace agreement with Arafat. As I stated in a previous chapter, then Shin Bet head Ami Ayalon, and his external assistant, academic Dr. Mati Steinberg, claimed that there was a chance of signing an agreement with the Palestinians, on the basis of a Palestinian state on 92 percent of the West Bank and the division of Jerusalem. They were very optimistic and estimated that, under these conditions, Arafat would forfeit his demand for the Palestinian "right of return." On the other hand, the research experts in the Military Intelligence Directorate were pessimistic and assumed that Arafat would not forfeit the right of return.

The Camp David Summit and post-summit discussions proved that the Shin Bet prediction regarding Arafat's position was wrong, while the Intelligence Directorate evaluation was precise. Even so, the erosion of Israeli positions continued. The Palestinians made no concessions regarding the right of return, and they initiated an attack on Israel in September 2000. Yet at talks held by Gilad Scher, director general of the Prime Minister's Office, and others, the Israelis upped the ante. If, at Camp David, discussions focused on giving 85 percent of the territory to the Palestinians, later this rose to 95 percent. If at the outset of the process there were talks of keeping the Jordan Valley, now there was discussion of giving up the entire region. Even regarding the refugees in Taba, Minister Yossi Beilin raised ideas that were totally different from the initial Israeli position, albeit in a "noncommittal manner," as Prime Minister Barak claimed. I regarded this dynamic of giving in with great severity, because of its security implications.

Here it must be noted that Barak, as prime minister and minister of defense, was present at both military and political discussions. His understanding of the political-strategic picture, alongside his operative and tactical military understanding, challenged us and turned our discussions into productive and creative sessions. A short while after his election he visited Central Command, which I headed, and we held a very serious discussion on all areas of our relationship with the Palestinians.

Clearly, he was not there just for the photographs. One of the meetings at my headquarters was held after he had tossed the idea of "separation" from the Palestinians into the air. At this meeting I and my officers presented the significance of this term as we understood its meaning and implementation, in various fields: territorial, political, economic, security, and more. At this meeting we learned much about Barak's intentions when he used the word "separation." On his part, he learned much from us, the military echelon, as those responsible for developing the knowledge in our field. In my view, this was an example of the correct relationship between the political and military fields.

Barak came across to the public as someone with a short fuse, and we cannot say that this claim was without any basis. Ehud Barak had no patience for stupid people or nonsense. He portrayed an air of boastfulness, as one who thinks that he knows everything. But this was only true until the person in front of him raised a challenging issue or a perspective. When this happened, Barak appreciated it and responded accordingly.

In general, I saw things the same way that Barak did. We had the same concern that we were going to war, and we agreed that we should maximize our chances for peace and prove, throughout the process, that we were doing everything possible to achieve peace. I understood that Barak had to take the path he did so that we would know where we stood, so that in case we needed to draft the nation to war, they would know what they were fighting for. The Israeli public had been brainwashed into believing that peace was only a stone's throw away and had been deferred because of us. The people needed a change in understanding, to make them aware of the need for battle.

But the truth became apparent in Camp David. After Arafat's true face was exposed and he himself initiated war against us, Barak did not lead the nation to war as was required. He did not stand up before the nation and tell them the bitter and complete truth. His government was narrow, and most of his ministers were the founding fathers and supporters of the Oslo Accords. They did not let him do what was needed: to declare Arafat an enemy. On the contrary, these ministers demanded that Barak offer more concessions, or, as some expressed, "to take another step in Arafat's direction." It seems that in order to survive politically, Barak let the people around him take that extra step toward Arafat. When it became clear that one step was not sufficient, they took another step, and when it became clear that two steps were not sufficient, they took three. This way, Barak himself blurred the truth that he had exposed. In order to survive politically, he created an ambivalent situation of a restrained war on the one hand, and withdrawal in political negotiations on the other; coping with Palestinian violence militarily while continuing to give in politically to Palestinian demands.

When Arafat saw this, once again, he identified our weakness. He knew that we knew that he had initiated war, and he knew that we were too afraid to say so. He knew that we knew that he was the enemy, and, despite this, we continued to call him a partner. That is why he concluded that he had no reason to agree to a cease-fire. His extortions had succeeded. The Israelis had proven, week after week, that they had no red lines. After each round of violence, the previous red line was erased and, in its place, a new red line was drawn. If this was the dynamic, then we could also erase the new red line and replace it – using violence – with the next red line that would be even more convenient. Muhammad Dahlan defined this perfectly: "You are like a squeezed lemon – but with you the juice never ends."

Two weeks before the attack that killed Staff Sergeant David Biri, I began my term as deputy chief of general staff. The day after the attack, on Thursday, September 28, 2000, MK Ariel Sharon visited the Temple Mount, a short visit that ended peacefully. We all went to sleep quietly.

But the next day, on Friday, September 29, on the eve of the Jewish New Year 5761, two major events occurred:

The first happened at 6:45 a.m., when Commander Yosef Tabega, a Border Police officer, was murdered by a Palestinian policeman while conducting a joint Israeli-Palestinian patrol in the Qalqilya region.

The second occurred in the afternoon: the violent uprising after prayers on the Temple Mount, which gave the opening signal for the Palestinian terror war (or Second Intifada), termed by the Palestinians "the Al-Aqsa Intifada."

In retrospect, I discovered that a meeting was held between Arafat and Barghouti, in which Arafat gave the signal to open fire. But, at the time, I did not know this. There was no official order to begin the Second Intifada. But, as claimed by Professor Yigal Eilam, a historian, in his book *Following Orders* (Keter, 1990), there was no need for such an order. There were understandings, there was the "commander's spirit." Barghouti clearly understood Arafat's intentions, and his people were on the Temple Mount. One day after Sharon's visit ended quietly, they purposely initiated the outbreak. Arafat identified the opportunity. He understood that the moment he had been waiting for had arrived. And he made sure his people understood that the great moment had come.

In his book *The Intifada – Explosion of the Peace Process* (2001) and in articles published beginning in September 2001, Arafat's advisor Mamdouh Nofal describes the meetings headed by Arafat just before Sharon's visit to the Temple Mount and on the night after this visit, in which he conveyed the spirit of war and the message to initiate an attack. Faisal Husseini defined the process as a Trojan horse: the Oslo Accords were the Trojan horse through which the Palestinians entered Palestine, and in September 2000 they came out of the horse's stomach.

I saw clearly that this was an initiated attack. But within Israeli society, many were still confused, and not only the public. The Shin Bet claimed that there was no proof that the attack was initiated – and this was true:

there was no written or taped proof. But the writing was on the wall. Whoever had eyes in his head could see this.

Yet even at this stage, when war had been declared on us, some refused to see it. Shimon Peres, then deputy prime minister and minister of foreign affairs, defended Arafat in internal discussions. "Why are you making him into such a strategist?" he accused us in the cabinet meeting. "He's just a poor guy who's lost control." Once again, the situation infuriated me. There was a war going on. Someone had initiated a war against us. The first thing that had to be done was to define him as an enemy – with all that is implicated in that title. But instead, we spent a whole week arguing about the definition of what was happening. True, Peres did not call us warmongers. But he claimed that the military leaders were "exaggerating," that our analysis was incorrect, and that Arafat was "a miserable wretch." He'd gone to some meeting with Arafat in the middle of the night and reported that he'd found an unfortunate soul who had lost control. I thought that we should send Arafat straight to Habimah Theater. The man was one of the greatest actors I have ever seen.

This situation continued for a week. There were attempts to prompt a cease-fire through meetings between senior officials on both sides, such as the one between GOC Central Command Yitzchak Eitan and the head of the Preventive Security Force, Colonel Jibril Rajoub. We thought that a cease-fire was accepted, but this was not to be. Arafat didn't really want it. That is why the ill-fated meeting was held between Barak and Arafat in Paris, sponsored by US Secretary of State Madeleine Albright.

The meeting was a farce. The Palestinians made false accusations against us, and we disproved them, one after another. Barak asked Arafat, justifiably, how such a violent outbreak could take place, after Camp David and after he had indicated consent to evacuate the entire Gaza Strip and most of Judea and Samaria, and to split Jerusalem. But the Palestinians did not respond. They tried to divert attention from the real problem and continued with their well-known tactics. Arafat told fake stories about his childhood with his aunt who lived next to the Western Wall, trying to show that he knew all about the area. He tried to claim that it wasn't possible to throw rocks from the Temple Mount down onto the Western Wall plaza, which is what happened when policemen were injured in the events preceding the terror war. In his meeting with Prime Minister Barak, Arafat said: "You are a general, and I am a general and also an engineer" (In Arabic: "*Int general, ve'ana general umuhandas kman.*") All this was done to divert the discussion from the main issue – in this case, to avoid a cease-fire, or more precisely, the cessation of terror attacks.

There was also an amusing moment during that meeting, which was held at the residence of the US ambassador in Paris. Arafat, Barak, and Albright were meeting behind closed doors. Suddenly we heard terrible screams. Arafat was going wild. The door flew open and Arafat stormed out, while the secretary of state shouted: "Stop him, stop him!" Arafat jumped into his Mercedes and sped to the gate, while Madeleine Albright shouted at the US Marines: "Close the gate! Close the gate!" She ran in her high-heeled shoes across the paved courtyard to the Mercedes, which was stopped in front of the locked gate. Then she opened the car door, grabbed Arafat by his arm, and dragged him out of the car and back into the ambassador's residence. This was a once-in-a-lifetime scene. Even the Palestinians laughed out loud.

In the end, after a very long day, a document was prepared, and it meant a cease-fire. Each leader was supposed to go back home and announce to the media that a cease-fire had been reached and we were returning to the pre-battle lines. We drove to the Champs-Élysées to receive the blessing of President Jacques Chirac. In the meantime, the agreement that both sides were supposed to sign was being printed at the US ambassador's house. Chirac's attitude was clearly hostile to us and supportive of Arafat. This was obvious from the moment we walked in, by the way he welcomed Arafat (with hugs and whispers) and also later, in the atmosphere and the way he spoke.

From the beginning of that day in Paris, I felt that Chirac supported Arafat and accepted his version – that we were the aggressors and they were the victims. The day started with Chirac meeting Arafat, and then he sat with our team. When it was our turn, it was clear that Arafat had already fed Chirac with fake stories and details. Chirac responded impatiently to Barak and others who tried to put things straight. One of the ridiculous accusations that he made was that most Palestinians injured in the first week of fighting were hit in the head, a fact that he interpreted as Israeli soldiers firing to kill. We tried to explain to him that most of the dead on the Palestinian side were Tanzim snipers, who expose only their head when they shoot us, and therefore are hit in the head. But he hastily rejected our explanation (which was true and exact).

At the end of the event at the palace, we returned to the US ambassador's residency to sign the document. But then we noticed that Arafat had disappeared. Barak waited, Albright waited, but there was no sign of Arafat… We waited and waited until we realized that he wasn't showing up. He would not sign. There would be no cease-fire.

All this happened on October 4, 2000. On that date, after five years of question marks, I finally saw the exclamation mark. From my point of view, there was no longer any possibility that the violent attacks initiated by Arafat would be the "last battle" before an agreement. I was finally convinced that he had chosen war to avoid the "two-state solution for two peoples, within the borders of the Land of Israel."

I remember that early the next morning, when we boarded the plane back to Israel, I realized that this would not be a clash of months but rather a war of years. Three, four or five years. I was finally aware that Arafat would never recognize the State of Israel as a Jewish state.

He would do all he could to avoid a permanent agreement and a "two states for two peoples" solution. We were facing a principled Palestinian refusal, which would have historical implications. After the second Palestinian refusal to the UN suggestion of partition in 1947, we were facing the third Palestinian refusal to the Israeli suggestion of partition in 2000. Just as the Palestinian leadership responded with violence to the previous suggestions, it was doing the same this time. We could expect many more years of blood, sweat, and tears. Yet the war we were about to enter was a direct continuation of the previous wars. The war of 2000 was a war of historical significance no less than the War of Independence. This was a war over the right of the State of Israel to exist as an independent Jewish state, a war over the right of the Jewish nation to have a national home.

Toward the end of 2000, when I confronted this situation daily in my role as the deputy chief of general staff, the general picture was slowly becoming sharper.

I understood the strategic danger of the Israeli policy of concession. The Palestinians felt that when they put pressure on Israel, Israel collapsed under the pressure and gave everything, meaning that violence paid off. As long as the Palestinians felt that violence was worthwhile, they continued to act violently against us. That is why, even if we came to some arrangement, it would be regarded as an Israeli surrender to Palestinian violent pressure. The arrangement would be only temporary, to be used as a starting point for the next round of violence. Instead of bringing peace closer, Israeli concessions encouraged the Palestinians to use more violence and turned this pattern into a strategic problem.

I understood that since 1983, we had been engaged in a battle of withdrawal and delay. This had to be stopped, as this type of battle is the most difficult to manage. In this kind of battle, you are not the initiator but the responder, and you have to time your withdrawal so that your enemies don't hit you while withdrawing. This type of battle leaves you without a goal to move toward or a line to protect. It is unstable, tactically very difficult, and strategically disastrous.

I realized that we had reached the moment of truth, and that if we wanted to stop this vicious cycle, we would have to turn this war into a turning point. We would have to switch – in the midst of battle – from withdrawal and surrender to the offensive. Otherwise, the cycle would continue – withdrawal from the Hezbollah encouraged the Palestinians, and withdrawal from the Palestinians encouraged the Hezbollah, in a vicious cycle. Slowly, others in the region took notice of the process and closed in on us, like hyenas tracking a dead deer. Entities such as the Iranian regime and Al Qaeda treated us like an injured and defeated animal, and once again started to figure out how and when to attack us.

I also understood that the world saw reality in a distorted manner. The world assumed that the Palestinians wanted a two-state solution and that Israel didn't, but it was exactly the opposite. Israel wanted a two-state solution and the Palestinians didn't. From their point of view, the border is not that of 1967, but the Mediterranean Sea. That is why they were not prepared to accept any solution that would give them a state within the 1967 lines and prevent them from aspiring to expand beyond these boundaries. If this was the situation, with or without an agreement they would continue to fight us at all costs, as long as they thought that violence paid off. Therefore, the need to prove to the Palestinians that violence was not worthwhile was a strategic need.

That is why I believed that the war of the twenty-first century was an existential challenge, but also a historic opportunity. We had an opportunity to turn things around strategically, to prove our strength and stability, and to renew our power of deterrence. From my point of view this was the purpose of the war – to switch from defense to offense. We had to ensure that all those who wished for our demise returned to treating us like a powerful country that could defend itself and protect the red lines of its security.

The Nakba events of 2000 led me to a certain understanding of this issue. That is why under my leadership, I defined Central Command's goal as creating an understanding among the Palestinians that violence did not pay off. But I formulated a general position on this issue only toward the end of 2000, and I warned Prime Minister Barak of the continued erosion of the Israeli position under fire. When the possibility arose to attend meetings in Taba, I regarded this as a grave mistake – again, because of the security implications of Israeli concessions. I realized that there was no chance of reaching an agreement, and that whatever we agreed to in Taba would be used as a starting point for the next round of violence and concessions. That is why I believed we had to stop. I thought that, under the circumstances, we had been right to go to Camp David, but we must not go to Taba.

In theoretical terms, in 2000 I identified a problem that was no less severe – the asymmetry between us and the Palestinians. I don't mean the usual asymmetry of power: we are strong, they are weak. Here I refer to an inverted asymmetry of expectations: we gave up on Judea, Samaria, and Gaza, but they did not give up on Haifa and Tel Aviv. They were fighting for it all, attacking it all, while we were still in retreat and delay, fighting for something that we had already given up. In the name of justice, they were fighting for their right over all of Palestine, while most Israelis were fighting for security in part of the Land of Israel. In the Israeli and international consciousness, it became accepted that the Arabs have a right to live anywhere in Israel, but there are areas that are "out of bounds" for Jews. This is a very problematic situation, which puts Israel at a strategic disadvantage in terms of its self-awareness. If we want to stand up to our adversary from an equal standing, we have to threaten it all. We must not accept that Judea and Samaria are theirs. Only this way will the game be open, and when the adversary threatens Haifa and Tel Aviv, we must threaten Hebron and Ramallah in return. This is the only way to create a symmetry which might lead to some balanced arrangement.

Regardless of the fundamental attitude toward Judea and Samaria, the claim to hold them creates a balance opposite the Palestinian claim for Tel Aviv or Haifa, until they are forced to waive this claim.

In the political climate that existed in Israel toward the end of 2000, this understanding had no chance of becoming a political goal. After seven years of the Oslo process and in an atmosphere where the dominant atmosphere was defeatist and irrelevant, it was not possible to expect an immediate change – in theory and in politics – in the Israeli position. The correct approach was to initiate a political offensive and state that if the Palestinians are fighting for all of Palestine, then the Israelis are fighting for all of Israel. But in the given political environment, it was impossible to do this. That is why I developed an approach that I call "building the wall." This wall tells the Palestinians: you won't achieve anything political or territorial with violence. If Israel did not launch a political counterattack, it would at least build a wall to stop their attacks and prevent them from gnawing away at Israel's positions, territory, and strength.

How do we build such a wall? On four fronts:

Military: We don't let terrorism succeed. We use all means available to the IDF and Shin Bet to prevent terrorism.

Economy: We ensure that the Israeli economy continues to thrive even in wartime situations, and that the Palestinians suffer financially as a result of their attacks.

Public: We ensure that the People of Israel stay strong. We don't have protests, don't count the dead, and don't blame ourselves.

Political: We do not give in to the Palestinians while they are attacking, and do not suggest attaining quiet by giving in to their extortions.

Through a combined effort, under a united and close leadership, we create a situation that would make the Palestinians lose, for the first time in twenty years – in military, financial, and political terms. Only then, when defeat is engraved in their consciousness and they realize that they are not facing Israeli spider webs but an Israeli wall, then we can return to the discussion table and seriously consider dialogue.

The idea of a wall was not a military concept in the narrow understanding of the term, but a strategic one. I reached this concept through thought processes that I underwent, first in the Central Command and then in the offices of DCOGS and COGS. These thought processes stemmed from my realization that as a military man, I must understand the relevant reality that influenced me and that I was trying to influence. Even though my mission seemed purely military, I had to be aware of the international circumstances, the internal Israeli constraints, and the Palestinians' view of the situation. As division commander, and even more so as GOC Central Command, DCOGS, and COGS, I knew that I could not rely only on the topographical map, aerial view photographs, or what I saw in the binoculars.

The routine situation assessments that the IDF conducted usually addressed the engineering aspect. They raised practical questions, as in the construction field. What materials were required and in what quantities? What and how many military companies were needed? What ammunition will be needed? How long would the construction (i.e., the military operation) take, considering the materials we had to work with? But I claimed that we could not work only as engineers. As an army, we could not be construction contractors only. We had to move from planning to design, and the design was cultural, theoretical, and conceptual. It required an understanding of the context, and it created a connection between context and the detailed military plans. Including the design as a stage in the evaluation process, before the planning stage, enabled me, first as GOC Central Command and then as COGS, to stay relevant. Foreign armies learned this innovative idea and adopted it.

In late 1999, at Central Command we defined the context as such: Israel and the Palestinians are Siamese twins joined by the navel. Israel is the strong twin of the two, but it is connected to the weaker one. The two are going through a process designed to bring about separation. This route is like a tunnel. The Oslo Accords carved out the tunnel, and the international system set it in concrete. This concrete tunnel should lead the Siamese twins to separation through an agreement to end the conflict, but this is not what Arafat wants. Arafat does not want to separate at the end of the tunnel, he wants to blow up the tunnel. That is why a war will break out, and our role in this war will be to stop Arafat from blowing up the tunnel and getting out. Our role in the war will be to force Arafat to return, grudgingly, to the tunnel.

In late 2000 and early 2001, thinking about the context in which the conflict broke out led us to the idea of the wall. To some extent, the wall was a continuation of the tunnel. The wall was meant to stop the hole that Arafat was trying to create in the tunnel through his violent attacks against us. That is why the wall was not an alternative to the political process, but a means to achieve a political process on a solid foundation. The intention was to put Arafat in a no-choice situation that would force him to abandon violence and return to the political table.

CHAPTER 9

ARAFAT: THE REVOLUTION IS ME

Yasser Arafat was the main Palestinian personality I faced after I began the term of head of the Intelligence Directorate in June 1995, and until his death in November 2004. Arafat had power, as expressed in his slogan: "The Palestinian revolution is me." I clearly remember a photograph of him standing on a balcony in Nablus, the crowds cheering him while he saluted them. Behind him was a large photograph of himself in an identical position: Arafat saluting the crowds and the crowds cheering him. His keffiyeh-wearing image embodied the Palestinian struggle, and as long as he was alive, it was impossible to separate the two.

Undoubtedly, Arafat registered many historical achievements to his name. He united the Palestinians in the 1960s. He put them on the international map in the 1970s, and despite many mistakes, he led them from one success to the next. He constantly used manipulations and lies, but from his perspective, his maneuvers were wise and promoted the Palestinian cause, which he served with total dedication. His understanding of European sensitivities in the postcolonial era enabled him to describe the issue of occupation in terms that blurred the historical truth and delegitimized the State of Israel. In September 2000 as well, when he initiated terror attacks against Israel, he succeeded in creating a false image and the impression that Israel was the aggressor.

In Israel, many claim that Arafat brought disaster on his people by causing them to miss another historical opportunity to split the land and establish a Palestinian state. I deeply doubt that the Palestinians see things this way. From their perspective, they are marching forward. Despite the damage and suffering caused to them during the period of continued dispute in the twenty-first century, they still believe that they are marching toward the goal. They regard Israel as withdrawing from one red line after another and from one position after another, while they have not been forced to forfeit even one of their basic demands. This Palestinian success is taken directly from Arafat's teachings. Thanks to him, the Palestinians are perceived by the world as a people fighting for national freedom, despite the fact that they are actually fighting to annul the national freedom of the Jewish people and the State of Israel.

In this regard, I had severe criticism for the ninth president of the State of Israel, Shimon Peres, who was one of the architects of Oslo. Peres was the one who brought Arafat to Israel. He was the one who convinced Rabin, in many ways, to gamble on Oslo and give Yasser Arafat a foothold in the Gaza Strip and in Judea and Samaria. Further, at several junctions along the way, when asked to make brave decisions in dealing with Arafat, Peres was also the one who chose not to make them. He always underestimated the dangers that Arafat embodied. He found justifications in favor of Arafat's behavior. To some extent, Peres acted like an advocate in his defense, emphasizing his good points and covering up his bad points. I can understand his rationale. I can understand his need to go to Oslo to investigate the possibility. I can understand that later, and for a long period of time, it was difficult for him to drop his choice of Oslo. What I cannot understand is why in 2000, when everything became clear, Peres did not stand up and say, Arafat is the problem and not the solution. Arafat took us for a ride.

I expected something different from Shimon Peres. I expected him to stand up before the nation and make a clear statement about this man with whom we had signed a treaty, and demand that he return the Nobel Prize for peace. If Peres had done this, he would have achieved fame and glory. In a single moment he would have changed Israel's international status by creating a clear picture, both globally and in Israel, regarding the nature and essence of the conflict. He would have made good use of his reputation and his unique status to serve his country's most vital interest.

Arafat's strategic goal was "a Palestinian state from the [Jordan] River to the [Mediterranean] Sea." He never gave up on the idea of a complete Palestine. He regarded himself, in historical terms, as an Arab-Muslim leader who was leading his people to victory over the State of Israel and not to a compromise with the Zionist state. But he read the international map very well, and so he did not declare his goal, but constantly maneuvered. Maneuvering was his greatest talent. He maneuvered the Eastern Bloc countries, with the Europeans, and finally with the Americans. He maneuvered Israeli public opinion and the Israeli leadership. Even within the Arab world he succeeded in maneuvering, as in Palestinian society. He pushed away and then pulled close, pulled close and pushed away again. In this sense, he was a true artist. He juggled people like tennis balls. But in all his tricks and maneuvers, he never lost sight of the strategic goal. He always strived for the same goal: replacing the State of Israel with Palestine.

My feelings toward Arafat were ambivalent. On one hand, I couldn't help but admire him. On the other, I despised his wily personality. I spent years studying the files on him. I read every scrap of information about him. I learned that he had dedicated himself, heart and soul, to the Palestinian issue. He was a formidable opponent. I despise lies, but I must admit that his lies worked very well. They yielded great achievements for his people, and he was able to transform himself from a nobody into an omnipotent leader. He brought destruction with him wherever he went – to Jordan, Lebanon, and the State of Israel – but this wasn't destruction for its own sake. He visualized the goal from within the ruins, and through them he marched toward it. Although he was surrounded by corruption, he himself followed a modest lifestyle. He also exploited corruption – of Palestinians as well as Israelis – to act on behalf of his nationalist goal. The good life did not interest him. Everything he did was for the Palestinian cause. He was completely dedicated to it, totally identified with it. Some say that he used corruption as a method of tempting individuals on the enemy side. He used this method against numerous entities in Lebanon during 1970–1982, and also against senior Israeli figures, mainly through his confidante, Muhammad Rashid. I was very worried about the business connection between Arafat and his supporters and former members of the Israeli defense establishment, such as the late Yossi Ginossar, and even more so by the connection between him and close advisors to our prime ministers, such as Omri Sharon and Dov Weisglass.

History will be the judge of whether Arafat was right. If Israel turns out to be a Jewish state that exists in peace, then Arafat was wrong. If not, then Arafat was right. But in any case, we have to view this issue with intellectual honesty, and recognize that the Palestinian ethos that Arafat formulated does not rely on the establishment of a Palestinian state within the 1967 lines. Rather, it requires the destruction of the State of Israel in order to construct something else upon its ruins. True, this will happen in stages, but the most important stage is the destruction of the State of Israel. This was Arafat's goal throughout his career, and this is the heritage that he left behind for future generations of Palestinians.

Even while managing the trivial details of daily life, Arafat never lost sight of his overarching goal. One of the incidents that reflects his involvement and control over the finer points took place during a meeting I had with him. While I was commander of Central Command, I was called upon to implement one of the "further redeployments" (FRD), as one of the stages in implementing the Oslo Accord. For this mission, I had to meet with General Haj Ismail, commander of the Palestinian National Security Forces in the West Bank, to transfer responsibility for areas in the Jenin region to the Palestinian Authority. The night before implementation of this phase, Prime Minister Ehud Barak accepted a recommendation to make a small change in the agreement that previously been made with Arafat. I was asked to present our request for this change at the beginning of the meeting. I was certain that General Ismail would not be able to make this decision without Arafat's permission, and I wondered whether Arafat would be willing to authorize it by phone, or if he would want to see it with his own eyes. The meeting was held on a Friday, and the prime minister instructed me to do everything I could to complete the process before Shabbat began on Friday evening, and not put it off until Sunday. Accordingly, I had a helicopter at the ready in case I would need to fly to meet Arafat, following phone authorization for this from the chief of general staff and the prime minister.

As expected, after I presented our request to General Ismail, he spoke with Arafat by phone, and the latter insisted that the matter be brought to him directly. I suggested that I fly out to meet him immediately so we could carry out the FRD phase as planned. Arafat agreed. On that day he was in Hebron, and our meeting was held in his offices there (before he was confined to the Mukata'a, Arafat had offices in all the major cities in the West Bank). We arrived at his office when he was in the middle of the Friday prayers, so we had to wait for a few minutes. At last the meeting proceeded, and Arafat authorized our request for the change without objection.

While we waited, I noticed about forty men of various ages, a few of them in uniform, sitting in the waiting room. I asked General Ismail who they were, and he referred my question to Arafat's chief of general staff. The answer was astonishing: "They all have requests for the Ra'is ["chairman" or "president"], and they're waiting for his answer." Curiosity piqued, I asked, "What kind of requests?" The COGS replied, "One wants to open a business here in Hebron, and he's asking for the blessing of the Ra'is. Another wants to send his son to study in Saudi Arabia. He also wants the blessing of the Ra'is."

The list went on. When I noticed an officer in uniform among the group, I asked, "And what's the colonel waiting for?"

"His Land Rover," came the reply.

During Operation Defensive Shield, we found evidence in the Mukata'a that documented Arafat's obsession for detail. His signature appeared on even the smallest payments in the hundreds of shekels to terrorists, Fatah Tanzim activists, and families of "martyred" terrorists (*shahidi*). He controlled both the grand vision and the picayune details, at one and the same time.

This is why I knew that he was the one who had lit the flame of violence in September 1996, and that the opening of the Western Wall Tunnel was only an excuse. The terrorist attacks in the spring of 1997 resulted from the terrorist organizations' interpretation of Arafat's statements on the night of March 9–10, which they understood as a "green light." I had no doubt that he was responsible for inflaming the fires on September 29, 2000, and Sharon going up to the Temple Mount was only an excuse.

Arafat would not have succeeded if certain Israelis had not played into his hands. I call these individuals "terminal." These are the people to whom the facts are not important. Even if reality slaps them in the face and rocks their existence, they will never change their opinion.

Arafat succeeded because we suffered from a culture of self-blame. This point must be clarified: the Israelis and the Arabs are completely at odds in all matters concerning self-criticism and self-blame. The Arabs do not blame themselves at all. The guilty party is always on the outside – Israel, the USA, the West, but never them. On our side, on the other hand, we suffer from an almost opposite condition. On our side many blur the difference between self-criticism and taking responsibility, and self-blame. Self-criticism is an important and positive Jewish term.

Taking responsibility is a correct Western term. But when self-criticism and taking responsibility turn into a mental situation where I am always at fault and all blame is on me, there is something wrong. We have seen these situations in the past. Some Jews blamed themselves during the Holocaust. Other Jews blamed themselves during the Bolshevik period, even when they were taken to the gulags in Siberia. This indicates a very deep pathology of the victim identifying with the attacker, a sick tendency to say: "We probably deserve it," "We must be wrong." One of our greatest poets, Natan Alterman, spoke about this phenomenon in his poem "Then Satan Said" (published posthumously):

> Then Satan said: How do I overcome
> this besieged one?
> He has courage and talent,
> implements of war and resourcefulness.
> He said, I will not take away his strength
> Nor curb him with bit and bridle.
> I will not implant cowardice in his mind
> Nor weaken his hands as in days of yore.
> Only this will I do: I will dull his mind
> and cause him to forget
> the justice of his cause.
> So Satan said.
> The heavens blanched in terror
> As they saw him rise up
> To carry out his plot.[1]

---

[1] Poem used by permission of Nathan Slor and Yael Slor Marzuk. Modified and expanded from translation in Sarah Honig, *Debunking the Bull: For Seekers of Another Tack* (Jerusalem: Gefen Publishing House, 2012), 85.

In our relationship with the Palestinians, this phenomenon repeats itself, like the expression of a characteristic embedded in our genetic code. But in this case, our tendency to blame ourselves clashes with the Palestinian tendency to blame only us. Along the way, a strange symmetry is created. The Palestinians say that only the Israelis are to blame, and the Israelis also say that only the Israelis are to blame…

We have completely distorted our understanding of reality, and we are the ones leading this process of distortion. In handling our sense of helplessness regarding problems on the other side of the fence, it is much easier to blame ourselves, because no personal decision on our part will ever change the destructive goals of the Palestinian struggle. No decision of ours will change the terrorist nature of the Palestinian struggle or of extremist Islam. But it's easy to say: "It's all my fault. If I change my ways, everything else will change." That is why throughout the years of war against Palestinian terrorism, many Israeli factors have felt comfortable blaming the IDF, the government, and other Israelis. Almost all these accusations were baseless. They derived from the unholy alliance between the Palestinian need to blame others and the need of many Israelis to blame themselves.

More than once, Israeli politicians have been the first to blame the IDF in "torpedoing opportunities for a cease-fire" through military action, mainly after a targeted assassination. The Palestinians use this in their propaganda. One of the most prominent cases was after the killing of the head of the Hamas military wing, Salah Shehade, in a July 2002 air force raid. In this case, the first one to blame the IDF for torpedoing an opportunity for a cease-fire was MK Yossi Beilin. A short while after the attack, Beilin made an announcement to the press. He claimed that before the attack, negotiations had been conducted between the Palestinian Authority and Hamas to bring about a cease-fire. He claimed that the negotiations had been close to completion, but that the killing of Shehade caused them to collapse. Several days later, MK Haim Ramon sent a question to then minister of defense Binyamin (Fuad) Ben-Eliezer, claiming that the head of the Intelligence Directorate, Major General Aharon Ze'evi (Farkash), had concealed information from the defense minister regarding these negotiations, and so the minister had approved the attack without knowledge of the opportunity for a cease-fire.

These claims were totally unfounded and were denied by the minister of defense, by myself as chief of general staff, and by the head of intelligence. As this was sensitive intelligence information, we avoided publicizing details about what was really going on between the Palestinian Authority and the Hamas – what two members of the Knesset called a "near-agreement for a cease-fire." I demanded that the matter be brought before the Sub-Committee for Intelligence and Secret Services of the Foreign Affairs and Defense Committee, where discussions of this kind can generally be held without leaking of information. In the discussions, the head of intelligence easily refuted MK Ramon's claim regarding the concealment of information from the minister of defense, and emphatically denied the claim of "near-cease-fire." Unfortunately, the Knesset members involved did not bother to apologize, and the claims were not erased. This is only one example of many.

Arafat knew that we were aware of the fact that he was toying with us by enabling the existence of secondary agents for terrorism, such as Yahya Ayyash and Muhammad Deif. On the Israeli side, we heard statements that Arafat interpreted as signals of weakness, such as "We will strive for peace as if there is no terrorism and we will fight terrorism as if there is no peace." In addition, we never insisted on an ultimatum that demanded clear actions and statements against terrorism as a condition for continuing the political process and implementation on the ground. Arafat apparently understood that the Israeli politicians who had signed an agreement with him had become his hostages.

The question regarding Arafat's level of control on the ground was repeatedly raised by us and by the Americans. As head of intelligence, I was asked this question by two secretaries of state: Warren Christopher and Madeleine Albright. The first time Christopher presented this question was during his visit to Israel in the summer of 1995. During this period, buses were blowing up regularly in Israeli cities, mainly in Jerusalem, in attacks that Ayyash instigated from the Gaza Strip under Arafat's control. Following a review that I presented to Prime Minister and Minister of Defense Yitzchak Rabin, he asked: "Do you think the problem with Arafat and his failure to deal with terrorism is a matter of willingness or a matter of capability?" My reply was unequivocal: the problem results from lack of willingness, and not from a lack of capability to cope with terrorism. To support my response, I gave examples of incidents in which Arafat had challenged Hamas, whenever Hamas threatened him and the Fatah. The most obvious examples were firing on and killing Hamas members who had publicly challenged the Palestinian Authority after Friday prayers in Gaza. Another was the arrest of senior Hamas leaders and the shaving of half of their beards and moustaches as an act of humiliation. Clearly, whoever dared to take such steps was not scared of Hamas, and most definitely would fight against it, if he so desired. Later more evidence accumulated proving that in fact, Arafat maintained a complicated relationship with Hamas. Arafat did not want to neutralize Hamas's terror abilities, in order to use it as a secondary agent when needed. This applied to all other organizations as well.

One event related to the question of Arafat's willingness or ability to handle terror organizations involved a diplomatic incident between myself and the US ambassador to Israel. After the terrorist attack at Apropos Café in Tel Aviv (March 21, 1997), Secretary of State Albright announced that she recognized the fact that Arafat was making a 100 percent effort to fight terrorism, but that there was no such thing as "100 percent success." That statement became the accepted reality and released Arafat from responsibility. But it infuriated me, because according to the intelligence information that I had, the attack had been a result of the Hamas understanding that it had received a "green light" from Arafat. So, instead of pressuring Arafat and pushing him into a corner, the secretary of state released him from responsibility!

In a meeting with US ambassador to Israel Martin Indyk, I made my argument on this matter, and detailed the serious implications that underlay the secretary of state's announcement on Arafat's behavior. The ambassador exploded in fury at my audacity in criticizing the secretary of state. Eventually, we patched things up.

I wondered if the secretary of state's comment resulted from a lack of knowledge of the situation, or from intentionally ignoring the situation, mainly the intelligence information. In a later trip to the US, I asked to meet with CIA entities who covered the Palestinian situation. The meeting was traumatic. I discovered that these officials were basing their analyses and estimates on reports sent by their representatives in the region, US diplomats, and the Arab and Israeli media. Their main source of press information in Israel was the English newspaper *Ha'aretz*. Following this meeting, I understood that there might be another possible explanation for the secretary of state's remark.

In 2006, after my release from the IDF, I spent several months as a research fellow at the Washington Institute for Near East Policy. In a seminar held following the Hamas victory in the January 2006 elections, I met with State Department researchers on the Palestinian situation. This time I was not surprised by the level of ignorance on the issue. I realized that beyond the influence of the abovementioned sources, most of these researchers are graduates of Middle East Studies departments at American universities, where the position is generally not pro-Israel. Some claim that this approach results from Arab funding of these departments.

Until the capture of the *Karine A* weapons vessel, Arafat had the benefit of the doubt. This incident changed the attitude of President

George W. Bush toward him, but not necessarily that of the researchers in the State Department and the CIA.

⁂

If things had been up to me, I would have delegitimized Arafat back on September 29, 2000, after we had already missed several earlier opportunities. I would have said publicly that he was responsible and to blame for starting the war. I would have defined him as an enemy and refuted the baseless story about the 1967 "occupation" as the cause for the conflict. I would have built a strategic "wall" by explaining to the Israeli public that we were fighting for our survival. I would have recruited support from the international community for this existential battle. I would have asserted that the only way to advance was through blood, sweat, and tears. I would have declared loudly and clearly that we must regard this war as a direct continuation of the War of Independence.

But things weren't up to me. As one who wore the IDF uniform, I had to accept the constraints and guidelines of the political echelon. I had to face the fact that they were not doing the same work of understanding the context as we were in the IDF, or maybe they were seeing things differently. That is why I formulated the idea of the strategic wall as a relatively modest suggestion. It was not intended to change the fundamental situation in Israel, but to be used on our side during the conflict, so that it would end with the two Siamese twins returning to their march through the reconstructed tunnel of the political process.

But it was difficult to stabilize even the most minimal wall. At the end of 2000 and throughout 2001, we faced several test moments. The government should have adopted the idea of the wall and proceeded accordingly. But politically, Ehud Barak could not come out directly against Arafat. I understood the logic that guided him in going to Camp David and placing the most sensitive and problematic topics on the table. Mainly, this meant ceasing the "salami" process in which we were kept giving significant assets and receiving empty words in return, such as Palestinian commitments that they had no intention of keeping. By placing these issues on the table, we would have been able to clarify whether Arafat sincerely intended to make peace with us. This would expose his true face, which was extremely important to the international community, but was even more important inwardly. Israeli citizens had been brainwashed about Oslo and Arafat. We had to convince Israelis that our leadership "had turned over every stone on the way to a peace agreement," and prove that the failure was not due to our leadership. We also had to prepare Israel for imminent war. This is the way I saw the situation.

But despite all, Barak did not succeed in convincing anyone that this was the situation. Senior ministers in his narrow government continued to defend Arafat. Their main claim was that terror and violence were results of Arafat's weakness and loss of control, so we must strengthen him! Some even blamed Barak for "precipitating matters" at Camp David when Arafat was not ready for an agreement. They blamed the IDF for an overly powerful response to Palestinian terrorism and violence ("The IDF was too ready for these events"). To strengthen their claims, they quoted Major General Amos Malka, then head of intelligence. Malka reported that on a visit to Central Command, he asked how many bullets the Command had consumed during the first month of confrontations. The response was: "one million bullets." This number reflected the demand by command units for supplementary ammunition to complete their quotas, and definitely did not refer to the actual number of bullets that were fired. But it was added to the list of claims and accusations toward the IDF regarding its supposedly exaggerated response.

Ariel Sharon replaced Ehud Barak as prime minister in March 2001, but even he was not successful in leading Israel on a total offensive against Arafat, even though he had no doubts about the man in front of him. That is why Israel never took a proper stand in public relations against the Palestinians and repeatedly agreed to give Arafat another chance. For this reason, even after the horrific terrorist attack at the Dolphinarium in Tel Aviv, on Friday night, June 1, 2001, Israel did not go on the offensive – despite twenty-one Israelis murdered, mostly immigrant youth, and more than one hundred injured. Throughout this period I had tried to create a strategic wall and hoped that now we would succeed. But then I discovered that the wall was made of ice, and Arafat could melt it easily. Israeli politicians were also undermining it and helping Arafat to bring it crashing down.

The terrorist attack at the Dolphinarium was yet another opportunity for the government of Israel to declare Arafat as an enemy and embark on a military and political offensive. At the Cabinet meeting that convened the next morning, a Saturday, Prime Minister Sharon was striving to achieve this. He wanted to convince the Cabinet to approve a military campaign against the Palestinian Authority, as well as a political campaign to put pressure on Arafat as the one responsible for the attack. Foreign Minister Shimon Peres objected, claiming that we must not blame Arafat, but rather the suicide bombers and those who sent them. During the meeting, which continued for several hours, Peres had communications with the foreign minister of Germany, Joseph Martin "Joschka" Fischer, who happened to be on an official visit to Israel at that time. As a result of these contacts, the Cabinet was informed that Arafat was ready to do what he had avoided since the outbreak of hostilities – to announce a cease-fire, in Arabic and on Palestinian media. Based on this, the military attack was cancelled. As for the political response, Foreign Minister Peres objected to the prime minister's demand to declare Arafat an enemy. As a compromise, the Cabinet approved a statement claiming that Arafat "operates terrorism and supports terrorism."

Arafat's commitment to declare a cease-fire on the Palestinian media, in his voice and using his people's language, was supposed to take place on that same day – Saturday, June 2, 2001. At five p.m., a press conference was held with Arafat and Miguel Moratinos, a representative of the European Union. We waited for Arafat to make his announcement. Instead, we watched Moratinos declare a cease-fire in English, while Arafat stood beside him, nodding his head but not saying a word. Arafat's message to his people was clear: the war goes on. Once again, we had been deceived – or we had deceived ourselves.

Prime Minister Sharon then approved the distribution of the document known as the "White Booklet." This document had been prepared by the Intelligence Directorate immediately after the outbreak of the hostilities, but at first it was not approved. The booklet clarified the Intelligence Directorate's opinion regarding Arafat's responsibility for the terrorist attacks and violence, based on whatever available intelligence information did not endanger the sources of information. In addition, the prime minister demanded that the minister of foreign affairs instruct his ministry's officials in Israel and around the world to wage a political campaign to clarify Arafat's responsibility for terrorism and violence. Peres did not like this idea at all. He even tried to convince the Cabinet members to direct the political campaign against suicide attacks, and not against Arafat in person. His suggestion was rejected. In order to clarify his intention, the prime minister demanded to convene foreign media representatives the next day and instruct them on Arafat's responsibility for the terrorism and violence.

The briefing for foreign journalists was set for the next day at the Ministry of Foreign Affairs in Jerusalem. I was given the responsibility of briefing them on the military aspect of the situation and was placed last on the list of speakers, even though I was the first to place the responsibility with Arafat. Speakers of the Ministry of Foreign Affairs, headed by Minister Peres, condemned the suicide bombers, but did not speak out against Arafat. It was embarrassing to me and to the State of Israel. We had given the wrong impression, as if the deputy chief of general staff had a personal vendetta against Arafat that was not in line with the policies of his government. In fact, the situation was the opposite: the minister of foreign affairs and his officials were the ones diverging from the policies of the prime minister and the majority of the government.

Before, during, and after the round of hostilities, I heard several claims against the IDF and its officers, expressing doubt for their understanding that they were under the authority of the political echelon. I have several criticisms regarding the level of influence of IDF officers on decisions that lie in the gray area between the political and military fields. I believe that the occasional lack of balance derives from the weakness of the political echelon and the civil servants. There have been very few cases in which IDF officers exceeded their authority or did not obey the political officials. Not one IDF officer, for example, dared breach the political decision not to publicize the "White Booklet," until the Cabinet decision changed this ruling. But in the case of that briefing, I witnessed a government minister disobeying a Cabinet decision and instruction by the prime minister.

The terrorist attack of September 11, 2001, or 9/11, created a one-time opportunity to build the strategic wall. In the first weeks after the attack on the Twin Towers, even Arafat was scared. He understood that the rules of the game had changed, and that his dabbling in terrorism had become dangerous. Suddenly the world was divided into "good guys" and "bad guys." Arafat was at risk of being included with the bad guys, and it was very important for him to join the good guys. He even was photographed donating blood for the injured in the attack. To me this was pathetic, especially due to his medical condition. We had to make good use of this moment. I suggested pushing Arafat into a corner, so that he would say to his public, in Arabic and in unambiguous terms, that all expressions of terrorism would be stopped. But we missed this opportunity as well. Several emissaries visited Miguel Moratinos during that time: former

Senator George Mitchell, CIA Director George Tenet, General Anthony Zinni. I warned them all that they would fail in their mission, because Arafat did not want to stop violence. Without a wall built in front of him – both Israeli and international – the violence would not stop. At that time, such a wall had not been built.

I dared to predict the failure of these emissaries in their mission, because I had learned about the incorrect perceptions that most had about the dispute, and mainly about the Palestinian leadership. I met most at the start of their mission and told them that they were due to fail.

One fundamental error was their perception of Arafat as wanting a two-state solution. Another error was assuming that he wanted to stop the fighting but could not, and in order to help him control the situation, Israel must make concessions, i.e., concede to him on various matters, strengthen his security forces, even give them more arms and ammunition. This error derived from a typical Western misperception of Arafat's approach as an accountable leader. Meanwhile, Arafat was maneuvering nonstop to avoid and deny responsibility.

I remember another typical Western error, which I called the "chicken and egg trap." A typical example of this error was presented during General Zinni's visit to the region. He identified the IDF roadblocks as a factor that was encouraging terrorism, because of the humiliation that the Palestinians underwent when being checked by IDF soldiers. He recommended that the roadblocks be removed, or at least for the young soldiers serving there to be replaced by older servicemen. He accepted the Palestinian propaganda approach that terrorism was because of the roadblocks – he did not understand that the roadblocks were there because of terrorism. I discovered that there are many people with good intentions and Western ways of thinking who cannot understand this complex situation. They try to find a simple reason and a simple solution. I do not claim that the roadblocks are devoid of negative implications. I learned that every use of power has a price, not only a benefit. But we certainly cannot claim that terrorism is due to the roadblocks – if only because when the confrontation broke out in September 2000, there were no roadblocks throughout Judea and Samaria, other than along the border seam.

This distorted perception was not unique to foreigners. It also characterized the understanding of the situation by many Israelis, mainly in politics and the media. These individuals claimed that the IDF – not Arafat – was responsible for the escalation of the situation in September 2000, that the IDF was "warmongering and thwarting every opportunity for a cease-fire," and similar accusations.

In December 2001, Arafat felt that things were closing in on him, and he decided to lower the level of violence. We had about two months of "relative quiet": a drop in the number of terrorist attacks, but not a total moratorium. During this period, eleven Israelis were murdered in a suicide bombing on Ben Yehuda Street in Jerusalem, fifteen were murdered on bus number sixteen in Haifa, and many other attacks and attempted attacks took place.

During this "quiet" period, we discovered that Ra'ad Karmi of the Tulkarm Tanzim was preparing a serious attack against a senior Israeli individual. What should we do? If we sent up a combat helicopter and attacked him, they would again blame us for raising the level of violence and ending the relative calm. Even so, we could not sit and do nothing while a serious attack was unfolding before our eyes. We decided to attack him in a way that would be perceived as a "work accident." This way, we would prevent a terrorist attack, while the Palestinians, who were interested in maintaining quiet, would be pleased at the removal of the provocateur who endangered that quiet. On a routine visit to his mistress, Ra'ad Karmi was killed by an explosive. The Palestinians often avoided responding to "work accidents," and it was most probable that they would overlook this one as well. But the Israelis could not keep quiet. The political echelon leaked out information designed for political gain, which meant that Israel took responsibility for the attack. As a result, Arafat and Barghouti were released from the international pressure that was closing in on them, and they permitted terrorist attacks at a wedding in Hadera and near the Ma'ariv building in Tel Aviv. On the Israeli side, the IDF and Shin Bet were blamed automatically for warmongering and held responsible for breaking the calm.

This was the situation leading up to the major terror attacks of early 2002. March was the bloodiest month, with seventeen attacks and 135 dead. Finally, after the mass murder on Passover night at the Park Hotel in Netanya, Arafat was declared an enemy. Finally, we switched to a full offensive. The government approved Operation Defensive Shield, which intended to regain control over Palestinian areas in Judea and Samaria. For the first time since the Oslo Accords, we took full responsibility for our security.

CHAPTER 10

From Defense to Offense

The Oslo Accords entrusted the Palestinians with security responsibilities. But this led to the breakdown of security for the Israelis. Treating the Area A zones as if they were under Palestinian sovereignty prevented the IDF and the Shin Bet from operating in them for a long time. Military operations in Area A were defined as "across the border" operations, which required approval from the political echelon (the Security Cabinet).

As the Palestinians intensified their violations of the agreement, many of us – and especially those in the army – realized that ultimately, we would be forced to take military action in areas controlled by the Palestinians. That meant we would have to enter Palestinian cities.

Fighting in built-up areas deters any army. A built-up area is advantageous to the defender, and it presents the attacker with significant challenges. The defender has the advantage of knowing the terrain. The defender can utilize houses, alleyways, tunnels, and ditches as hiding places and shelters. They can use these sites to kill the attacker and booby-trap traffic lanes. Fighting in a built-up area is the most complicated type of warfare. I personally experienced combat in built-up areas in the city of Suez during the Yom Kippur War, in the villages of southern Lebanon during Operation Litani, in Beirut during Operation Peace for Galilee, and during other operations.

In preparation for the possibility of taking over Palestinian cities, we carried out various assessments about the nature of the fighting, our chances of success, and the price it would cost us in fallen soldiers. We began to prepare for this possibility immediately after the events of September 1996 ("Western Wall Tunnel events"). The IDF and Shin Bet chiefs' trust in the Palestinian will to fulfill the Oslo agreement had slowly eroded, until the Western Wall Tunnel events shattered the illusions. In their wake, the IDF boosted its preparation for the possibility of regaining control of territories that we had transferred to the Palestinian Authority, and particularly the large cities. As a result, the Central Command, led by Major General Uzi Dayan, began to prepare a plan called "Field of Thorns." This plan aimed at preparing the command units for the possibility of retaking all of Area A, meaning the Palestinian cities, and reassuming responsibility for security there. When I entered Central Command in June 1998, I continued this work, which my predecessors had begun.

During the Oslo years, Israel decided not to engage each and every terrorist individually. Our security outlook was that the Palestinian Authority was responsible for Area A, and all that Israel had to do was demand that the Authority exercise its responsibilities. When the war broke out in September 2000, this concept had not changed. Our slogan was: "The PA is the address for this," and so the IDF's actions were intended to motivate the Palestinian Authority to act. For example, in the wake of the lynch in Ramallah (in which two Israeli reservists were killed by a frenzied Palestinian crowd, after the reservists accidentally entered the city in their civilian car), Israel carried out a series of attacks on PA institutions to pressure the PA to act.

Even before Operation Defensive Shield, we began to change this modus operandi. We entered Area A, made arrests, and began direct contact with terror centers. However, these first actions of transition from defense to offense were limited. Although it was obvious to the military echelon that the Oslo era security strategy had collapsed, and that we had to replace it with a different approach, the political echelon did not permit us to take comprehensive action to retake responsibility for security. Finally, after the developments in American relations with Arafat in 2002 and the bloody terror attacks against Israel in March of that year, the political echelon changed the line of approach it had followed for such a long time.

Effective war on terror must be offensive. It is not possible to win in this war when you are waiting for the suicide bomber at the entrance to the Dolphinarium in Tel Aviv, or at the entrance of a pizzeria in Jerusalem. To stop the suicide bomber before he strikes, you must trap him in his bed. To do this, there is no choice but to enter Palestinian population centers and to operate within them. But when these population centers are closed to army units and Shin Bet forces, they become hatcheries for terrorism. When the incubation process takes place undisturbed, terrorism gains strength and becomes a strategic problem, like the one we faced at the beginning of 2002.

The political leadership's attempt to "save the peace process" after the outbreak of the Palestinian terror war prevented offensive military operations. But as the conflict continued, the leadership approved limited offensive operations, mainly by infantry divisions (Paratroopers, Golani, Nahal, and Givati) and special units. We carried out division operations on the various fronts, especially in Jenin, Nablus, and Tulkarm. Essentially, these were raids: our forces took over areas for a limited time, made arrests, and killed terrorists when there was resistance. We detected, collected, and destroyed weapons and explosives laboratories. In each case, our forces pulled out from the field after completing the mission.

We accumulated a significant reserve of operational experience in the course of these operations. From platoon leader to brigade commander, our personnel developed combat techniques and practices for dealing with the terrorist challenge in a dense built-up area. Thus, for example, we developed the technique of moving through homes by breaking down walls, instead of entering through doors and windows or advancing through alleys, as these might be booby-trapped. In these military actions, we also developed various tactics for taking control of a region, a refugee camp, or casbah. We changed our methods frequently in order to surprise the terrorists each time.

The commanders requested special weapons to deal with the challenges. Among other things, we developed and provided the forces with launchers designed to detonate mines in streets or alleys.

We accumulated experience, and the success of our operations between October 2000 and March 2002 meant that the field commanders and senior command were growing increasingly confident. We also sustained a low number of casualties to our forces in these operations. Yet despite this, concern still hovered in the air concerning the launch of a broad and comprehensive action to take over all of Area A. Such an operation would enable comprehensive treatment to uproot terrorist capabilities. The main concern was the casualties that our forces would sustain in military actions where most of the fighting is done in densely built-up areas.

The fear of Israeli casualties has become a difficult limiting factor to the IDF's use of force. The aim of sustaining as few Israeli casualties as possible is right, of course, both for ethical and utilitarian reasons. Ethically, the sanctity of life requires that we protect our lives. From the utilitarian aspect, a mission with a high number of casualties raises the question of utility. However, some situations require us to endanger our lives for the sake of performing a mission. Of course, the price in casualties must be an important consideration of every commander and political leader. But Israeli society has gone very far in avoiding actions that are necessary to perform a mission, because we wish to avoid casualties.

At a tactical level, to neutralize an enemy threat, carrying out an assault is sometimes preferable to any other option, even when doing so involves a definite risk to our fighters. Likewise, on a strategic and operational level, in some situations it is imperative to operate at a certain risk to our forces. In such cases, we act because the alternative is more expensive in terms of lost human lives.

It is difficult to explain this to our society, because the necessary military action usually involves a definite and immediate risk. On the other hand, the repercussions of the failure to act will be felt only in the medium and long term.

Israeli society, and as a result, the leadership, went even further in many cases where approval was required for a military action that involved short-term risk. By preventing such action, they mortgaged the future. This is how we should see the public pressure to leave Lebanon, given the casualties which we would have sustained had we stayed there. This is how we should view the decision to leave the Gaza Strip, and our decision to refrain from approving a ground operation in the Second Lebanon War. This is also how we should see the political leadership's hesitancy to launch more substantial ground operations to fight terrorism in the Gaza Strip. These hesitations all belonged to the period prior to approval for Operation Defensive Shield. After the massacre on Passover night at the Park Hotel in Netanya, on March 29, 2002, these hesitations evaporated.

The question of legitimacy for military action is another component in the political echelon's considerations. I think that this is a positive element. In general, both ethically and in terms of benefit, the use of military force should be a last resort, after all other means have been exhausted.

In a democratic society, the leadership needs the people's support for its decisions, and particularly for the decision to go to war or to launch a widespread military operation. People want and need to be convinced that "the jig is up." This is why it is difficult for democracies to go to war, and it is even more difficult for democracies to initiate a "preventive war," for better or for worse. In a democratic country, the political leadership must explain to its citizens that a military move is essential, and it must cultivate public support for such a move.

In our era, international legitimacy for military action is also needed. The international community is not tolerant of military aggression. When it does not support the military action taken by a given country, it has the power to harm this country using political activity, sanctions, or even military intervention against it.

The need for international legitimacy underscores the importance of public diplomacy. The State of Israel has done too little in this arena, especially as pertains to the Israeli-Palestinian conflict. When most of the world accepts the Palestinian narrative about the "occupation" and "apartheid," Israel and the IDF's freedom of action become limited.

The Passover night massacre and the hundreds of Israelis killed and wounded since September 2000 granted legitimacy to Operation Defensive Shield. The Dolphinarium attack in 2001 could have been the event that legitimized the transition from defense to offense. In fact, the beginning of the terror war on September 29, 2000, could also have been the legitimate grounds for the IDF's takeover of Palestinian cities. It all depends on the Israeli political context. The story that the leadership wishes to tell springs from this context. In September 2000, the leadership wanted to "save the peace process," and therefore did not use the beginning of the terror attacks as a pretext for a counterattack. After the Dolphinarium attack, the government was divided on this issue, and again, an offense was not approved.

Operation Defensive Shield marked a transition for the IDF and the State of Israel, from a defensive position against the Palestinian terror war, to offense. The operation began following the bombing of the Park Hotel in March 2002. But three basic elements that had evolved over a long period before that massacre set the stage for Operation Defensive Shield:

1. The bloody terrorist attacks against Israel from September 2000 and onwards.
2. The Karine A incident on January 3, 2002.
3. The IDF's preparation for the possibility of escalation, which began after the September 1996 events (the Western Wall Tunnel events) and intensified after 1999.

The military rationale for Operation Defensive Shield had been clear to us for years. When we predicted the beginning of this war, we concluded that we would be forced to reclaim security responsibility for the territories that we had transferred over to Palestinian responsibility. In practice, we assessed that we would be forced to undermine the security concept behind Oslo, which gave responsibility for Israel's security to the Palestinians. The premise behind the Oslo Accords was that the Palestinians would have an interest in maintaining the calm and cooperating with us to prevent terrorist attacks. This premise was never proved. From 1994 onwards, any quiet or cooperation to speak of was the result of direct self-interest, based upon a specific "give and take." It was not the result of the Palestinians' commitment to the agreement that they had signed at Oslo. All along, since the signing of the agreements and until the present, there has been no true Palestinian commitment to prevent violence. The Palestinian conduct did not resemble Jordan's behavior against terrorism in any way. However, when it became clear that there was going to be war, we also realized that the complex game of "give and take" that the Palestinians were playing with us had reached its end. The Oslo security structure was collapsing, and there was no way to avoid turning back the wheel and creating a different security regime in Judea and Samaria, one that would return control of the territory to Israel. Without creating this military regime, there was no way to curb the wave of violence and to stop the suicide attacks that struck central Israel.

Once the war broke out, this military rationale was crystal clear to the top IDF command. Then came the incident of the *Karine A*: the IDF captured a vessel carrying Iranian weapons sent for delivery to the Palestinian Authority. This assisted in the implementation of the military rationale. The *Karine A* incident finalized Arafat's delegitimization in the eyes of US president George W. Bush. There were two components to this issue. First, the connection between Arafat and the Iranians proved his essential nature and intentions. Second, Arafat lied and attempted to deny his connection to the ship that he himself had financed, and this caused President Bush to permanently lose faith in Arafat. The *Karine A* did what the Israeli government had not done: it created a strategic wall. After this incident, Americans unequivocally understood who Arafat was. So, when the wave of attacks struck at the beginning of 2002, the IDF was prepared to carry out Operation Defensive Shield, and the US administration was already in a new state of consciousness. It recognized Israel's need to launch an operation. A year and a half after Arafat initiated his major offensive against Israel, Israel was ready at last to define him as an enemy and to start a counterattack. President Bush had been ready to define Arafat as an enemy in February 2002. The Israeli government did so only after the attack at the Park Hotel on March 29, 2002. The defensive phase in the war had ended. Israel assumed the initiative and began to act.

After the Passover night massacre, the Cabinet voted unanimously to approve the IDF offensive – Operation Defensive Shield. The public supported this move substantially, and the operation began. I asked myself and others, "What has changed in the eighteen months between September 29, 2000, and March 29, 2002? What brought those who had opposed the move then to declare Arafat an enemy now? Has Arafat changed? Has his strategy changed?" My answer was, "Arafat has not changed and his strategy has not changed. We are the ones who have changed, and we have changed our approach to him." Moreover, the decision demanded of those who had refused to recognize Arafat's responsibility for the Palestinian terror war: why did we need a year and a half, and hundreds of victims of terrorism to recognize this?

The number of reservists who reported for the operation was impressive. Relative to the magnitude of forces at IDF's disposal, the mobilization required few reserve units. Many of the commanders of reserve units expressed resentment that they were not called up – as befits those who want to take responsibility. Some of them knocked on the door of my office, and some even came to my house at night, hoping to meet me there and convince me to enlist their units.

Unlike in the Second Lebanon War, in Operation Defensive Shield the IDF's senior command was well acquainted with the strengths and weaknesses of the regular and reserve units. As deputy chief of general staff, I found it necessary to intervene and comment on the division of powers and tasks at Central Command. GOC Yitzhak Eitan made changes accordingly. I knew which units were more familiar with certain cities, so I adjusted the plan. Also, we determined that the regular units would fight first, as they were experienced in fighting in built-up Palestinian areas. The reserve units would go out into combat a few days later, to enable them to train and practice before military action. During this time, the reserve units could learn from the experience accrued by the regular units in fighting of this type. This example also clarifies the meaning of "the art of command" and "the art of war."

Despite the military operations that we had carried out in Palestinian cities prior to Operation Defensive Shield, the terrorists still felt that they could use the casbahs, refugee camps, and crowded city neighborhoods as shelters. They presumed that the IDF would not dare to take over built-up areas because of fear of Israeli casualties. But within a few days, the IDF forces took control of Palestinian cities, in rapid action and with a small number of casualties, except in the Jenin refugee camp.

We assigned the takeover of the Jenin refugee camp (April 1–11, 2002) to a reserve infantry brigade. Two days after the start of the operation, I realized that it was not going smoothly. There were dozens of armed terrorists in the Jenin refugee camp, and they had booby-trapped many houses and streets.

This was the case in other cities as well, but unlike our rapid action in other cities and refugee camps, Israeli forces in Jenin acted cautiously and slowly. This meant that the terrorists fought our forces from house to house, street to street. After nine days of fighting, we achieved complete clearing of the camp.

Because I realized that the battle in Jenin was problematic, I visited the area almost every day. Chief of General Staff Shaul Mofaz also made many visits. Unlike in the Second Lebanon War, the media did not publicize my visits, comments, or orders, and so these were not perceived as an expression of lack of faith in the GOC and his subordinates. The officers understood that our shared goal was to win, and not to engage in the politics of criticism and allocation of responsibility and blame while fighting.

The battle in the Jenin refugee camp was decided after nine days. Twenty-three of our officers and soldiers were killed. On the Palestinian side, fifty-three were killed, the vast majority terrorists. The number of Palestinian civilians killed during fighting was probably five. I do not know if they were killed by our forces. The terrorists' shots were often imprecise, and the refugee camp was booby-trapped with explosive devices, which probably also resulted in the killing and injury of Palestinian civilians.

These data did not prevent the Palestinian blood libel about the "Jenin massacre." This blood libel was created by false information that was spread about "indiscriminate killing" carried out by the IDF, and false claims that hundreds or even thousands of people were killed in the refugee camp. The libel was the handiwork of Palestinian officials, including Dr. Saeb Erekat, whose lack of credibility I had encountered earlier. He spoke out on various forms of media, mainly television channels, and spread the "Jenin massacre" libel.

The international media agencies were overjoyed to report on the "Jenin massacre," as were many international aid organizations, human rights organizations, and members of the UN bureaucracy. I witnessed personally how these parties participated in spreading this blood libel.

On the eve of Yom Hazikaron, Israel's Memorial Day, after the battle in Jenin, Defense Minister Binyamin (Fuad) Ben-Eliezer phoned me. He told me that Foreign Minister Shimon Peres had phoned him following a call that Peres had received from the UN secretary general's representative for the Middle East, Ambassador Terje Rød-Larsen. Larsen had been called into action due to reports of a massacre in Jenin. He spoke about a Palestinian claim that there were "three thousand missing persons in Jenin" and he complained that the IDF did not allow entry of trucks carrying food and equipment to the refugee camp. The defense minister asked me to investigate these claims. A few hours earlier, I had spoken by telephone with the GOC of Central Command about the humanitarian situation in the refugee camp, so I was fully updated. I told the defense minister that according to the GOC's report, food trucks had been allowed entry into the camp. As for the number of missing persons in Jenin, I answered that Larsen's numbers seemed extremely exaggerated. The defense minister requested that, given the sensitivity of the issue, I travel to Jenin and report to him personally.

Meanwhile, the Palestinian narrative of the massacre in Jenin was being spread worldwide. The UN representative's report fanned the flames.

A few minutes after the phone call from the defense minister, I received a call from Gideon Meir, deputy director of public relations at the Foreign Ministry. He told me that Steven Rubenstein and Nancy

Haberman were in Israel. Rubenstein and Haberman were senior experts from a well-known public relations firm in the United States that the Foreign Ministry had hired to combat the false Palestinian propaganda. Gideon sought to coordinate his tour with them in the Jenin refugee camp in order to rebut the story about the massacre. I told him that I intended to fly to Jenin the next morning, and I suggested that he and his two guests join me.

The next day we flew to the Jenin refugee camp. When we arrived at the camp, I asked the helicopter pilot to fly above it so we that could observe what was going on from the air before we landed. Our observation from the helicopter refuted the lie about the entry of food trucks to the camp. Trucks bearing the United Nations logo were dispersed throughout the camp, and next to them there were a few people, mainly children. After landing, we set out by car to tour the camp. There, I learned that food trucks had entered the camp over a day ago, and that the distribution of food had ended (which explained the lack of lines near the trucks). I received reports that traffic to and from the refugee camp was open, except for a small area with a few houses, which remained closed due to booby traps that had not yet been neutralized.

During our tour, we came to a paratrooper battalion checkpoint. It was blocking access to a handful of homes where our detonations experts were working to neutralize the booby traps and explosives set there by terrorists. At this checkpoint, the American guests and I witnessed firsthand how a false and biased report is created: UNRWA (the United Nations Relief and Works Agency for Palestinian Refugees, which is responsible for the refugee camps) and a foreign television channel crew (staffed primarily by Palestinians) tried to enter the blocked area. Had the soldiers allowed them to enter the booby-trapped area, the UNRWA and television crews would certainly have been hurt. I'm not sure they really wanted to get in. But the television crew filmed the IDF soldiers blocking them and the UNRWA staff from entering the area, and then reported on "the closed refugee camp." The insinuation was, "Who knows what's going on behind the checkpoint..." Of course, they presented this as an example of how Israel obstructs humanitarian aid to the refugee camp. We saw with our own eyes how a "blood libel" is fabricated.

I asked the head of the District Coordination and Liaison (DCL) Administration, who was an IDF officer with the rank of general, to explain the report about "three thousand missing persons in Jenin." He replied that he had no idea where these numbers came from. He knew that about fifty Palestinians had been killed as a result of the nine days of fighting – and the vast majority of these were armed.

I do not know who tripped up Terje Rød-Larsen with false reports, but it is worth noting that the UNRWA mechanism employs more than twenty-five thousand Palestinians. Most of the foreign television crews are also staffed by Palestinians, which may partly explain the source of the problem. Larsen apparently rushed to use these false reports without checking them.

During the tour, I also visited the local hospital, which operated during the fighting with the assistance of the IDF. In my presence, the hospital director (a Palestinian) thanked the DCL commander for his aid in supplying drugs, oxygen, and other supplies during the fighting. I underscore this because afterwards I saw several completely different stories in films, including *Jenin, Jenin*.

There is an addendum to this incident. When the UN secretary general appointed a commission of inquiry to investigate the "Jenin massacre," Foreign Minister Shimon Peres and Foreign Ministry officials recommended that we recognize the commission and cooperate with it. Chief of General Staff Mofaz objected. The subject came up at the cabinet meeting, and we agreed that we would not recognize the commission and would not cooperate with it, because its establishment was rooted in a lie. I have no doubt that if we had recognized the commission, it would have been utilized for the false and distorted reporting of events in a manner harmful to the State of Israel and the IDF. We would have had to cope with a situation like the Goldstone Commission's false report after Operation Cast Lead.

As part of our war on Palestinian terror, I met with several international organizations, including human rights organizations. Here is the place to mention that my experiences made me suspicious of them. Amnesty International reports published during my tenure as chief of general staff alleged that "hundreds of Palestinian children" had been killed by Israeli soldiers. Given my sensitivity to the issue of injury to innocent civilians during battle, I established a rule that I would investigate any incident of killing of a Palestinian civilian who was not involved in the fighting. The number cited in the Amnesty report astonished me, because I knew every incident in which a Palestinian child had been killed during the fighting. If there had been hundreds of such killings, then I should have received hundreds of investigations.

I requested that Amnesty forward to us the list of all the "children." It took some time until I received a partial list. The list revealed that according to the report:

1. A "child" is defined as anyone under the age of eighteen.
2. Most of the "children" were armed terrorists aged sixteen to eighteen.
3. Some of the "children" were suicide bombers who blew themselves up and killed Israelis. But until the matter was clarified, Israel was unjustly slandered.

In other cases, I encountered organizations staffed mainly by young, naive liberals, who perceive the Israeli-Palestinian conflict solely in terms of the human distress of the Palestinians. They accept the usual slogans about "the occupation" and "Israeli apartheid" literally, without really understanding the essence of the conflict. Against this background, they side with the Palestinians because they conceive of them as victims in need of humanitarian assistance. This makes them take a politically hostile stand against Israel. Despite the fact that Palestinian terror attacks Israeli civilians, and the IDF protects Israeli civilians from terrorism, the staff members at these organizations perceive the State of Israel as the aggressor and the Palestinians as victims.

However, the difficulties – and sometimes the failures – on the propaganda forefront should not blind us to the main point: the only way to suppress terrorism is to attack it. In terms of national security, the best defense is offense.

The first significant achievement of the offense that we launched on March 29, 2002, was evident before the first shot was fired. We had attained the full mobilization of reservists and the Israeli people's full support for the army. This was of great significance. In a strategic sense, our retreat and capitulations since 1983 are based on our assessment and that of our enemies that we have become an affluent society, no longer willing to fight as we were in the past. When Rabin went to Oslo, he did so, in part, with this view. He feared that the people were tired and no longer ready to go into battle. At every stage of the conflict, our leaders had similar concerns. They feared that the reserves would not report when called up, that parents would not support the soldiers who had to fight. They also feared that at the moment of truth, our soldiers would not have the fighting spirit. There was great concern about this, and it was discussed quite openly. Hezbollah leader Hassan Nasrallah was not the only one who likened us to a spider web. Many Israelis thought the same thing, and therefore we lacked boldness. We grappled with the Palestinians in a very cautious way. Then suddenly, the day after the Passover night massacre in Netanya, there was a turning point. Citizens who had not even been called up reported for reserve duty.

People fought over every spot in every tank and APC. In many units, the attendance rate was about 130 percent. That was a great demonstration of strength, even before going out to battle. Operation Defensive Shield began as a manifestation of power. It proved that we were not spider webs, and that when necessary, we knew how to fight – both the army and the society.

Operation Defensive Shield's second achievement was in the professional military sphere. In the year preceding the operation, I was uncertain about the military's ability to enter inhabited Palestinian territories. I was not worried about the brigade, battalion, and company commanders. But among the generals and brigadier generals, some doubted our ability and thought that we wouldn't succeed. Senior officers believed that if we entered refugee camps, for example, we would suffer many casualties and we wouldn't be able to take control of the area. Reporters and military analysts frightened the Israeli people with warnings of the heavy losses that such a move would incur. The field ranks were confident and determined, but there were senior officers who were strongly opposed to the planned moves. Although our early successes in Tulkarm, Jenin, and the Balata camp proved that it was possible to enter a refugee camp without complications, a cloud of doubt remained in the air.

Finally, when we launched the operation, it was encouraging to see how impressively the IDF operated. Very quickly it became evident that this was a honed army at all levels – from soldiers to squad leaders, platoon leaders, company commanders, and up to brigade level. Our military action was professional and precise. Correct tactical initiatives were conducted, from the bottom up. The army found creative solutions to the unique problems of fighting in built-up territory. The entire system worked in a way that surprised even me. Therefore, apart from the entanglement in Jenin, there were no significant complications. Many in the senior command were surprised by the relatively limited number of casualties. Years of thought about the war and training troops for it had borne fruit. In Operation Defensive Shield, the IDF was at its best. With no excuses and no "buts," the IDF fulfilled the mission that had been assigned to it. With this, Israel reclaimed its deterrent power and self-confidence.

Operation Defensive Shield's third achievement was intelligence. Israel had lost much of its intelligence capabilities in the Palestinian territories since Arafat's entry into Gaza in May 1994, and our transfer of the cities of Judea and Samaria to the PA's responsibility at the end of 1995. Just as the security premise was that the Palestinian Authority would be responsible for our security, the intelligence premise was that cooperation with the Palestinians would replace the previous intelligence gathering methods in Judea, Samaria and Gaza. This assumption collapsed: during the suicide attacks in 2001–2002, Israel was at an intelligence disadvantage. Palestinian intelligence agencies were trying to locate our intelligence sources, particularly human sources ("collaborators"), rather than thwart terrorism. This reality required us to be cautious in providing intelligence information to the Palestinian entities. It certainly did not allow for the required cooperation which is a given between friendly countries. Operation Defensive Shield changed this intelligence situation quickly. Our entry into Palestinian territory and the subsequent arrests created a kind of intelligence snowball, which intensified during 2002 and 2003. The result was that one year after the operation, Israeli intelligence had achieved absolute intelligence superiority in Judea and Samaria.

Soon, these three achievements of Operation Defensive Shield were translated into a comprehensive systematic achievement. The number of attacks inside Israel dropped dramatically. After seventeen serious attacks in which 135 Israelis were killed in one month (March 2002), and 453 deaths during that year, a downward trend began in the number of Israelis killed in attacks. In 2003, 212 Israelis were murdered in Palestinian terror attacks; in 2004, 118 were killed; in 2005, fifty were killed. In 2006, twenty-nine Israelis were murdered in Palestinian terror attacks, while in

2007, this number was down to thirteen. Terror was transformed from pursuer to pursued. Our well-trained soldiers, equipped with precise intelligence, penetrated every cell of territory in Judea and Samaria and caused the terrorists to lose their balance.

Step by step, we identified and struck the terrorists' infrastructure. Rather than wage a campaign against the Tanzim and Hamas at the door to a bus in Hadera, we waged it in the doorways of the terrorists' homes. The new fighting methods which we developed resulted in close cooperation between the IDF and the Shin Bet. Military Intelligence and the Shin Bet achievements meant that fighters had accurate intelligence in real time, which in many cases allowed them to strike the enemy without suffering damage themselves. The IDF achieved almost full security control of the West Bank with a relatively low "signature" – without continuous, noticeable military presence. Arrest operations that in early 2002 had required a force the size of a brigade were now performed by a platoon.

In Operation Defensive Shield, the IDF lost twenty-nine combat soldiers. According to the UN report, 497 Palestinians were killed in the operation.

The flexibility and sophistication with which our forces operated produced one of the most outstanding military accomplishments that any army has achieved in the war against terrorism. In the summer of 2003, a year after the beginning of Operation Defensive Shield, we could declare that Israel had succeeded in fending off Arafat's terrorist attacks. Security returned slowly to city streets. The economy began to grow once more. Israel was able to stabilize itself and recover from the damages incurred since Arafat launched his offensive on September 29, 2000. We had not yet achieved a strategic victory, but we achieved tactical and operational victories, which removed the pressure from Israel and greatly expanded the political echelon's freedom of operation. Individual attacks still occurred and claimed victims, but Operation Defensive Shield created a clear turnaround in the war on terrorism. The operation, and the new security regime which was introduced in the West Bank in its wake, meant that after three years of battle, Israel had the upper hand.

Belatedly, and after great effort, we had finally succeeded in building that wall.

CHAPTER 11

The Ethics of War

The results of the battle in Jenin during Operation Defensive Shield again raised questions concerning ethics in warfare. As IDF commanders, we were confronted with criticism over our decision to conduct house-to-house combat in order to avoid casualties among Palestinian civilians. Indeed, most of those killed on the Palestinian side were armed terrorists, but we paid a heavy price for our ethics: twenty-three of our fighters fell in battle.

Most of the criticism came from bereaved families. As deputy chief of general staff, I agreed to several families' requests to meet with them and to address their claims. Some of the bereaved parents, wives, and siblings espoused political views that were "against the occupation," or against the IDF policy of use of force in fighting terrorism. But when it came to their own family, their criticism was that the IDF risked their sons' lives instead of deploying artillery and air assets – even if doing so would have come at the expense of Palestinian civilian casualties.

As IDF commanders, we and the political echelon that had approved our actions were well acquainted with the questions posed following the battle in Jenin. On a purely ethical level, some situations justify harming innocent civilians. In such a situation, the decision maker is aware of the high degree of probability that his decision will result in injury to civilians or collateral damage. Yet the decision may be justified ethically, when the price of protecting the enemy's civilians is higher – in terms of human lives on our side – than the price of harm to the enemy.

It was on these grounds that US president Harry S. Truman justified the decision to drop atomic bombs on Hiroshima and Nagasaki at the end of World War II. His decision resulted in the killing of some 150–200,000 Japanese citizens. Truman explained that in the assessment discussion that led to this decision, he understood from the experts that winning the war against Japan by means of atomic bombs would claim fewer lives than conventional warfare. If conventional means had been used, the expected number of casualties among the US forces was one million, with at least an equal number of Japanese casualties.

IDF commanders and the political echelon have often had to make decisions that would almost certainly result in civilian casualties. A prominent example is the decision to attack Hezbollah's Fajr rockets in the opening strike of the Second Lebanon War in 2006. The air strike was executed according to a plan that I helped to prepare when I was chief of general staff.

We discovered that Hezbollah had placed Fajr rocket launchers (for Fajr 3 rockets with a twenty-eight-mile [45 km] range and Fajr 5 rockets with a forty-seven-mile [75 km] range) in residential villages and towns in southern Lebanon. The rockets were placed in homes, and they were aimed at Israeli communities in the north. We knew that failing to strike these rockets would lead to attacks on Israeli civilians. We also realized that bombing the rockets would harm the occupants of the homes where the launchers were installed.

During and after the Second Lebanon War, we described these homes cynically as having a kitchen, bathroom, living room, bedroom, children's rooms and "rocket room." We also said, "Someone who goes to sleep with

Iranian rockets in their home shouldn't be surprised to be woken up by an Israeli missile."

Hezbollah's challenge to us reflects the cynicism of an organization that deliberately launches rockets against our citizens and uses its own citizens as human shields. But this situation confronted us with an ethical dilemma. This challenge reflects the contempt that an organization like Hezbollah holds for our values, including the sanctity of human life, adherence to the international laws of war, and following our ethical rules of military engagement. Hezbollah deliberately abuses the rule enshrined in our combat ethics and in international treaties regarding the distinction between combatants and civilians.

During the Second Lebanon War, we witnessed many instances in which Hezbollah operated among civilians. This includes the incident in Kafr Qana, when we observed the members of a Hezbollah cell fleeing into a home after firing a Katyusha rocket at a civilian target in Israel. In this case, our troops did not know that there were civilians in the home. Because our forces had called for residents of southern Lebanon to leave the combat zone, the commander who authorized the attack assumed that the home was empty of civilians. If there were civilians in the home, the Hezbollah cell members obviously knew it when they entered. (Some claim that the whole affair was orchestrated by Hezbollah.)

In both cases, the strike on the Fajr launchers and the strike against the Hezbollah cell in Kafr Qana, our decision to attack civilian homes was ethically justified. Here I would like to discuss another aspect of the decision-making process in matters of this kind – the utilitarian aspect.

The decision to use force, especially when it comes to matters of life and death, should be ethical. But it should also be beneficial. The decision maker must determine that the use of force will lead to, or at least contribute to, defeating the enemy and removing the threat. We have learned that in some situations, a tactical victory does not necessarily bring victory in the war. In cost-benefit terms, applying more force or causing more deaths to the other side does not necessarily bring victory in the war.

The Kafr Qana incident is an example of an event that gave us a tactical achievement (a successful strike against a Hezbollah cell that had been launching Katyusha rockets). But it also caused strategic and political damage, which constrained our freedom to maneuver, both politically and militarily. (Following the event, the prime minister decided to halt air strikes for forty-eight hours. International criticism against Israel flared, the military's zone of operation was reduced, and Israel's ability to insist that the enemy meet its demands in cease-fire negotiations also diminished.)

Similar dilemmas arose in operations in the Gaza Strip, such as Operation Cast Lead in 2009, Operation Pillar of Defense in 2012, and Operation Protective Edge in 2014. Hamas intentionally fired rockets against Israeli civilians and used residents of the Gaza Strip as human shields. The political echelon and IDF commanders were tasked with formulating an operational response that would protect Israeli citizens and the Israeli forces, but that would not lead to international intervention that would limit our freedom of operation.

In my experience, in an era when wars are broadcast from the battlefield directly to viewers around the world, the military commander must consider the enemy's manipulations. The commander must refrain from providing the enemy with "ammunition" for propaganda that he can use for these manipulations.

I also learned that the use of force requires legitimacy. The political and military maneuverability zones are based on three circles of legitimacy:

A. Moral legitimacy. Does the planned use of force stand the test of my personal values and our values as a society? Does the use of force stand the test of tension between the biblical precepts "Thou shalt not kill" and "If someone comes to kill you, rise up and kill him first"? I call this test the

"Mirror Test" – will I be able to look at myself in the mirror at the end of the military operation?

B. Internal legitimacy. Does our society support the planned use of force? The question of internal legitimacy includes moral questions based on society's fundamental values, as well as ideological and political positions. A prominent example of this is the political debate in Israeli society on Palestinian terrorism. Those who see the territories of Judea and Samaria (and formerly Gaza) as "occupied territories" and see Palestinian violence as "resistance," generally oppose the use of force and demand that Israel make territorial concessions. Those who claim that these areas are "liberated territories" and that the Palestinian's claim of "occupation" applies to the entire Land of Israel demand that Israel adopt an uncompromising policy position, and they support the use of more military force.

C. International legitimacy. In the past, Israel's political leadership has been under an international steamroller of pressure, and it may be in this situation again in the future. This can lead to political and economic isolation. I have witnessed instances in which US presidents have demanded that the government of Israel stop military action. On April 18, 2001, for example, President George W. Bush demanded from Prime Minister Sharon that Israel withdraw from Beit Hanoun. In September 2002, Bush again demanded that Sharon stop the IDF's military action at the Mukat'a, Arafat's headquarters in Ramallah.

In this sphere, global public opinion plays a large role, and this public opinion may be manipulated to support false propaganda and benefit one side in the conflict. This was the case in claims that the IDF used excessive force in situations such as the Second Lebanon War, in the Gaza Strip in the winter of 2008, in the "Jenin massacre," and in the "Rafah massacre." In these cases, public opinion influenced political leadership.

On the international playing field, considerations are not necessarily ethical. They rely mainly on the interests of various players who follow the rules of the often hypocritical game of international politics. On this field, we find ideological attacks on Israel's very right to exist as an independent Jewish state, prejudice, European guilt, and more. I witnessed the international community's hypocrisy up close when I served as commander of the Judea and Samaria Division.

In January 1993, Israel arrested a Hamas member known as Sheikh Salah, a Palestinian who carried an American passport. He landed at Ben-Gurion Airport on a mission for Hamas leader Moussa Abu Marzouq, who was then living in Virginia. Salah's mision was to restore the Hamas'ss terror infrastructure, in the wake of Israel's arrest and deportation of 415 members of the movement to Lebanon in December 1992.

Salah entered Israel on his American passport and he circulated freely in Gaza and the West Bank. He met known terrorists such as Salah al-Arouri (who has since advanced and become deputy head of Hamas'ss political bureau) and Adel Awadallah (director of Hamas terror activities in the West Bank). He gave each of these terrorists about forty thousand dollars, which they used to rent safe houses, buy weapons and explosives, recruit and activate other terrorists, and carry out attacks. When Salah was arrested, about six hundred thousand dollars in cash were found in his luggage.

Salah's arrest interested me, and I asked the late Gideon Ezra, the Shin Bet head of the Judea, Samaria and Jerusalem zone, for permission to meet the detainee. One night, Gideon and I traveled together to see and talk to him in the detention center. In that conversation with Salah, I realized that Hamas headquarters is actually located in Virginia. The organization had concluded that situating its headquarters in Judea, Samaria, or Gaza endangered its survival, and so it had decided to move its HQ elsewhere. Moreover, the organization's decision-making method involved consulting its senior members (*shura*). Some of these were located in Judea, Samaria, and Gaza, while others were in Arab countries (mainly Damascus) or elsewhere.

The day after my visit with Sheikh Salah in his detention cell, I had a meeting scheduled with representatives of various American research institutes, who were touring Israel. The researchers asked to meet me in a Jerusalem hotel, but I insisted on hosting them at division headquarters in Beit El. After the briefing, it was time for questions. One of the researchers posed a question that I might well have requested in advance: "Why doesn't the IDF carry out an air strike and destroy the Hamas headquarters?" In fine Jewish tradition, I replied with a question: "Do you know where Hamas headquarters are located?" "No," he replied. Then I pulled the rabbit out of the hat: "Virginia, the US of A!"

I explained my words to the surprised listeners, although I'm not sure I convinced them. My claim sounded strange to them, but it was the truth.

When I was appointed head of Military Intelligence, I acted to outlaw the associations and institutions that Palestinian terrorist organizations use in the United States and Europe. Ramadan Shalah, head of the Palestinian Islamic Jihad (PIJ) was summoned to lead the movement in 1995 after his predecessor, Fathi Shiqaqi, was assassinated. Until then, Shalah had headed a research institute in Tampa, Florida (not far from the US Army Central Command Headquarters, which carries the brunt of the burden of the war on global Islamic terror). Moussa Abu Marzouq also operated from the United States, and he was later deported from there.

As head of Israeli Military Intelligence, I invested great efforts to try to convince our allies in the United States, Britain, Germany, and other countries to ban nonprofit organizations that funnel money to support terrorism or assist the families of so-called "martyrs." But my attempts hit a brick wall. These countries explained that they opposed my request due to human rights issues and the difficulty of passing legislation to close these foundations and nonprofits.

After the suicide attacks on September 11, 2001, the US passed laws that changed the situation completely. Other countries also adopted legislative initiatives that crippled the "charity" foundations that finance terrorism. In Britain, however, one of the foundations whose closure I had requested in 1996 continued to operate for years, even after 9/11. The UK political system woke up to the terror threat only after the severe bombings in London and Manchester in 2017. In the wake of these attacks, Britain acted to change its legislation, and finally prioritized security and human lives over other human rights.

The 9/11 suicide attacks led to an important change in the international arena. Until then, in most cases, Western countries treated terrorism as a criminal incident requiring police handling. The 9/11 attacks turned terror into a target that is handled by all intelligence branches, internal security services, police, and armed forces of countries in the free world.

Nevertheless, the terror that still plagues us is treated differently by various parties. Those who accept the arguments of Hezbollah, Hamas, and Fatah about the Israeli "occupation" refer to this terrorism as "resistance to the occupation." They distinguish it from the terror of global extremist Islam. This diagnosis is wrong, yet it reflects on the legitimacy of the actions of the State of Israel and the IDF when taking protective measures against terrorism. So, when Israel defends itself against Hezbollah's rockets or against Hamas, Islamic Jihad, or Fatah suicide bombers from Gaza or Judea and Samaria, Israel is accused of using "excessive" or "disproportionate" force.

This distinction narrows the legitimacy zone for necessary military action. But in my opinion, it also affects the interests of the international community in protecting the world order. The State of Israel, and especially the Foreign Ministry officials, must lead the political, diplomatic, and propaganda battle on this issue.

During our offensive in Operation Defensive Shield, the considerations that I outlined above were factors in the decision-making process on how to operate in Jenin and in other cities. We also had to consider the need to achieve moral, domestic, and international legitimacy.

Twenty-three dead soldiers is a very heavy toll, which provokes the question of whether it was moral to risk the lives of so many soldiers and officers in order to avoid harming Palestinian civilians. From an ethical and moral perspective, the question is appropriate, but only in hindsight. The decision makers had projected that the price we would pay in fallen soldiers would be lower. Indeed, the price was lower, in every other battle in that operation.

In terms of internal legitimacy, I am certain that most of the Israeli public would have backed the IDF and the political echelon for a more massive use of force, at the price of harming more Palestinian civilians. However, internal legitimacy is not a permanent factor. It varies, and it is influenced by the leadership. It is also affected by the "narrative" that the leadership imparts to its civilians, and the general public's level of confidence in the leadership's discretion and integrity. Internal legitimacy is also a function of public discourse and is greatly influenced by the media – and of course, by the events themselves. The Passover Seder night massacre at the Park Hotel in 2002 legitimized Operation Defensive Shield. This legitimacy did not exist in September 2000, when Arafat launched his terror war. We did not have an agreed-upon narrative as to the nature of the war and the responsibility for initiating war. Nor did we have enough fatalities to warrant action, as in the case of Defensive Shield. (I am not justifying the situation – I am merely presenting the picture as I read it.)

In order to create internal legitimacy for the use of force, the leadership must mobilize the people to support the course of action. This is the nature of democracy, as well as its advantage – it is no coincidence that democratic governments are not eager for war. But this is also democracy's weakness, because it is difficult to garner public support to wage war or carry out a preemptive action against a threat that has yet to materialize. I also assessed that Israeli society would not tolerate the use of force involving significant harm to civilians. I concluded that victory in battle might lead to defeat in war, due to loss of internal consensus in Israel.

One case in which I (as COGS) was forced to end a military action for fear of losing the national consensus was in Rafah in May 2004, during Operation Rainbow. This operation aimed to impair arms smuggling from Sinai into the Gaza Strip. To do so, an IDF division took control over part of the town of Rafah, to enable us to detect and demolish the tunnels that the smugglers were using.

Terrorist groups and smugglers had positioned the tunnel openings on the Palestinian side inside private homes, forcing the inhabitants to abandon them. The enemy then booby-trapped the homes with explosives that targeted the IDF soldiers who were searching for the tunnels. The smugglers believed that they would thus deter us from approaching the tunnel entrances. Our response to this threat was to demolish the empty, booby-trapped homes. In a few cases, we attacked these homes from the air. In this operation, we pinpointed several houses that had tunnel openings inside them.

During the operation, an Israeli television channel aired a report that described the demolition of the homes, presenting the move in a negative light. One of the pictures showed an elderly Palestinian woman picking through the ruins of one of the homes. Following the publication of the photo, then justice minister Yosef (Tommy) Lapid, said publicly that the old woman reminded him of his grandmother who had perished in the Holocaust.

Following Lapid's statement, I decided to stop the action, for two reasons. First, my mission was to carry out military action approved by the political echelon – and now a minister in the government and Cabinet member who had approved the operation had renounced his support for the mission. Second, I understood the implications of the loss of Israeli consensus for the IDF's activity. I knew that such a situation could have long-term impact on the legitimacy that Israeli society grants the IDF in its war against Palestinian terror. I understood that this could become another instance where winning the battle leads to defeat in the war. Still, I remain ethically satisfied with the decision to demolish the homes. Today as well, I am convinced that this military operation was important to prevent the smuggling of weapons that might harm our citizens and our soldiers. I had expected the prime minister to reprimand Minister Lapid and express public support for the IDF operations. When I realized that the prime minister would not be providing such a public statement and public support, I halted the action. Today I still think that this was the right decision.

X

One of the issues that frequently arise in the context of battle ethics is targeted killings. A great deal of criticism is directed against these operations. Some have called them "assassinations" and "extrajudicial punishment," and defined them as "war crimes."

Ethically, it is certainly possible to justify targeting terrorists for their actions in the past. Such strikes also aim to deter potential terrorists in the future. Yet we have chosen to restrict ourselves to harming only those terrorists who have plans to carry out attacks in the future. We do not kill terrorists as punishment for past deeds. Moreover, this measure is a last resort, when there is no other way to stop the terrorist.

We prefer to arrest a terrorist, rather than kill him, due to both ethical and utilitarian considerations. Ethically, killing is a last resort, when there are no other options. From a utilitarian viewpoint, when we arrest the terrorist rather than kill him, we can interrogate him and obtain further information which allows us to stop other terrorists. Also, arrest does not arouse the same sense of revenge provoked by killing, which fans the flames of violence among the enemy.

Some would add into this equation the value of deterrence obtained when killing a terrorist. I do not dismiss this element entirely, but in this case, it is difficult to deter by killing terrorists, because the Palestinian culture sanctifies death and promises the suicide killer (the *shahid* or "martyr") the reward of paradise. Death may deter those who do not believe in this, but in the Palestinian case, arrest, prosecution, and imprisonment deter more killers – provided that we do not release the prisoners. Releasing prisoners harms the deterrence achieved by imprisonment, especially lifetime imprisonment.

Due to this complex set of considerations, we designed a decision-making process and authorization procedure that allows us to examine all aspects of the targeted killing operation. These include the legitimacy of the operation as it pertains to the terrorist who is the target of the operation, the absence of operational alternatives that would allow us to arrest the terrorist, and the aim of avoiding harm to innocent civilians, as well as other criteria.

The IDF generally carries out arrests when it is possible to surprise the terrorist at the time of his arrest. There was a time in the West Bank, mainly before Operation Defensive Shield, when it was difficult to surprise terrorists in their hiding places because the IDF lacked freedom of operation in Palestinian cities, so the IDF carried out targeted killing operations in the West Bank. Once the IDF attained freedom of operation, and could surprise the terrorists and arrest them, the need for targeted killing operations in that area decreased. However, because the IDF lacks similar freedom of operation in the Gaza Strip (along with other considerations), we are forced to carry out multiple targeted killing operations there.

In this regard, I will mention that Israel's Supreme Court heard a petition demanding the halt of targeted killing operations, and it handed down a fundamental ruling in this matter. The High Court determined that under certain conditions, there is legal and ethical legitimacy for such operations.

The decision to strike Hamas leader Sheikh Ahmed Yassin reflects the indecision of the political and military echelons regarding such targeted killing actions. The discussion to target Sheikh Yassin focused on ethical and utilitarian issues, and at one point, legal aspects as well. My view was that when taking on a terrorist organization such as Hamas, the distinction between the political and military echelons was irrelevant. We had solid intelligence that indicated that Sheikh Yassin was the dominant entity in determining Hamas'ss terror strategy. He was the one who approved their terror attack policy (such as whether to carry out suicide bombings and rocket attacks on Israeli communities in the Gaza Strip and elsewhere). He bore significant overall responsibility for terror attacks.

Those who were opposed to striking Sheikh Yassin compared him to a representative of the Hamas political echelon, like the political echelon in Israel or in any other country, which authorizes military action. The accepted practice in relations between countries – even hostile ones – is to refrain from attacking the political echelon.

This topic can be argued back and forth with justifications on both sides. The main question was how great a risk we faced of exposing our own political echelon to a terrorist threat as retaliation for a strike on Sheikh Yassin. We recalled all too well the murder of then minister Rehavam (Gandhi) Ze'evi by the Popular Front for the Liberation of Palestine (PFLP) in retaliation for our killing of Abu Ali Mustafa (Mustafa Alhaj). The PFLP considered Abu Ali Mustafa not a military leader, but rather a political leader.

Ethically, it was easy to justify the killing of Sheikh Yassin as a person who had personally issued religious directives (*fatwa*) and operational orders that led directly to the murder of so many Israelis. But in terms of the cost and benefit of such a targeted killing, a disagreement arose between those who believed that attacking the Hamas leader would offer greater benefit than cost, and those who feared that the cost would outweigh the benefits.

The benefits included eliminating Yassin as a terrorist operative, deterring others, and deterring the organization. A popular saying held, "If we can get Sheikh Yassin – we can get anyone on the scene." The possible costs included several opposing considerations. First, the attack on Sheikh Yassin would promote feelings of hatred and revenge. Second, the organization would try to deter us with a wave of new terror attacks. Further, striking someone who is considered a religious leader would likely inflame the Arab Muslim street. Finally, the resulting vacuum meant the possibility that even more radical leaders would take Yassin's place.

Since Prime Minister Sharon also wanted the approval of the attorney general, the discussion process lasted almost a year. Toward the end, the issue was brought to the Cabinet for its approval. The Cabinet decided to authorize five ministers to make the decision. Finally, the decision was made.

The first opportunity to implement it came on a Saturday afternoon. A few hours earlier we had received information about a possible meeting of Hamas senior officials, led by Sheikh Yassin, which would take place in a private home in Gaza City. Evidence of the meeting continued to arrive, until we were certain about the meeting and its location. The meeting would be attended by Sheikh Yassin, his senior aide Ismail Haniyeh, veteran terrorist Muhammad Deif, and other known terrorists such as Adnan al-Ghoul and Ahmed Ghandour.

The meeting took place in the three-story family home of a Hamas activist. We were not sure if the family was at home. We assumed, with a high degree of likelihood, that the family was not there for reasons of compartmentalization and secrecy. Even if it turned out that the family was there, striking the Hamas leadership justified harming others present. But as luck would have it, five yards from the home stood a large, five-story residential building. Our understanding was that the building was inhabited. We estimated that some forty families lived in the building. We were particularly certain that people would be inside in the afternoon, as children would have returned home after school.

Israeli Air Force performance evaluators carried out an analysis of the target. They determined that in order to destroy all three floors of the target building, we would need to drop a one-ton bomb (containing approximately 770 pounds [350 kilograms] of explosives). But doing so would also cause great destruction to the residential building next door. It would have been possible to carry out a surgical strike against the target, without collateral damage, by dropping a quarter-ton bomb, but this would not have destroyed the target completely. The smaller bomb would have leveled only the building's top floor.

We carried out the decision-making process and the debate under pressure for time, because we knew that the Hamas meeting would not last long. Once we had made our decision, our aircraft and pilots hovered in the air and waited to receive the order. We held a telephone conference call with Prime Minister Ariel Sharon; Defense Minister Shaul Mofaz; Shin Bet chief Avi Dichter; Major General Yoav Galant, military secretary to the prime minister; and myself. I advised against the strike, given the assessment of the enormous damage that a one-ton bomb would cause to the nearby populated residential building. Neither was I in favor of using a quarter-ton bomb, because of the performance evaluators' assessment – if we used a bomb of this size, they did not guarantee the desired outcome. I recommended that we wait for another opportunity. Sharon and Mofaz accepted my position, and the attack was not authorized.

Of course, we felt a certain sense that we had missed an opportunity to strike the entire Hamas leadership. But I was satisfied with my recommendation.

Ten minutes after we made the decision, the head of the Shin Bet phoned and reported that we had received new intelligence that the meeting would take place on the building's third floor (the top floor). This meant that we now had the opportunity to strike the top floor of the house with a quarter-ton bomb. Again, we held a telephone conference call. This time, the strike was approved.

The pilot struck the target accurately. The Air Force performance evaluators had made an accurate assessment: the home's upper floor was completely destroyed, with no surrounding damage. But it turned out that the meeting had taken place on the first floor. All the participants fled the house without serious injury.

The sense of missed opportunity was even greater than it had been before, because our strike proved our ability to reach the Hamas leadership. From now on, they would likely take additional precautions that could prevent another such opportunity.

We can only speculate about what would have happened to Hamas after a strike that destroyed their entire top leadership. We might wonder how Hamas would look today without some of its leaders and senior commanders, some of whom are still active. But to me, the more important question, and particularly in retrospect, is what was more ethical and beneficial: to refrain from attacking the Hamas leadership at the price of their continued functioning, or to attack the terrorist leaders at the price of dozens of Palestinian casualties, including children.

There are instances that might justify such an attack, both in ethical and utilitarian terms. Yet in this case, my assessment that there would be another opportunity in the near future to attack the terrorist leaders, together or separately, tipped the scales in favor of refraining from attack. A strike that would have resulted in the killing of dozens of Palestinians, including children, might have turned out be a Pyrrhic victory – a victory in battle but a defeat in war. This was due to the lack of legitimacy for such an action in Israeli society, and of course, in the entire international world.

On the morning of March 22, 2004, we had another opportunity to attack Sheikh Ahmed Yassin. He had spent the night in the mosque near his home because he feared military action against him while he was in his house. We located Yassin and struck him while his companions and bodyguards escorted him from the mosque back to his home.

Yassin's killing ignited the Middle East, but it also strengthened Israel's deterrence. In fact, a series of strikes against Hamas leaders who were considered "the political leadership," such as Ismail Abu Shanab, Mahmoud al-Zahar (who survived the strike) and Abdul-Aziz Rantisi, led the Hamas leadership to agree to an unconditional cease-fire, and produced a long lull in attacks.

Those who understand that fighting terrorism has no immediate solutions but rather involves a long-term strategy, should not be frustrated that the problem is not resolved in a "quick fix" – a single military operation.

One of the common claims about Israeli interests in the conflict with the Palestinians is that "occupation corrupts." I agree with this claim: controlling another nation, ignoring the rights of its people, or, heaven forbid, oppressing these people – all of these corrupt. For this reason, I have no desire to control any other nation.

This does not mean that Jews are prohibited from living anywhere in the Land of Israel, and this does not mean that "disengagement," "convergence," or unilateral "separation" will ensure the Jewish people security in their country. Under the circumstances, I think that offering more concessions to those who still do not recognize the right of the State of Israel to exist as an independent Jewish state only worsens our situation. Concessions can only diminish the chances of attaining security and peace. I have addressed this matter extensively in other chapters.

Our attempts to "break up" with the Palestinians by means of an agreement or unilaterally (in order not to rule over them) have failed. Given this, it is very important for Israeli soldiers and other security forces engaged in defense work among the Palestinian population to operate in a way that preserves our ethical values. This is important ethically (the "Mirror Test" I mentioned earlier) and it is also beneficial. Military force that does not enjoy legitimacy internally and internationally may lead to losing the war.

Ben-Gurion's statement that the way to beat the enemy is "with courage, wisdom, and purity" has always resonated with me. In the IDF and security forces operations among the Palestinian population, our commanders are faced with an enormous challenge: to educate, and to ensure that the troops subordinate to them act in a proper and ethical manner. In every war, there is the danger that an individual may be overcome by his personal emotions. Our sages addressed this danger when they said, "Who is a hero? He who conquers his own evil will."

War creates situations that elicit sharp emotions – hatred, fear, an emotional desire for revenge. A person, and especially a young soldier, who sees a friend fall in battle, or sees civilians killed or injured in a terror attack, could translate these experiences into actions that stem from his emotions.

Among the civilian population, war creates anger and frustration. You know that your country possesses immense military power, but you cannot make full use of it. Sometimes the use of force works against you. The battle is daily, and there is no end in sight.

In warfare conducted among the civilian population, soldiers may be tempted to loot, and even to justify it as a punishment against the enemy. It has happened to us. There also may also be cases of rape. This has not happened for us.

Waging battle among the civilian population creates gray areas. But young soldiers tend to see life in black and white terms. Who is the enemy? Are the citizens on the other side the "enemy"? Do they support or help terrorists? If so, "They are all enemies, and they all need to be killed," or at least "Everyone should pay the price." Battling an enemy who operates under a different ethical code poses an enormous challenge: "If they kill civilians indiscriminately, why don't we do so?" "If they use ambulances to infiltrate a suicide bomber or explosion, or they infiltrate a suicide bomber pretending to be a patient on his way to the hospital – why should we treat them as human beings?" These are some of the questions raised.

Fighting such an enemy, and the type of experiences that a young soldier undergoes, might lead to dehumanization of the enemy. The rationale behind this effect seems to have some sense: "A society that sends suicide bombers to kill women and children and idolizes these killers is a society of animals, not human beings – so it is only right to treat them accordingly."

The war being waged daily at the checkpoints, in searches, patrols and arrests, is draining, corrosive, and can lead to numbness. But precisely in such a war of necessity, officers must make every effort so that at end of the war, we will be the victor, and still remain human.

I added that sentence to a page that I distributed to the commanders of my units when I served as commander of the Judea and Samaria Division, and later on, as COGS. The page included a poem by Natan Alterman from 1948, in the "Seventh Column" op ed that he published regularly in *Davar* (the Histadrut newspaper). The poem is titled "Al Zot" (About This):

Across the vanquished city in a jeep he did speed –
A lad bold and armed, a young lion of a lad!
And an old man and a woman on that very street
Cowered against a wall, in fear of him clad.
Said the lad smiling, milk teeth shining:
"I'll try the machine gun" and put it into play!

To hide his face in his hands the old man barely had time
When his blood on the wall was sprayed.

My friends, a scene from the battle of freedom, behold!
There are worse – nothing is hidden!
Our war demands song, it must be told
To sing of this we are bidden.

We will sing of "delicate incidents"
Whose name, don't you know, is murder.
Sing of conversations with sympathetic listeners,
Of snickers of forgiveness that are slurred.

Let it not be said, "Only individuals are responsible for the glorious story."
Individual and society are an inseparable pair
If society listens to the individual who tells it
instead of putting him in chains!

For those in combat gear, and we who impinge,
Whether by action or agreement subliminal,
Are thrust, muttering "necessity" and "revenge,"
Into the realm of the war criminal.

War is cruel! Says the innocent preacher
Its fist hits him back in the face
The charge of justice and mercy
Would that it would be so cruel.[2]

---

[2] First, second, fourth, and sixth stanzas modified from translation by Ralph Mandel, published in *Ha'aretz*, March 18, 2016.

I also added the letter that Ben-Gurion sent to Alterman after reading the poem:

> 19 Cheshvan 5709 (November 21, 1948)
> Dear Alterman,
> Congratulations on the moral validity and the powerful expressiveness of your latest column in *Davar*. You have become a pure, faithful mouthpiece of the human conscience. If our conscience does not beat in our hearts in times such as these, we will be rendered unworthy of the great wonders we have merited until now.
> No armored column in our army exceeds yours in battle strength! I ask your permission to have 100,000 copies of your column printed by the Defense Ministry for distribution to every soldier in Israel.
> With appreciation and thanks,
> D. Ben-Gurion

This challenge of command requires officers to indoctrinate soldiers with values that confront a daily, intensive test in the burden of warfare. The commanders must use every tool at their disposal to prevent ethical deterioration: education, supervision, monitoring, enforcement, and punishment. Commanders should never forget that the saying, "He who is merciful to the cruel, ultimately is cruel to the merciful" – applies first and foremost to ourselves. We must defeat the enemy and still remain human.

PART III

Hamastan

CHAPTER 12

DISENGAGEMENT

For six years I was on the Israeli front line in addressing the Palestinian threat – from the summer of 1999, when I realized that we were facing a war with our partners in the Oslo Accords, until the summer of 2005, when Israel was due to conduct a unilateral withdrawal from the Gaza Strip and Northern Samaria. These six years can be divided into four periods of time:

First period (1999–2000): The IDF leadership and Prime Minister Ehud Barak understood the possibility of a clash and prepared accordingly, even though public discourse and political awareness were in a completely different place, anticipating peace and an end to the conflict.

Second period (2000–2002): Israel fought against the terror campaign initiated by Arafat in a frustrating attempt at defending itself, with its hands tied behind its back and without any inner Israeli internalization of the challenge which we were facing.

Third period (2002–2003): Israel stood up to the Palestinian terrorist offensive, and upgraded from a defensive approach to successful offense, mainly in Judea and Samaria, but also in the Gaza Strip.

Fourth period (2004–2005): Israel was lured into the so-called magical solution of the disengagement and addressed only with this issue, instead of using its military success from Operation Defensive Shield and onwards on a political level.

These four stages of the conflict occurred while I was serving in the IDF. After I ended my term as COGS, a fifth stage developed. The disengagement took place in August 2005. About four months later Hamas won the elections in the Palestinian Authority (January 2006) and eighteen months later, they took total control over the Gaza Strip (June 2007). In 2006 and 2007 we did not see terror return to our streets, but we did witness Gaza turning into an armed Hamastan, firing Qassam rockets at Sderot and the western Negev and making life in the south unbearable. Since then the rocket range gradually increased: Ashkelon and Ashdod, Be'er Sheva, Rishon Lezion, and, finally, Tel Aviv and farther north.

During these years, we also witnessed Israel's political achievements of 2002 and 2003 slowly melt away. Instead of President Bush's speech of June 24, 2002 – we got the Annapolis Conference, which was the continuation of the Oslo approach that had failed. Instead of a growing international understanding that the Palestinians must implement fundamental reforms before giving them additional land, if at all – pressure was put on Israel to waive all demands without any conditions and continue the withdrawal process, even though the result was the establishment of terrorist bases that could endanger our future.

Just as I had predicted when I warned against the disengagement, the unilateral withdrawal gave tailwind to radical Islam and terrorism. It presented Israel with a much greater Palestinian threat than we had faced before the implementation of this irresponsible move. But the disengagement caused additional damage, no less severe: it created a political avalanche that put Israel at a political disadvantage against the Palestinians. After our intense efforts in 2002–2003 succeeded in erecting a political wall between Israel and Arafat, this wall cracked in 2004–2005, and collapsed in late 2007. This false and dangerous paradigm for Israel led to the eruption of the Palestinian terror war (Second Intifada) in September 2000 (Al-Aqsa Intifada, according to their story). In the first decade of the twenty-first century, many understood its falsehood, but it once again became dominant after almost seven years of a slow and painful learning process.

If Prime Minister Sharon believed that by leaving Gaza, he would buy the credit he needed for Israel, in order to shift the burden of international pressure to the Palestinians, he was gravely wrong. The disengagement that he initiated, and the policy of unconditional concessions bolstered by his successor, Ehud Olmert, led to great satisfaction among Arafat's heirs and followers. Seven years after Arafat attacked Israel, they could assert that the offensive had succeeded. While the IDF and Shin Bet stood up to terrorism, Israeli society withstood terrorism with resolve, and Israel's economy flourished as the Palestinians' economic situation worsened – in the end the Israeli leadership was not wise enough to cope with reality. Lacking any comprehensive national strategy and an agreement over the narrative of the conflict, Israel missed its historical opportunity in 2003–2004. There were no reforms in Palestinian society, no changes in Palestinian basic positions. The old Palestinian method of combining armed conflict with political struggle had proven its success. After many years of dealing with the Palestinians, and following a period when this approach seemed to bear fruit, I was deeply concerned for the future that awaited us, should we fail to come to our senses.

What had happened here? What had failed us? Why had such an impressive Israeli achievement slipped between our fingers and turned into a stinging failure?

The immediate cause for the deterioration of Israel's strategic situation vis-à-vis the Palestinians was an incorrect, surprising, and unexplained decision of former Prime Minister Ariel Sharon. I have no doubt that

Sharon's decision derived from external considerations. Following criminal allegations against him and a decline in popularity, he found himself suffering from personal and political distress. Sharon decided to turn the tables and initiate a dramatic move that blatantly contradicted his political beliefs and deviated from his perception of reality.

In his attempt to save his political future, Sharon put Israel on a strategic path that had no purpose and no future. Perhaps he convinced himself that his actions were helping Israel and would give it some credit points in the international arena. But from my professional acquaintance with Sharon, I can unequivocally say that the idea of disengagement was foreign to him, in total contrast to his way of thinking. Furthermore, the way the idea sprouted was strange, as well as the way it was handled.

What led me to suspect Sharon's motives for the disengagement was the order of events. Let us reconstruct them concisely.

The highlight of the Israeli counterattack against the Arafat offensive of the early 2000s occurred in the summer of 2003. At this stage, about one year after Operation Defensive Shield, the operational results of this campaign were clearly visible. The terrorism curve had dropped substantially, and Israel's cities were enjoying relative quiet. We still suffered from terror attacks, but the numbers had dropped dramatically since early 2002. We put continuous pressure on terrorists in all areas of Judea and Samaria. We cleaned out the terrorist cells in the cities and pursued the terrorists in their own areas. We showed initiative; our intelligence was slowly improving and our operational achievements, based on real-time information and operational flexibility, were unprecedented.

But our most significant achievement was in the political arena. The political atmosphere that had been created among the Palestinians following the IDF and Shin Bet's success was completely different than that of 2001–2002. This was clearly visible when Arafat planned to visit the Jenin refugee camp in May 2002, one month after the battle there during Operation Defensive Shield. Protestors awaited him, heckling him and carrying signs with slogans that attacked him. He cancelled his visit to the camp to avoid an embarrassing incident, and also at the recommendation of his security guards, who feared he might be harmed. Popular criticism against him was widespread and authentic. At the same time, Arafat was severely criticized by the Palestinian leadership. Senior officials – including Abu Mazen – who had disparaged his terrorist strategies from the outset, were now bold enough to speak up. In closed circles, which were growing wider, they now claimed that Arafat's chosen terror approach was leading them to destruction. An influential group of Palestinians set out to find another way.

I regarded these developments from a broad perspective. In early 2003, the US attacked Iraq. The extreme forces in the region felt that they were under pressure. Operation Defensive Shield and its ensuing success were part of this comprehensive pressure. For the first time in a long period, a feeling arose in the Middle East that the Western forces had taken an offensive approach instead of a defensive one. On the other hand, the forces siding with extremism and terrorism lost their glory and the support that they had enjoyed. Suddenly they were perceived as dangerous, even repulsive. Some even felt battered and in retreat.

I regarded the combination of these circumstances as a one-time historical opportunity. The military achievement of 2002–2003 could have been leveraged into a political process that would bring Israel out of the current situation with the upper hand. I recalled the realization that I had publicly expressed in 2000, a short while after becoming COGS: this conflict must end with the Palestinians learning that violence does not pay. We must engrave into their consciousness that violence is not worth their while, not only for us, but for future generations. Sometime in the future, the Palestinian pattern of constantly demanding more had to stop at the sovereign boundaries of the State of Israel, a defensible border that represents its own interests.

But for the conflict to end with such an understanding, there must be an alternative to the reign of terrorism and Arafat's ideology of terrorism. Abu Mazen was this alternative. The government he founded in 2003 created an opportunity to realize this success and strengthen the Palestinians who did not believe in violence.

But Abu Mazen's leadership did not last long. Some claim that it failed because Israel was not generous enough toward it. I also felt then that Israel should have taken steps to strengthen Abu Mazen and clarify to the Palestinians that their lives would improve significantly under a more moderate leadership. Among other moves, I supported transferring cities in Judea and Samaria to the responsibility of the Palestinian security forces, even though this involved a significant security risk. Even so, Israel was not responsible for Abu Mazen's failure in the summer of 2003 – not exclusively, and not even mainly. His defeat resulted from his own weakness, and from the internal Palestinian circumstances in which he operated, mainly from Arafat's tricks and maneuvers while still serving as Ra'is. I had no illusions about Abu Mazen's strategic approach, which denied Israel's right to existence as a Jewish state. But I did think we had convinced him that terrorism did not serve the Palestinian interests, and he should be given a chance to practice what he had been preaching: against terrorism and in favor of "one authority, one law, and one weapon."

Even though Abu Mazen's attempt failed, the basic conditions showed that Israel's situation within the conflict was gradually improving. The low point in the security situation was far behind us, and evidence was now showing that Israel was recovering from the 2001–2002 economic slump. The obvious military improvement, gradual economic rise, comfortable international environment, and resolute US actions in Iraq meant that Israel had no reason to initiate hasty or perfunctory actions. Israel's basic strategy since the outbreak of the conflict – no negotiations under fire and no compromises under fire – had finally yielded results. Now Israel needed strong nerves, clear political thinking, and patience.

Just at this critical moment, in the fall of 2003, the disengagement appeared on the horizon.

Sharon never held an organized discussion with me on the disengagement. In preparation for the Fourth Herzliya Conference (annual global policy gathering at the Interdisciplinary Center Herzliya [IDC]) in late 2003, he asked for my opinion as COGS on the evacuation of three villages: Netzarim, Morag, and Kfar Darom. This move, initiated by Minister of Justice Tommy Lapid, was supposed to demonstrate Israel's good will and improve our position in the world. After the collapse of the Abu Mazen option, there was a strong sense that we had hit a dead end. There was some political distress, which I did not take lightly, but I also did not believe it to be too serious. In any case, I did not think that it justified the total breakdown of the strategy that had been guiding us for the past three years. Therefore, when Sharon asked for my opinion, I told him that I opposed any retreat under fire. I described the sequence of events since 1983 and explained to him that from a Palestinian point of view, the Jibril Agreement had led to the Intifada, the Intifada to the Oslo Accords, and the Oslo Accords to the year 2000. After the major efforts we had invested and the blood we had spilled, if the Israeli-Palestinian conflict once again ended with us retreating under fire, then the Palestinians would learn that violence is worthwhile, that "the Jews only understand force." The result of the evacuation of three villages in the Gaza Strip would be an additional use of force against the Jews. What would we have achieved? With what result would we be ending the struggle between us and them?

Sharon said nothing. He listened. But I quickly realized that other reasons were guiding him, unconnected to the specific political and security considerations. In one of our meetings, Sharon's head of office, attorney Dov Weisglass, tried to convince me to support the disengagement. He said that Sharon was losing political favor and had to make a move. I clearly did not feel comfortable presenting such considerations to the chief of general staff. It made me feel that politics had no limitations. In the background, investigations were being conducted against Sharon and his two sons for criminal acts. Therefore, before the plan was made fully public – without consulting with me as COGS or with other senior military officials – I had the feeling that Sharon might take steps that would save him politically and personally, even at a high strategic price. By that time, I had already witnessed corruption. I had experience and knowledge of this phenomenon and its influence on decision makers in Israel. I saw the connection between major economic interests and the pressure put on the government and the defense establishment to implement a policy that would serve these interests. Prior to the 2003 Herzliya Conference, I realized, even though I had not been specifically told, that Sharon was diverting policy in a different direction. In order to pull Israel out of the current, but bearable, political situation, he was about to change the strategy that we had adopted and destroy the wall that we had worked so hard to build.

As a COGS who had worked harmoniously with the prime minister and with a certain level of closeness, I can testify that from the moment the idea of the disengagement was born, Sharon stopped being Sharon. His behavior was different, work at headquarters was different, his leadership spirit was different. Sharon was clearly determined to promote and realize the disengagement, but it was also clear that he was not totally in favor of it. He was acting on hidden interests.

These facts led me to believe that there were much broader forces underlying Sharon's decision and that led him to do what he did. These forces ultimately caused Israel to fail and lose what might have been a victory, even one with historical implications.

What do I mean? In my years as deputy COGS and COGS I became closely acquainted with the juxtaposition between the political and military echelons. I saw from up close how decisions were made. I felt the pressures that were put on the country's leaders and the considerations that guided them. My magnified vision of the political leadership gave me not only a personal sense of unease, but also made me fear for our national future. This was not only because the processes of decision making that I had witnessed were hasty and superficial, and not only because the quality and moral integrity of some of our leaders was questionable. Rather, I was afraid because even when our country's leaders see the current reality and try to address it as best they can, they are surrounded by a ring of pressure from leading power groups in the Israeli society, two of which hold authority without responsibility.

The first group is the business tycoons. A small but powerful group of wealthy individuals has emerged in Israel in recent decades, and the power they hold is tremendous. They are joined by a small group of foreign investors who try to connect with the government and influence it, not necessarily from Zionist motives. In this group I do not include most Israeli and Jewish industrialists, who earn their money honestly, make a major contribution to the Israeli economy, and even donate from their earnings to the Zionist enterprise in diverse fields. Because of the weakness of the political system and the low quality of some parts of the government and political system, no public entity has sufficient weight to stop or restrain these wealthy individuals. Therefore, prime ministers, ministers, and Knesset members are unreasonably influenced by the personal opinions and interests of these people.

With regard to the Israeli-Arab conflict and the resulting security problems, the tycoons' positions in the years following the Oslo Accords correlated smoothly with their immediate interests. Most wanted quiet that would enable their businesses to continue flourishing and the stock market to continue rising. For this reason, they were against any policy that risked the immediate calm in the country. Those wealthy individuals had no interest in Israel standing up for its vital needs, as this might have caused friction and jeopardized the calm required for business. Some powerful non-Israeli industrialists had (and still have) economic interests with our neighbors and enemies, and some Israelis had economic interests with the Palestinians. There were, of course, other influential individuals who had a different approach and understood that for their own good, it was better to address our long-term national security and not strive for a false, short-term quiet at the price of mortgaging their future. Even so, the former group swayed Israel's leaders in one clear direction. At most junctions, they supported concessions to buy time, and did not insist on fighting for national interests that might cause conflicts, risking immediate personal and business interests.

The second power group that wields authority in an irresponsible manner is the media. In all free countries, a free media is the lifeline of democracy. Media is vital to ensure the flow of information, the expression of different opinions in public debate, and pluralistic and critical thought. But unfortunately, during my years in the IDF leadership, I learned that the Israeli media does not always fulfill its role on the democratic playing field. I learned firsthand that information provided by the media is not always exact. Sometimes it is slanted, even fabricated. The media does not always present the full picture in all aspects and complexities, in a fair and professional manner. Some media entities are beholden to certain trends of thought. They ignore alternative options, or even prevent the public from accessing them. Instead of encouraging pluralistic and critical thought, the Israeli media has often encouraged almost unified thinking that exhibited strong criticism of one sector and extreme forgiveness toward others.

As a result, the picture of reality that the Israeli media consumer receives is severely distorted. Selective presentation of facts, distortion of opinions, and the adoption of double standards toward certain personalities and institutions cause the media to betray its professional and democratic role. It blinds the public from seeing reality as is and puts heavy political pressure on the state leaders.

Prime ministers in Israel have been challenged to fight the media, realizing that they would end up paying a high, and sometimes fatal, price – losing the next elections. The media can "treat someone with kid gloves" or they can challenge them and even ruin their political career. But when the time comes, when it becomes clear that the policy that the media blatantly pushes is placing Israel in great danger, then no journalist, television reporter, or editor is released from taking responsibility for the damage caused, directly or indirectly. The lack of binding ethics and norms in this field has turned the triumvirate of capital, government, and media into a wild jungle that lacks any responsibility. When media sources are owned by capitalists, the rules of the democratic game become even more imbalanced.

I am aware that it is difficult to demand accountability from those who do not have the right to make decisions. But it is possible – and necessary – to demand that the media uphold journalistic ethics. One senior journalist publicly called to "protect the prime minister like an *etrog* in a box" (a citron, used ceremonially during the Jewish holiday of Sukkot), because the prime minister was about to take steps on a controversial issue, and the journalist supported Sharon's policy. I would expect that his colleagues would be devastated by his comment, which stains the entire media profession. I would expect them to condemn and denunciate him. But this did not happen. Only a handful of journalists criticized this phenomenon. It was specifically because of this that I believe in the importance of an independent public broadcast entity that is free of interests and pressure by capitalists and politicians.

But in recent years we have witnessed the opposite trend, which is no less worrying. Ministers and Knesset members, supported by Prime Minister Netanyahu, attack the media in an attempt to control it. ("What is the corporation worth if we do not control it?" said Minister of Culture Miri Regev.) They set the public against the left-wing media, presenting it as a fifth column that is undermining the foundations of the State of Israel's existence.

In recent years, the media map has changed drastically, and this is a positive development. Newspapers such as *Yisrael Hayom*, *Makor Rishon*, *B'Sheva* and Channel 20 can hardly be accused of left-wing tendencies, and now occupy a much more central position in public media. Journalists and editorialists who identify with the right host popular current affairs programs on the radio and television, alongside their left-wing peers. The media today is more heterogenous than it was fifteen years ago. But that does not stop the relentless attack of right-wing politicians against it. The most significant challenge for free media in Israel today is Netanyahu's ambition to control the media.

The third power group is the legal system, headed by the Supreme Court. Unlike the first two power groups that I mentioned, I am confident that the court operates with due authority. I support the rule and preeminence of law. I disagree with relentless attacks on the Supreme Court, which have become common recently. But in my position as deputy COGS and COGS, I could not help but notice that during Aharon Barak's term as president of the Supreme Court, an atmosphere developed within the judiciary that "everything could be judged." As a result, often the court interfered with state matters that were not within its realm, such as the "neighbor tactic" (a method used to entice terrorists to leave their homes by having a neighbor knock at their front door) or decisions regarding the route of the security fence. Its decisions regarding the difficult battle we were waging against the Palestinians weighed heavily on the government, the IDF, and the Shin Bet. I certainly understand the importance of human rights in our lives and the need to protect those rights, even during a conflict, but sometimes I had the feeling that the Supreme Court judges were not sufficiently aware of the security

GOC Central Command

With Prime Minister and Minister of Defense Ehud Barak *(center)* and COGS Shaul Mofaz *(right)* at Central Command

As GOC Central Command at training grounds

Signing the second FRD (steps of the Oslo Accord) in Jenin, with General Haj Ismail, commander of the Palestinian National Security Forces in the West Bank

With my Bureau Chief Major Yair Kules on patrol in Hebron

As GOC Central Command giving a briefing to Border Patrol officers in Judea and Samaria

Chief of General Staff

Change of command ceremony for COGS at the Prime Minister's Office. From left: outgoing COGS Shaul Mofaz, Prime Minister Ariel Sharon, Minister of Defense Binyamin Ben-Eliezer, entering COGS Moshe Ya'alon.

Honor parade for receiving the position of COGS at the Kiryah base in Tel Aviv

Training Exercises

Arriving for a tour of the field

Observing a training exercise of a reserve ground forces brigade

A tank exercise

With First Lieutenant Amir,
a reserve officer from Grofit, during a tank exercise

With Major General Yoav Galant at an exercise of a regular brigade.

A paratroopers brigade exercise, with, *from left:* COGS Shaul Mofaz, Brigade Commander Gadi Shamni, and Head of Military Intelligence Aharon Ze'evi (Farkash)

Observing an exercise of a regular armored brigade

Exercise of a reserve armored brigade

As COGS, speaking with soldiers during an exercise in the Golan Heights

Keeping fit; commanders' run at Wingate Institute

Visiting the site of a terror attack in Avnei Chefetz

Conversation with a soldier at an observation post in the Gaza Strip

Speaking to Givati soldiers during an operation in the Gaza Strip

Visit to the Golan Heights

An observation officer giving an update at a post in the Golan Heights

As COGS, speaking with new immigrant soldiers in the Nativ conversion course

Conversation with a cadet

Reviewing cadets during a visit to GOC Army Headquarters

Speaking to soldiers of Battalion 890 before making
a parachute jump with them

Meeting with veteran paratroopers before the jump. Center: Lieutenant Colonel Micha Ben-Ari of Unit 101. During the Six-Day War, I helped his wife Aviva with farm duties in Kfar Bialik while he was serving.

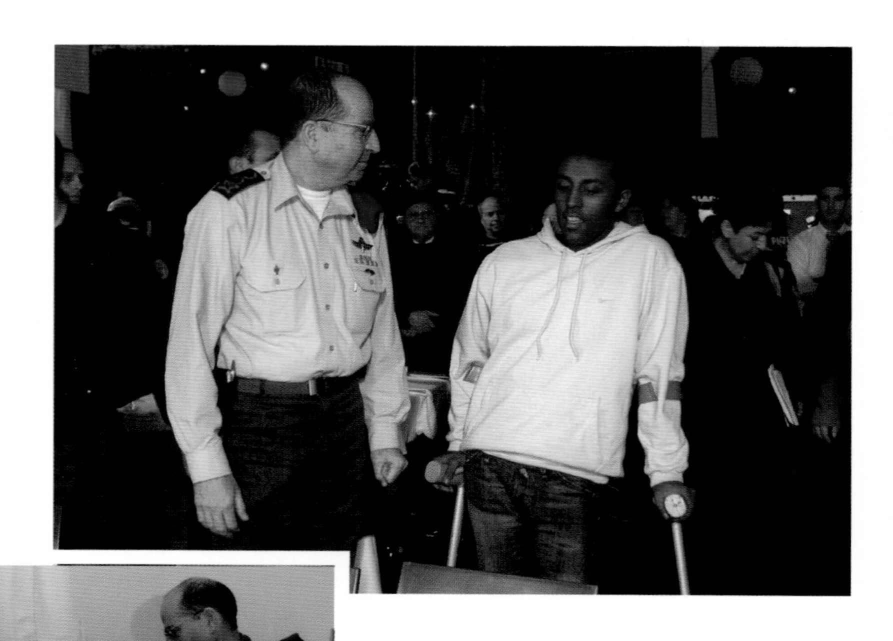

Top: With First Lieutenant Shmuel, an engineering officer who was wounded in action in Gaza

Center and bottom: Visiting the wounded at Barzilai Medical Center in Ashkelon

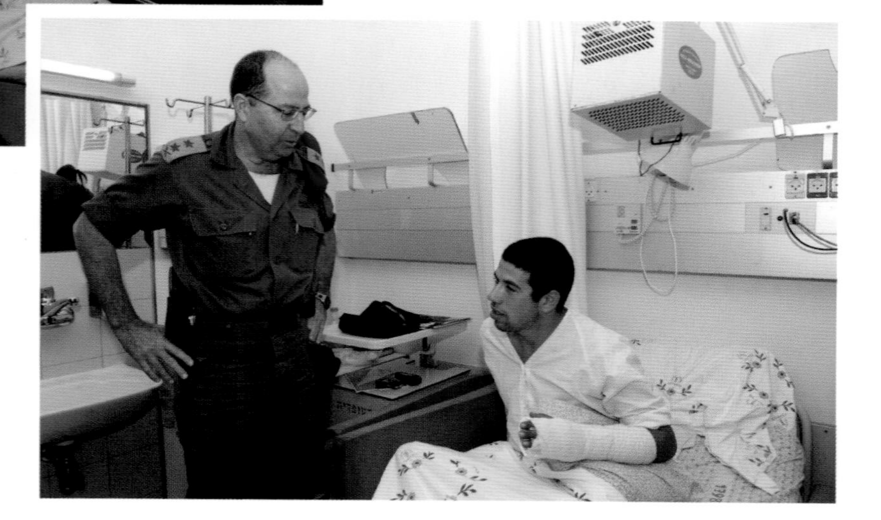

Awarding Families of Fallen Soldiers from Garin Ya'alon and Kibbutz Grofit with the insignia for the Attrition War

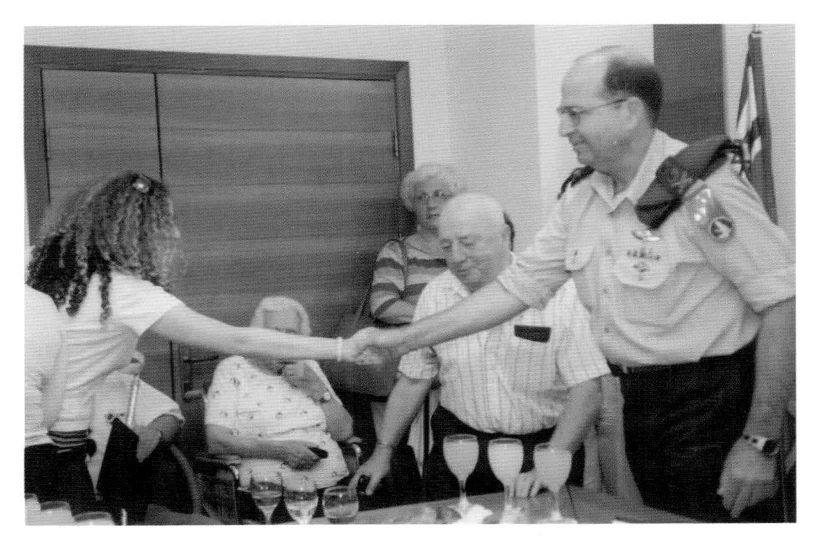

The family of fallen soldier Dudik Kimmelfeld

The family of fallen soldier Shlomo Svirsky

Meetings with VIPs

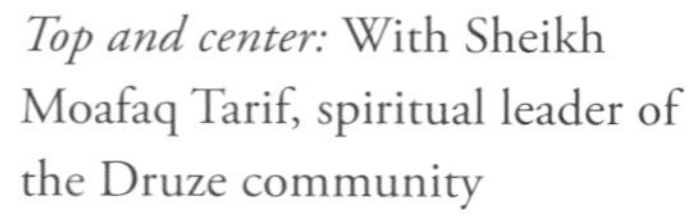

Top and center: With Sheikh Moafaq Tarif, spiritual leader of the Druze community

Bottom:
With Sheikh Ouda Abu Muamar, the legendary late leader of the Bedouin community

Visit to Poland

COGS delegation visiting death camps in Poland; at the entrance to Auschwitz (I am center in dress uniform with red beret)

The delegation in Birkenau (I am center in dress uniform with red beret)

Saying Goodbye

Parting parachute jump

Parting parachute jump with paratroopers from the armies of Israel's allies

I take my leave. The sign reads: "To Lieutenant General Moshe Bogie Ya'alon – Go in Peace and Good Luck."

and political implications of their decisions. Many times, the fear of the Supreme Court and the shadow that it imposed on decision makers caused serious damage to the state and diminished its ability to properly protect itself.

I have no doubt that the Supreme Court acted with full integrity and did what it believed to be right to protect the values of the State of Israel as a Jewish and democratic state. The status of the Supreme Court in Israel and around the world was also a source of support for me in making decisions that received its backing. This support is also important within the world of international law. But I believe that the judicial activism in the 2000s caused the legal system to frequently exceed its boundaries and penetrate the political and security arena, which were the realm of the military forces and not the judicial system.

Still, I do not agree with the unconstrained attacks on the reign of law in general, and on the Supreme Court in particular, that were initiated by the government of Israel in recent years and mainly after the 2015 elections. I was witness to the cynical political events in which the government passed its responsibility to the Supreme Court. I saw ministers and Knesset members who attacked the Court and delegitimized it, supported by Prime Minister Netanyahu. It is correct to define the balance between the judicial and the legislative authorities, but under no circumstances must the superiority of the law be impaired, and one of the important conditions to ensure this is to maintain the status and independence of the Supreme Court.

Unfortunately, in recent years the pendulum has swung from one extreme to the other. Politicians declared war against entities that are part of the system of checks and balances in a democratic regime. They attack them, delegitimize them, defame their status and present them as "elite groups that do not permit the government to govern." This is true regarding attacks on the media, the Supreme Court, and civil servants.

The balance was breached in a way that endangered the future of the State of Israel and the democratic regime.

During one of the customary interviews I held at the end of my term as COGS, I was asked, "What keeps you awake at night?" The interviewer expected me to answer, "Iran possessing an atomic bomb." But instead, I answered, "Corruption." Sadly, I found myself giving the same answer more than a decade later, toward the end of my term as minister of defense – and today I must give the same reply. I will discuss this further in subsequent chapter.

During the ten years of my service at the IDF General Staff, in all positions from head of intelligence to COGS, I witnessed a dismal reality. I smelled the stink of skunks rising from positions of leadership and power in Israel. The picture was not always clear, and I did not have all the details or the proof, but many question marks bothered me, and some continue to do so until today. In some cases, I shared my suspicions with the law-enforcement and auditing authorities.

I was concerned by the fact that a foreign tycoon had succeeded in connecting with influential people in the Prime Minister's Office, who became wealthy from this liaison when they left their jobs. When money controlled the media as well, the information reaching the public was filtered by personal interests. I heard many complaints from honest journalists about instructions given and pressure placed out of consideration for the capitalist-government relationship. Very few journalists were prepared to fight the phenomenon, because they were scared to lose their source of income. The result was the corrupted and dangerous relationship of capitalism, government, and media. This relationship helped to raise those who had fallen. It treated immorality with kid gloves and did away with rivals. The reality that was formed stifled any opinion that did not serve the interests of these powers and prevented the creation of an appropriate alternative to the reigning government.

I saw then, and I see today, a political leadership whose ultimate goal is its survival behind the governmental steering wheel, and for this purpose it is prepared to jeopardize national interests. Beyond the reflection of this disastrous state of affairs in certain decision-making processes, we can see politicians in various situations striving to weaken important and worthy power sources, such as the legal system, the attorney general, the state attorney, the Israel Police, the IDF, and other civil servants.

We must view with severity the damage to the law enforcement system, which comes from several directions. Mudslinging against the legal system undermines public trust. Attacks on the state attorney's office harms it. The Israel Police is weakened by budget cuts, unprofessional considerations in the appointment of senior officers, and politicians under investigation who attack their investigators.

This is also true of public culture. I believe that the majority of Israeli society understands the unethical nature of the culture of handing out jobs, bribery, and shady business plans. But there are some who choose to "join the party" and try to benefit from it. Their attitude is "If you can't beat them, join them," or "Eat and drink for tomorrow we die."

We are talking about a cultural war on the image of Israeli society, on public ethics and norms in the State of Israel. It is being waged on all systems, including the IDF and the Israel Police. If we do not succeed in changing this situation, they will beat us from within. That is why I claim that this threat was, and still is, worse than an Iranian atomic bomb.

When Sharon was first elected as prime minister in January 2001, he was the most veteran and experienced politician in Israel, along with Shimon Peres. Sharon had a deep awareness of conditions on the political playing field, certainly beyond my own. But while I regarded the situation with sadness and concern, Sharon analyzed the state of affairs like a poker player. Together with his cronies, known as "the Ranch Forum" (named after Sycamore Ranch, Sharon's home in the south) he analyzed the advantages and disadvantages of the other players, and considered how to exploit them to extract him from his legal and public difficulties. The direct result of this analysis was the disengagement.

I had always admired Ariel Sharon – as a military leader. As a young major in the First Lebanon War (Operation Peace for Galilee), I did not like the way Sharon, then minister of defense, led the war. In a previous chapter, I described one event which almost caused me to decide to leave the army. In Sharon's dealings with the senior IDF commanders, I witnessed instances that revealed a lack of integrity and reliability. I later found out that these attitudes were also expressed in his dealings with then Prime Minister Menachem Begin and other ministers in the government. Sharon's style of managing the war and his behavior toward the echelons both above and below him synchronized with what I had read and heard about his past.

In this regard, it seems fit to mention that David Ben-Gurion – who highly regarded Sharon as a warrior and military leader – was also aware of these characteristics. On November 24, 1958, when Sharon was given the rank of colonel, Ben-Gurion wrote in his diary: "I asked [Sharon] if he had been weaned from stating untruths.... [Sharon] admitted that several times, he had not told me the truth, but [he claimed] that he had been weaned of this." On January 29, 1960, Ben-Gurion wrote, "He [Sharon] has something of [Orde] Wingate – except for Wingate's moral nature." (Wingate was a senior British army intelligence officer in Mandate Palestine, who became an ardent Zionist. He founded and trained squads that conducted counterattacks on Arab saboteurs.)

But when I started working directly with Sharon in the spring of 2001, he as prime minister and myself as deputy chief of general staff, I found that he was a very serious interlocutor. Sharon was clear and lucid. Our conversations did not deal with tactics, but with strategy. Sharon always had his own ideas and manipulations, which I didn't like. I also didn't like the way that he disempowered the Security Cabinet. In this regard I acted with great sensitivity, because I didn't want to be a partner – even a passive one – in a move similar to that of the First Lebanon War, in which Sharon maneuvered the entire government. But as a national leader, he had a correct way of thinking and vast experience. We did not have a close intimate relationship, but we worked well together, and I allow myself to claim that this was also out of mutual appreciation. He frequently consulted with me during discussions, at meetings, and on the telephone. He would ask for my opinion on sensitive topics, and have me write it myself by hand, so as not to share it with anyone, not even a secretary who might type it. Of course, I updated the minister of defense on all of these. The working relationship between Sharon and me was good, possibly even very good, until the disengagement severed our good rapport.

But I was never part of Sharon's "gang." For many years, he was surrounded by a regular group of supporters. From their viewpoint as well as mine, I was not one of them. One day during my term as GOC Central Command, a good friend came to visit me. He asked why I didn't have a good relationship with Sharon, and said, "It's worth your while to have a good relationship with Sharon." I said, "If Sharon wants to visit me to hear about the situation – no problem, but only with the approval of the minister of defense and chief of general staff." Indeed, unlike several senior officers whom I knew, I and most of the other senior officers did not hold late-night meetings with politicians or disclose classified information to them as a long-term investment in a future promotion. Several days later Sharon did, in fact, call me. He suggested that we become friends. But when I said that I would agree to meet him only with the approval of the minister of defense and COGS, his excitement cooled. That was not what he meant. I understood that he wanted to bring me in, to be one of his group. We never held that meeting.

I was never wanted as part of the Ranch Forum. When the chief of general staff appointment was discussed in 2002, they preferred Dan Halutz to me. At first, the Ranch Forum was not totally against me, but they weren't in favor either. They did not know what to do with an officer like me. They did not know how to work with an officer who was meticulous about instructions, regulations, and proper administration, who made sure that matters were conducted above board – not below. They realized that with me, there would be no monkey business.

Over the years, I became increasingly concerned by the behavior of Sharon's gang. Many events caused me to ask questions. After so many years when he had unequivocally refused to purchase gas from Egypt, why would he suddenly change his mind by 180 degrees? Why did Advocate Dov Weisglass, the prime minister's right-hand man, promise to give back Jericho in its entirety to the Palestinians, plus commit to removing the security roadblocks that were in place even before September 2000? He did this in opposition to the position of the defense minister, head of the Shin Bet, and the COGS, and without holding any discussion on this matter – but it served the interests of the casino owned by his close confidants. There are endless examples of this. I had the feeling that I was looking at an enormous puzzle, but I could see only some of its pieces. What was more, the puzzle did not look good. There was something corrupt about it.

There were times when I believed that the behavior of Sharon's men crossed the boundaries of reason. I could not explain exactly what was behind this behavior, but things were done that should not have been done. The Palestinians were promised things that they should not have been promised. The Americans were told things that they should not have been told. We had the feeling that the head of the Prime Minister's Office, Dov Weisglass, was managing Israel's business in an irresponsible manner. This conduct included statements that were unclear and even contradictory. Sometimes it seemed that impractical personal and external considerations were affecting decisions regarding Israel's security, and these decisions came at the expense of Israel's best interests.

One event that was managed by the Prime Minister's Office in a most surprisingly improper manner occurred in the summer of 2003, during Abu Mazen's term as prime minister of the Palestinian Authority. During this period, it was agreed that responsibility for the Palestinian cities would be gradually transferred to the Authority. The first city in this process was Jericho.

During discussions with me as COGS, and then with Minister of Defense Shaul Mofaz, the following process of transfer was approved: the city would be transferred to the Palestinian Authority, including removing the security roadblock and opening the route from Jericho to Ramallah. But the other roadblocks would remain as they had been before September 2000. This plan, as agreed upon and approved by the Minister of Defense, was supposed to be presented to the Palestinians by the regional division commander, Brigadier General Tal Russo, during his meeting with General Haj Ismail.

In the meantime, I learned that Weisglass had met with Dr. Saeb Erekat and promised to transfer responsibility, while removing all security roadblocks around the city (including south toward Jerusalem, north toward the Jordan Valley and east toward the Jericho bypass road). When I heard about this, I contacted Mofaz, who was on an official visit to France, to check if he agreed with this. The minister of defense was disturbed to hear my news and resolved to handle it immediately upon his return to Israel. I also contacted the prime minister's military secretary, Major General Yoav Galant, and requested that he check this information with Weisglass. The military secretary reported back to me, saying that Weisglass had denied the claim.

When Mofaz landed in Israel, we held an urgent meeting in his office, where information about Dov Weisglass'ss commitments were presented. Mofaz was furious and undertook to check with the Prime Minister's

Office. In the meantime, he confirmed that the plan for transferring responsibility to the Palestinians would be presented at the division commander's meeting with General Ismail, as Mofaz had outlined previously. In other words, the roadblocks, excluding one, would remain in place.

After Mofaz checked the situation with the Prime Minister's Office, he told me that Weisglass had denied the information regarding his commitments to Erekat. The division commander met with General Ismail as planned and detailed the process of transferring responsibility for Jericho to the Palestinian Authority. Unsurprisingly, the meeting exploded when the Palestinian officer claimed that Weisglass had given Erekat a specific commitment to remove all roadblocks around the city.

Even after the meeting failed, Weisglass continued to deny his commitment. Another meeting was set with the Palestinians, but it also ended in a dead end when the Palestinians insisting on receiving the commitments that they claimed they had been promised. After the second meeting the minister of defense asked me to see what I could do to solve the problem, even if it meant making some concessions toward the Palestinians.

Eventually the Palestinians accepted our demands. Even they understood that it was not reasonable to remove roadblocks that had been in place around Jericho even before September 2000, when the local casino had been active, and even if only to prevent the unwanted entry of Israelis into the city.

Even though the Palestinians lied several times during our meetings, in this case I have reason to believe that their claims regarding Weisglass'ss commitment to Erekat is correct. If so, why did Weisglass make such a commitment? Did the casino have anything to do with it? Was it merely a coincidence that Weisglass represented businessman Martin Schlaff, the central figure in Casinos Austria, owners of the Jericho casino? Or that

Weisglass's office handled Schlaff's business in Israel? I have no proof, but I have not disregarded this as an option.

This event was added to the list of others that caused me to question Dov Weisglass'ss behavior as head of the Prime Minister's Office, mainly in connection with his American ties. Several events reminded me of the late Yossi Ginossar's mission in meeting with Arafat. I was never sure that the messages he delivered between the prime minister of Israel and Arafat were faithful to their original spirit, content, and language.

On Thursday, September 19, 2001, the security cabinet approved the operation to surround Arafat's office in Ramallah (the Mukat'a), following the attack on a Dan bus on Allenby Street in Tel Aviv. The operation began in the evening, under concern that the Americans would get involved and demand that we back off. As COGS, I thought that terminating the operation because of American intervention was against Israel's interests. I regarded such an intervention as giving US immunity to Arafat. I preferred to halt the operation before the US might publicly intervene.

Two days after the operation began, on Saturday night, the first signs of US dissatisfaction became apparent. I contacted the minister of defense and the prime minister's military secretary and expressed my concerns. The military secretary reported back to me a short while later and said that Weisglass, head of the Prime Minister's Office, had checked the matter with US administration officials and that "we had nothing to worry about."

But the very next day, Sunday, US president George W. Bush appeared on television from his family vacation home in Texas. He made it extremely clear that he was dissatisfied with the operation.

Once again, I contacted the minister of defense and prime minister's military secretary. Once again, I received the reply that Weisglass was checking the matter with US Secretary of State Dr. Condoleezza Rice, and that we had nothing to worry about. The public messages were for specific purposes and we should ignore them.

On Tuesday, US ambassador Dan Kurtzer visited the prime minister's sukkah. Kurtzer delivered a loud and clear message regarding the US administration's demand to stop the operation. Sharon immediately ordered termination of the operation.

At the end of the operation, I was curious about the messages that were conveyed from Washington to the Prime Minister's Office. I wondered whether Weisglass had actually checked the information, as he had claimed.

Another event was connected to the "Roadmap," which was supposed to lead to implementation of President Bush's policy, as stated in his speech on June 24, 2002. During 2003, when information on its preparation was accumulating, we discovered that Arab and European officials were involved in formulating the Roadmap. They were trying to influence its wording in a way that would erode the principles set by President Bush in his speech.

The Military Intelligence Directorate, the Mossad, and National Security Advisor (and former Mossad director) Efraim Halevy warned Prime Minister Sharon about the preparation of this document and the erosion of our interests due to the involvement of outside officials. This matter was brought before the prime minister in a meeting. He contacted Weisglass, who was responsible for liaising with the US administration and asked him to what extent this information was true. Weisglass responded that he knew about the document, that he had checked the information, and that it should not be taken seriously.

In October 2003, at the end of the prime minister's visit to Washington, he was given the Roadmap document, which included Arab and European demands that contradicted the spirit of President Bush's speech. Weisglass's avoidance of the warnings led to a document that was bad for the State of Israel – and this document became a cornerstone of US policy regarding the Israeli-Palestinian conflict.

Then the prime minister, and mainly Weisglass, presented the document for approval by the Israeli government. This process also involved diversions and deceptions. An Israeli attempt to amend the document was warded off by the US administration. An Israeli attempt to attach fourteen Israeli comments to the document was also repulsed. Yet when the head of the Prime Minister's Office presented the document in a superficial and manipulative manner, the government approved it.

This event and similar ones resulted in the resignation of National Security Advisor Efraim Halevy. Clearly, Prime Minister Sharon was aware of the behavior of his head of office. I also found opportunities to voice my criticisms of Weisglass's behavior. But the prime minister preferred him over others, which caused me to suspect that he had ulterior motives.

Until late 2003, Israel's achievements under Sharon were significant. Although the transition from defense to offense against the Palestinians was implemented with great delay, it was done well. Cooperation between the various security organizations was excellent. Sharon took a sensible view of reality and understood our situation. His professional and military understanding also meant that working with him was practical and high level. But I did not like the way he treated the Arabs, which was simplistic and aggressive. He exhorted us not to ignore their power as the enemy, but he regarded them with unsophisticated generalization. Nevertheless, when Sharon had to make a decision, he did so in a very impressive manner. From my perspective as DCOGS and COGS until the end of 2003, he led the various state systems with skill.

But then came the disengagement. From the moment the disengagement was put on the table, Sharon was another prime minister. While previous discussions with him were comprehensive and methodic, and enabled all professional bodies to voice their opinions, now there were no discussions at all. To coin a phrase taken from the IDF Armored Corps, it seemed that Sharon had "closed off all openings." For reasons of his own, he chose the disengagement route and refused to hear any other opinion. Yes, there were discussions on the plan, but they were operational, not strategic. They addressed the forces, tasks, and administrative work, but not the strategic purpose or implications of the plan.

Physically there were also changes in Sharon. At first, I did not notice them, but others mentioned them to me and said that he looked sick. He had truly become another person. He lost his vitality. Previously there had been reports of him falling asleep during meetings, but now this became more common. Sometimes he would even close his eyes during one-on-one meetings. Sometimes he spoke out of context. The disengagement was not just a title given by Sharon's public relations advisors to the unilateral withdrawal from Gaza – it was also a fitting description of Sharon's behavior in his dealings with the Palestinians from 2004 onwards.

CHAPTER 13

RESIGNATION LOOMS

The first time that Sharon mentioned the concept of "disengagement" was in December 2003 at the Fourth Herzliya Conference. At this stage, it was still an abstract concept that expressed a direction and a state of mind– not a coherent plan. When Sharon delivered his speech at the major policy conference, I imagined that he was referring to an idea that he had discussed with me regarding the evacuation of three isolated settlements in Gaza: Netzarim, Morag, and Kfar Darom. It was only a few weeks later, in mid-January, that Defense Minister Shaul Mofaz told me that the intention was to evacuate the entire Gaza Strip.

It was at the end of a routine work meeting. Mofaz asked me to remain in the room. After all the aides had left, he dropped the bombshell. Mofaz said that evacuating only three villages would not make a significant difference either way. Therefore, he had advised the prime minister to either conduct a full evacuation of the Gaza Strip, or to abstain from any evacuation. I was shocked.

At this point, Mofaz asked me to keep the matter secret, to refrain from reporting it to the general staff officers and from holding any discussions on the matter. I demanded an audience with the prime minister. I told

Mofaz that I had something to say about the matter, and that I considered it imperative to conduct an orderly and comprehensive discussion with the prime minister before making any irreversible decisions. Mofaz agreed with me and said that it went without saying that such a discussion ought to be held. But in the meantime, he said that I must keep what he had told me a strict secret. I kept the secret until February 2, 2004, when Yoel Marcus publicized Sharon's decision to evacuate all Jewish settlements in the Gaza Strip, in the Israeli daily newspaper *Ha'aretz*. My heart sank. Sharon had committed to a move with far-reaching strategic ramifications without conducting a proper discussion of this initiative, and without consulting with me or with the other parties in charge of Israel's security.

It was only on February 17, 2004, two weeks after the cat was already out of the bag, that the prime minister called the first discussion on disengagement. At this point, it was clear to me that the Americans had been in on the secret since November, and that the Egyptians had also known about it since December or January at the latest. The only ones kept out of the secret were those responsible for Israel's security. Even Defense Minister Shaul Mofaz had been let into the secret at a late stage in the decision-making process.

Another fact came to light that February. Not only had the Americans been informed of the planned disengagement long before the responsible parties in Israel, but the promise to the Americans had also included a significant retreat from the Judea and Samaria region. Somehow, the Americans had received the impression that Israel would retreat not only from the Gaza Strip, but also from most of the West Bank territory. In February 2004, the IDF conducted an analysis of the alternatives to the disengagement and concluded that such a retreat was not an option. We would have to approach the Americans again and convince them to support a partial version of the disengagement plan. The head of the National Security Council, Giora Eiland, described this process as "an attempt to put the toothpaste back in the tube." Beyond the fundamental argument about the propriety of carrying out a one-sided retreat, the way that the process was managed was unbearable. The prime minister's advisor, Dov Weissglass, managed the political contacts concerning the disengagement in an amateurish and irresponsible manner. At times, it felt as if Weissglass had compartmentalized all the factors related to the issue so that he could navigate the process according to his wishes, and that he was not telling the entire truth even to his boss, the prime minister. Weissglass' lack of integrity and flighty management caused unbelievable damage to vital Israeli interests.

In the discussion, which was held at the prime minister's residence, I made it clear that the disengagement must not be a unilateral move. I said that if we had already started the process, it would be right to use unilateral action as a threat against the various players, but we must not fall in love with it. I explained that the unilateral option was the worst option, since it would mean conceding valuable assets while receiving nothing in return, not even a commitment from the other side. How would the disengagement threaten Arafat? By having Israel flee from him? And if Israel fled the Gaza Strip, how would we behave in Judea and Samaria?

During the discussion I didn't present an ideological stand, but rather a professional one. I said that if the disengagement was already a given, and if from a political standpoint we couldn't get out of it, we should at least receive real compensation from the Americans. I explained that if the Americans were to make a clear statement in favor of Israel on the issue of Jerusalem, or the settlement blocs, or the Jordan Valley, or anything related to the right to return, this would at least serve as slight compensation to us for the Palestinian achievement in Gaza. Only if the Palestinians knew that they had paid a high political price for the disengagement, would it be possible to cope with their conception of unilateral retreat as a huge victory for terrorism.

As COGS, I brought up the Philadelphi Route dilemma. I will explain the importance of this route. The Philadelphi Route (or Corridor) as defined in the Oslo Accords is a narrow strip of land at the southern end of the Gaza Strip on the Egyptian border. First, the name "Philadelphi" that appears on IDF maps was randomly selected by a computer and has nothing to do with the US city of Philadelphia. For security purposes, the Oslo Accords define this route as sovereign Israeli territory. It runs almost nine miles (14 km) in length from Kerem Shalom on the southern corner of the Gaza Strip between Israel and Egypt, to the Mediterranean Sea in the north. Its width is between 75 and 110 yards (70–100 m). The Accords defined this narrow corridor as a means for maintaining Israel's security because it provides Israel with control over every passage between Egypt and Gaza. In effect, it serves as an Israeli-controlled buffer zone between the Gaza Strip and Egypt.

The Philadelphi Route's full length as defined on Israeli maps is about 124 miles (200 km). It begins in Israel near Eilat, and from there it runs northwest along the border with Egypt. Inside the Gaza Strip, the route's eastern side passes through the Palestinian half of Rafah, and on the western side it goes through Rafah's Egyptian half. The route ends beside the ruins of Rafiah Yam, the most southwestern of the evacuated Israeli settlements of Gush Katif. The Philadelphi Route also includes the Rafah border crossing, designed to allow Gaza Strip residents to cross to Egypt, while providing Israel with supervisory authority over the individuals crossing the border to ensure that they do not smuggle weapons or otherwise endanger Israeli security.

During that same discussion with Sharon, I explained that if we did not leave the Philadelphi Route (the segment that borders the Gaza Strip from Kerem Shalom up to the sea), and if we did not allow for a ground border crossing from the Gaza Strip to Egypt, we would not be conducting a true disengagement from Gaza. We would still be held responsible for everything that happened there. On the other hand, if we were to leave the Philadelphi Route before Gaza established a responsible and efficient leadership, we would soon have Hamas-stan, Hezbollah-stan, and Al-Qaeda-stan in the Gaza Strip.

Full disengagement would mean cutting off the Gaza Strip from the West Bank, and from the Palestinian point of view, this would have been a high price to pay. It would have eradicated the concept of "safe crossing" between the two areas and annulled the concept of the Gaza Strip and the West Bank as one territorial unit. But I understood that during his contacts with the Americans and Egyptians, Weissglass had pledged that this would not happen, so this advantage had already slipped away from us. I also saw an advantage in the financial aspect of a full disengagement between the State of Israel and the Gaza Strip. But I realized that Weissglas had already sent clear, soothing messages to Egypt about this issue as well. Weissglass had pledged that the State of Israel would continue to provide electricity, water, and merchandise to the Gaza Strip, while maintaining the joint economic principles between Israel and the Palestinian Authority in accordance with the Paris Agreement. I realized that we were about to enter the worst of all possible worlds.

To my mind, the disengagement would have two additional serious repercussions. First, retreating from the very last millimeter of land created a dangerous precedent to determining the border in Judea and Samaria. In the West Bank, defensible borders are requisite – and the 1967 border lines are not defensible. Second, conceding control of the borders shattered an Israeli principle on which we had insisted even during the Taba discussions. Moreover, in practice, this move constituted an Israeli concession of our demand to demilitarize the Palestinian territories.

But beyond these specific points, I assessed that the disengagement was a serious mistake because it would boost terrorism, strengthen Hamas, and greatly weaken Palestinian moderates. I saw the disengagement as significantly strengthening the false Palestinian narrative that "the problem is Israel's 1967 'occupation' of the territories." In my assessment, the Arab world would view disengagement as a defeat for Israel in its battle against terror. That perception would cause damage not only to Israel, but also to the United States and to other Western countries. I knew that the combination of demonstrating Israeli weakness in Gaza and American difficulties in Iraq would encourage radical Islam and have serious repercussions for events in the Middle East. While 2003 was a record year in the offensive against extremist forces in the region, 2005 was about to become a year of dangerous retreat from them. Such retreat would not bring peace, and even the quiet that it might yield would be short-lived.

The discussion held on February 17, 2004, was positive. Alongside the political pressure placed on Sharon, it started the process that led to the publication of President Bush's letter to Sharon in April 2004. For the first time, the United States recognized that Israel would keep the settlement blocs in its possession under a final status agreement. However, this letter did not give a reasonable solution to the defects inherent in the disengagement concept. I watched Sharon during the discussion, and I realized that we had already crossed the Rubicon. Sharon had made a decision, and now he had to execute it. Sharon understood that he could not blink, because if he blinked, his entire political future would be in jeopardy. My assessment was that strategically, Sharon did not believe in the disengagement. It was entirely contrary to his worldview. But in order to save himself politically, especially in light of the investigations that he and his sons were under for suspected acts of corruption, Sharon realized he had to complete this mistaken process. For him, the battle over disengagement became a personal political battle – life or death.

Sharon was right to believe that if he fed Israeli media the fat bait of disengagement, the media would let him off on corruption. In this respect, the disengagement truly was successful.

I did not invent the use of the term "protect like an *etrog* (citron)" regarding Sharon. It was coined by senior journalist and commentator Amnon Abramovich, who guarded Sharon like a precious ceremonial citron. In other words, he protected Sharon from accusations of corruption so that he could carry out the disengagement undisturbed. He did this knowingly and intentionally, and even boasted about it. But what the term *etrog* really implies is corruption. It means that the press has ceased to play the accepted role that it ought to play in democratic regimes. Sharon understood the nature of the media at that time in Israel, and he manipulated it cunningly.

I can imagine that Sharon justified his actions by saying to himself that because only he could save the State of Israel, he should do everything possible to ensure his own political future. Sharon truly believed that the other Israeli leaders around him were irresponsible and lacked judgment and nerve. The events that have transpired since Sharon's departure do not refute this assessment. But from my perspective as COGS, the prime minister had suddenly turned in an irrational direction in terms of security and strategy. I was not certain that Sharon could see the whole picture. I was not sure that he understood the implications of his move on the strengthening of radical forces in Israel's immediate and more distant environments. I was very worried, and I asked myself what my duty was as chief of general staff.

X

My tenure as COGS was not easy. I conducted a complex and difficult battle against terrorism. Even in my previous positions I had often experienced "commander's loneliness." Heavy responsibilities had been entrusted to me also in my previous positions. But never in my life had I suffered from insomnia. My insomnia began in the spring of 2004. I worried over Israel's future and I could not sleep.

I considered resigning. On sleepless nights, I wondered whether my resignation would be beneficial. At first, I hoped that this runaway train would stop at a station. I believed that the government might halt the process, or that the Knesset would do so. During that period, the possibility of carrying out a referendum also came up. But when I saw that the train was not stopping, I thought that if my resignation would stop it, I would take this unprecedented step.

But my assessment of the situation led me to the opposite conclusion. Resignation would be possible and even imperative in a case of manifestly illegal decisions or actions. Yet despite all my objections to the disengagement, I could not define it as illegal. Therefore, in this case, resigning would approach the level of a military coup. My resignation would have undermined the strength of Israeli democracy. After the terrible harm to the democratic system caused by the murder of Yitzhak Rabin, I was determined not to do anything that could be interpreted as a blow to democratically elected people and institutions – even if, in my eyes, the path they chose was wrong.

I have often participated in conversations that raised the question of whether there is a possibility of a military coup in Israel. The conversation almost always ends with agreement that democratic values are deeply rooted in Israeli society and the IDF, and therefore there is no chance of this happening. Until the signing of the Oslo agreement, I used to say in these discussions that Israeli democracy was strong, so there were two types of antidemocratic events which I did not believe could ever transpire in Israel: political assassination of a prime minister and a military coup. After the signing of the Oslo Accords, I changed my assessment pertaining to the first option, which unfortunately materialized.

I could see the threat of surging internal antidemocratic reactions in Israeli society in general, and in the army in particular. I was aware of every call and decision to refuse military service, and I ordered that these be handled with a firm hand.

I instructed commanders to discuss the issue with their soldiers. I myself did so in my visits to units. I also met with rabbis, and heads of yeshivas and pre-military institutions, and I conveyed to them my position about refusal to serve. I believe that because my opposition to the disengagement process was leaked, this helped me to convey my determined position against refusal to serve.

I knew that once the decision to carry out the disengagement had been accepted and approved by the political system, the IDF's performance became a test of Israeli society and democracy. Fortunately, the IDF and Israeli society passed this difficult test.

As an officer, I always made sure to play by the rules of the democratic process. In my senior positions, I made certain not to come out publicly against a decision made by the political echelon, even if I thought or recommended against the decision. In this case as well, I was careful not to make public statements against the disengagement. But pervasive leaks, even from the most closed forums, resulted in the publication of my objections. Some took advantage of my public statement at the Herzliya Conference in early 2003, long before the decision on the disengagement, and turned it into a political poster. Indeed, I foresaw a danger that the disengagement would give a boost to Islamic jihad and terrorism, and I said so in closed forums in which the COGS is expected to present his professional opinion. The words quoted on the poster were said at the Herzliya Conference, in answer to a question about the possibility of evacuating a settlement like Netzarim in Gaza in order to save the battalion that protected it. I answered that I opposed any withdrawal under fire. I explained that what might appear to be saving a battalion would require us to send a whole division as reinforcement, since withdrawal under fire would give a boost to terrorism. All this happened long before the disengagement plan was on the agenda.

Although I was careful not to express myself publicly against the political echelon's decision, I realized that some individuals were trying to incite the prime minister and the defense minister against me. I learned that the prime minister avoided reading newspapers and documents, and instead received oral reports about their content. I knew that this could be used as a means of manipulating Sharon, and I suspected that Dov Weisglass, the head of the Prime Minister's Office, was using it.

As COGS, I was very limited in my ability to attend entertainment or cultural events. One evening mid-week, the Tzavta theater hosted a book launch, and my wife Ada asked me to join her. The location was near my office in the Kiryah, so I agreed.

Before I entered the theater, I received a phone call from the IDF spokesperson, Brigadier General Ruth Yaron, regarding a report by Channel 2 commentator Amnon Abramovich on the prime minister's intention to dismiss me for "public statements against the disengagement" – statements that I had never made. I was forced to spend the evening outside the theater, talking on the phone in an attempt to clarify the matter. After studying the contents of the report, I phoned Defense Minister Mofaz and the prime minister's military secretary, Major General Yoav Galant, and then I asked to speak to the prime minister himself.

Sharon sounded angry in our conversation and claimed he had been informed that I had made public statements against the disengagement. I denied this claim outright. The prime minister asked me to deny it publicly in my own voice on the radio the next morning, or to release a message through the IDF spokesperson retracting these words. I clarified to Sharon that I did not intend to retract words I had not said. I suspected that such a retraction would be exploited by Sharon's people, who would present my words as an expression of support for the disengagement. This incident had repercussions for our relationship.

Prime Minister Sharon and his gang of supporters completely disregarded my loyalty as chief of general staff to the government and its decisions. As far as Sharon and his Ranch Forum were concerned, I had become a strategic threat. Sharon and his forum were entirely invested in the disengagement. They saw disengagement as the ultimate goal for Israel. Given that values such as statesmanship and proper management did not run in their veins, it was difficult for them to understand how a senior officer could be very critical of the process they were leading, but still determined to implement it properly. Sharon and his circle attached paramount importance to personal loyalty as a value. The Ranch Forum was not able to understand or appreciate the values of loyalty to state institutions, government decisions, and the law.

But beyond the matter of the disengagement, there was another issue that soured relations between the prime minister and myself – namely, the Ranch Forum's attempts to intervene in the military, particularly in the appointments of senior officers. One of many striking examples was the appointment of the prime minister's military secretary. This is a highly sensitive appointment, which affects the way the political leadership relates to the military leadership on issues of Israel's security. As is customary, I made a list of candidates who I believed were worthy and qualified for the job. I met with Defense Minister Shaul Mofaz to discuss the list, and he confirmed it. I took the list and the candidates' personal files to a working meeting with the prime minister. We discussed several issues during this meeting. When it came time to discuss the appointment of the prime minister's military secretary, Sharon wanted to know which candidates I recommended. I had prepared a detailed evaluation of each of the candidates. Sharon wrote the five names on a note, placed it in his pocket, and said that he had no time to discuss the matter. That ended the discussion. A few days later, Defense Minister Mofaz told me that "they" were saying that the list that I had submitted could not be considered under any circumstances. "They" were asking why I had not included a certain sixth candidate. My response was sharp. I did not understand who "they" were. More accurately, I understood, but I refused to accept it. I did not know how it was possible to reject a whole list without discussing it in an orderly fashion. I did not understand how it was possible to take a professional matter of first-class security importance and turn it into yet another topic that the Ranch Forum discussed and tried to manage. I realized what was behind this: those who were friends of Omri Sharon stayed on the list, and those who were not his friends were disqualified. The candidate "they" wanted was someone whom Omri Sharon knew from his military service – a good officer, but not ripe yet for this position, in my professional opinion.

The military secretary affair was one of many. In 2003 and 2004, as Sharon's political power increased, and members of his group felt that they controlled the country, I noticed an unacceptable attempt by government officials to meddle deep within the IDF. Omri Sharon and Dov Weisglass, and perhaps even the prime minister himself, maintained direct and inappropriate contact with senior IDF officers. They did not respect the requisite separation between the political leadership and some of the senior officers. A process of corruption was taking place. Officers received invitations and offers similar to those I had received years earlier, and not everyone was resisting the challenge. An increasing number of officers understood the message conveyed to them from the top: their promotion would not be determined in accordance with their professional work and its results, but based on their closeness and their loyalty to the Ranch Forum. To me, this message was disastrous. It turned the improper phenomena that we had witnessed previously into an accepted norm – the corrupt and corrupting norm of the Sharon family.

In early 2005, things deteriorated further. The appointment of the head of the Military Intelligence Directorate and of GOCs were on the agenda, and Sharon and his people were trying to take over these appointments. I realized that they were trying to carry out a coup and ensure that a significant part of the General Staff would be under their complete control.

I decided to put the brakes on this. Since it had not been decided whether I would continue in my position for another year, I thought it would not be right for me to determine the composition of the next chief of general staff's headquarters, so I delayed the new appointments. I realized that extension of my term was contingent on my willingness to appoint whoever "they" wanted. This infuriated Prime Minister Sharon, Weisglass, and the prime minister's son Omri. I had dared to raise serious questions about the strategic rationale of the disengagement, and now I was adding insult to injury: I blocked them in action. I did not let them take over the IDF's top brass.

At that time, a large part of my conflict was with Omri Sharon and Dov Weisglass, directly and indirectly. I confronted Omri, who was a member of Knesset, in the Foreign Affairs and Defense Committee, and I could see Weisglass'ss fingerprints in many events. But in retrospect, I realize that the main responsibility for the disruption of norms lay with Sharon himself. Ariel Sharon had acted that way as an officer, he acted that way as a politician, and he exhibited the same behavior as defense minister during the Lebanon War. He had no respect for the law or ethics, for rules or regulations. Sharon did not really understand the meaning of democracy or a state governed by civil law. As soon as he felt strong enough, he tried to weaken the prosecution, the police, and any other system that could challenge him. He tried to ensure that the primary loyalty of all the people occupying sensitive positions in government was to him. At a certain point, after achieving this goal in the police, Sharon's appetite increased and he wanted to take over the IDF. But as COGS, I was the barrier to this process. Sharon knew very well that I would not allow him to turn the IDF into a subsidiary of Sycamore Ranch. As far as Sharon was concerned, he was left with no choice: he had to get rid of me. He had to remove the obstacle from his path.

During the same period, the relationship between the minister of defense and myself also disintegrated. Mofaz and I had worked together splendidly when he was COGS and I was his deputy, and also at the beginning of my term as COGS, when he was defense minister. To my mind, Mofaz was a good COGS. I did not like his conduct, but as a commander, he knew how to make decisions and implement them.

However, in his new position as defense minister just after his tenure as COGS, Mofaz could not adjust. When I came to him for discussions, I naturally brought the military outlook to the table, assuming that he would represent the civilian system and give insights from that perspective. I had worked with several defense ministers – civilians and former military personnel – who brought the civilian perspective to discussions. In contrast, Mofaz did not adopt the civilian approach. Meetings with him were meetings between a COGS and a former COGS, and not with a defense minister. As a result, I was very concerned that military thinking would dominate the political-strategic discourse, and the danger inherent in this. I myself often had to raise nonmilitary aspects in the discussion, because no one else raised them. The COGS needs a civilian partner, and in Mofaz's days as defense minister, this function was not filled. Instead, he tried many times to function as COGS. I did not allow him to do this, and this caused conflicts between us.

This acute problem was not the only one. Mofaz was an appointed defense minister. He was not a member of the Knesset, and at that time was essentially devoid of political power. He became dependent on Prime Minister Ariel Sharon – basically one of Sharon's lackeys. Any lackey of Sharon's also became a lackey of Sharon's disciples – chiefly, Sharon's son Omri and his bureau chief Dov Weisglass. They called Mofaz the "operations officer" (who executes the commander's decisions). I observed the situation from the sidelines and understood Mofaz's behavior, so I was not surprised when Mofaz and Sharon began looking frantically for the opportunity to get rid of me. They maneuvered to make this happen.

On February 14, 2005, near Netanya, there was a dinner for wounded soldiers from the Army Combat Engineering Corps. At the end of the evening, Defense Minister Mofaz, several other officers, and I held a consultation in a small side room, about an operational matter. At the end of the consultation, Mofaz asked me to remain alone with him in the room. After the others had left, Mofaz told me that the prime minister and he had decided that from now on, the chief of general staff's tenure would last for only three years and would not be extended to a fourth year as had been the case till then. This decision, Mofaz said, would be effective immediately.

I asked Mofaz whether something was wrong, whether he had reservations about my work as COGS.

"Not at all," said Mofaz. "We have great respect for you. This respect will also be reflected in the report to the press that we will soon release announcing the end of your tenure. The decision is one of principle."

We were sitting in the event hall manager's office, surrounded by plates of bourekas pastries and half-filled soft drink bottles. There was something right in the fact that this wrong deed should be done in this manner, in the wrong spot and with the wrong timing. Mofaz was clearly embarrassed, but he had been given a task and he did it. He apologized for the timing and the location but said that since Dov Weisglass had been involved in the discussion, he feared that the news would be leaked, and he did not want me to hear about it in the media. He felt it was his duty to inform me personally.

I had mixed feelings about the news. On the one hand, I felt great relief. For a long time I'd felt that I had been caught between a rock and a hard place because of the disengagement, the corruption, and the way state matters were being managed. Then here comes Mofaz, as Sharon's emissary, and releases me from this pressure. But on the other hand, I was outraged and insulted at the scheming way in which they rationalized my removal on grounds of "principle" (limiting the term of office of the COGS to three years). As expected, they gave the media other reasons – my opposition to the disengagement and claims that I had failed as COGS.

The spin flew out of control, and I was delegitimized. The press celebrated the disengagement, and they were fueled by Sharon's and Mofaz's bureaus and largely accepted this power move. A serious, ethical press should not have accepted it. Only a few journalists asked pointed questions.

Sharon, in his political wisdom, distanced himself from the move. At first, he did not even speak with me about the decision to end my tenure. He let Mofaz do the job. Two weeks later, Sharon phoned me personally and invited me to lunch at the prime minister's residence for a private chat. In the phone conversation, Sharon heaped praises on me and thanked me for all I had done. I queried, "So why did you choose this time to decide to limit the chief of general staff's tenure to three years?" Sharon said that Mofaz had contacted him and said that he could not continue to work with me anymore. Sharon even offered to help if I were interested in obtaining another position. I declined the offer politely and told him that I had other plans for after the end of my military service.

In a work meeting with Mofaz later the same day, he inquired, "How was the meeting with the prime minister?" I told him that Sharon had told me that Mofaz was responsible for the decision, due to my strained working relationship with the defense minister. "What?" Mofaz jumped as if he'd been bitten by a snake. "That's what he said?"

I knew who had planned the move and who had carried it out. I realized that all those involved were lying – even to each other.

Ultimately, this aggressive move not only harmed the accepted norms of governance in Israel, the position of COGS, and the fabric of the relationship between the political and military leaderships. It also meant that a professional officer, who stood his ground against the prime minister and defense minister while maintaining absolute loyalty to the elected government, was replaced with a chief and deputy chief of general staff whose main merits were that they were intimates of the prime minister and his family. I have no doubt that this move affected the outcome of the Second Lebanon War.

As fate would have it, the same week in which Sharon and Mofaz notified me about the end of my tenure, I presented the disengagement implementation plan to the defense minister for his approval. I had labored on the plan for months. Mofaz approved the plan with no comments. At the same time the press published "explanations" for the need to replace me, with the reason: "Lieutenant General Ya'alon is not preparing the IDF properly to carry out the disengagement."

When I realized that the intended date for replacing me, July 9, 2005, was near the planned date of the disengagement, I decided to bring forward the completion of my tenure. I did this to allow my successor, Dan Halutz, to prepare personally for this complex mission.

From the moment the end of my tenure was declared, I was flooded with letters of encouragement and a wave of public sympathy. Everywhere I went, I met cheering and supportive crowds, even outside the IDF, when I went privately to attend a theater performance. In those days, I could not run on the street or the beach, as I usually did, because people I didn't know stopped me to shake hands and say something. The public reaction was my source of inspiration and hope, because I realized that it was not possible to fool the entire public with "spin." The public has its own wisdom.

I never saw myself as a professional soldier, but rather as someone who became a professional soldier out of duty. I did not attend a military boarding school, and during my compulsory military service I did not attend an officers' training course. I did not see warfare as my purpose in life. But things turned out differently. Ever since I was a soldier in compulsory service in Paratroopers Battalion 50 of Nahal, and throughout my years in the military, I served on the frontline of Israel's struggles against its Arab enemies in general, and its Palestinian enemies in particular. I fought in the War of Attrition and pursued the enemy in the Beit She'an Valley, Jordan Valley, and the Arava during 1969–1970. I took part in the war on terror in Gaza in 1971–1972. I participated in Operation Litani in 1978 and the First Lebanon War in 1982, and I participated in depth raids, some against the Palestinian terrorist headquarters. In addition, I was commander of the Judea and Samaria Division from 1992–1993.

But it was not until June 1995, when I was appointed MI chief, that I mounted the command bridge from which the Israeli campaign against our Palestinian opponents is managed. From then and through the end of my tenure as COGS – for ten consecutive years – I was part of the senior Israeli team responsible for the State of Israel's security and its plan for facing the Palestinian challenge. Therefore, when I took off my uniform and with it, the responsibility entrusted in its wearer, I was able to look back from the perspective of a participant in information processing and decision making.

I looked back on how Israel conducted itself during an extremely important decade in the face of its closest and bitterest enemy. The 1990s were years of illusion. After September 1993, most of the Israeli leadership assumed that Arafat's PLO was Israel's strategic ally that would assist us to take steps toward a "two states for two peoples" solution and would ultimately realize it. The concept that guided the Israeli government and the IDF top brass was a version of Yasser Arafat who had given up his dream of annihilating Israel. Israel thought he had become a rational actor who sought to establish a Palestinian state that would live alongside Israel, and not replace it. Although we had accumulated a large amount of information that contradicted this conception, the decision makers did not internalize it or bring it to the public's attention. When I took up my position as head of Military Intelligence, I was very surprised to discover that the intelligence material that reached my desk often starkly contrasted the public mood, media reports, and worldview that guided the country's leaders. This gap made me think seriously about how public discourse is conducted and how national policy is formulated in Israel.

After only a few months as chief of military intelligence, I realized that we had a dangerous tendency to close our eyes and lead ourselves astray.

More than the Palestinians deceived us in the 1990's, we deceived ourselves. However, the illusion of the 1990's was for many an illusion in good faith. In a sense, as I mentioned earlier, even today I do not totally disapprove of the Oslo move. I thought that given Israel's reality, it was important to investigate the option of peace with the Palestinians to clarify for ourselves whether there was a Palestinian partner for this possibility. If it turned out that this was not the case, I believed that we ought to close ranks around this issue and minimize internal divisions and polarization. Although today I am certain that the Oslo process was wrong, I can understand the logic behind it. I understand the need to try the path of compromise and mutual recognition. I believe that this test also helped Israel in retrospect in several ways, but it was not fully exploited.

For me, the grave process that occurred in the Israeli governmental and political system was not the choice to pursue the Oslo peace process, but rather ignoring its failure. Evidence of its failure kept accumulating. At some point in the mid-1990s, the illusion ceased to be in good faith. Rabin went into partnership with Arafat with eyes wide open, a sober perception of reality, and butterflies in his stomach. But even when it became clear that it had become fraudulent, those who replaced him continued the partnership. Government leaders, military officers, government officials, and journalists at the most senior level lent a hand to the conspiracy of silence, which was designed to continue to foster the illusion of Arafat even when it was clear that the illusion was shattered. In the face of this reality, I found myself alone and isolated, along with a small group of other people. I found that trying to speak the truth to those who do not want to hear it leads them to label and discredit you. I discovered that Israel was acting out of complete blindness to what was happening around it. Senior Israeli officials systematically cultivated and preserved this blindness.

Against this background, the year 2000 created a critical historical moment of immeasurable importance. Until 2000, we could try to rationalize Arafat's behavior one way or another. After 2000, the excuses became hollow. Until 2000, Israel could nurture the hope that further concessions would satisfy the Palestinians' seemingly unrelenting hunger. After 2000, it was obvious that no concessions would bring the Palestinians to true recognition of Israel as a Jewish state. But even at this late stage, when Israel was under Arafat's terror war that aimed to undermine and defeat the State of Israel, the members of the conspiracy of silence did not demonstrate the intellectual courage required of them. They did not admit their error and did not stand up assertively against Yasser Arafat. As a result, Israel's war on terror from September 2000 until March 2002 was indecisive and ineffective. Even when Israel launched a counterattack in 2002, it still had not achieved internal consensus on the narrative of the Palestinian conflict. Many still insisted on sticking with the remains of the old worldview. Reality had proven in the most brutal way possible that this was not a conflict about the conquest of territory in the Six-Day War, and that the Palestinians did not accept the existence of Israel as a Jewish state. Yet the disillusioned insisted on preserving the gentler forms of illusion. So, Israel was unable to translate the military success it achieved in 2002–2004 into a sustainable diplomatic achievement.

Again, the Israeli public discourse returned to outdated concepts such as "permanent arrangement – now" or "two-state solution – immediately." In my opinion, this is why Prime Minister Sharon ultimately decided to carry out the disengagement, which contradicted his entire worldview – thus shattering the same strategy that he himself had formulated and navigated. He apparently knew that such a decision would earn the support of influential parties in the media, academia, and politics – and he was not wrong. So, after seven years of bitter struggle with Palestinian extremism, Israel was trapped in a position where it was led instead of leading, withdrew instead of winning. Instead of utilizing the strategic achievement it had earned, which could have led to a historic turning point, Israel dropped the ball of achievement and deepened the sense that it was in a difficult situation of retreat and delay.

The Hamas victory in the Palestinian elections in January 2006 and its takeover of the Gaza Strip in June 2007 are a result of Israel's strategic inconsistency. These two events occurred after I completed my tenure as COGS. But both events are tied deeply to the crucial mistakes that Israel made during my tenure, and against which I had protested. It is true that these events are also associated with profound processes taking place in the Arab and Muslim world, but I have no doubt that Israel made a decisive contribution to their occurrence. The origin of this contribution is not the failure of a military operation of one kind or another. Rather it is the Israeli leadership's deep conceptual failure to recognize the historical truth in which Israel exists. Intellectual dishonesty, the tendency to deceive, and the desire to impose an irrelevant paradigm on reality, had a gloomy result. At the end of a decade of struggle against the Palestinian terrorist challenge, Israel's situation had not improved. It had worsened.

To a large extent, this failure reflects the inability of Israeli government systems to deal rationally and effectively with the country's main problems. During the ten years that I served in key positions in the IDF top brass, I had a front-seat view of how Israel manages its struggle with the Palestinians, and more importantly, of the state's behavior in numerous fields.

What I saw during those years was not a pretty sight. Most heads of government under whom I worked – Rabin, Netanyahu, Barak, Sharon (especially early in his career) – conducted serious and appropriate discussions about fateful questions and knew how to make decisions. But for the most part, the mode of operation of the Prime Minister's Office and the government system as a whole provoked my criticism and concern. While the IDF conducts organized staff work and tests alternatives before making a decision, the civilian system to which the

IDF is subordinate often tends to be superficial, amateurish, and tainted by extraneous political considerations.

Looking back at how Israel acted during those years, I can state unequivocally that the three power groups – the wealthy, the media, and the activist court – made it difficult for the country's leadership to properly address the threats it faced. At least two of these three groups – the wealthy and the media – were partners in building and preserving a false image of reality. Both were active partners in setting an irrelevant political paradigm.

As COGS charged with managing a complex, multidimensional war on Palestinian terror, I felt almost daily how a distorted picture of reality and a groundless self-serving or ideological paradigm caused serious difficulty for those who were fighting for Israel's existential interests. I felt that the main problem I faced was not in front of me, but rather behind me. A lack of sober recognition of reality and repeated need to blame the Israeli side for everything became heavy burdens and hampered me in carrying out my mission. To this I add the fact that many of the politicians to whom I answered in the government and the Knesset did not demonstrate an appropriate level of responsibility and acted not out of overall national interests, but to advance personal or political interests.

As a result, I often felt the rug being pulled out from under me. I felt that the Israelis themselves were toppling the wall that I thought should be built to protect Israel's security. Some of those Israelis acted in good faith to promote their beliefs. Others acted cynically and recklessly. Both groups did not allow those managing the battle to do so as a country should wage a battle for its survival. Ultimately, the direct and indirect pressure that those individuals and power groups applied on the national leadership caused it to break down at a critical moment. Israel has paid a high price for this breakdown, and in 2008, that is what pushed me to go into politics.

CHAPTER 14

Arrogance and Complacency

After I completed my tenure as COGS in June 2005, and after Israel carried out the disengagement in August 2005, in the best possible way as far as the IDF was concerned, I understood that Israel must prepare for another terror offensive that would be launched against it from the north or the south. While our unilateral withdrawal from Gaza had earned praise within Israel, the hostile elements that surrounded Israel saw it as a sign of weakness. The Middle East does not tolerate weakness and is unforgiving toward the weak. So, I predicted that within a short time, Hamas, or Hezbollah, or both, would challenge Israel. I knew that once our enemies realized that Israel was unable to withstand the pressure exerted on it, they would try to renew that pressure in order to gain further achievements. As soon as they reached the conclusion that violence pays, I knew that they would use violence to strike Israel again and push us to further withdrawals. In Hamas'ss view, this would bring Israel closer to destruction.

Based on this assessment, I thought that if I were still COGS, I would be putting the military into an emergency state of readiness. In 2000, the high command prepared the IDF for the terror war that broke out in September of that year. The IDF had accurately predicted this war. In the same way, at the end of 2005, after carrying out the disengagement, the IDF senior commanders should have prepared the armed forces for the test that would inevitably arrive in 2006. But unfortunately, and to my astonishment, the COGS who replaced me, Lieutenant General Dan Halutz, did not see the situation as I saw it and as senior general staff officers saw it.

In 2006, Israel held elections. Prime Minister Ariel Sharon had suffered a stroke and was replaced by his deputy, Ehud Olmert. The new ruling party was Kadima, which had promoted disengagement and convergence. It boasted about the achievements of the disengagement and offered to continue it through convergence – another unilateral, extensive retreat from Judea and Samaria. When this is the agenda of the ruling party, when elections control the atmosphere, and when most of the public believes the story that the media tells it about the success of the disengagement, it is very difficult to swim against the current. It is difficult to face the prime minister and tell him that he is detached from reality. It is hard to face the public and tell it that it has been fed an illusion. Further, it is tough to disobey the power groups of wealth and the media, which had turned the disengagement and the convergence into veritable "golden calves."

Chief of General Staff Halutz did not swim against the current – rather, he swam with it. He ignored the sober analysis of reality that the army itself had made. He ignored intelligence warnings. In his public speeches and in his manner, he conveyed a sense of arrogance and complacency. The message he conveyed was, "Our situation has never been better." This message matched the political interests of the chief of general staff's superiors. It was also consistent with the spirit of the time and the desires of the leading power groups. Halutz created a situation where the COGS was lauded as the hero of the disengagement, and he won favorable treatment from the media. This message was not only false – it was also destructive. Halutz caused the IDF system to become complacent. Instead of training, preparing for the future and being primed for conflict, the IDF began to show signs of weakness.

Ben-Gurion once said that in order to be victorious in battle,

> We need three things: courage, wisdom, and purity. We need courage to create and build, to defend ourselves, to demolish the terrorists. But we also need reason at this mad hour, in this bloody tangle... We must find the way to increase our helpful allies and reduce the number of our enemies as much as possible. We also need purity... Our strength lies in the Jewish people's great asset – our moral heritage, the moral purity of our lives, of our children, our aspirations, our ways of engaging with the world. We will stand with these three qualities – courage, wisdom, and purity – all the way to victory.

Unfortunately, after my term as COGS, these three foundation stones were replaced by arrogance, a sense that we know it all, a conviction that no one else is as worthy as me.

This new approach was unacceptable to me. I do not believe that certain people know everything. I cannot believe in a person who is so self-confident that he does not need to hear the opinions of others. When I see these types of people, who radiate superficial and arrogant charisma, I know that they will end up falling. I heard about this spirit in the army before the outbreak of the Second Lebanon War, and I was not tranquil. I saw signs that something had gone deeply wrong in the IDF's conduct.

Three flaws bothered me in particular. The first was the tendency of senior commanders not to go into detail. They engaged only in the macro. The perception was that the COGS was like a chairman of the board, and therefore he did not need to get to the bottom of specific events. But in the State of Israel and the IDF, when the supreme commander conveys that he has no interest in the details, his subordinates develop laxity in dealing with details. The art of command requires providing maximum freedom of action to the troops, but commanders must be knowledgeable about the details, and they must be able to intervene when necessary.

Several events that occurred between the summer of 2005 and the summer of 2006 indicated that the COGS was disconnected from the field. He was unfamiliar with the particulars of sensitive combat operations and significant situations of tension in the border areas. As a result, the high command inhabited its own world. This was not the world of the soldiers and commanders in the field, and it was not the reality they had to face.

The most notable instance of this disconnect that was exposed to the public was Halutz's statement in a press briefing immediately after the kidnapping of Gilad Schalit. He announced that there had been no warning of the attack. A few hours later, one of the soldiers injured in the attack was interviewed and said that there had been such a warning. This fact was confirmed by senior officers and the head of the Shin Bet (ISA). In the Israeli reality, it was inconceivable to me that the COGS would not know about this warning or ignore it. It should have led him to conduct a site visit, to check the troops' level of readiness, or at least to speak on the phone with the GOC to check the level of readiness of forces on the ground. He should have verified what special measures were being taken to prevent the terrorists from carrying out their plot.

The second flaw was even worse. Since I had been appointed GOC of Central Command in the late 1990s, I had learned that one of the challenges I faced was to define for myself the reality in which I was working. I had to stay relevant. We live in a world of constant change and clashes that change shape frequently, and this mandates continuous and intense analytical work. We must constantly "read the map" and formulate the correct operational patterns for that map as it changes.

One of the things I learned at Central Command and brought with me to the Joint Chiefs of Staff is that we must think, and we must value thinking. The successes we achieved in the war against terrorism between 2000 and 2005 were largely the result of such thought processes. The proper preparation for the execution of the disengagement was also based on the thought processes carried out by the senior command, under my leadership. Statements such as "the military's role is to execute and not to think," and "the IDF is the execution contractor, and the political echelon should do the thinking" reflect a failure to understand the general staff's role regarding strategic thinking in the interface between the military and the political echelons. They also reflect a lack of understanding of the general staff's operational thinking role in the interface between the general staff, military branches, and subordinates. In the Second Lebanon War, we witnessed the consequences when the general staff, headed by the COGS, failed to fill this function.

Twentieth-century challenges require leadership that is participative, not tyrannical. Participative leadership means encouraging a corporate culture in which the commander does not know everything. Subordinates are required to be proficient in their field, to develop knowledge, and to teach the commander – not only to provide information. In such a culture, the commander encourages his subordinates to voice their opinion, even if it is critical of him, in the spirit of the slogan "Freedom of thought and expression – obedience in action." But after I retired from the army, a different command style took over. This style was based on quick decisions based on intuition, without consultation or thorough examination of the situation which they affected. After years in which the IDF had developed a thinking culture, which to the best of my judgment proved itself, came a COGS who destroyed this culture in one fell swoop. He replaced it with a charismatic and arrogant type of populistic leadership.

The third flaw was ethical. The new chief of general staff, Halutz, and his deputy Moshe Kaplinsky (Kaplan) were members of Ariel Sharon's Ranch Forum entourage. The same publicists who served Sharon also served Halutz and Kaplinsky. The same entourage of wealth and media that surrounded the government – especially since the disengagement – surrounded Halutz and Kaplinsky as well. This resulted in a dangerous blurring of boundaries between the political and military echelons. Norms that belonged to the world of politics seeped into the army. Adherence to the principle of telling the truth weakened. Adherence to the atmosphere of modesty and ethics in the military also became lax. Once more, the situation proved that there is nothing stronger than a personal example – whether positive or negative. When I examined the IDF, I felt that within a very short time, moral and professional norms had been eroded among some military leaders. Brigadier General Miri Regev replaced General Ruth Yaron, the professional and experienced IDF spokeswoman whom I had appointed. Yet Regev acted as the chief of general staff's public relations' aid, and not the IDF's spokeswoman. Certain senior officers mingled with senior government officials. During my tenure as COGS, I had worked diligently against corrupting processes. But after I left, these processes intensified. The criminal subculture raised its head, and many officers accepted the message transmitted to them by the system: those with connections will advance. Those with connections to government, money, and the media were carried on their shoulders. In this reality, the biggest rewards were not given for real work and telling the truth, but for participating in the internal political game, which was both corrupt and corrupting.

These deficiencies led to my great disappointment in my successor, Dan Halutz. I had known Dan as an excellent air force commander. To his credit, he pushed the IDF forward in many fields and was responsible for the integration of the air force in the combat against Palestinian terrorism to an unprecedented extent. Under his command, the air force also excelled in providing a solution to other challenges, less known to the public. During my tenure as COGS, Dan was my deputy for nearly a year, and performed the task very well. There were things I did not like about his behavior, and we discussed this during his service as well as during the transition period. I believed that after he was appointed COGS and given the weight of responsibility that comes with the mission, Dan would undergo the necessary change. So, I supported his candidacy for the position, along with the other candidate, Gabi Ashkenazi. But unfortunately, I was disappointed. My disappointment in Dan Halutz's behavior arose before July 12, 2006.

The Second Lebanon War exposed all the failings in Halutz's personal conduct, at great cost. I believed that he should have resigned (along with the political echelon) immediately after the war. When he did not, I was forced to call for his resignation.

On July 12, 2006, Hezbollah militants crossed into Israel from Lebanon and ambushed two IDF vehicles, killing three soldiers and capturing two other soldiers, provoking the Second Lebanon War. At that time, I was in Washington, DC, writing a research paper for the Washington Institute for Near East Policy. The events on that day were not surprising. For years, we had prepared for the scenario of a kidnapping by Hezbollah. Anyone who observed the processes that occurred in the Arab world after the 2005 disengagement could conclude there was a high probability of such abductions in 2006. Therefore, on the day of the kidnapping and over the next two days, I was not particularly worried. I knew that the IDF had analyzed the Hezbollah challenge in depth, had formulated a comprehensive operational plan for dealing with this challenge, and had trained our forces well in preparation for the required task.

My first encounter with Hezbollah was during the First Lebanon War, after Operation Peace for Galilee in early 1983. As commander of

Battalion 890, I first faced the organization and its agents a few months after the end of the operation, when they began to carry out terrorist attacks against our forces in Lebanon. These consisted mainly of setting explosives (Improvised Explosive Devices or IEDs) against IDF vehicles on the roads, shooting at our convoys, and firing Grad rockets directly at IDF posts. Later, they also attacked with larger explosives. In one attack, they destroyed a building used by the IDF and the Shin Bet in Tyre.

I confronted Hezbollah as a battalion commander in the Tyre military area and afterwards in the Sidon area, and we had many successes in those regions. I complete the battalion's operational deployment tour with no casualties among our forces, while the other side suffered many thwarted attacks and many terrorists killed.

One of my first encounters with Hezbollah terrorists was with a cleric who led a squad, and to me it shed light on the organization's development. Here is what happened.

During the deployment of Battalion 890 under my command in the Tyre region, Hezbollah launched several attacks on an IDF post near the village of Ma'aroub, which was in the area of an IDF reserve battalion. They fired Grad missiles, straight on. To my frustration, our pursuit of the attackers yielded no results. We repeatedly lost their trail during the chase. I asked the regional brigade commander, Colonel Ofer Ben-Zvi, to allow Battalion 890 to pursue the terrorists after the next attack.

The next Grad rocket attack on the military outpost was not long in coming. This time it happened on a Friday night. I deployed the battalion for the chase. The previous day had been very rainy, and the ground was muddy and wet, so the tracks were clear. Early in the morning, after a chase over several miles, the tracks led to a house in the Shi'ite village of al-Hallousiye al-Tahta.

There was light in the house, and inside we could see the squad sitting down to a meal (post-operation). Outside there were clothes hung out to dry, and in the yard, we located a secret weapons cache where they had hidden the weapons and equipment that they had used in their terror attacks. We broke in and surprised the cell. After we captured the diners, it turned out that they were indeed the squad that had fired the Grad rockets that night. The landlord was a twenty-four-year-old Shi'ite cleric, who was also in charge of the terrorist cell.

In our searches of the young cleric's home we found a large sum of money in a drawer – American dollars and Lebanese pounds, with a total value of ten thousand dollars. We also found a few issues of *Penthouse*...

We took the detainees to the Shin Bet interrogation compound at brigade headquarters in Tyre. Meanwhile, we imposed a curfew on the village to allow us to carry out further detentions, in case our investigation yielded the names of other terrorists. In the interrogations, we learned that beginning in 1980, after the Khomeini revolution, our young cleric had spent over two years in the city of Qom, Iran, to pursue "religious studies." As part of his study program, he was trained by the Iranians and others to establish Hezbollah in Lebanon, as part of the strategy of exporting the Iranian revolution. This was before Operation Peace for Galilee. He underwent religious and operational training to establish armed terrorist cells. I am emphasizing this detail to refute the argument that repeatedly comes up in our region, that Operation Peace for Galilee and the expulsion of the PLO from Lebanon created Hezbollah. This argument is often voiced by those who tend to blame ourselves for all our problems. Hezbollah used the IDF presence in Lebanon to promote its interests by presenting itself as a resistance organization against the "Israeli occupation in Lebanon." But the fact is that Hezbollah was not created because of us. Evidently, as an arm of Iran, Hezbollah would have attacked us even if we had not carried out Operation Peace for Galilee. They would have attacked us on the grounds of "the Israeli occupation of Palestine."

Another detail that came to light during the interrogation was that some members of the cell had participated in earlier firing incidents against an IDF outpost in Ma'aroub, and that there were other terrorists in the village who had participated in these attacks but had not been arrested.

When the Shin Bet agent conveyed this information to me, I prepared for the arrest of the additional terrorists. Since early that morning, when our activities in the village were exposed, we noticed that young people were fleeing to the mosque. I assumed that these were the additional terrorists, and that they were in the village mosque. After consulting with the coordinator, we flew the cleric by helicopter from the Tyre headquarters to the village. We intended to use him to help identify the wanted terrorists and to persuade the young people to leave the mosque so that our forces would not have to storm it.

A Shin Bet agent "convinced" the cleric to ask the young people to leave the mosque. He also persuaded him to identify the wanted terrorists, by threatening to expose the fact that we had found *Penthouse* magazines in his bureau drawer. Just in case, the Shin Bet agent took the magazines with him, tucked under his coat.

When the helicopter reached the mosque, the Shin Bet agent sensed that the young cleric was hesitating. So the Shin Bet agent exposed a corner of the magazines. The cleric immediately did what was required of him. The operation ended shortly, after the young people left the mosque and we arrested the wanted terrorists.

I have always learned – and taught – not to underestimate the enemy, but also not to overestimate its strength. In Israel's attitude toward Hezbollah and its leadership, we have gone too far in the amount of power that we attribute to them. The case described here reminds me that even in the most extreme ideological organizations, there are people with weaknesses. As head of military intelligence, I learned to exploit these weaknesses.

Hezbollah is a social, political, religious, and ideological phenomenon that has become an inseparable part of the life of the Shi'ite community in Lebanon. Hezbollah has a sophisticated and well-organized military wing, but we cannot isolate it from the overall Lebanese regional context or from radical Shi'ite Islam. There is no way to destroy Hezbollah or to eliminate it with the stroke of a single military operation, because it is impossible to uproot it from the hearts of those who belong to it or support it. It is also very difficult to defeat the Hezbollah guerrilla army infrastructure because it is well positioned to conduct asymmetrical combat. Moreover, it is constructed in such a way that a regular army, no matter how sophisticated, will be challenged to destroy it without causing heavy and unreasonable harm to the civilian population of southern Lebanon.

Given these basic facts, the approach that we developed during my tenure as IDF DCOGS and COGS was that we must fight Hezbollah primarily by exploiting its political vulnerabilities. Since it is not possible to defeat the organization with one military operation, we aspired to weaken the organization to such an extent that the Lebanese political system would be able to contend with it, and eventually Hezbollah would be disarmed. As a strategic planner, I knew that if the organization kidnapped Israeli soldiers or attacked the Galilee with Katyusha rockets, Israel would have to respond, and that in order to maintain and strengthen Israel's deterrence, the response would have to be impressive and overwhelming. Yet we were familiar with the complexity of the Lebanese entity and with Hezbollah's capabilities and its weaknesses. I and my partners in the general staff understood that we must not cause an uncalculated response to the organization's provocations, which would lead to Israel fall into the trap that Hezbollah was preparing for it in Lebanon.

Given this, we formulated the following plan. If Hezbollah were to attack northern Israel, we would immediately respond with an air attack, while recruiting reservists and concentrating troops along the northern border. If the air offensive and the concentration of forces drove the international community and the Lebanese government to apply political pressure on Hezbollah, eventually leading it to disarm – all the better. If these moves did not achieve the required result, the IDF would enter southern Lebanon in a calculated fashion and for a predetermined period. We would seize control of territory, stop the anticipated firing of rockets into Israel, and cause international and Lebanese pressure, which would lead to a cease-fire under conditions that served our interests.

When I became COGS in 2002, the premises of the IDF plan that I prepared were based on a thorough understanding of Hezbollah's challenge to us. Any Israeli action would cause Hezbollah to launch a massive firing of rockets on northern Israel. Our air force would not be able to neutralize the short-range Katyusha rockets. We could only damage Hezbollah's strategic arm (the longer-range rockets).

I assumed that in order to stop Hezbollah from firing rockets, we would have to enter Lebanon by ground, but this entry would have to be mostly on foot (without tanks or armored personnel carriers). I understood that time would be a major factor in such an operation. Israel would have to act quickly to initiate political processes that would eventually provide a comprehensive response to the problem of Hezbollah, while intensifying the strike on Lebanon in a calculated and intelligent manner.

Based on these assumptions, I prepared the IDF plan called "The Land of Israel Shield." After I completed my tenure, this plan was changed, and rightly so, given the developments in the second half of 2005. My plan was replaced by Operation Heavenly Water. I later discovered that the readiness for this plan was not completed.

To prepare our forces for the unique battle with Hezbollah, the IDF established a dedicated training camp in the north. The camp simulated the geography of southern Lebanon and Hezbollah's deployment there. I instructed the commander of the Nahal Brigade, Colonel Noam Tibon (later general) to develop the tactical exercises and battle techniques necessary for this unique combat arena. The operational response that we developed and practiced was based on foot soldier or helicopter operations. It aimed to control all of southern Lebanon and sever the region from the north. In the first stage, we would not use tanks or armored personnel carriers, due to Hezbollah's advantage in the field of anti-tank missiles and road mines. In the first stage we would also avoid fighting in built-up areas. After the ground invasion and after we had taken control of the area, we would deploy the tanks and armored personnel carriers, and purge the built-up areas. This mission was assigned to Major General Eyal Ben-Reuven as part of the Northern Command. The relevant units, in regular and reserve service, were trained and prepared for the expected battle in the north. At the same time, the air force planned and prepared for air strikes to intercept Hezbollah's Zilzal and Fajr rockets. We had obtained precise intelligence information regarding their location.

Given that I knew these facts, the dreadful events of July 12, 2006, did not lower my spirits. Of course, it pained me that soldiers were kidnapped and killed that day. But I was convinced that from an overall strategic perspective, there was no reason that Israel should feel in distress. On the contrary – with the correct management, based on our advance planning and the vast experience that the senior command had gained, we could have used the events of July 12, 2006, as a positive lever. We could have taken advantage of the opportunity to strike Hezbollah and prove to the fanatical forces surrounding us that Israel still wields great power. Finally, we could have proved that our unilateral pullouts from Lebanon and Gaza did not prove Nasrallah's claim that Israel was as resilient as a spider web. I saw Hezbollah's provocation as an opportunity to strike the organization hard and to weaken it. This would have made it easier for the Lebanese opponents of Hezbollah to contend with it politically. I saw this an opportunity to stimulate a wave of Lebanese protests against Hezbollah. This would have been like the wave of protests that led to the Syrian withdrawal from Lebanon in April 2005 without a single shot being fired. I saw the opportunity to gravely harm Iran and

Syria's interests, and to rehabilitate the damage done to the perception of Israel's deterrent power after our withdrawal from Lebanon in 2000 and the disengagement in 2005. Considering all these opportunities that we could have exploited, undoubtedly the Second Lebanon War was a major missed opportunity.

CHAPTER 15

Failure, Flight, and Missed Opportunity

On the seventh day of the war, I realized that something wasn't quite right. The air force attack had been planned for several years and succeeded above and beyond expectations. But the army divisions weren't called up, and the public was led to believe that it would be possible to defeat Hezbollah with an extensive air strike. I realized that it was impossible to overthrow Hezbollah by military means alone – all the more so by air battle alone. The message transmitted from the government in Jerusalem, the Defense Ministry and the General Staff Headquarters in Tel Aviv was that Israel was about to achieve a "deluxe" victory: quick, decisive, elegant, and practically bloodless.

From conversations I held in Washington, I understood that the Americans had received a similar message. The White House, the State Department, and the Pentagon had the impression that the Israelis had a trick up their sleeve – a military plan that was about to bring Hezbollah to its knees. On the seventh day of the war, I heard from my American friends that all Israel wanted was time – "A couple of weeks or a couple of months to crack down on Hezbollah."

I knew that the Israeli request for time was foolish. It stood in complete opposition to Israeli interests. The entire logic of combined military and political action against Hezbollah was based on the fact that there was no time. As time went by, the efficacy of an Israeli military operation would decrease, we'd miss the quality targets, and the risk intensified of a "Kafr Qana–style" mishap (as it was named in the status reports and exercises) – whether a real incident or one fabricated by Hezbollah. We recalled the events of April 1996 during Operation Grapes of Wrath, when an artillery battery was ordered to fire shells to assist in evacuating a special forces team. Instead, the fire hit a group of refugees in a UNIFIL camp near the village of Kafr Qana in Lebanon. Some one hundred civilians were killed, including many women and children, and over one hundred were injured. After this, Israel had to end the operation without having fully achieved its defined goals.

So although Hezbollah leaders searched for a way to achieve a cease-fire in the first few days, the senior political and military echelons in Israel were not prepared with a definition of the desired final status or with an exit strategy. I noted rhetoric that raised expectations and lack of coherency in decision making, which created confusion within the IDF. I saw this as proof that the decision makers did not properly understand the fundamental components of the battle they were waging. They did not understand the limitations of power or how to apply it. They did not define the targets that could be attained through the power at their disposal. In my view, the public declarations of Prime Minister Ehud Olmert and Defense Minister Amir Peretz on the goals of the war seemed disconnected from reality. They created a threshold of expectations that were obviously unattainable to anyone versed in the issues. The unrealistic expectations they created, both in Israel and in Washington, harmed Israel's trustworthiness and image of deterrence.

When I identified the problematic nature of this manner of handling the conflict and realized that the leaders did not intend to conclude the military operation within a short time, I flew back to Israel. I tried to do everything I could to understand what was going on and help change the way the war was being managed. I offered my assistance to Chief of General Staff Dan Halutz – but he preferred not to meet with me.

After I landed, I met with the prime minister's military secretary, Major General Gadi Shamni. I tried to understand the logic of how the battle and its objectives were being handled. I described to him at length my evaluation of the situation and presented my recommendations. I offered my services for any need. Several hours later, he called and said that he had delivered my analysis and recommendations to the prime minister, and that Olmert thanked me.

During my stay in Israel, the IDF carried out its first ground entry operations into Lebanon. This was done in a disorganized, imprudent manner, which infuriated me. The entanglement in local battles in Maroun al-Ras and Bint Jbeil were diametrically opposed to the rationale of the plan I had worked on for years with my colleagues at General Staff headquarters and the Northern Command. As the days went by, it became apparent that the IDF was being managed in a scandalous manner. The leaders had no clearly defined political goal for the military operation. Achievable goals were not outlined. Instead, they improvised, over and over again. Instead of reaping political goals at the right moment, they continued to apply force. But applying excessive force in such a situation is destructive and becomes a double-edged sword. When you turn a screw, you reach a certain point where you have to stop. If you keep turning, the screw will fall out. This is what happened after the second week of the war. The prime minister, defense minister, and chief of general staff were helpless in the face of reality. This was because the goals were not defined correctly and clearly, and the time frame was not properly thought out. In addition, the limitations of force were not understood and internalized. Further, there was no connection between military and political actions. When they understood that the promise of an air victory was false, they became frustrated and pressured. Unreasonable expectations had been raised at the beginning of the war, and leaders had made public declarations of unachievable targets without thought or serious discussion. Now these same leaders were under pressure, as they were unsuccessful in achieving results. They began to search desperately for any process that would create a feeling or image of victory.

This resulted in a series of ill-advised actions. At first, they spoke about a ground operation that would create a security strip at a half-mile depth along the border. Then they initiated the local ground operations. The most important of these was the battle at Bint Jbeil, due to its symbolic value – this was where Hezbollah leader Hassan Nasrallah had delivered his "victory speech" after the IDF had retreated from Lebanon in the summer of 2000. But these ground invasions were all hesitant, arbitrary, and unwise. They were not part of any overall plan. They did not aim toward a clear strategic goal that we had a chance of achieving. These were mostly shots in the dark, the foolish attempts of a rudderless leadership to grasp at straws.

Here I should clarify – there are failures in war, and there are mistakes. This happens in any war. In principle, it's important to back the political leadership as well as the military command for reasonable errors and failures – up to a certain point. But the problem with the way the Second Lebanon War was managed was that there was no organized roadmap, so the orders were constantly being changed. In many cases, the field commanders did not know what their leaders wanted from them, or why they were fighting. As a result, a feeling of confusion and helplessness spread throughout the IDF. Commanders and soldiers lost confidence in the leadership and command ranks, as these did not understand reality or properly define goals. Instead, they managed the war on a day-to-day basis. This reflected negatively on their performance, because sticking to a mission can only be accomplished toward a defined goal.

One of the major problems that characterized the Second Lebanon War was that it was not even defined as a war. The senior command headquarters was not operated according to the proper format for war. At first, some of the emergency warehouses were not opened. The COGS directed the war from his office, as if this were not actually a war. The message trickled down: the Northern Command, the air force and the various units were ordered to carry out battle missions, but also to operate using the resources and terms of ordinary, everyday security. This lack of clarity characterized not only the war goal, but also the very understanding of war status. This also influenced decisions regarding the home front. Therefore, there was no internalization of the strategic importance of ongoing strikes against cities and settlements in northern Israel. These strikes brought daily life to a standstill in a sizeable portion of the state, displaying to our enemies an image of a bleeding Israel that could not defend itself and reflecting the negative consequences of the time aspect on this image.

In parallel, severe problems were revealed within the chain of command. When distress was felt in the Northern Command, the officers managing the battle did not receive backup from senior command, and some felt that their commanders were denying responsibility. They felt their commanders were stabbing them in the back during battle by holding them responsible for the lack of success. The highly publicized appointment of the deputy chief of general staff to the position of head of Northern Command did nothing to support commanders and fighters. Instead, it created a feeling of mistrust and extensive infighting. In general, the atmosphere among the IDF commanders was gloomy and suspicious. The General Staff was not convened for organized meetings and did not discuss the war in any depth. The media at its various levels was dishonest and acted with impropriety. The spin culture that prevailed outside the military penetrated within and clouded the management of the war.

Things came to a head in the final days of the war. To the best of my understanding, the ground operation that concluded the war was based more on internal political considerations of the defense minister and prime minister than on state and security considerations. The process that the Cabinet authorized at the late date of Wednesday, August 9, was based on a certain logic and state and security considerations. But by the time it was implemented two days later on Friday, August 11, those considerations were no longer relevant. On that Friday evening, after the forces had been sent on their mission, it was no longer possible to improve Israel's position against the proposed UN decision, which was formulated before the ground attack was set in motion (as then US ambassador to the UN John Bolton has asserted several times since).

The ground attack surprised me personally, because on Friday, August 11 at six p.m. (Israel time), I was already aware of the agreed text for the proposed decision in the UN Security Council. This text had been formulated, accepted by Lebanon and Hezbollah, and was to be put to a vote within several hours. My American friends who reported this to me viewed the upcoming decision as the conclusion of the military operation. Thus when I found out about the ground attack, I was surprised. I didn't understand the logic, and I felt that this was a last-ditch Israeli attempt to improve the concluding picture. When I learned the details about how the decision was made, I realized that it was motivated by political considerations, not state and security ones. I learned that on that Friday, Defense Minister Amir Peretz had informed the Labor Party ministers about the upcoming UN decision in anticipation of the end of the military operation. Some of his party's ministers criticized it harshly, and even said that if the operation ended in that manner, he would be "finished politically." After hearing this,

Minister Peretz asked to call Prime Minister Olmert. Following that phone conversation, Peretz traveled to Olmert's home. Olmert had objected to the ground attack throughout the operation and had managed to avoid implementing it in various ways. But he felt the political sword on his neck. Apparently, he had read the harsh criticism of him in the Friday papers and observed the sharp decline in support for him in the opinion surveys. The defense minister and IDF commanders supported the ground attack, which had already been approved by the cabinet, while Olmert was the lone objector. Thus, we may assume he realized that the blame for any outcome of the war would be placed squarely on him – and the outcome was not promising. In my view, this was the main motivation for implementing the ground attack. The Winograd Commission report did nothing to contradict this impression.

The prime minister and minister of defense were responsible for initiating the ground attack based on political considerations. But it was the military command that erred in carrying out the attack, as it did not change the plan despite knowing that the enemy was aware of it. On Wednesday evening, IDF forces prepared for attack, revealing their intentions and the main focus of their efforts – crossing the Saluki Valley. Postponing the operation by twenty-four hours and the additional preparation of IDF forces enabled Hezbollah to organize for the attack with its own forces and numerous anti-tank missile launchers. The senior IDF officers upheld the original plan without adapting it to the new circumstances, and this permitted Hezbollah ample preparation time for attacking the IDF forces, which came from an expected direction. This was a mistake of the senior IDF command, so it bears responsibility. To this criticism, I add my reservations about using tanks at this stage of the battle.

Following Israel's lack of success in the Second Lebanon War, the Israeli public furiously attacked the government, the IDF senior command, and to a certain extent, the IDF as well. This wave of anger was justified at heart, but it did not distinguish between issues of strategic management and problems in the water supply; between shortage of high-tech vests and the absence of realistic war goals. The public found fault in everything: Israel's behavior in the six years before the war, the division commanders sitting in front of plasma screens during the war, the level of readiness of the fighting units, the home front, the logistics system, and the IDF fighting spirit.

This sweeping criticism was understandable, but not always right. It did not distinguish between primary and secondary issues, between what was truly wrong in management of the war and unpreventable problems that were part and parcel of every war, or of Israeli reality and its constraints. As a result, some of the barbs of criticism were not only misplaced, but also dangerous. They could lead to drawing incorrect lessons from the war, and as a result, the IDF would not be correctly prepared for future challenges.

The most disturbing criticism was of overthinking and over-sophistication in the military language used by the IDF in the past decade. Several veteran major generals called for a "return to the sources" – to simple language, old-school tank formations, and basic IDF values. I myself come from that world of basic IDF values. I did most of my military service in the field with field units. In many ways, the old IDF from the period between the Six-Day War and the Yom Kippur War serves as my formative pattern. But as a commander who was attentive to changes in the region, in the relevant threats, in technological combat abilities, and in the conceptual understanding of warfare, I realized we had to formulate new, contemporary types of warfare. As deputy chief and COGS, I did much to develop these new types of warfare and introduce them in the IDF. An army that falls asleep on its watch cannot be a victor. An army that rests on its laurels cannot prepare for future wars. So although I appreciate the attempt to preserve the values of warfare in which we were educated, I warn against the trend of going back in time, preparing ourselves for the last war rather than the next one. Using plasma screens to control the modern field of battle is justifiable. Use of creative terms to understand the face of battle in the twenty-first century should not be condemned. Tanks and more tanks are not the answer to the challenges that Israel will face in the coming decade. We must not permit the criticism of failures discovered in the summer of 2006 to cause fear of innovation and withdrawal into a fossilized kind of military conservatism.

Still, we must ensure that terms that are innovative and important on the strategic and operative level do not trickle down to the tactical level. I will explain.

The tactical level requires language that is mainly physical: "The force will occupy," "The force will defend," "The force will destroy the enemy." The strategic and operative levels require abstract thinking, and address processes and power centers. The encounter between the strategic military echelon and the political echelon obligates discourse, from which the military side must understand the goals and constraints of the political side. The responsibility of the strategic military echelon (General Staff headquarters, headed by the chief of general staff) is to work with the political echelon to formulate a clear goal for the war, translate it into a concept, and derive a plan and tasks that the operative and tactical echelon can implement in a coherent manner so as to achieve the goal. Sometimes high-level language must change due to developments in threats, opportunities, and capabilities. At the same time, the senior echelon also bears responsibility for preventing this language from penetrating the tactical level, which requires clear, straightforward vocabulary. As COGS, I encouraged development of high-level language on the strategic and operational level, and I ensured that this language would not reach the tactical level. After I identified this problem among several officers, I initiated a workshop on this topic for officers at division level and up.

Instilling new skills and concepts requires the involvement of officers, alongside examination and criticism of the process and its results. In the past few decades, the IDF has developed innovative skills in operations, intelligence, and C^5I (Command, Control, Communication, Computers, Cyber, Information) in a manner that has enabled and even demanded change in its operational concept. I realized that I personally had to take responsibility for teaching these skills in a controlled, supervised manner. Some of the skills were developed and imparted during the tenure of my predecessors, from the time of Lieutenant General Dan Shomron and onwards. Others were tried in exercises and in the laboratory of battle, but were yet to be incorporated in the units, much less in operations.

Operation Days of Penitence took place in 2004 during my tenure as COGS and serves as an example of a controlled and supervised process of assimilating new methods. In this operation, a brigade-sized force occupied the northern end of the Gaza Strip up to the edge of Jabaliya refugee camp, after Qassam rockets were fired on Sderot from this area. The officers of Southern Command (GOC, division commander, and brigade commander) felt that the brigade headquarters could absorb new skills and put them into practice. The air force and intelligence (Military Intelligence and GSS) commanders agreed. I instructed the commanders to prepare for this possibility before the operation. Then I announced that I would visit the field to examine preparation and decide whether to permit the capabilities at brigade level. After I arrived in the field, I examined the individuals involved and authorized the change. The operation was crowned a rousing success in terms of implementing the new capabilities in the operational concept. I understood that this success should be multiplied by teaching the skills in additional brigades. I also realized that in war, when several divisions are activated, we would not be able to equip each brigade with these skills. We repeatedly witnessed that command and war are an art, and that success, luck and victory are located in the smallest details.

Another criticism focused on the assertion that the IDF did not train enough in the years preceding the war. An army always needs to train, and it always needs to train more than it does. Due to the constraints we faced in the early twenty-first century, we had to decide whether we would slash the overall budget, thus endangering Israel's economy (which faced serious danger in 2002–2003) or take certain calculated risks in the organization of forces, inventory, and training. To my best judgment, the decision we made at that juncture was correct and justified. It did not mean that the IDF would be unprepared for war, but rather that it would need several days of honing skills before going out to war. Unfortunately, the Israeli government and senior command did not internalize this fact. They did not call up the reserves on time and did not insist that the reserve formations polish their skills before going into battle. The problem discovered in the war was not lack of training, but lack of judgment. Even while acting under harsh budget constraints that it did not define, the IDF was prepared to fulfill the tasks it should have been given during the Second Lebanon War – if only its commanders and leaders had acted with wisdom and based on true acquaintance with the arena and the system, in all its strengths and weaknesses.

Another point of criticism asserted that it was wrong to permit Hezbollah to accumulate power for six years and remain undisturbed while building a rocket system that would threaten northern Israel. This critique mainly focused on a statement attributed to me, that what Israel had to do against Hezbollah rockets was to "let them rust." This inexact quote was apparently intended to goad me personally. The phrase I had actually used to characterize our policy was to "make the rockets rust" – in other words, to act militarily, politically, and diplomatically in a process that would lead to the disarming of Hezbollah. This was the policy of the Sharon government, and I considered it correct and wise. Some critics of this policy who failed in their management of the Second Lebanon War, such as Olmert, moved to supporting it when they became members of

Sharon's cabinet. In the best case, this critique stemmed from political interests and spin, based on the assumption that most of the public had a short memory. In the worst case, it stemmed from misunderstanding of the limitations of power. This superficial criticism considered the entire prewar period as one block, under the title "six years" – from the unilateral retreat from Lebanon in May 2000 until the Second Lebanon War in 2006. It did not permit a serious, deep discussion of the numerous events and periods under the various leadership terms.

Even today, Syrian missiles are aimed at Israel, but we do not attack them. Iranian Shahab missiles are aimed at Israel, but we don't attack them either. Hezbollah has also rearmed with rockets that threaten Israel, but the same leadership that criticized its predecessors does not rush to attack. Why? Because the use of military strength is a last resort. We cannot use it casually. To use military force, we must analyze the process in cost-benefit terms. We must identify a legitimate and rational strategic context, and all in a situation where we have no other choice. Such a context did not exist against Hezbollah. Furthermore, we did have a choice: the possibility that in an internal conflict inside Lebanon, we would weaken Hezbollah and force it to put down its weapons. Further, when I was COGS, I understood that Hezbollah was an entrenched phenomenon, and that no one single military operation could erase it. I realized that against the rocket threat, there was no individual military operation that would solve the problem. I therefore supported a combined political, military, and diplomatic operation that would eventually lead to disarming Hezbollah as a result of a process inside Lebanon. I suggested that we act in a political and limited military manner to contain Hezbollah, reduce its maneuvering field, and delegitimize it inside Lebanon. Wiser Israeli leaderships followed this path – those that led Operation Accountability in 1994 and Operation Grapes of Wrath in 1996. In my view, the Second Lebanon War merely proved the judiciousness of this approach. As proof, those who argued vociferously in July 2006 that we must not accept the existence of a Hezbollah rocket system never repeated this argument later, when the organization restored its capabilities and reconstructed a rocket system that covered sizeable portions of the State of Israel.

During the failed attempts of those responsible for the Second Lebanon War to avoid responsibility, they tried to place the blame for the failures of the war on the military forces, primarily the ground forces, and on their predecessors, including myself. Before the battles subsided, senior government officials and commanders hinted that achievements were difficult because "the IDF did not deliver the goods." And why was that? Because in previous years, its commanders had not prepared it appropriately for war.

This critique infuriated me, not only because of the attempt to muddy my name, but also because it meant slandering the entire IDF. The IDF was and remains a good army. It performed Operation Defensive Shield in an optimal manner and defeated Palestinian terror in Judea and Samaria, to the amazement of military experts around the world. The IDF also implemented the disengagement from the Gaza Strip efficiently, rapidly, and without mishaps. In the difficult conflicts that it experienced in various areas between 2000 and 2005, the IDF was revealed as a fighting army that was honed, creative, and victorious. It appeared that way after the Second Lebanon War as well, in its operations in the Gaza Strip – when it was managed correctly. So the argument that the IDF is the source of the problems revealed in the Lebanon War is groundless. It is unfair toward our high-quality soldiers and dedicated officers, from the highest levels down to the lowest. It is unfair toward the entire system, which has proved its efficiency and professionality over many years. But it is correct toward the senior commanders of the Second Lebanon War, headed by the COGS.

It was hard for me to stand by and watch the failure of outstanding officers whom I knew personally. It is difficult for me to shake the feeling that certain generals would not have failed had they been under my command. Even if they made mistakes for which they were responsible, it was the senior political and military leadership of the war that made them fail.

I am not asserting that in an IDF under my command, there would be no defects. I do not argue that there is no room for improvement. I am not stating that the IDF is perfect – it was never so, and it never will be. But it must be clear to all that the true failures of the Lebanon War were not caused due to inabilities of soldiers and officers, but rather due to the failure of the senior political and military echelon. If the senior leaders had adopted a sober conception of reality, including recognition of the IDF's strengths and weaknesses, a realistic strategic plan, and an appropriate ethical attitude, the results of the war would have been very different.

A series of pointed assertions were made against me personally. The argument was made that I had prevented the development of an anti-rocket system and thus exposed Israel's cities to Katyusha hits. The truth was that the Nautilus anti-rocket system that was demonstrated to me involved a sizeable investment, while its anticipated efficacy was relatively small. Its capabilities were focused and limited. My position was that if Israel would invest millions to produce protective gear for every citizen and become a "bunker state," it would not survive economically. I thus preferred to invest the limited resources at our disposal in developing intelligence and offensive capabilities. I enabled the Nautilus project to continue even after doubts arose about the ability to make this system operational and efficient, because I thought it was important to develop the technology to the fullest. The decision to end the project was made several months after I completed my tenure and was fully justified. Today as well, we must avoid the illusion of technological solutions of active defense against simple rockets such as the Qassam and the Katyusha. Even if we overcome the technological challenge, we must consider equipping ourselves with such systems based on their efficiency and cost. We cannot "defend ourselves to the death" – and that means economically.

After the technological and operational feasibility of the Iron Dome system was proven and at a reasonable price, the decision to acquire it was correct. To the credit of the Administration for the Development of Weapons and Technological Infrastructure (Maf'at) in the Defense Ministry, mainly the engineers and technicians at Rafael Advanced Defense Systems, they succeeded in transforming an idea into an efficient operational system within a relatively short time. But so long as there is no cheap and efficient defense solution, we must adhere to the rule that "the best defense is offense." In this case, this means that either we exact a price from the side that is attacking us, of a size that will force it to suffer the consequences of using this weapon, or our forces take control over the launching areas.

Another assertion made was that I shared the conception that placed excess weight on the air force and precise weaponry. In my assessment, the air force and precise weaponry had proven themselves in the Palestinian arena as well as the conflict in Lebanon. But I did not delude myself. I knew the limits of air capability. That was why I prepared a ground plan and trained forces for it. That was why I believed in a combination of military and diplomatic efforts. I was not thrilled to implement the ground plan. Therefore, I also thought it right to exploit the power of our advanced intelligence capabilities to identify targets, and the capability of precise fire to destroy them, mainly from the air. This I believed would lead us to a political achievement within a short time. I also realized that if this process did not produce the anticipated achievement, there would be no choice but to implement the ground operation. At any rate, I thought it was important to prepare this process in advance and use it as both a threat and a means of pressure on the various entities.

The fact that the air force was not prepared to solve the problem of the short-range Katyusha rockets came as no surprise. We needed the air force and its precise weaponry for other, more weighty tasks. That is what they had prepared for in the past, and the same is true today. The Lebanon War should not confuse us on this issue and should not cause us to turn our back on the air force, which defends Israel's security. The investment in building power in the air force and intelligence are the most preferable in cost-benefit terms. Investment in these branches and in acquiring skills in intelligence and precise attack provides solutions in all types of warfare: conventional war against armies, war against terror and guerrilla tactics, handling rockets and missiles, and attacking targets in countries both near and far.

Yet another criticism raised was that I had accepted the atrophy of the reserve forces and that I was responsible for the disgraceful state of the emergency warehouses. The decisions regarding the reserve forces stemmed from budget constraints that were justified in terms of overall national security. In the economic reality of late 2002, it was correct to cut government spending, including on security, to prevent an economic crisis. At that highpoint in the battle against Palestinian terror, after Israeli society had absorbed hundreds of dead and thousands of wounded and proved its resilience, I considered the economic situation as the weak link in the chain of national strength. I feared that the economic crisis might lead us to an incorrect and inappropriate political surrender or concession. I realized that we had to cut, even if I didn't agree on the size of the cut that the Finance Ministry demanded, and to cut meant to take risks.

On the Israeli side, the IDF was at the height of a successful pushback against Palestinian terror. Meanwhile, the Americans had launched a successful attack in Afghanistan, and we anticipated another stage in the American offensive. In consideration of these factors, I thought it right to take risks in everyday expenses, including training, supplies, and ongoing security – but without harming the long-term buildup of power. I assumed that training and supplies could be completed as

The official photo: Lieutenant General Moshe ("Bogie") Ya'alon

In the United Kingdom

With Pakistani officer at the Command and Staff Course at Camberley, Surrey, United Kingdom

Training exercise with the British Marines

Class photo with foreign officers from the Camberley course (I am in the front row, second from left)

In Jordan

With the Jordanian COGS, General Khaled Al-Sarayra, during a visit to Amman

On a visit to Jordan, with the Jordanian COGS and other officers

In the United States

With General Richard B. Meyers, chairman of the Joint Chiefs of Staff of the US Armed Forces

With US Congressman Tom Lantos (11th district, California)

Lecturing to students at the US National Defense University

Receiving the US Legion of Merit award

Shaking the hands of senior officers following honor parade at the Pentagon

In Germany

With Joschka Fischer, German minister of foreign affairs

With the German COGS, at the honor parade during a visit to Germany

In Turkey and Romania

With the head of Turkish military intelligence, during a visit to Ankara

With the head of Romanian intelligence, during a visit to the Stasi in Bucharest

In China

Honor parade at the reception in Beijing

With the COGS and head of military intelligence

Visiting the Great Wall of China

the situation analysis changed, while abilities that required development and equipment could not be made up within a short time limit.

I understood that a change in the situation analysis of late 2005 would require a change in the IDF's work plan, emphasizing completion of training and supply gaps throughout 2006. The change in the situation analysis was required in light of three significant developments in the area: the departure of Syrian forces from Lebanon, the American failure in Iraq, and completion of the disengagement from the Gaza Strip. The senior command was aware of the situation, and yet in 2006 it had failed to enable more training time for the units in anticipation of northern and southern scenarios. Thus, after the decision for a military operation was made on July 12, 2006, it was more important than ever to call up the reserve units immediately so that they could prepare and train for the scenario.

We may compare this to the situation before the war on Palestinian terror that broke out in September 2000. Then as well, the IDF acted under budget constraints. Awareness of deficiencies in training and supplies led then chief of general staff Shaul Mofaz to decide on a change in priorities that year, including completing supply quotas and training the regular and reserve forces in preparation for the possibility of war.

I remain content with the decisions I made then. I see no significant connection between them and the failed manner of operation of the regular and reserve units during the Second Lebanon War. The impression among the public that the IDF had not trained for this scenario is false. Various entities attempted to create the sense that the IDF had not trained for six years – but this is untrue. Even in a reality of more training, we still must enable regular and reserve units to "remove the rust" and refresh training exercises and battle techniques designed for the area. Before the Six-Day War as well, the reserve troops needed time to refresh training, and therefore they used the three-week waiting period before the war for exercises. One training session per year for a reserve unit in a certain arena such as the Golan Heights does not abolish the need for the unit to refresh training before entering battle. This is even truer with regard to an unfamiliar arena such as Lebanon or Gaza. Even a highly polished unit of the regular army that transfers from fighting in Gaza or Nablus to Lebanon requires sector-specific training. When there is no time to train, such as in the Yom Kippur War, which I experienced as a reserve soldier, the troops pay a price in the first hours of battle until the rust is removed.

Reports of problems in emergency provisions at the beginning of the war surprised me. When I left my position, the emergency warehouses of the reserve units were full. I was informed that "crucial equipment" was taken from some of the warehouses to reinforce regular units during battle, mainly in the Gaza Strip, and particularly after the kidnapping of the soldier Gilad Schalit. In addition, I found out that such equipment was taken from reserve unit stores to serve regular units sent to Lebanon after the kidnapping of soldiers there. As far as I am aware, this equipment was supplemented in the units before they entered battle. Assertions of another kind were heard regarding equipment quality. To the best of my knowledge, the fighting units were equipped with appropriate, functioning equipment. Assertions that some of the reserve units had equipment of lower quality than other units are true, but it must be understood that the IDF, in the past as well as the observable future, is not financially capable of exchanging all of its equipment each time a new type is purchased. For this reason, there are some tank units that fight in the Merkava 2 or 3 tank, while others use the Merkava 4. Some pilots fly new F-35s while others fly old model F-16s. The same is true for bulletproof vests, stretchers, and night-vision equipment.

In retrospect, the units that were activated correctly, without distinction between regular and reserve units and with the given level of equipment and training, fought well and completed their battles with the upper hand. In general, when the units were given clear tasks, they carried them out smoothly. When the tasks were not clear, and mainly when a clear goal was not defined, then implementation was in accordance. It is difficult to speak of "sticking to the goal" when there is no goal to work toward, all the more so when the high command improvises, and changes missions every other day.

A general criticism raised against me was that during my tenure as COGS, the IDF overemphasized the conflict with the Palestinians, and as a result, not enough attention was paid to the IDF's readiness for conventional warfare in other arenas. A political tone was added to this assertion, hinting that the IDF's tasks in the Palestinian sector diverted it from preparation for wars of another type. I reject this assertion. In my view, the Palestinian threat was and remains the most important existential threat to Israel in the nearby region. The Iranian strategic threat – both from unconventional weapons as well as from its proxy Hezbollah – and the Palestinian threat are the two main challenges that Israel must face in the current period. For this reason, it was supremely important to focus efforts on the Palestinian arena, so as to prevent Israeli collapse under a terror attack. On the military level, this goal was achieved almost fully. Unfortunately, Israel failed miserably on the diplomatic level in this field. But in any case, focusing our efforts on the war against terror did not harm the IDF's preparedness for war. On the contrary, as a result of the battle experience they earned, the combat units honed their skills. As a result of adopting and implementing sophisticated means and new methods of warfare, the IDF developed impressive skills that improved its ability to operate in a comprehensive war. The investment we made in the Palestinian arena produced impressive direct results in the war on terror, but also indirect results that improved the overall combat system and prepared the IDF fully for handling challenges of any type.

In the same way, I do not accept the argument that the IDF was not prepared for war in Lebanon because we had to carry out the disengagement. Despite my objection to the disengagement on principle,

I am thoroughly convinced that implementing it did not harm the IDF's operational ability or its morale, as certain circles attempt to assert.

It was not fundamental weaknesses within the IDF that caused the lack of success in the Second Lebanon War, but rather the failure of the leadership in utilizing the IDF and in the overall management of the war. In 2000, the IDF senior leadership led the preparations and battle against Palestinian terror competently and did not look to blame others for creating the situation in September 2000. But the political and military leadership of the Second Lebanon War did not follow this line. Instead of taking responsibility for their failure immediately after the end of the war, they tried to avoid responsibility by deflecting it to their predecessors or to the combat units under their command. The refusal of the prime minister, minister of defense, and chief of general staff to resign at the end of the failed military campaign and their attempt to avoid responsibility caused even more damage to the IDF than that caused during the war. The leadership trio avoided taking responsibility and instead placed responsibility on the lower ranks, mainly on the ground forces, which caused deep damage to the IDF's deterrence image as well as to the self-image of many officers. Following the war, the decline in willingness to participate in the officers' training course and to join the permanent army are a result of the leadership's preference for personal survival over and above the good of the state.

X One of the questions that has repeatedly arisen throughout the IDF's existence is that of the position of the commander in battle. Should he be in the middle of the battle arena together with his soldiers, or is it preferable for him to remain at the command post, where he can control all the forces under him? This is primarily a professional question and should be discussed as such. However, it has implications that extend beyond the narrow professional field, mainly in terms of morale and trust in commanders.

This question was discussed frequently in the investigations that followed the Second Lebanon War, and entered public debate mainly with regard to the positioning of division commanders at rear command posts at their desks – "in front of computer screens" to quote the term that was used. In my view, the public debate mostly expressed a popularist tone. Some of it reflected a release of anger by subordinates (low-level soldiers and commanders) who justifiably felt frustration after the war, and took out their anger on their commanders – not always justifiably.

To clarify my position on the matter, I'll relate four incidents in which I was involved as commander.

The first incident took place when I was commander of the Paratroopers Brigade Reconnaissance Company during Operation Litani in 1978. The IDF invaded South Lebanon in two stages. In the first stage, we reached the Ras Biada line. After a pause of several days, we implemented the second stage in which we continued up to the Litani River line.

After the first stage, Battalion 50 under Lieutenant Colonel Yair Rafaeli was ordered to perform searches in several villages to the north, beyond the line of our forces. A truck from the brigade communications unit coming from Israel traveled north up the coastal highway. When it reached the northernmost checkpoint on that road, it continued north, without realizing that it had crossed the line of our forces. The soldiers at the checkpoint allowed it to pass, because they thought it was going to Battalion 50. Because Battalion 50 was operating in the villages east of the coastal road, the truck continued without disturbance. When it reached the outskirts of Tyre, south of Rashidaya, it encountered a terrorist unit. The surprised terrorists fired RPGs (rocket launchers) and light weapons and hit the truck, which stopped with one soldier killed and several wounded.

A Battalion 50 support company under company commander Captain Yiftach Ayin (who was killed along with Captain Nir Zehavi in Operation Shalechet on June 8, 1978) was first to arrive at the site, along with the deputy battalion commander, Major Reuven Hecker.

I was with the Reconnaissance Company in another sector, but when I heard about the incident over the radio, I took the physician, Captain Dr. Gideon Man, along with me, and rushed to the site in my jeep. On the way, I instructed my deputy, First Lieutenant Moshe (Moishele) Tov, to load the rest of the company into APCs and advance toward the site. My main fear was that the terrorists who had attacked the truck would take soldiers as prisoners. (At that time, they hadn't yet thought up the idea of taking bodies for bargaining purposes.)

I identified the site of the incident quickly, as there was only one route along the coastal road, and the exchange of fire between Battalion 50 and the terrorists was easily heard. I stopped at some distance behind the truck and left the doctor to care for the wounded. Then I verified Deputy Commander Reuven's position and ran to him through the orchard east of the coastal road.

Reuven was in the line of fire. When I reached him, I understood the battle scenario. The Battalion 50 force had taken position behind cover (mainly irrigation ditches and dirt mounds) in the orchard and fired at the terrorists, who were behind a wall of another orchard. The two orchards were separated by the access road to the village of Buraliya and an open agricultural field that was several dozen yards wide.

Reuven told me that Yiftach, the company commander, had been wounded in the leg as he was trying to cross the coastal road to the west. He had been attempting to take position in a house overlooking the road so as to secure the area of the damaged truck.

When I understood the battle scenario, I thought that the best plan would be to outflank the terrorists from the west and reach them from behind, from the west side of the road. But I had no soldiers with me, because I'd come in my jeep accompanied only by the physician. I asked Reuven for a few soldiers to carry out the outflanking maneuver, and received under my command the deputy company commander, First Lieutenant Ze'ev Hayut, and five other soldiers. After I organized them rapidly, we retreated out of the terrorists' line of fire. Then we crossed the road to the west and advanced among houses and orchards to the point where we could see the terrorists' backs as they fired at our forces.

We opened fire, surprising them. After several were injured, they identified our position and tried to return fire. They fired a machine gun in our direction at short range. I threw a grenade at the machine gunner and took him down. The remaining terrorists retreated, leaving their comrades' bodies in the field. The battle was over.

After the battle I heard praise, but also two types of criticism. The first was from the team commanders and sergeants in the reconnaissance brigade, who complained that I hadn't taken them along. The second was that I'd acted too hastily in going to the site on my own in a single jeep and with only Dr. Man along.

I rejected these two critiques out of hand. In the heat of the moment, the time factor was crucial. Every minute that passed could determine the results of the battle, so it was vital to reach the site as rapidly as possible without waiting for the force to get organized. In battle, situations sometimes arise in which you must make a decision under conditions of uncertainty, taking a risk that in retrospect might be the one that led to failure or loss of life. This is true for your location as commander as well as the direction of a maneuver or battle plan. In battle, a single decision might result in "citation or demotion," as the IDF saying goes.

The second incident took place in 1979 in an operation in Jordanian territory. We received information that terrorists had accumulated weapons in dugouts in a dry riverbed that flowed into the Dead Sea from the east. Our mission was to scan the entire riverbed and the area of the dugouts to locate the weapons or disprove the information.

There were fourteen combat soldiers in the force under my command (again as commander of the Paratroopers Brigade Reconnaissance Company). We crossed the Dead Sea in rubber boats operated by navy commando soldiers. One of the problems that I had encountered previously in operations in Lebanon was a lack of precision in navigating in these boats. To verify that we had a clear shared language regarding the target landing point on the Jordanian side, during preparations for the operation I took the navy commander up to an observation point. We identified a large, prominent rock in the landing area, and agreed that during landing he would inform me whether we had landed north or south of it. (To navigate, the navy force commander used a radar system set up on the Israeli side, which tracked the movements of the boats. This outdated, inaccurate method has since been replaced by satellite navigation.)

The operation was overseen by the deputy commander of the Jordan Valley brigade, Lieutenant Colonel Shmuel (Shmil) Golan (later brigadier general), from the command post in the Ein Gedi area.

The landing on shore was slightly late, due to delays in the movement of the boats. At landing time, the navy force commander informed me that we'd landed south of the big rock, so I had to move north to reach the entrance to the riverbed. After landing and rapid organization, I began to advance toward the target with the force. As we moved, I began to have doubts about our location, because despite the darkness, I noticed incompatibilities between what I'd learned before the operation about the shoreline and what I found in the field. When I reached the opening of the nearest riverbed, I realized that we were far north of the riverbed we were supposed to enter. Apparently, we'd landed north of the big rock, not south of it, and as a result of the boats' deviation and the faulty assumption of the navy force commander, our walk had taken us farther from the target rather than closer.

This error led to an additional delay in the schedule. But according to the calculations and plan, I had not yet passed the latest deadline for carrying out the mission. (This deadline was fixed based on the timeline for performing the mission, returning to the shore, and traveling by boat back to our territory before dawn.)

Moving rapidly back south to the target destination, I reported the navigation error and the delay in schedule to the deputy brigade commander at the rear command post.

As I approached the opening of the target riverbed, I smelled a strong odor of camels. I stopped the force and scanned the field using night-vision equipment. I advanced slowly until I found several camels at rest, which raised the suspicion that there were people around as well. I did not find any people in the area, but of course we had to go around the camels to avoid the risk of revealing our force.

Now I had almost reached the final deadline for performing the mission. I deliberated whether to report the camels and the delay to the deputy brigade commander. Finally, I decided not to report, fearing that at this stage, reporting would lead to additional delay for the purpose of investigation, and the final deadline would pass. Even if the deadline did not pass, it was likely that I'd receive an order to abandon the mission and return to Israel. I realized that I was taking full responsibility for my decision, and that I'd have to explain myself after the mission was over.

After circling the camels, I went into the riverbed for the survey, and completed the mission almost at the last moment – not without queries from the deputy brigade commander about the delay in schedule. The return trip went smoothly.

After landing on shore near Ein Gedi, I met with Shmil, deputy brigade commander of the Jordan Valley, for a preliminary briefing on the mission. I reported the camel incident to him at once. He was angry that I hadn't reported to him in real time. I knew that his anger was justified. He viewed my behavior as irresponsible and reflecting lack of trust in him, and he asked the GOC of Central Command to summon me for an inquiry. I was also asked to explain my decision to my direct commander, Colonel Amnon Lipkin-Shahak, commander of the Paratroopers Brigade, who gave me full backing.

The inquiry with Moshe Levi, GOC of Central Command was more like a personal conversation, and I explained my deliberations. I argued that if my brigade commander had been sitting at the command post, I would have reported to him, because after many training exercises and operations, the level of acquaintance and trust between us was intimate. I was certain that he would have accepted my recommendation to continue the operation. But the Jordan Valley deputy commander and I did not know each other, and I had feared that reporting the camels would cause him to cancel the mission. I explained my view of the mission's importance and my assessment that reporting to the deputy commander would not have helped in fulfilling it. Instead, there was every chance that reporting would have led to aborting the mission. The GOC of Central Command accepted my version and demonstrated understanding of my decision. Further, after another mission or two in the Jordan Valley, the level of acquaintance and trust between Shmil and myself rose.

This story reveals the complexity of the relationship between commanders at several levels. It includes several issues. First, personal relationships and trust between a commander and his subordinates are always important, and crucial in times of crisis. Second, a commander must observe the delicate balance between adherence to the mission and reporting to the superior rank. Third, the commander must take responsibility, in this case sole responsibility, for the decision not to report, in order to ensure performance of the mission. Last, a commander must decide the question of his position in battle – behind or in front.

In this case, as in similar ongoing security operations, the deputy brigade commander supervised the mission from a command post in our territory. In such cases, locating the command post inside our territory is correct, because from this position we have better control than if we were in a location in enemy territory. Optimal information about the enemy and our own forces can be sent to the command post, and this enables the commander to make the right decision. Since that operation in the late 1970s, improvements have been made in our intelligence capabilities and in tracking our forces in such a way that expands command capability from this position and makes it even more important.

This is not to say that commanding from up close has no significance. There are situations in which a brigade commander must command from very close, like the commander of a platoon, company or battalion. But in most cases, commanders from the level of brigade and up can make better decisions from the command post and not on the front line.

One example that clearly demonstrates the advantage of the command position is the story of Operation Crate, in which Sayeret Matkal kidnapped senior Syrian officers. (I did not participate in this mission.) The Unit commander at the time was Ehud Barak, and he has described this failed attempt to carry out the mission when he commanded the operation in the field, as compared to the successful performance when he commanded from the command post.

Major General Yishayahu (Shaike) Gavish related how he commanded the Southern Command during the Six-Day War from inside a half-track. The command and control systems used by Central Command today are a vast improvement over their 1967 equivalents. Those acquainted with these systems understand the need and advantage of commanding from inside a command post at a desk. This does not mean that the commander should always stay inside the command post. He has to go out into the field on occasion, in a vehicle or a helicopter, to meet the forces and mainly the other commanders face to face. This is important for morale. But only in a command post can the major general receive the optimal data for making his decisions.

The following story demonstrates the occasional need to command from inside the field.

On May 27, 1985, when I was deputy commander of Brigade 35 (regular Paratroopers Brigade), I was wounded while pursuing terrorists in Lebanon. A few days earlier, Nehemiah Tamari had taken over as commander of the brigade, and it had retreated from the Nabatiya region and completed its deployment in the sector south of the Litani River. From June 1985 until Israel's unilateral retreat from Lebanon in May 2000, this area was our security strip in South Lebanon.

Nehemiah and I were in the brigade command post near Kibbutz Yiftach when we received a report of an explosive device activated against an administrative convoy of paratrooper Battalion 202 at the top of the Saluki River, near Kfar Shakra. The report came just a few minutes before the start of Nehemiah's first meeting with the other commanders in his new position. I suggested that he hold the meeting and allow me to handle the incident.

When I reached the site, I met the commander of Battalion 202, Shamai Ran (Kastenberg), whom I had known when he was a soldier in Battalion 50 (he was also the officer who replaced me in commanding the Paratrooper Reconnaissance Company). I also met the deputy battalion commander, Meir Klifi (later major general and military secretary to Prime Ministers Olmert and Netanyahu), two company commanders from the battalion, and the brigade physician, Dr. Itzik Ashkenazi. Soldiers from the administrative convoy that had been attacked were also at the site.

As soon as I arrived, I realized that the terrorists had activated the explosive from a post that overlooked the route, from inside the ancient fortress of Kalat Dubay. With the help of trackers, we located their position rapidly. Organized preparation for pursuit meant waiting for forces to congregate, helicopters to arrive, and deploying an advance command post. I knew this would enable the two terrorists to flee and disappear in one of the surrounding villages. I thus decided to commence pursuit immediately with the improvised force at my disposal. I was in front next to the tracker. The battalion commander was to my right, the deputy battalion commander was on my left, and the other commanders, signal operators, and combat soldiers took up the rear.

After a mile of pursuit in Wadi Jimel, we met up with the two terrorists. Apparently, they saw that we were approaching, and decided to hide behind some rocks on the banks of the riverbed. Then they began to fire at us from a range of seven yards to our left. We returned fire while taking cover. When I identified them, I ordered everyone to get up and attack – but then I realized that I couldn't get up. I'd been hit in my right leg. We killed the terrorists, and I was the only one of our forces wounded in the incident. When GOC Ori Orr came to visit me in the hospital, as expected he asked, "What were the deputy brigade commander, battalion commander, and deputy battalion commander doing at the front?" I explained the circumstances and he accepted my explanation. We all took it for granted that the decision to make the pursuit in that manner, with the senior officers in the front, had been correct. Any delay would have reduced our chances of carrying out the mission.

An extreme example of the dilemma of the commander's position took place in the village of Anza in Samaria on December 10, 1992. In a Yamam (special counterterrorism unit) operation for the arrest of an Islamic Jihad terrorist, the wanted man hid inside his home and began to shoot at our force. The Yamam force surrounded the house and shot back. In the crossfire, several barrels of olive oil caught fire, and the house went up in flames.

Yamam head commander Dudu Tzur, sector brigade commander Colonel Amal Asad, and myself as commander of Judea and Samaria division all thought that the house had been burned thoroughly, and that there was no chance anyone was left alive inside.

After the fire died down, a fire truck was called to extinguish the flames so that we could search the house to find the terrorist's body. But when the Yamam unit went in to search the house, they were met with bullets. A Yamam officer and supervisor, Sasson Mordoch, was killed, and three other combat fighters were wounded. The force evacuated the house. From a short investigation that I conducted with the fighters after they left the house, I concluded that the terrorist must have taken shelter in an attic that had an opening to the outside. This saved him from the conflagration and allowed him to continue breathing normally.

Instead of instructing a force to go look around the building for such an opening, I thought the simplest and fastest way to accomplish this was to do it myself. Taking my signaler with me, we circled the building to the corner that I thought might be the source of the shooting. I saw a small window that looked like it could lead to such an attic. I reported my position over the radio and said that I was going to throw a grenade. The first grenade missed the small opening, but the second one went into the hole and exploded. Afterwards, we found the terrorist's body in that spot, a small attic that permitted him to survive the flames and shoot at the search force.

In this case as well we might ask, was it right that a brigadier general and division commander take this on himself? Had I been wounded, of course this question would have been asked forcefully. But in this case as well, I thought the commander's place was at the position where he could decide the battle. In the special circumstances that developed and considering the risks and opportunities, I thought it was the right thing to do.

The incidents above indicate the complexity of the dilemma of the commander's position. I hope I've clarified that this is not a black and white issue, and that the decision depends on the circumstances of each individual incident.

I did not like the criticism against the "desktop commanders" following the Second Lebanon War. Retrospectively, it is true that some of the commanders were placed too far back. This mainly resulted from the highest senior command's failure to understand that this was a war and not an ordinary security event. But in the public debate, assertions were made that implied that senior commanders should not be sitting at their desks. The critique of their position portrayed them as cowards who preferred to remain in the rear. From my acquaintance with them in battle, I can state confidently that this was an injustice to most.

I am hardly inventing the wheel when I say that a commander must choose his position in such a way that will influence the outcome of the battle. In other words, he must locate himself where he can make decisions optimally to lead to victory in battle. To date, from the level of squad or tank commander up to the level of battalion commander, the commander goes in front. From the level of brigade commander and up, sometimes the commander is in front at the scene of battle, but mostly he is at the optimal position for decision making. If the command post with the computer screens can be up front, all the better. But this is not always possible. The screens enable the commander to make decisions in the best possible conditions, because they give him the full battle picture. They are where he obtains optimal data in real time, enabling him to make the decisions that will win the battle.

PART IV

The Netanyahu Government

CHAPTER 16

Welcome to Politics

When I ended my term as chief of general staff and was discharged from the IDF, I was not ready to leave the public arena. The experience I had amassed, especially in the most recent positions, my familiarity with the Palestinian issue, and my disillusionment following the Oslo Accords inspired me with a sense of mission to bring my experience and insights regarding the country's future to the public sphere.

My brush with politics while still wearing my army uniform was not very positive. I knew that for my trip from the Kiryah to Jerusalem, I needed to have anti-nausea pills handy. I saw how politicians were cynically twisting comments that I had made. I witnessed ridiculous situations, like when I was participating in a meeting of the Foreign Affairs and Defense Committee, as director of Military Intelligence or COGS, I received false "leaks" of comments that I had allegedly made at that very meeting. My personal term for the twenty-four hours after my report to the Foreign Affairs and Defense Committee was "twenty-four hours of preparing to take a hit." Sometimes, part of the Israeli public expressed their agreement with what I hadn't said, while another part was opposed to what I hadn't said. At one meeting, this situation reached an all-time high. I began my overview with a statement saying that I saw both opportunities and risks in the current situation. One of the media outlets reported my statement under the headline: "Director of military intelligence is optimistic," while another reported: "Director of military intelligence is pessimistic."

Yet, I realized that the important decisions in our lives are made in politics, and that I needed to contribute my experience to the country. Therefore, despite all my reservations, I chose to enter politics. I decided to join the Likud. I had already changed my vote back in the 1996 elections, behind the curtain at the ballot box. The change took place following my disillusionment with the Palestinian issue. As far as I saw it, our own self-deception regarding the Palestinian situation was a tangible hazard, even an existential threat. During the intelligence assessment in 1998, I had already said that if we continued to follow this path and ignore reality, the Palestinian problem would put the State of Israel's existence at risk. I was resolute about dealing with the problem differently.

I had grown up in a Mapai home reading the *Davar* party organ, and accordingly, I had voted for the Labor Party for years. I searched for individuals who could bring about change and free us of the approach based on self-deception. It wasn't that I abandoned the Labor Party; the Labor Party had abandoned me.

After I was discharged from the IDF in June 2005, I was contacted by various political entities, but I rejected anything that demanded a political connection, because I had decreed a cooling period for myself. I met people who wanted to hear my opinions regarding current state and security issues, including Benjamin Netanyahu, who was then a member of the opposition. The conversations centered on the challenges that faced the State of Israel.

My cooling period was over in November 2008, and elections were to be held in March 2009. I met with Netanyahu for our first political conversation regarding the possibility of joining the Likud Party. I was offered a reserved spot on the Likud's list, but I turned down the offer. I asked to compete in the primaries, even though they were just three weeks away.

The first primaries were a good experience for me. I felt good in the Likud, with the people, the relationships, and the support I was receiving. Here and there, I identified negative phenomena. Some people who asked to meet with me were on the hunt for a job or some other favor. After each such encounter, I told my political advisor that I would no longer meet with that person. Unfortunately, over time, the phenomenon became more common, and even affected the positive figures. Vulgar, provocative Knesset members such as Oren Chazan and David Bitan attract most of the public and media attention. They overshadow serious, diligent Knesset members who remain almost anonymous, such as Sharren Haskel.

I was elected for the seventh spot in the primaries. I had joined a party whose members reflected my perspective with a hawkish security approach on one hand, and as social liberals on the other hand. I quickly connected with Benny Begin, Dan Meridor, and Ruvi Rivlin. At the Likud party meeting during that period, the rule of law was undisputed.

Over time, matters deteriorated in this area as well. Extremism became more prominent, and the dominant voice was no longer national, but rather nationalistic, with certain voices even expressing a racist approach. The rule of law was trampled. But during the first term, and part of the second term as well, when I was defense minister, the support I received in the Likud made me feel at home, and I was able to deflect the negative influences.

After the 2009 elections, I contemplated whether I should try for the position of defense minister or education minister. The prime minister was aware of my deliberation. The role of defense minister was promised to Ehud Barak when the Labor Party joined the coalition, but I wasn't appointed as education minister either.

Instead, I was appointed as vice prime minister and minister of strategic affairs. I gave my all to the position and I saw positive results. I became familiar with the lacunae in government work, the issues that fall between the cracks, including state public relations matters. I proposed to the prime minister that a national staff for public relations be established as part of his office. When he decided against this, I took the responsibility for this area, which had been neglected due to a deterioration in the functioning of the Foreign Ministry. I was very active in fighting BDS, the delegitimization and boycotting efforts against the State of Israel. For example, we held a seminar in Israel attended by representatives of 150 organizations that fight Israel's public relations war around the world. We ran summer seminars for Jewish students who came from various universities worldwide and Israeli emissaries learning or working overseas, and armed them with knowledge and tools to fight on this front.

The government that began its term in 2009 was a good government. The State Security Cabinet functioned well. I assumed a highly influential position on the "forum of seven," alongside Netanyahu, Barak, Benny Begin, Dan Meridor, Eli Yishai, and Avigdor Lieberman. Although he was foreign minister, Lieberman barely attended any of the discussions. He was the only negative entity. On Fridays, we closed ourselves off in the Mossad headquarters, where we had less disruptions than at the prime minister's office. We reviewed issue after issue – Iran, Hezbollah, Palestinians, Gaza, Judea and Samaria, the entire region; we heard in-depth surveys and held discussions and follow-up discussions. The prime minister attended these discussions and was attentive and open. In this manner, we handled critical issues. Without leaks, without politics, without headlines, and without comments for the transcripts.

There were arguments, but they were all for the common good, for the benefit of the country. Some of the issues discussed will only be permitted for publication fifty years from now. I felt that I was making an impact, and I saw that joining politics had been a positive move.

Over time, events took place – at first, small and seemingly marginal, and later, more significant ones – that exposed me to the ugly side of politics. On the political playing field, it is easier to explain the extreme. Complicated and diverse issues are harder to explain. It turned out that making sense of a politician like myself was not at all simple – a hawk in state and security issues who also believes in a Jewish democratic state that values the rule of law and citizens' rights, similar to Begin and Jabotinsky. As time went on, I watched as a certain sector tried to depict me as extreme and unenlightened, while a different sector viewed me as a leftist and an enemy of the settlement movement.

Sometimes, my words were taken out of context to deliberately harm me. One of the first events where this happened was in August 2009, at the beginning of my term as a minister, when I made rounds of the nationwide Likud offices. On one occasion, I was invited to the Likud branch in Jerusalem. No one told me that the office was being used for a conference of the Manhigut Yehudit ("Jewish Leadership") Party, headed by right-wing maverick Moshe Feiglin. Following the event, the word spread that I was collaborating with Feiglin, which of course was false.

At that conference, I presented my worldview. I said that cognitively, it is difficult for us to understand the reality with the Palestinians. We don't realize that we do not have a true partner to work with, so we try time and time again to conduct peace negotiations and reach agreements, and then we pay the price. I emphasized that this process stems from positive intentions and from the basic desire for peace in every human being. It is natural for people who have experienced wars, like I and most Israelis, to want peace. This desire lives inside each of us like a virus, I said, and therefore, this dream of peace is skewing our cognitive perspective.

In response to a question from the audience, I said that due to this peace virus that lives within us, some people want peace now. A few days later, the Friday newspaper blared the following headline: "Ya'alon: Peace Now is a Virus." That was a complete distortion of what I had said. I saw how easy it is to manipulate words when they are deliberately taken out of context to depict someone as a delusional extremist.

I also noticed this phenomenon when I visited Samaria settlements with other ministers on a tour that was meant to show the absurdity of the Talia Sasson Report. This report had been initiated by Ariel Sharon and his supporters in preparation for the disengagement. My interpretation is that Sharon used this report as a means of punishing the settlements for their refusal to cooperate with him during the disengagement (more about the report and its significance later in this chapter). During the tour, we arrived at the ruins of the settlement of Homesh in northern Samaria, which was evacuated as part of the disengagement. Homesh was not included in the report and was not part of the tour's itinerary, but it grabbed headlines in a manner that made me suspect manipulation between the reporter and Netanyahu's office. I understood that there were entities in the prime minister's office who wanted to harm me and most of all, blemish my good name. I was also surprised by the lack of mutual support between the ministers and their petty, premeditated behavior. It was disappointing, but I had long before learned to stick it out and deal with it.

In May 2010, tension peaked when peace activists on Turkish vessel MV *Mavi Marmara* tried to break the IDF blockade of the Gaza Strip. Three weeks earlier, I had read intelligence material and understood that the activists' plan was unusually audacious: a flotilla of ten ships would attempt to reach Gaza (in the end, there were six vessels). I tried to check whether someone was acting to stop the flotilla through diplomatic means and was told that the Defense Ministry was handling the matter. I held a meeting at the Ministry of Strategic Affairs attended by representatives from the National Security Council, the Mossad, and the military to discuss preparations for the flotilla, and I discovered that proper preparations were not being made. I contacted the prime minister, but he said that Defense Minister Barak and Foreign Minister Lieberman were handling the matter.

A day before the flotilla arrived, Netanyahu flew to Canada. Before his trip, he convened a public relations meeting about the flotilla. At that point, I was already burning with anger. Was this what we had prepared? I understood that we were heading into a mess.

While the prime minister was in Canada, I served as his replacement because of my official position, but the truth is that the replacement only functions when there is no contact with the prime minister. The *Marmara* incident was managed entirely by the prime minister while he was in Canada, and I was only notified of his decisions. The attitude toward the flotilla was not serious on any level, beginning from the top. The chief of general staff wasn't even in the Pit, the war room at the Kiryah military headquarters in Tel Aviv, where the top brass usually convenes during an important incident. The entire weight of responsibility fell on the naval commandos who overcame the vessels and acted courageously, with dedication and discretion. It could have ended in a massacre.

The end of the story was that during the encounter between the naval commandos and the violent, extremist activists on the *Marmara*, nine activists were killed. Ten IDF soldiers were wounded. A public outcry raged in Israel and worldwide. Israel was criticized internationally and by the UN Security Council, and a severe crisis developed in our relations with Turkey.

We should not have been surprised by the incident. We should have been ready for it. Right after the incident, Netanyahu and his people attempted to hold me responsible, in briefs to the reporters, because I had been the prime minister's replacement at the time, although Netanyahu himself had managed the event from Canada. This did nothing to fortify the relationship between us, which should have been built on trust.

My big disappointment with the Likud took place during the elections for the Nineteenth Knesset in January 2013. When Benny Begin, Dan Meridor, and Michael Eitan did not reach realistic spots during the primaries, I understood that there was a problem. Begin paid the price for trying to intervene to help the residents during the crises of Migron and Givat Ha'ulpana. The residents of these settlements were evicted by government order. They were tricked by those who did not believe in the rule of law.

The Migron settlement and the construction in Givat Ha'ulpana neighborhood of Beit El were illegal activities that had taken place before our government began its term. They were determined to be illegal in investigations that we conducted following petitions to the Supreme Court. We would have to evacuate the settlers and destroy the buildings. The situation was complex, because some of the settlers had been unaware that they were constructing illegally, and they had invested in the projects. Minister Benny Begin took on the task of handling the issue. He formulated a plan that included evacuation and destruction as well as offering alternative housing to the evacuees. Some political elements (including some in the Likud) caused incitement among the settlers and their supporters. By failing to present the full picture, they acted inappropriately and unfairly against Begin.

I held the prime minister responsible for allowing the events to take place and not behaving like a leader who sets limits. If individuals such as Miri Regev, and during the next elections, Oren Chazan as well, are given the opportunity to dominate the discussions during the party meeting, their tones become the primary legitimate dialogue. The result is that the Likud became a party to which even Jabotinsky and Menachem Begin would not have been elected, where people such as Benny Begin, Ruvi Rivlin, and Moshe Arens are perceived as leftists.

After the elections, I was appointed defense minister. As part of my role, I had to handle another event, after which some again attempted to depict me as extreme and unenlightened. In 2004, when I was chief of general staff, I heard that a new organization had been established under the name "Breaking the Silence." It publishes testimonies from discharged soldiers of illegal activities, violence, and damage to property that took place during their service in the territories. The first testimonies came from discharged soldiers from a Nahal battalion involved in noncombat operations in Hebron. I raised the issue for discussion at General Staff and added that we were dealing with a serious problem, regardless of whether the stories were true or false. If the testimonies were true, it was obvious that the matter needed to be examined in depth and, if necessary, investigated by the Military Police Criminal Investigation Division. In any event, if IDF soldiers are discharged feeling that the operations they did in Judea and Samaria were illegal and immoral, we have a problem. Their commanders should have processed the meaning of serving in Judea and Samaria as a necessity that should not be criticized. I can sympathize with a soldier who feels uncomfortable after patting down an Arab or searching his home at two a.m. with little children crying in the background, but terrorists must be stopped, even if that means operating in this manner. The educational and command activities of the commanders, from the level of the platoon commander up to brigade commander, include ensuring that soldiers are not discharged from the army feeling that they committed illegal or immoral deeds.

I instructed the military attorney general to contact Breaking the Silence, to ask that the soldiers who testified to them also testify before a Military Police Criminal Investigation Division investigation, because they were reporting allegedly criminal activities. Very quickly, I discovered that Breaking the Silence was not willing to disclose the identities of those who had testified. Until recently, none of the soldiers who had testified to Breaking the Silence also met with the IDF on this matter. (The recent exception was the organization's spokesperson, Dean Issacharoff, who claimed that during his service as an officer in the Nahal Brigade, he beat an innocent Palestinian. In April 2017, he was summoned to a police investigation for this act that he allegedly committed according to his public statement.)

Following our request to hear the soldiers' testimonies, Breaking the Silence launched a media campaign purporting that the IDF was persecuting them. I understood that this was a political move and did not stem from a sincere concern for the IDF's image. If Breaking the Silence were truly concerned about the IDF's image, and if they were motivated by a sense of morality, they would help the IDF investigate criminal events that allegedly take place in its framework and harm it, and they would cooperate with it.

When I discovered that the organization was taking its operations overseas and slandering us, as chief of general staff I gave orders to sever all contact with them and forbid them from any access to the IDF. This organization opposed the government's policy in Judea and Samaria, and the IDF cannot allow itself to bring politics into the picture. If an entity that is opposed to the "occupation" is brought into the military, an organization with the opposite political viewpoint must be brought in as well. But in the IDF, there is no room for the former or the latter. Later, when I lectured at universities and Jewish communities in the United States, I encountered the activity of Breaking the Silence again, and I saw the damage that they were causing to the IDF and the State of Israel.

When I returned to government as defense minister, I again encountered the issue when the parents of soldiers started to complain that their sons were being exposed to the activism of Breaking the Silence while in the IDF. I contacted Chief of General Staff Benny Gantz and asked him to check what had changed. It turned out that certain units were permitting them access to the soldiers, as a local initiative of the education officers. Furthermore, representatives of the organization were making rounds at schools, meeting with students before their recruitment and carrying out a slander campaign against the IDF. The chief of general staff refreshed the existing orders that prohibited Breaking the Silence's activity with the IDF.

The IDF encourages many activities that purposely raise moral dilemmas for discussion. Some of these are facilitated by external, professional entities. These discussions are legitimate. The IDF handles them within the units, in squad commanders' courses, and at the officers' cadets school (Bahad 1 training base). We don't "shut mouths" and we don't prevent soldiers from addressing moral dilemmas that they will have to face during their operational activities. But when an organization comes with a clear political agenda against the "occupation," they are crossing a red line.

At the same time, I am opposed to any attempts to say that Breaking the Silence is illegal. I have heard voices in favor of such a move, even within the Likud. The organization's members have the right to express their opinions even if they contradict mine – but not inside the IDF. They also have the right to receive the support and funding of philanthropic institutions – but funding from foreign governments is a red line that may not be crossed, regardless of whether the organization is Breaking the Silence, Zochrot (which promotes awareness of the Palestinian Naqba) or Adalah (Legal Center for Arab Minority Rights in Israel, which promotes Palestinian human rights). Some Israeli organizations that receive funding from foreign governments undermine the state's very right to exist as a Jewish and democratic state.

Therefore, when the law governing nonprofit organizations was proposed, I reasoned that foreign government funding for organizations at the heart of the political battlefield should be prevented. Does anyone think that the State of Israel should be funding the Basque underground or political organizations operating in Sweden or Norway? I recognize the right of these organizations to raise donations in the accepted way, but not from foreign governments. A diverse range of voices is an inseparable part of democracy.

One of the challenging areas that I addressed as defense minister was related to settlement and preserving the rule of law in Judea and Samaria. The gradual deterioration within the Likud extended to this area as well.

My position on the matter is decisive: I support the settlement of Judea and Samaria, in accordance with the government's policy, in specific areas, and most importantly – according to the law. It is our right to settle anywhere. Someone who is willing to waive that right in Judea and Samaria will waive it in Tel Aviv as well. In the Balfour Declaration and in other international declarations, no one limited the national homeland of the Jewish people to the 1967 lines. Those lines are the result of war, and from a security perspective, they are not defensible lines. Israel cannot abandon itself to "Hamastan" rule in Judea and Samaria. If we return to the 1967 lines and forfeit Judea and Samaria, we will leave the next generations with a strategic security problem that could turn into an existential threat.

I also believe that wherever there is no life, there is no security. The country's borders were determined based on settlement. Jewish history has proven this since the days of the Partition Plan and the "tower and stockade" method of settlement used in Mandatory Palestine, in which Jewish groups established settlements in strategic locations. Today, we know that wherever there is a kindergarten, there will be security. Where there are no towns, there is no military presence. This is a philosophy that I formulated over the years based on my experiences, and this was also Yitzchak Rabin's outlook.

The struggle for land in Israel is in part a struggle with crime, because in places where the land is not inhabited by Jews, it is liable to be illegally seized. This phenomenon is apparent in the case of the Bedouins in the Negev Desert – who have tried, unsuccessfully, to seize IDF firing zones or JNF forests.

In the Galilee, the complex reality has different causes. As agriculture begins to dwindle, sometimes Arabs take control of land that was abandoned by Jewish farmers. Arabs also purchase land from Jewish farmers who are at risk and decide to sell at high prices. Such sales are sometimes backed by foundations such as Al-Quds, which operates in the Gulf states. Instead of conquering the country with tanks, they are conquering it with land purchases.

For all the reasons that I listed, there must be Jewish settlement in Judea and Samaria, but it must be administered by the state according to the law. The members of Gush Emunim can claim that if they had adhered to the law, places such as Sebastia, Kedumim, Elon Moreh, and other settlements would never have been established. Unfortunately, I cannot refute that, but that claim needs to be posed to the previous governments. Today, settlement must exist based on government decisions and according to the law, and not as each person sees fit.

I encountered attempts to portray me as an extremist based on this position as well. I found myself almost entirely alone on all fronts related to the struggle to preserve the rule of law: demolition of illegal construction, protecting the position of the Supreme Court, and more. It was as if I were standing on the other side of the fence.

Back when I was appointed as Judea and Samaria division commander, some thought that a "kibbutz leftist" had arrived to "fight the occupation." Quickly enough, they realized that this "leftist" also knew how to fight terror and protect the law. Settlers understood that with me, they couldn't play tricks by adding a new trailer here or there, or by building an illegal outpost in memory of a terror attack victim. Over the years, from the days of Gush Emunim in Sebastia and until I was appointed defense minister, the settlement movement had developed the attitude they could establish facts on the ground. They thought they could use the "tower and stockade" method of settlement under the nose of the Israeli government, as if it were the British Mandate. I was vehemently opposed to this conduct.

When I entered the position of vice prime minister and minister of strategic affairs, I had to address a reality determined by previous governments that Judea and Samaria were occupied territories, a temporary deposit that we would one day give up. The Supreme Court rendered its decisions based on this approach. After all, if they are "occupied territories," then in the court, a local Arab takes precedence over the temporary, "occupying" Jew. I resented this approach as well.

As defense minister, I had to deal with illegal construction on one hand, while on the other hand, I had to curb the effects of the Talia Sasson Report. According to the report, any settlement for which the approval stage of the planning and construction process had not been completed was illegal. This led to a list of over two hundred "illegal" settlements and outposts. Some of these had been approved by the authorities, but the planning and construction procedures had not been completely finalized. At the time, I claimed that not all the settlements with incomplete planning and construction procedures should be considered illegal. Lehavot Chaviva, for example, was established in 1949, but its urban construction plan (which regulates use of the land) was only approved in 1981. The urban construction plan for Beit Shemesh was only approved in the 1990s. Before approval, were those settlements considered illegal?

This is a different policy approach, which did not correspond to the policy of the elected government, and therefore, we promoted a resolution that effectively threw the Talia Sasson Report into the garbage bin. A decision was reached to examine all outposts based on defined criteria: any settlement built on private Arab land would be removed, and any settlement built on government land would be considered for authorization.

In addition, in conjunction with MK Benny Begin and attorney Zvi Hauser, who was serving as government secretary, I initiated the establishment of a committee led by late Supreme Court Justice Edmond Levy. The committee, which was composed of former Foreign Ministry legal advisor Alan Baker, a specialist in international law, and former district court judge Techiya Shapira, examined the entire issue of settlement in Judea and Samaria based on the political approach of the Likud government. The most important section in the report determined that in terms of international law, there was justification for defining the area as a "disputed territory" instead of "occupied territory." This was resolved by a government resolution on November 29, 2011. The date was no coincidence – this was the date of the UN partition resolution in 1947.

This resolution was the most important element. The rest were bureaucratic issues, and as far as I was concerned the government system would handle them according to the law. It would remove settlements that had to be removed and examine the possibility of authorization when possible. This was the keystone that obligated both the state attorney and the Supreme Court. Indeed, changes were made. Justice Asher Grunis, former president of the Supreme Court, mentioned the Edmond Levy Report in his rulings on construction in Judea and Samaria. He gave us time to authorize construction in the settlements and even prodded us when there were delays in the authorization process. We built the proper legal infrastructure to advance the issues.

But there are always extremists in the settlements, those who do not accept the legal approach in any way whatsoever because as far as they are concerned, the land was given to us via a heavenly sales deed recorded in the Bible. With such fanatics, I cannot hold any dialogue. If the land is registered in the Land Registry under the name of an Arab, what does it matter that it was promised to our forefather Abraham?

When I was defense minister, I did not permit the establishment of illegal settlements. In 2016, when settlers entered the Beit Rachel and Beit Leah buildings in Hebron, I was angry. In order to settle in Hebron, both state and security authorizations are required, as well as proof that the purchase was made legally, which was not the case this time, as the documents were discovered to be false. I gave the inhabitants an ultimatum for evacuation – and they vacated the homes a few hours later, on a Friday morning. But soon enough, I discovered that I was on my own. On Sunday morning, while pressure was applied from within the Likud and by the Jewish Home (Bayit Yehudi) Party, Prime Minister Netanyahu opened the government meeting by stating that he hoped that the defense minister would allow the settlers to enter the homes within the week. I felt that I had been abandoned. I was at the front and I was serving as the bulletproof vest.

This scenario repeated itself during the evacuation of the Dreinoff project in Beit El. A felonious contractor had constructed illegal buildings without any authorization – and to the dismay of the neighboring residents, who complained about the illegal construction. He exacerbated the matter by deviating from Beit El's boundaries and spilling over to the private land of a Palestinian, which led the landowner to appeal to the Supreme Court. This was the reality that I inherited: on one hand, illegal construction, and on the other hand – a government that bows under pressure and promises to try to authorize the buildings, plus the Supreme Court threat. Under the prime minister's nose, MKs Betzalel Smotrich and Oren Chazan set up parliamentary offices in illegal buildings, and Netanyahu, as usual, didn't call them to order.

I announced that the matter was not up for discussion. The only option was to demolish the illegal buildings, and there was no need to wait for the Supreme Court ruling. But when the issues reach the prime minister's doorstop, he prefers to hand the responsibility back to the Supreme Court and then blame it, via his emissaries, for activism and leftist tendencies. The event turned into a battlefield between myself and right-wing entities in the Likud and Jewish Home. This time, I was portrayed as coming out against the settlement movement and working to destroy it.

The clash became very serious when it touched on what I viewed as a breach of the rule of law. During one of the discussions, I said that blood that was shed due to the failure to uphold the rule of law was on our hands. Those who do not respect the rule of law, those who ignore the fact that during the Dreinoff project incident, teens threw rocks and bags of urine at soldiers and police officers, those who do not speak out against this and instead attack the Supreme Court – should not be surprised when these teens later slash the tires of the company commander's jeep or the police car, uproot olive trees, light a mosque on fire, or burn a Palestinian family.

Again I was deemed an extremist by both sides. As far as the leftists were concerned, I was a right-winger working to approve settlements in Judea and Samaria, but among a certain group of the settlers, I was a leftist working against them and trying to evacuate settlers. I admit that it is a bit difficult to put me into a box. If I'm on the right, that means I must be unenlightened, extreme, and flaut the law – even violent and racist. But if I abide by the law – I must be a leftist in the eyes of the extreme right.

Toward the end of my term as defense minister, the issue of the settlement in Amona was also placed on my desk. This was a twenty-year-old legacy that no government had properly handled. In this case, the facts were clear, no matter who was reading them – Benjamin Netanyahu, Avigdor Lieberman, Naftali Bennett, or Ayelet Shaked. Amona was located on private Arab land that was registered in the Land Registry under an Arab's name. Settlement was not possible there. Menachem

Begin had set down the rules in 1979: 1. Establishment of settlements will be on state land only. 2. Expropriation of land from an Arab will be carried out only for public purposes and for use by both sides – Jews and Arabs.

Therefore, my position on the issue was unequivocal: the settlers would not be able to stay in Amona. However, because some of them were misled by government institutions, we would take responsibility for that as the authority. The fact that the government paved roads and built additional infrastructures had led them to believe that the settlement was legal and therefore invest in their homes. Thus, we proposed to the settlers who wanted to stay together as a community that we would establish an alternative neighborhood for them in Shiloh. We promised compensation to those who had invested money. At the same time, though, our message was clear: no one would be staying in Amona.

Even after I left office, the prime minister and the ministers followed this position. Then suddenly, the message changed. Why? Because of pressure from the extreme right. Instead of behaving like leaders, they conducted political maneuvering and argued over who had contacted the Supreme Court first to request an extension – Netanyahu or Bennett. That is not leadership – that's survival politics that only invites additional pressure.

In the end, the incident was resolved with the Regulation Law (a law intended to retroactively approve Israeli construction on private Palestinian land). This occurred after all realized that there was no chance this law would get past the Supreme Court, even if it was voted on three times. The attorney general declared that it was unconstitutional and asserted he would not defend it at the Supreme Court. But the coalition members (except for MK Benny Begin) all voted in favor of the law. Lieberman was even quoted as sarcastically saying that he had voted in favor because he knew that the Supreme Court wouldn't be approving it anyway. The rest of the process involved attacks on the "leftist Supreme Court," presided over at the time by Judge Miriam Naor – the justice who had grown up in a right-wing Revisionist home; whose husband, Dr. Aryeh Naor, was the government secretary in Menachem Begin's government; and whose son, Naftali Naor, is a Likud activist.

This is politics that pretends and manipulates. It is a dangerous process, and we are paying for it dearly. Because of the Regulation Law, former US president Barack Obama did not veto the harsh resolution against the settlements in the United Nations. Must we pay for the political tricks of Bennett and Netanyahu as each try to prove he is the bigger patriot? We got out of it fairly unscathed – but we will pay a heavy price in the long term. "If not for the fear of authority, man would swallow his neighbor alive" (Ethics of the Fathers). That's where we are headed with this conduct.

Alongside the illegal activity of various entities on the issues of construction and settlement, the problem of the Price Tag movement (violent revenge acts by Jewish extremists) and Jewish terror intensified. Violent activity was focused at several flash points in Judea and Samaria: Yitzhar, Tapuach, Bat Ayin, and Southern Har Hebron. This was violence based on ideology, and many of the individuals who participated were youth. They were called "Hilltop Youth" since much of the illegal construction was done on the tops of the gently rolling hills in the region.

One of the leaders of the Hilltop Youth was Rabbi Yitzchak Ginsburgh, a Chabad chassid and leading expert on mysticism who is also president of the Od Yosef Chai Yeshiva in Yitzhar. I became acquainted with this rabbi when I served as commander of the Judea and Samaria Division. I read his books and turned green. His rabbinic worldview belonged alongside that of *Mein Kampf*. It states that the Jews are a superior race while the Arabs are an inferior one. When I was GOC Central Command, I went to meet him, and I found him to be an intelligent, charismatic individual.

I understood why people flocked to him – he promotes a fascist, racist worldview with polish and charm.

After I was appointed minister of defense, I discovered the extent of the Hilltop Youth phenomenon. The disengagement had caused a crisis and caused the fringes to expand. Dozens of Hilltop Youth filled illegal outposts in the Binyamin and Samaria regions. Some came from outside Judea and Samaria, but aside from several educational initiatives, the leadership was unable to handle the phenomenon. The result: Jewish youth damaged Arab property, spray-painted Nazi slogans on the walls of the Trappist monastery in Latrun, and set fire to the Church of the Multiplication of the Loaves and Fish in the Galilee. All connections led to that same network of extremists, some of whom follow Rabbi Ginsburgh or his student Rabbi Yitzchak Shapira, head of the yeshiva in Yitzhar, while some are even more extreme. They damage Arab property in revenge for terror attacks or government acts, such as evacuating illegal outposts.

These acts disgusted me. My mother was a Holocaust survivor, and I was educated to believe that every human being was created in God's image. I learned to fight my enemies without hatred or delegitimization. I live on the axis between "You shall not murder" and "If someone tries to kill you, rise up and kill him first." This axis guided me in making thousands of decisions related to taking life. I am not exaggerating when I say that there are very few people in Israel, and fewer in the Knesset, who have encountered as many enemy soldiers and terrorists as I have – and been forced to kill them. But even when I operated in that arena, my activity was moral.

We cannot in any way accept intentional damage to property. When I read the memoirs that my grandfather wrote about the pogroms in Ukraine, I see before my eyes the Jewish pogrom carried out in Israel against Arab property. We must use force when there is ethical justification. But damage to property, and even more importantly, harm to individuals, is an unethical act that society cannot accept. I take this for granted – it is my backbone. It's how I grew up and was educated. With these acts, the morals of Israeli society, in which I was educated and which I taught to others, are falling apart in front of our eyes.

Beyond the severe moral and ethical problem, in terms of efficacy every such incident is a "bullet in the leg" of the settlement project – if not in the head. It provides ammunition and fuel to those who attempt to delegitimize the settlements. Settlement leaders who are considered supportive of the state understand this and suffer from it as well. They are also the victims of tire slashing and other vengeful acts.

As defense minister with responsibility for the rule of law in Judea and Samaria and the Jordan Valley, I addressed the escalation in acts of Jewish terror with several steps. I closed the yeshiva in Yitzhar, and I sent a Border Police company to the site after a series of Price Tag activities and attacks on military officers. This process also encouraged the law enforcement entities, which observe policy and leadership and ask that as leaders, we speak clearly. I spoke clearly, and the result was a drastic decline in Price Tag actions.

But before I was able to do so, Jewish terrorists stepped up their work and succeeded in carrying out two atrocious murders. In July 2014, Palestinian youth Muhammad Abu Khdeir was murdered in revenge for the 2014 kidnapping and murder of three Jewish youths, Gilad Sha'ar, Naftali Fraenkel, and Eyal Yifrach. In July 2015, Molotov cocktails were thrown at the home of the Dawabshe family in Duma, causing the deaths of Sa'ad and Riham Dawabshe and their toddler son Ali, and severely wounding their son Ahmad, age four.

Here I must emphasize: these were two terror attacks performed by Jews, compared to hundreds of attacks carried out by Arabs. That was why I was outraged by any attempt by international entities to speak in a balanced manner about "violence on both sides." But from our viewpoint, even those two attacks were two too many.

Our greatest fear was realized. An extremist faction, kippah-wearing fanatics that had no God, carried out a horrific act that represented a distortion of the Jewish worldview. I knew that these youth had not sprung from a vacuum. A definitive, authoritative statement was needed, both to encourage the Shin Bet and the police in the investigation, and also toward all those who were involved in the incident or who were considering becoming involved in similar incidents in the future.

Within a few days, investigators of the Duma murders realized that this was an act of Jewish terror. I reported this to the cabinet, and I was attacked with accusations: "Who said it's Jewish terror?" "Maybe it's an electrical short?" "Maybe it's an internal settling of accounts among the Palestinians?" I firmly declared that we would not avoid responsibility.

I saw the clear connection between the forgiving attitude toward Price Tag acts by Hilltop Youth and contempt for the rule of law, and the escalation in Jewish terror, just as I saw the revenge connection between the burning of the Dawabshe family and the 2015 murder by Hamas of Rabbi Eitam and Na'ama Henkin of Neria. This is what happens when we are not careful in upholding the rule of law. Blood is on our hands.

The Shin Bet knew that the perpetrators of the Duma attack were connected to a group of thirty fanatics whose ideology is even more extreme than Rabbi Ginsburgh's. These are hard nuts to crack. They have been trained to avoid breaking under interrogation, to uphold the right to remain silent, admit nothing, and hide evidence. It took a while, but following administrative detentions, the interrogators finally deciphered the murder and obtained a confession.

During the interrogation, accusations were made that the young Jewish detainees were tortured. A campaign of lies began, asserting that the confessions were inadmissible because they were obtained under torture. Of course, the detainees were not tortured. Following the recommendations of the Landoy Commission (1987 investigation into extreme force used by the Shin Bet), under certain circumstances the head of the Shin Bet may authorize interrogators to use special means. This refers to physical and emotional pressure, such as preventing sleep (pulling out fingernails is not permitted). Everything is carried out under legal supervision.

Knesset members and ministers had difficulty accepting the painful fact that this was Jewish terror. I was disgusted to discover that certain politicians visited the family home of the youth who admitted the arson. When Abu Mazen sends condolences to the family of a terrorist, we complain. But here among us, there are those who behave exactly like him.

In December 2015, I brought to the cabinet a terrible video that circulated on social media. The clip shows extreme right activist youths dancing ecstatically at a wedding, weapons held high, celebrating the Duma killings and even stabbing the photo of murdered toddler Ali Dawabshe. At first everyone was shocked. Then some raised the possibility that this was a Shin Bet conspiracy.

I was amazed to discover the deep rift that had opened between us, the complete disconnect between politicians and events in the field. Instead of being shocked by the phenomenon growing under our very noses, by Jews dancing at a wedding over the blood of a baby as if they were Hamas or ISIS fighters – they suggest conspiracy theories. The prime minister used the term "Jewish terror" only after Bennett preceded him in daring to mention the phrase.

In such extreme incidents, a statesmanlike declaration has great importance. Our leaders must define and clarify our moral values, and support and breathe the fighting spirit into the law-enforcement entities – the Shin Bet, the Israeli Police, and the attorney general. Witnessing the failure of statesmanship in the face of Jewish terror, I realized that due to short-term political considerations, we would pay a heavy price in the long term. I felt that I remained almost alone on the battlefield.

X Another challenge I addressed as defense minister was the wave of terror of stabbings and vehicle ramming attacks that began in September 2015. This new development surprised both sides. We had prepared for an uptick in attacks around the time of the Jewish High Holidays, because every year during this season, Palestinian organizations and the Islamic movement in Israel would fan the fires of the Temple Mount issue. But we weren't prepared for the continuous series of attacks carried out by individuals acting alone. Even the Palestinians were caught unprepared. The spontaneous, lone wolf attacks were unfamiliar, unpredictable, and difficult to control.

Except for a few incidents, such as the band of three terrorists from Qabatiya who decided to commit a stabbing attack together in Jerusalem, most of the attacks were individual initiatives. These individuals made an "on the spot" decision, often inspired by an incitement video they had watched the night before on social media, or due to personal pressure – unrequited love, a personal or family crisis, failing exams, and so on. The idea of escaping the problems of this world and moving on to the next world as a martyr enticed them.

This new wave of attacks broke out in the wake of the quiet that followed Operation Defensive Shield. Since then, the terror organizations had not managed to lift their heads – not because their motivation was any less, but thanks to our intelligence control and our operational freedom of action. We continued to attack whenever necessary, arresting anyone who we discovered was planning an attack, and striving to nip any terrorist activities in the bud. The terrorists lacked the ability to carry out a large attack, but their motivation to do so continued, and so knifing and vehicle ramming incidents by individuals became prevalent. It is possible that the ISIS decapitation videos disseminated around that time were also an influential factor.

As always, the wave of violence began with the Temple Mount. The fire is always kindled in the area of the Temple Mount, on Rosh Hashanah (the Jewish New Year) or on Passover. Recall that Arafat decided to start a war after the Western Wall Tunnel incident and after Sharon ascended to the Temple Mount. That's where it all begins. It's easy to ignite the spark there.

On Rosh Hashanah 2015, the Temple Mount riots broke out. They started with a group of thirty young men, Hamas members, who barricaded themselves inside Al-Aqsa Mosque at night, along with a supply of pipe bombs, rocks and Molotov cocktails. The next morning, just as the first group of tourists stepped onto the site, the Hamas attacked. The Palestinian media and websites immediately joined in the incitement with the slogan: "Al-Aqsa is in Danger." It was a portent of what lay ahead. We started to suffer three or four individual knifings and car ramming attacks every day in Jerusalem, Judea and Samaria, and later in other areas throughout Israel. Terrorist attacks are contagious, especially when they result in the murder of Jews.

This phenomenon posed a greater challenge than we had known in the past. When a team of terrorists organize themselves, need to buy weapons and create bombs, we have time to track them. But if someone decides to commit a terrorist attack on the spur of the moment, without divulging his intentions to anyone, like the fifteen-year-old teen who entered Otniel and stabbed Dafna Meir to death in her own home, our ability to issue an alert or to thwart it is minimal. Knives and cars are readily available weapons. No alerts are involved. Anyone is allowed to own a knife, and anyone can drive a car. It's a complex security challenge.

Our response was expressed on several dimensions. The first dimension was an attempt to identify various entities involved in incitement – pirate radio stations, Facebook accounts, websites – and stop them. Our abilities in this area gradually became more sophisticated. Using intelligence operations, we pinpointed the inciting entities, located people who intended to attack, and arrested them in time.

The second dimension involved deploying more forces in areas where Jews and Arabs interact, locations that became prone to attacks, such as Gush Etzion Junction, Tapuach Junction, and the industrial zone in western Binyamin. In these areas, skilled forces and protection measures were added as reinforcement, including protective concrete blockades to prevent vehicle ramming attacks at bus stops. Some cabinet ministers and other politicians criticized the use of protective measures and called to "switch from defense to offense," "launch Defensive Shield II" and "carry out targeted aerial killings in Judea and Samaria." These are examples of empty slogans that may earn "likes" on Facebook but are disconnected from reality. After all, since Operation Defensive Shield in 2002, the IDF has had offensive freedom of action throughout all areas of Judea and Samaria, including Area A. Any information that alerts the army of an intention to carry out a terrorist attack is quickly translated into an operation to thwart it. To do so, a large operation is not necessary – a small, highly skilled force is deployed. This is the daily operational routine. Therefore, aerial attacks are also unnecessary.

Another means that we applied was extending punishments to family members of terrorists who killed Israelis, as a deterrent. This included demolition of homes; revocation of work permits, including those of second-degree relatives of the terrorist's family; denial of exit permits to Israel, and even outside of Israel, for first- and second-degree relatives. These efforts were meant to encourage the families to avert terrorist attacks. It worked. There were families who prevented attacks and even turned in family members who were about to commit an attack.

In villages such as Qabatiya and Bani Na'im, which have produced a series of terrorists, the Coordinator of Government Activities in the Territories Unit (COGAT) and his staff got involved on the ground. They entered the villages and convened public leaders, mukhtars, school principals, and parent committees. They demanded that these leaders take responsibility for handling the attackers. The initiative was successful. The Palestinian Authority did the same thing. They searched for knives in students' backpacks and organized talks at the schools to explain why committing a terrorist attack was not a worthwhile move.

It was important to avoid pushing the rest of the population into the circle of violence. We did that, despite pressure within the cabinet to react strongly. Many claimed that we could not stand by with our hands tied behind our backs while they were stabbing us. Cabinet members called for closures and curfews "to choke the Palestinians." Heavy-handed suggestions were made, such as demolishing twenty high-rise buildings in the Issawiya neighborhood of Jerusalem, a hotbed for terrorists; ordering the IDF that after any vehicle ramming attack from a village, the army would remain inside the village for seven days; and blocking all Palestinian traffic on the main highways. These suggestions were accompanied by populist cries such as, "Why don't we enter every village, neighborhood, and city? We aren't we turning over every stone?"

The cabinet is not supposed to be involved in resolutions such as these, and furthermore, its suggestions were illogical and dangerous as well. Certainly, any village that had served as a starting point for a terrorist was immediately closed off, and the individuals involved were arrested. But how would it have helped for the army to remain there for a full week? Had we adopted these measures, we would have easily been dragged into a third Intifada. We would have pushed the entire Palestinian population into the circle of violence.

Another front that I had to handle was the issue of the terrorists' bodies. The government decided not to return the bodies of terrorists, in contradiction to the opinions of the professionals, who pointed out the dangers of such a move. This was without even considering our ethical position that we do not use bodies as bargaining chips. While we keep a terrorist's body, the mourning tent in his honor remains active and constitutes a point of friction and violence. After the government decided against returning bodies, contrary to my judgment, fifteen such tents were active in Hebron. To the public, I was depicted as the leftist who wanted to return the terrorists' bodies to their families.

In my case, this is an especially sensitive issue, because of my personal connection with the family of Hadar Goldin, my own relative. Hadar was killed while fighting terrorists in 2014 in Operation Protective Edge in Gaza, and his body has not been returned. The family was provoked with statements such as: they have your son's body, but we're returning their bodies?

It should be recalled that the decision not to return bodies contradicts the Israeli interest of treating Judea and Samaria separately from Gaza. If we make this dangerous connection, we encourage Hamas to get involved in the issue of the bodies of terrorists from Judea and Samaria – an issue that should remain between the Palestinian Authority and ourselves. We will be acting against our own interests. The distinction between bodies of terrorists from the Gaza Strip, as an open issue between Hamas and ourselves, and the bodies of terrorists from Judea and Samaria, is very important to us. I explained this to the Goldin family in our frequent conversations. Sometimes, they accepted my explanation, while at other times they did not.

Of course, in Judea and Samaria the bodies must be returned with stipulations. We cannot allow the funeral procession to become an incitement procession. We must demand that the family limit the funeral's duration and prevent it from becoming a mass event. But we should not be involved in bargaining with bodies.

I also blocked suggestions such as imposing a closure or curfew in Judea and Samaria. If Palestinian workers don't go to work in Israel, this harms the Israeli market as well as the Palestinians. When people sit in their homes idly, the ground becomes volatile.

Had they been accepted, delusional suggestions such as these would have caused immense damage to Israel. I again stood strong in the face of that dangerous cabinet, whose members were having a criticism contest. When the security issue is pulled away from Prime Minister Netanyahu, he joins in the criticism and breaks, because he is easily influenced by pressure. Such criticism can inevitably lead to unintended escalation, because if Hamas is worried that Israel is planning something, it is liable to try to preempt it.

Members of the cabinet repeated the claims that we were taking a defensive approach instead of an offensive one, that we weren't creative enough, and that we were conservative and fixed in our ways. These assertions were incorrect. We were not in the same situation as we were prior to Operation Defensive Shield. Back then, we hadn't entered on the ground for an extended period of time, and it had become a launch pad for hundreds of suicide bombers. Today, when we have information about a terrorist, we go wherever we need to and arrest him. This is an ongoing offensive operation.

In the end, the wave of terror was successfully averted. Representatives from different countries suffering from terror came to us to learn how we managed to stop the wave of knife terror attacks. Part of the answer is making sure not to push the population into a corner, and to make the distinction between the bad apples and those who are not involved.

During such events, which are a blow to the public morale, we must stand strong and do what is right, not necessarily what is popular. I was on duty as deputy chief of general staff during many severe suicide attacks. After an attack that claims many lives, the blood boils. In such cases, I became accustomed to push back against a mental state that I call "kicking your bare foot into the wall." In the wake of the public outcry to "do something," the easiest thing for a leader to do is to make a rash decision and deal a forceful blow to the Palestinians. The most natural impulse is to kick your bare foot into the wall, until your foot finally breaks.

When the blood boils and dangerous suggestions are raised that stem from a desire for revenge, a good leader knows how to stand back and remain calm. When political interests prevent this, our national interests pay the price.

CHAPTER 17

Professional Military, Political Cabinet

I began my role as minister of defense with a positive attitude and a sense of mission. I arrived after a difficult period of tension between Minister of Defense Ehud Barak and Chief of General Staff Gabi Ashkenazi. I had followed previous events from the side, as one who understood the issues. At first, I thought that Barak and Netanyahu were responsible for this situation, as they had permitted this tension to exist. Then I realized that they both were waging a battle with the aim of harming Chief of General Staff Ashkenazi. They wanted to destroy him politically, in case he was planning to run for election after leaving the military service.

I was hardly surprised by this, because I'd seen it happen to previous COGSs, especially toward the end of their tenure. They were manipulated for the purpose of harming their reputations, in the event they might want to compete on the political playing field, a common process in Israel for former COGSs. One of the reasons for the waiting period that was set between the date when the COGS removed his uniform and his entry into politics was to prevent this erosion of his reputation. This law was also necessary to prevent the COGS from political considerations while he was still on the job.

During Shaul Mofaz's tenure as COGS, the government decided on a waiting period of six months, but during Dan Halutz's term, it jumped to three years. Still, it became clear that even this did not help. Political elements began to gnaw at Chief of General Staff Gadi Eizenkot at the height of his tenure. Either way, I think that a two-year wait period is enough.

When I entered the Defense Ministry, the atmosphere was gloomy. It stunk of dead meat. I was easily able to clear the air. In that period, the media editorial columns wrote that the Kiryah towers (one for the Defense Ministry, another for the general staff) had moved closer together and the air was purified. This is true. Egos were left outside the building, discussions remained relevant, and Chief of General Staff Benny Gantz and I had a trusting relationship. We did not fight over credit or public status, and we cooperated fully. The message came through and was understood fully by everyone around me.

Despite this, during that time the political cabinet was very different from the one I'd come to know in the previous term. This was a shallow cabinet, full of political ambition. It included ministers who did not read up on issues, did not listen, and did not bother to stay in the room until the discussions had ended. Politics entered the holy temple – the forum that discusses matters of life or death. Instead of supporting the prime minister, they tried to destroy him. Some of the ministers searched for ways to damage the prime minister and catch him out. They tried to harm me, so I wouldn't inherit his position. Netanyahu no longer trusted his cabinet, and with good reason – everything that was said inside leaked out and was exploited for political use.

Dealing in politics in the place where the most important, fateful decisions are made is extremely disturbing. The guilty party in this situation is the prime minister. I've been acquainted with cabinets since

1995, ever since I was head of Military Intelligence, under five prime ministers: Rabin, Peres, Netanyahu, Barak, and Sharon. I observed Yitzchak Rabin and Ariel Sharon in similar situations. When someone made them angry, they knew how to set limits.

The intensive discussions among the top seven ministers that I'd experienced in the previous term were no longer held. Instead, the serious discussions took place in my office. Since I had served as GOC, I'd held regular discussions at different levels, and I organized them like planning a building. A building begins with the architecture and design stage, continues to the engineering stage that determines the type and quantity of materials, and ends with the construction stage that carries out the plan. Similarly, I usually began my meetings with a discussion of design, where we first examined the overall situation. A too-rapid descent into the details of planning leads to loss of eye contact with entities that influence the events. There are external events that we cannot influence, but they influence us, and we must take them into account – such as elections in the United States and in the Palestinian Authority, crisis among the Palestinians, or a visit of the US Secretary of State to the region. A design discussion is at the macro level – a forum for thinking. It includes thinking out of the box, high-level cognitive thinking that is not weighted down by the details of arrangement of forces in the field.

In the cabinet formed after the 2013 elections, it was impossible to hold such discussions. During Operation Pillar of Defense (2012), another government ruled, although it was led by the same prime minister. Then we held very serious discussions, in the cabinet and mainly in the forum of top seven ministers, about what we should do in case of an escalation with Gaza. We knew that sooner or later it would come, and we had to prepare for it.

Of course, first we examined the possibility of acting on the political level to prevent escalation, but this option was ruled out because Hamas was not a partner for negotiations or a decision for a cease-fire. From the Hamas point of view, a cease-fire would be only temporary, while in return Hamas demanded that we retreat to the 1967 lines and divide Jerusalem. So back during my tenure as minister of strategic affairs, the diplomatic opportunities had been discounted and we knew that we had to prepare operational plans in case of escalation.

During the cabinet meetings prior to Pillar of Defense, we concluded that the option of occupying Gaza was not a top priority – to put it mildly. Instead, it was a last resort. The IDF is capable of occupying the Gaza Strip. But if we do so, we must take responsibility for whatever happens there, because no one else will do it for us – not Abu Mazen, nor the Egyptians or anyone else. Occupying Gaza bears a price tag: the price of rebuilding, of the victims that will inevitably result from deploying our best units there, and of sinking into the Gaza muck. We would gain all this, but without stopping the rockets, because the enemy can continue to shoot even when we're inside.

Occupying Gaza in such a reality would be a flawed deal. Operation Pillar of Defense ended with an Egyptian-brokered cease-fire without us entering Gaza. Instead, we conducted counterattacks. When the new government took office and a new cabinet was formed, it inherited the understandings reached by the previous cabinet.

This was the state of affairs in 2014 when we began Operation Protective Edge.

I had addressed the issue of attack tunnels when I served as deputy COGS. Although we'd invested much thought and billions of shekels on the subject, we still hadn't found the perfect solution. The Americans have been living with the problem on the Mexican border for many years, but even the superpower comes to learn from us. We were facing an unsolvable problem. We built an operational and technological defense system that aimed to reveal anyone coming out of the ground, to prevent another incident like the kidnapping of Gilad Schalit or an attack on a settlement. We prepared and practiced for this scenario. We never neglected the issue – as was later asserted. We also worked to locate tunnels that penetrated our territory, and we succeeded in identifying four such tunnels before Operation Protective Edge began.

In April 2014, we realized that Hamas was considering the tunnels in a new way, intending to carry out a massive attack on a scale much larger than before by exiting several tunnels simultaneously. We concluded that Hamas was planning such an attack, but that it was not yet ready to carry it out. We realized that this might require us to act against the tunnels in combination with a land operation, and we began to organize for this on the operational level. We began to prepare the brigades, we readied equipment, and we began exercises – each brigade on its own schedule – for locating and neutralizing tunnels.

No one anticipated the escalation that took place in July. Military Intelligence and the Shin Bet determined correctly that Hamas was not planning escalation and was not preparing for it. But as can always happen, a chain of incidents finally led to war. The state comptroller did not predict it during his work on the report following the operation, because his job does not include examining the other side. Hamas deteriorated into escalation. Had Hamas wanted to surprise us, it would have done so. But we also boiled the pot. We pushed Hamas into escalation through steps that we took.

The deterioration began with the kidnapping of three youths, Gilad Sha'ar, Naftali Fraenkel, and Eyal Yifrach, on June 12, 2014. Subsequently, in Operation Brother's Keeper, IDF forces searched for them in Judea and Samaria. Meanwhile, political pressure increased, to intensify measures against Hamas and arrest Palestinians who had been released in the Gilad Schalit prisoner exchange deal. This pressure was mainly initiated by the Jewish Home Party led by Naftali Bennett. Over fifty Palestinians were rearrested. This act, along with the decision to cancel the Israeli defense system's plan to pay salaries to the public sector in Gaza, were among the steps that led to escalation.

The plan to pay the salaries was hatched after we identified an economic crisis in Gaza. Following the counter-revolution in Egypt, Hamas had no financial support, and did not pay salaries to public sector employees in Gaza for three months. I feared that the economic situation there would blow up in our face, so I proposed a mechanism for paying salaries to the civil servants. Qatar was willing to put up the money. We worked with UN representative Robert Serry to formulate a road map. A list was prepared of some twenty-three thousand physicians, teachers, and clerks who were supposed to receive salaries in an organized manner. We authorized the list, but when Minister of Foreign Affairs Avigdor Lieberman found out about it, he ran to the prime minister, declared the UN representative an "unwanted person," and torpedoed the process. This stepped up the pressure on Hamas.

In the cabinet meeting on June 30, 2014, after the bodies of the three kidnapped boys were found, Bennett suggested a preventive strike against the tunnels in Gaza, before escalation and before any shots were fired from the Strip. Thanks to his connections in the Givati Brigade, Bennett was aware of the existing plan, and in effect leaked it and presented it as his own. Chief of General Staff Gantz and myself objected to a war in Gaza at our initiative. Global opinion would be against us, and the Israeli public would also refuse to support what it would consider a "war of choice." These aspects, not tactical issues, are what should be discussed in the cabinet, as well as the question of what would happen if we destroyed the tunnels. Would Hamas simply begin digging again? Those who suggested the preemptive strike had no answer to this. The only way to prevent it was to retake control of Gaza, and this option had been rejected in cabinet meetings previously, because we understood its price.

An absurd situation was created in the cabinet. One minister, Lieberman, demanded that we destroy Hamas, but he didn't even remain to discuss his own proposal. He threw it out and then left to leak it. Another minister, Bennett, called for destroying the tunnels, as if the tunnels were the solution to everything. Politics began to get in the way of managing the battle.

Our pressure on Hamas in Judea and Samaria led it to activate other organizations in the Strip that fired rockets randomly into our territory. On July 6, we attacked what we thought was a rocket-launching cell that we had erroneously identified as planning to shoot. In fact, it was a Hamas team responsible for preventing shooting by rebel elements. After this incident, Hamas made the decision to engage us in a full-scale operation. For the first time since the deterioration, we recognized that Hamas intended to push us to escalation. We identified a terrorist unit on its way to carry out a major attack in the Kerem Shalom area, through a tunnel. We destroyed the tunnel as well as the terrorist unit in an air strike and prevented the planned attack. We realized that Hamas was initiating war. From this point on, Hamas began to fire rockets on a massive scale, and we began to carry out air strikes and call up our reserve forces.

When the war began, I had no desire to begin ground deployment. I wanted to attack them from the air, the sea and the ground by standoff weapons, so that they would pay a heavy price and request a cease-fire. Indeed, this is what we did for eight days. I proposed reaching a cease-fire as quickly as possible, even without destroying the tunnels, unless we had no other choice. I knew that destruction of the tunnels was not the factor that would lead to a cease-fire based on our conditions and without any gain for Hamas. Rather, such a cease-fire would result from the amount of damage caused to Hamas and the price it would pay in battle.

On July 15, the eighth day of the war, the Egyptians proposed a cease-fire. From my viewpoint, at this stage it would have been possible to reap the fruits of our achievements and abandon the war with a cease-fire under our conditions, while meeting the complex goal we had defined: to leave a Hamas that was weakened and deterred but also responsible and effective, that could impose the cease-fire on the rebel forces without Israeli occupation of the Strip (to avoid governing the Strip and deploying our forces in the field). I believed that the blow we'd dealt to Hamas was strong enough to reinforce deterrence. At this stage, we had not one casualty. The cabinet voted by majority in favor of the cease-fire – but Hamas did not accept it.

The background to this was American behavior, which caused us damage. While we were coordinating with the Egyptians and their initiative, which did not permit Hamas any achievements, Turkey and Qatar began another initiative, which promised Hamas enormous achievements. The head of the Hamas political bureau, Khaled Mashal, informed his subordinates in the field that the Americans were sponsoring this second initiative. He thus instructed them not to accept the Egyptian cease-fire proposal. In addition, he asserted that in any case, the Jews would break down, and so there was no reason to reach a cease-fire with them at that point.

When we identified the problem, the prime minister asked US Secretary of State John Kerry to clarify that the Egyptian proposal was the only one on the table. Kerry issued this statement, but he added that if the Egyptian proposal failed, then there was a Turkey-Qatar initiative... We asked him to remain on the sidelines and permit us to complete the process with the Egyptians.

On July 17, two days after Hamas rejected the cease-fire, a cell of thirteen Hamas terrorists exited a tunnel near Kibbutz Sufa, at the southern end of the Gaza Strip. The IDF thwarted the attack attempt, just as it had foiled every other attempted tunnel attack on Israeli settlements abutting Gaza. In combat against the terrorists who exited the tunnels, our soldiers were killed and injured, but no Israeli citizen was harmed as a result of the tunnels. We succeeded in stopping an attempted attack by sea from Zikim Beach (July 8), and an air attack using armed drones and parachutes. We were well prepared for every scenario. In parallel, we attacked the enemy and exacted a heavy price by damaging Hamas's capabilities, property, and buildings used for command posts, communications, and weapons storage.

Following the failure of the cease-fire initiative and the tunnel attack attempt, we no longer had any choice. The cabinet decided to enter Gaza and address the tunnel problem. Handling took much longer than the IDF estimated. It took a week just to reach the opening of some tunnels.

Because the M-113 APCs ("Zelda") are not armored against heavy explosives or RPG missiles, we deploy the heavy armored vehicles at the front – the Namer (Merkava APC) and the Achzarit (armored APC). When the Golani Brigade entered the field, one of the APCs in the line got stuck in the town of Sajaya and took a direct hit from an anti-tank missile. Seven soldiers were killed in this incident, including Staff Sergeant Oron Shaul. His vest was found in the field and the evidence on it showed he was no longer alive, but no bodily remains were found. He was later declared as a fallen soldier whose burial place is unknown.

This incident developed into a stormy political debate surrounding the question of why our forces were still using the M-113 APCs, when we had the Namer APCs which offered better quality and protection. This is how things work in building the IDF's weaponry. When we purchase F-35 airplanes, we don't throw out the old F-15s. When we upgrade to Merkava IV tanks, we don't immediately replace all the tanks. The same is true for heavier APCs. We can't replace the entire set of armored vehicles simultaneously, as this would be enormously expensive. We arrange the weaponry so that soldiers entering the field at a stage with a high probability of friction travel in a Merkava IV or Namer. Those entering when the probability of friction is lower go behind, riding in lighter vehicles or walking. During the Yom Kippur War, I traveled to the Suez Canal in a bus.

At the height of the war, Secretary of State Kerry intervened again and sent us another version of a cease-fire plan. The cabinet met to discuss the new initiative, and our faces fell: it was the Turkey-Qatar proposal. We rejected the American proposal unanimously.

At this stage, we had realized that when Hamas spoke about cease-fire, it was referring only to ending the rocket fire and air strikes. It intended to continue attacking our forces that remained in the field to complete our mission, arguing that this was Israeli aggression. Aside from short breaks in the fighting for humanitarian reasons, we were unable to reach a cease-fire agreement.

On Thursday, July 31, 2014, Kerry proposed a general humanitarian cease-fire for twenty-four hours that would be extended at a later point. We asked him for clarifications, so that it would be clear that the cease-fire also covered our forces remaining in the field to complete the destruction of the tunnels. We needed this assurance that Hamas would not harm these forces. Kerry confirmed that the cease-fire applied to our forces in the field as well, but we insisted that he check this again. He did so and got back to us with the declaration that the cease-fire unequivocally included the forces in the field. We asked him and UN Secretary General Ban Ki-moon to clarify this in writing and in public, and they did so.

We informed the forces that a full cease-fire would go into effect at six a.m. the next morning. The forces would not advance or shoot, but they would continue to handle the tunnels and leave Gaza only after they had finished this mission. Retroactively, I blame myself for this. From my acquaintance with Kerry, I should have known that he often cut corners in negotiations. It was a mistake to permit him to be involved throughout the process. We should have kept him out of it altogether.

On the morning of August 1, a Friday, I held a situation assessment meeting with the chief of general staff and generals following the start of the cease-fire. Suddenly the COGS's head of office burst into the meeting, carrying a note: incident at Rafah. The enemy fired at our forces. We have some dead and apparently one abducted. I called off the meeting. The COGS went down into the Pit, the command bunker at the Kiryah, while I waited in my office for updates. We found out that the enemy had fired on a Givati reconnaissance platoon, and we had two dead and one abducted. The Hannibal directive (code name for the IDF response to an abduction) was implemented, and the fighting was still going on.

I asked to be updated as soon as the names of the soldiers killed and abducted were available. Three officers from my family were in the region at that time: my nephew was with Reconnaissance Battalion 35, and Tzur and Hadar Goldin, twin sons of my cousin Simcha, were also in the field. The COGS informed me that the abducted soldier was Second Lieutenant Hadar Goldin. I waited until the COGS finished his report and gave orders for the next steps. After the operational discussion ended, I informed Chief of General Staff Benny Gantz that Hadar was my cousin's son. I asked him to keep it to himself, so that Hamas wouldn't find out that they were holding a relative of the minister of defense. Gantz rushed from the Pit to my office. I reassured him that everything would proceed as planned. I understood the complexity of the incident, which was difficult in any case, and all the more so given that the abducted soldier was a relative of the minister of defense.

My relationship with the Goldin family is very close. I'd known Tzur and Hadar since their brit milah (circumcision ceremony). Shared events, such as a family dinner in the Goldins' sukkah, had become a tradition. When Tzur and Hadar were in eleventh grade, they invited me to speak to their class in preparation for military service. When they were deliberating whether to attend a pre-military institution and whether to join a battalion or a brigade unit, they consulted with me. Every time a soldier falls into captivity it is a tragedy. But for me, this tragedy became a personal and family event.

I asked to be informed when the Goldin family had been notified, and after that I called Simcha. I told him that we were employing all the means at our disposal. Simcha is a strong man with military experience. At this point he had not yet processed the tragedy, but he understood the situation. Meanwhile, my wife Ada went to the Goldin family home.

On Saturday, I traveled to visit Hadar's brigade, Givati, in the Gaza Strip. Although Simcha observes Shabbat (which means he does not use the telephone from sundown Friday until sundown on Saturday), we kept in touch. This was in keeping with the Jewish precept that it is permissible to violate observance of Shabbat in order to save human lives. In the meantime, we received findings brought by Lieutenant Eytan Fund. Fund was then deputy commander of the Givati Brigade reconnaissance unit. He had gone down into the tunnel in pursuit of the terrorists and received the Medal of Distinguished Service for this act. Toward the end of Shabbat, I was informed that according to the findings, and after they were reviewed by expert pathologists, Hadar Goldin was certainly dead. I convened an urgent hearing to summarize the findings for all parties involved, including the chief military rabbi, Brigadier General Rafi Peretz, who confirmed that according to the findings, Hadar was dead.

Earlier, at eight o'clock, I had seen that the Goldin family had come out of their home to speak with the media. Near the house there was a demonstration being held by members of the Bnei Akiva youth movement, with signs calling for the IDF not to leave Gaza until Hadar was brought home. I understood that entities that had been involved in previous prisoner exchange transactions with the enemy arrived to support the family and offer advice. The family had understood that on Saturday night the prime minister was planning to announce the IDF's departure from Gaza, so the Goldins wanted to express their opposition to the move.

After the IDF chief rabbi and the head of the personnel directorate informed Hadar Goldin's family that he had been declared fallen in action, I went to the Goldin home and described the situation. I said that according to the findings, it would be right to bury what bodily remains we had, to hold a funeral, and to observe the seven-day shiva mourning period, in parallel to continuing our efforts to bring home the rest of the body. It would be good to have a grave, I said. I succeeded in convincing the family in this intimate meeting. Some of the family members were angry at me afterwards.

In an interview with CNN, Khaled Mashal claimed that Hamas had not agreed to a cease-fire in Gaza. This contradicted Kerry's commitment to us in writing and in public. It turned out that Kerry had rounded corners again, as usual. Hamas had never accepted the plan that Kerry proposed. One hour before Hadar Goldin's funeral, the prime minister and I spoke with the US Secretary of State by phone. Kerry opened the conversation by expressing his condolences. It was a tense call. I snapped at Kerry that he was responsible for the incident. I made it clear that Hamas did not intend to cease their fire against Israeli forces in the Gaza Strip, and the evidence was Mashal's remarks in the interview with CNN after the Rafah incident. The phone call was cut short because I was hurrying to Hadar's funeral.

The fighting continued. Hamas discovered our weak point – the Iron Dome was effective against rockets, but it was not effective against short-range mortars. Media coverage, residents who spoke from the heart, and irresponsible municipal heads let Hamas know that the communities on the front line were not protected. So Hamas directed their fire there. Four-and-a-half-year-old Daniel Tregerman from Kibbutz Nahal Oz was killed, and just before the cease fire, two civilians were killed in Nirim – Ze'ev Etzion and Shachar Melamed.

One of the individuals whose behavior infuriated me throughout the fighting was Minister Naftali Bennett. Bennett went out to the field without coordinating the visit with the minister of defense, as required, and he uploaded pictures to his Facebook page of himself with soldiers in staging areas or a restaurant. I am not aware that he made any official visit or received any official briefing in the field, but later I learned that he tried to contact Colonel (later general) Eliezer Toledano, 35th Brigade commander; Colonel (Res.) Erez Weiner, who was on the planning team at Southern Command; and other officers from the religious sector. At the cabinet meeting, Bennett demonstrated proficiency in what was happening in the Givati Brigade and criticized the chief of general staff. Bennett said that the Givati forces were ready to fight and that the COGS was a "lazy horse who didn't order them to attack the tunnels." I found out that it was the late brigadier general (Res.) Avichai Rontzki, former chief military rabbi, who had updated Bennett. Rontzki had been active in the Jewish Home Party and had volunteered to serve as rabbi of the Givati Brigade, without being enlisted.

This was irresponsible conduct by a minister. The information that Bennett collected was misleading and unprocessed, and even though his behavior was inappropriate for a cabinet member, he was applauded for supposedly having saved the State of Israel from the tunnels. This is a lie that Bennett continues to use for political ends, to this very day.

It is important to emphasize that cabinet ministers who requested to visit the area received authorization, and they also received briefings in the units that they visited. That is how responsible cabinet ministers behave, when they do not see the battle as a political opportunity to promote their own interests at the expense of national interests, in a way that endangers human life.

At the end of the operation, we had seventy-four dead, of which sixty-eight were soldiers. The battle was not easy and the price was heavy. But after fifty-one days, and contrary to Khaled Mashal's prediction that we would crack first, it was Hamas who was broken.

"War is the realm of uncertainty," wrote Clausewitz, one of the founders of the theory of modern warfare, in his book *On War*. He was also the one who held, rightly, that war is not a science. There is no war, battle, or operation without mistakes or errors. Thus, it is vital to conduct investigations after the event and to learn the appropriate lessons for the future so that we can improve our performance in the next battle.

Unlike the state comptroller, we did not wait for two and a half years after the end of the war before we conducted investigations. We carried out in-depth investigations immediately after Operation Protective Edge was over – in the IDF, the Shin Bet, and NEMA (the National Emergency Authority within the Defense Ministry). The results of the investigations were presented to the cabinet. Basically, an investigation is aimed at the future, which means that it examines the events with an eye to learning lessons to be applied. In contrast, an inquiry is directed at the past: searching for guilty parties rather than lessons. The state comptroller's report on Operation Protective Edge erred in taking an investigative stance toward the war, even though doing so was not obligatory.

Another failure in the state comptroller's report was his decision to focus on two issues: the treatment of the tunnels and the cabinet's decision-making process. Such a narrow probe, done "through the tunnel shaft," cannot reflect the whole picture. In the battle, the political and military echelons were required to respond to the threat of rocket fire (Hamas fired more than four thousand rockets at Israel during the war) and attacks by sea and air, as well as attacks through the tunnels. We coped with all these threats successfully. We stopped marine attacks against our strategic and aviation assets. The enemy had planned to explode unmanned, precision aircraft over our facilities – and we prevented it. We protected civilians from the tunnels.

As I have said, the threat from the tunnels was not the greatest threat in the campaign. Every discussion about the tunnels had a demonic, primordial quality, as if the dark forces were suddenly bursting from the earth. But this was not the reality. When the terrorists came out of the tunnels into our territory, our army was prepared for them, and the fact is that the terrorists did not reach our citizens. Out of six tunnel events that took place in Israel during the operation, three were foiled with no casualties to our forces. In two of the events, soldiers and officers were killed and injured, as they were in the field and sought contact with the terrorists who emerged from the ground. There was only one event near Nahal Oz (on July 28), in which terrorists burst out of the tunnels and surprised our soldiers. Five of our soldiers, who had been participating in a section commanders' course, were killed. The event took place after we had already begun our ground attack and the entire defense system in our territory had become irrelevant, up to the Gaza border. (The defense system was effective as long as our troops were deployed on our side of the border, and not on the other side.)

Another narrow approach taken by the comptroller's team is its examination of the cabinet's decision-making process. Had the team examined only the process, and not the quality of the decisions that came out of it, it would have concluded that the cabinet operated by the book. The cabinet convened to discuss the right issues at the right time, both before and during the campaign. If the state comptroller had examined the full contents of the cabinet discussions, he would have realized the damage caused by some of the cabinet ministers who saw the war as an opportunity to attack the prime minister, the defense minister, and the chief of general staff. He would have also discovered that some of the cabinet ministers acted out of political considerations, in an irresponsible manner and during the war when human lives were at stake. The comptroller would have had to comment on this fact in his report. But the audit team chose to rely on the testimony of only some of the ministers, who continued to operate out of political motives in their testimonies, just as they had done during the war. The only thing that can be said in their favor is that they considered their own long-term political trajectory. Members of the state comptroller's team who had intended to examine the decision-making process, swerved from this path and instead addressed the content of the decisions. But they did so selectively, focusing only on the tunnel issue.

Another significant failure, which explains the gap between the report and the responsible and prudent management of the war stems from the fact that the cabinet is not supposed to manage the battle. The cabinet makes the important decisions, such as whether to go out to battle, defining the goals, and accepting or rejecting cease-fire proposals. All these were done by the book. In contrast, the management of the military operation takes place in limited discussions with the prime minister, situation assessments between the defense minister and the general staff in the Pit, at command headquarters, and in visits and situation assessments in the units. The state comptroller's report was biased and superficial because it took a narrow view of the management of the war through the cabinet decision-making process, based on biased testimony of politically interested parties.

When I learned of the comptroller's intention to audit and focus on the tunnels and on the cabinet's decision-making process, I recognized the potential for distortion and damage. I sought to discourage the comptroller from conducting the audit in this way. I argued that if we had failed in our management of the war, it would be better to establish a state commission of inquiry, headed by experts, to examine our functioning. I also said that if I had thought that we had failed – it would be incumbent upon us to resign. I knew that whoever dared to act out of political considerations during the conduct of the war would use the audit as a mouthpiece for their political ambitions.

I also warned against the phenomenon of inquiry and review commissions that castrate decision makers. During my years of military service, I met commanders and ministers whose actions had been investigated in the past in inquiry commissions. People who had undergone such an experience spoke in a different language. They spoke with an eye to the protocol and to the next inquiry commission. They avoided saying what they really thought, and they hesitated in making decisions and taking responsibility.

There is a price to establishing inquiry commissions or audits of the type that investigated Operation Protective Edge. When decision makers are forced to use lawyers in the testimonies that they give in various committees, they cease to be relevant. The lawyers try to shift responsibility to the level above and below. I saw this happen in the Shamgar Commission, which examined the massacre carried out by Baruch Goldstein at the Tomb of the Patriarchs. The political echelon shifted responsibility to the military, the chief of general staff rolled responsibility over to the GOC, who passed it on to the division commander, and the division commander transferred the blame to the brigade commander – and vice versa. The process also occurs from the bottom up. Is this how we learn from experience?

Despite the high cost involved, establishing a government inquiry commission is unavoidable only in certain situations, when failure demands examination and decision makers do not take responsibility. Even then, the commission should choose experienced people who are experts in the field.

In such criticism, there is an inherent tension between the public's right to know and the aspiration to transparency, and the need for confidentiality. It is most likely that a classified report could have been more effective. The state comptroller's report on Operation Protective

Edge, even after it was censored, caused serious damage because it disclosed information to the other side. Revealing the political considerations that were behind this kind of operation, which will not be the last of its kind, provides invaluable information to the enemy. Exposing intelligence issues publicly also caused significant damage. The political debate added to the damage caused by these exposures. When we look at the state comptroller's report in terms of costs and benefits, there is no doubt that the price we paid exceeded the benefits.

There are military analysts who claim that the IDF has not won a military campaign since the Six-Day War. I disagree with them. The IDF's swift victory in 1967 was indeed glorious, but the Egyptians resumed their fire three weeks after the end of the war, and the Syrians resumed their fire within six weeks. Since that victory, the Israeli army defeated terror in the Gaza Strip in the early 1970s, it defeated the terror campaign carried out by wanted terrorists in the West Bank from 1992 to 1993, and it defeated suicide terrorism in Operation Defensive Shield. In a war like Operation Protective Edge, it is not possible to display victory photos or albums. Our proof of victory in such a war is causing the enemy to accept the cease-fire in accordance with our conditions. That is exactly how Operation Protective Edge ended. Hamas did not attain any achievements, and we did not accept any of its demands. In fact, Hamas requested and received a cease-fire according to our conditions and respected it for a long time after the end of the campaign.

CHAPTER 18

Not at Any Price

The decision to release 1,027 security prisoners in exchange for the release of one IDF soldier, Gilad Schalit, was made at lighting speed, five years and four months after he was taken prisoner by Hamas. During the holiday of Sukkot, on October 11, 2011, I was on my way north when I received word that an urgent government meeting had been called: "Turn around and get to Jerusalem." That evening, a discussion was held over the decision, with no prior preparation. The considerations were known to all. It was a marathon meeting to achieve a majority and bring the decision for approval.

The prime minister acted to convince the ministers to vote for the deal. In a conversation before the meeting, he tried to convince me as well, saying that we had no choice and that he expected my support. I explained that from my viewpoint, this was a matter of principle that meant crossing a red line, and therefore I intended to vote against the deal. I did so. Three of us took the minority position – Ministers Uzi Landau, Avigdor Lieberman, and myself, against twenty-six ministers who supported the proposal. I was then serving as vice prime minister and minister of strategic affairs.

There is no question about the obligation of the State of Israel and the IDF to its soldiers and civilians who are taken prisoner (or abducted, as has become common in recent decades). The state and all arms of government and the security establishment must make every possible effort to obtain the release of the abductee, even while taking calculated risks. This was the case in the operation to release Staff Sergeant Nachshon Wachsman in 1994, or in operations to abduct "assets" for exchange, such as the Syrian officers in 1972, Jawad al-Katzfi in 1987, Sheikh Abdel Karim Obeid in 1989, and Mustafa Dirani in 1994. When it is not possible to release the prisoner in an operation, the possibility of a prisoner exchange deal comes to the table, and with it, discussion of the price that we're willing to pay.

Jewish tradition relates a relevant story about Rabbi Meir (the Maharam) of Rothenburg, a rabbi in thirteenth-century Germany. During his time, robbers and even the authorities frequently abducted Jews and demanded a sizeable ransom. Criminals and rulers identified the Jews' sensitivity to the issue of redeeming captives and exploited this as a profitable weak point.

The Maharam of Rothenburg was one of the great Jewish scholars of his time. He was arrested and imprisoned by the authorities, who demanded a high ransom for his release. The Jews collected the required sum and planned to pay it, but the Maharam objected strenuously. He based his decision on an ancient principle of Jewish law: "Do not redeem captives in excess of their value, for *tikkun olam* [literally "fixing the world" – i.e., as a precaution for the general good]" (Mishnah *Gittin* 4:6). Seven years after he was abducted, the Maharam died in captivity.

This general rule is based on the simple assumption that the willingness to pay an exorbitant price to redeem a captive is likely to encourage additional abductions. What the ancient Jewish Sages and the Maharam understood remains relevant today. Although the State of Israel stood firm and refused to yield during the arduous period of hostage attacks, beginning with the Jibril Agreement it began a series of capitulations to the demands of abductors, which has continued to this day.

Paying an inflated price for prisoner redemption creates an ethical conflict with the value placed on human life. As commander of Sayeret Matkal, I was required to carry out hostage rescue missions. I was taught that we must not give in to terror, because submission encourages more terror. Refusing to yield to hostage attacks – at Entebbe, Misgav Am, Kibbutz Shamir, and elsewhere – forced terror organizations to abandon that type of attack. By contrast, capitulation to terrorists' demands in exchange for release of prisoners and abductees has made abductions worthwhile. Today, the terror organizations are eager to carry out such attacks. Just as we made the terrorists understand that hostage attacks were not worthwhile, we must make them understand that abduction attacks are not worthwhile either.

The 1985 Jibril Agreement brought us to a breaking point. Unfortunately, Israel created a new reality when it agreed to release 1,150 terrorists in exchange for three IDF soldiers held captive by the Ahmed Jibril terror organization. Once terror organizations realized that Israel would give in and pay by releasing prisoners, the abduction of Israelis became an attractive possibility. The terrorists primarily targeted soldiers, but civilians were also considered valuable commodities. Even then, in 1985, I thought that capitulation was a terrible mistake. I realized that this would encourage additional abductions. In hindsight, the Jibril swap laid the real infrastructure for the First Intifada. The terrorists that were released in this exchange were the same ones who created the "popular committee" terrorist cells in the Palestinian arena during the two years until the outbreak of the Intifada in 1987.

For this reason, my position throughout the years was that we must do everything possible to free the abductee without paying the price in a prisoner release. As Sayeret Matkal commander, I initiated operations that aimed to abduct and bring to Israel individuals whom we could use as bargaining chips for the release of navigator Ron Arad, or to obtain information about his fate. The first operation that I commanded was the abduction of Jawad al-Katzfi. We caught him in Lebanon, in full daylight. He supplied the information that abducted IDF soldiers Yosef Fink and Rachamim Elsheikh were no longer alive. After him, the Unit brought other bargaining chips over from Lebanon, such as Sheikh Obeid and Mustafa Dirani. The declared goal was to try to solve the problem in an operational manner, to bring information or achieve a deal without releasing prisoners.

I do not accept the assertion that we must "release prisoners at any price." It is irresponsible and dangerous. Willingness to pay any price only encourages more kidnappings. Releasing terrorists from our prisons in exchange for freeing our prisoner or abductee endangers the lives of other individuals – additional abductees and victims of terror attacks carried out by the freed terrorists.

In prisoner exchange negotiations, the State of Israel must lower its level of willingness to pay a price for releasing its prisoners. It must insist on the principle that we pay for bodies with bodies, not with live prisoners. And when we release live prisoners in a deal, the payment must be proportional – not completely exaggerated. I am confident that such a policy will lower the motivation to kidnap Israeli soldiers and civilians, and it maintains the appropriate balance of tension between prisoner redemption and valuing human life.

In the Israeli reality, this issue is first and foremost a challenge of leadership. Demands from the families of the prisoners/abductees and the media impact of their pain put pressure on the leaders, who give in repeatedly to their demands. This solves the immediate short-term problem but reveals readiness to pay heavy prices over the long term.

Our behavior as a society on the issue of prisoner redemption is similar to our behavior in the political-strategic arena. It is characterized by the same severe faults: Israeli society wants a solution – right now! It is willing to exchange long-term interests for short-term benefits. As part of the privatization process, in the past few decades, Israeli society has transferred the center of gravity from society, its needs and interests, to the individual. (To my disappointment, my own movement – the kibbutz movement – has been swept up in this process.)

As a result of this, Israeli society exhibits weakness in its readiness to give in to terror. This weakness is expressed in almost every issue – prisoner negotiations, retreats on the ground, disengagement, convergence. Once again, I assert: I am certain that our readiness to concede to the demands of the terror organizations strengthens their image of us as spider webs (to use Nasrallah's expression), "dry wood" (as per the Iranian regime), and "the Zionist entity is getting old and won't survive another decade" (according to Bashar al-Assad and his entourage).

For this reason, I view the issue of prisoner redemption as having strategic importance that cannot be underestimated. Of course, the State of Israel, including the IDF, are obligated to make every possible effort and use all our abilities to free our prisoners and bring them home. But in no way must we do this "at any price."

In the case of Gilad Schalit as well, I remained faithful to my position that we must make every effort to bring him home without paying the price in release of prisoners. This time the decision makers had to face an unprecedented public campaign that included strategy, public relations, broad media coverage, and political and public activity to release the abducted soldier. Such political pressure involves many parties who act in their own self-interest and are not necessarily focused on the benefit of the abductee. Instead, they take advantage of the opportunity to put political pressure on the prime minister. The result, unfortunately, is that the prime minister capitulated to pressure and responded to Hamas's demands.

After the decision was made in complete opposition to my worldview, I realized that opposite the soldier going home – who had a name, face and family, and on whose behalf such intense public pressure was activated – stood victims who were as yet anonymous, who did not yet have names or faces, and whose families were not yet aware of the great disaster that awaited them. This is the price of the deal: the people who were murdered afterward by the terrorists who were released in the Schalit deal and who returned to the field. Today they have names and faces. One is Israel Police commander Baruch Mizrachi, who was on his way to the Passover Seder meal in 2014 when he was murdered by Ziad Awad, one of the terrorists released in the Schalit deal. The families of Hadar Goldin and Oron Shaul are also victims of this deal.

Many of the terrorists released in the Schalit deal have returned to their terror activities, like Awad. Mazen Fukha acted from Gaza until he was killed in March 2017. Fukha worked with his comrade Abd al-Rahman Ranimat to establish the "West Bank Headquarters in the Gaza Strip," which attempts to organize terror attacks in Judea and Samaria. The leader of Hamas in the Gaza Strip, Yahya Sinwar, was also released in the Schalit deal. Other released terrorists went to Istanbul, where they established the Hamas terror headquarters. I knew some of them personally – I had arrested them when I was commander of the Judea and Samaria division or as GOC Central Command, and as head of Military Intelligence, I had kept track of them. These were serious murderers with blood on their hands who had been sentenced to several life terms in prison, and I am well aware of what we had to do to put them in jail. When they were released, I knew we would pay a heavy price.

A campaign like the one waged to free Gilat Shilat is an exacting test of leadership: will it do what is right, or what is popular? Of course, it is difficult to withstand powerful public pressure. But all my life, I have learned that leadership means doing what is right, not what is popular. When representatives of the organization for freeing Gilat Schalit and organizers of the campaign contacted me, I explained my position to them. They did not continue their attempts to convince me, because they knew that I was consistent and stuck to my principles. When it came to the vote, they recognized that despite the pressure I would vote against the deal.

I believe in the saying by the great Jewish scholar Maimonides that "Truth will carve its own path." Even if someone seems unpopular and perhaps wrong in the short term, even if the surveys show otherwise, even if I might pay a political price for it – I will follow my own truth. In the final analysis, people will learn to value it. The problem is that irresponsible politicians exploit the public's short memory. The public wants the solution right now and does not see the damage caused in the long term. Prime Minister Netanyahu wrote a book about the war on terror. He knows that the decision he made encourages terror, but political pressure led him to make a decision that opposes his own belief. When a media campaign is waged and makes the impression that most of the public wants the government to bring Gilad Schalit home at any price, it's easier to make a decision that will satisfy the public will and ignore the future price that others will pay.

Sometimes I am asked the obvious question, "What would you think if it was your son who was taken prisoner?" I admit that I have not faced this test. But I am now facing the test in the case of Hadar Goldin, who is my relative, and it has not caused me to change my opinion. As I write these lines, over three years since Operation Protective Edge, the photos of First Lieutenant Hadar Goldin and Staff Sergeant Oron Shaul stand beside the desk in my office, and I feel responsible to bring them to burial in Israel.

I expressed this opinion to Gilad Schalit as well, when I appeared at an event at the Herzliya Interdisciplinary Center and he was in the audience. I can explain to the Goldin family today why we must not release prisoners in exchange for the bodies of Hadar and Oron, although this is not necessary, as they agreed with my position then and still do today.

I repeated this opinion in the speech I gave at the dedication ceremony for the Mitzpe Hadar archeological site near the village of Sal'it in April 2017. Following is an excerpt of my remarks:

> Over two and a half years after the war, I ask myself whether we have done enough to bring back Oron and Hadar to burial in Israel. Unfortunately, I can't give a positive answer to that question. As a person who believes in the value of redeeming prisoners on the one hand, and on the other, in the Sages' principle "Do not redeem prisoners in excess of their value," I objected to the Schalit deal. Because of my devotion to this principle, it is important for me to emphasize that I think we have not done enough to bring back Oron and Hadar, of blessed memory, to burial in Israel.
>
> Leah and Simcha Goldin face the supreme personal test, and they also call for upholding the principle in which I believe. For this bravery as individuals and as a family, they are worthy of the utmost praise. What do they demand? They do not demand the release of terrorists. They demand that we place pressure on Hamas. A legitimate, logical demand that is obligatory according to the values in which we have been educated: the obligation to our fighters and civilians who are in enemy hands, to bring them home or to bring them to burial.
>
> While observing the firm stance of the Goldin family, I have noticed that something within them has broken – their faith in the leadership, which was supposed to do its best to bring back the sons for proper burial. Their faith is broken due to promises that were broken, decisions that were not carried out, and so they feel almost alone in battle – the battle at home, in the global arena, and the battle against Hamas. In light of the Goldin family's

> nobility, the leadership should have exploited every possible way to put pressure on Hamas in the Gaza Strip. They should have used economic and political levers, and degraded conditions and family visits for Hamas prisoners in jails. They should have explored every opportunity such as the agreement with Turkey, Qatar's involvement in Gaza or Egypt's role as a broker between Israel and the Palestinian Authority, and Hamas.
>
> Between releasing terrorists as in the Schalit deal – to which I objected, and I will object to any similar deal in the future – and inaction, there is broad room for action. In this space, we must take the initiative to put pressure on anyone who inhumanely holds the bodies of our soldiers or Israeli civilians, such as Avera (Avraham) Mengistu. Leadership must make decisions that are not based on political pressure, because clearly, political pressure for us is likely to raise the price for them. Leadership must make decisions based on our values, even when there are no mass demonstrations in the streets, which raise the price in a way that opposes our interests. The behavior of politicians today puts the full weight of responsibility on the families. It's time to make decisions and implement decisions that were already made, to transfer the weight of responsibility to Hamas.

I also outlined my fundamental position to the Shamgar Commission, which was established to formulate principles for future prisoner exchange deals. I understood that on many issues, the members of the commission saw eye to eye with me, but they decided to publish their conclusions only after Schalit's release.

This was yet another political decision, a leadership event that is nothing to boast about. Principles were formulated, but they will apply to the term of those who come after us. Even after Gilad Schalit came home, the discussion of the Shamgar Commission's recommendations was postponed repeatedly. To this day, I do not know if it ever took place.

When I meet with civilians today, mainly youth, I tell them that they are subject to manipulation. I tell them that they must be critical and think rationally, not emotionally, about what should and what should not be done. I am not criticizing the public that called for Schalit's release at any price. I am certainly not criticizing his parents or the rest of his family. Rather, my assertions are directed toward the person who is supposed to lead and who bears the responsibility for behaving responsibly and drawing a clear line.

At the same time, as a society we also must criticize ourselves. For we might also conduct a reverse campaign to educate the public in right and wrong: on the one hand, Gilad Schalit, and on the other – the names and faces of all those who were murdered as a result of releasing the terrorists.

CHAPTER 19

ARAB SPRING, ISLAMIC WINTER

The process taking place in the Middle East has been correctly defined as "the greatest crisis since the time of Muhammad." I never defined these events as an "Arab Spring," but I was also careful not to call them an "Islamic winter." We face a very harsh battle, and it's still unclear where it will lead. There are already territories in which an Islamic winter is prevailing. These areas are under the control of radical Islamic groups that aspire to regional and global hegemony.

The uprisings began in Tunisia in late 2010. The background was economic, as in every event that arises as a result of public dissatisfaction from the current situation. The potential for revolution or takeover always stems from economic reasons. After street vendor Muhammad Bouazizi set himself on fire in protest against the Tunisian police for closing his market stand, protest demonstrations began and spread, leading to the overthrow of the Tunisian regime and igniting the entire Arab world. For the first time in the region, the street demonstrated against the government.

This was possible because today the Arab world is much more exposed to the external world. When Gamal Abdel Nasser ruled in Egypt, he handed out transistor radios that broadcasted a single radio station, which he controlled. He controlled the only source of information, and so he could manipulate it. There were no satellites, cellphones, or internet. But that age has ended. The regime has lost control over information. The public in the Arab states is exposed to information even though the regime does not want it to be exposed to that information.

When Hafez al-Assad controlled Syria, he did not permit ownership of cellphones or internet access. From his viewpoint, even walkie-talkies could enable a coup. When his son Bashar al-Assad opened the door slightly, a cold wind blew inside Syria. Suddenly, the public began to talk about democracy. Nonprofit organizations to promote freedom of expression were founded, with the support of Western countries. The atmosphere began to simmer. Citizens no longer bowed down to the ruler, and other opinions began to be heard. The wind became a storm.

From outside, the Americans pushed for democracy. They acted out of that same Western ignorance that motivated European leaders after World War I. Following the defeat of the Ottoman Empire, the British and the French divided the Middle East between them, and handed out states to their allies. One description documents British prime minister Winston Churchill drawing the new map. On it, we can easily see how Jordan's borders were drawn according to the Iraqi oil pipeline (IPC) and the desire to protect it. The result is countries that have Sunnis, Kurds, Shi'ites, Druze, Yazidis, Turkmens, Alawites, and numerous tribes without a shared national identity. We see the results of this today: religious, ethnic and tribal identity, and faith overpower false national identity, to the point of bloody warfare of one against another.

The Western leaders acted out of good intentions, but they did not understand that what was right for Europe was not right for the Middle East. Artificial nation-states created by Western leaders sprang up in the Middle East. The citizens of Libya, for example, have no national Libyan identity. That state has tribes, and it had a dictatorial regime that preserved its status through oppression. Nor is there a Syrian national identity. Either you are Alawite, or you are Sunni, Kurdish, or Druze. There are also several types of Sunnis – Muslim Brotherhood, ISIS, Al-Qaeda, or Sunnis who are not extremist.

When Western people interfere in the Middle East and try to impose democracy on the states here, everything blows up – in tribal battles in Libya or civil war in Syria, Iraq, and Yemen. Former US president George W. Bush began this interference with the downfall of Saddam Hussein in Iraq, and in pushing for elections there. Former president Barak Obama continued this policy in 2009 during his first visit to the region. In his speech in Ankara, Obama spoke about his model of modern Islam: democracy in Turkey. From there he traveled to Cairo, where he gave a speech in front of President Hosni Mubarak in which he advocated democracy. In his view, the Muslim Brotherhood was the authentic voice of the street. Obama did not understand what the Muslim Brotherhood was, but he backed it in his speech, essentially abandoning Mubarak. (I will discuss this in greater detail below.) The Cairo speech sowed the seeds of the revolution in Egypt.

The trend spread. Combined with the economic dissatisfaction on the street, the concept of democratization that came from the West led to riots and shock waves throughout the Middle East. In Egypt, this was called the "marriage crisis" – Egyptians didn't have the money to marry off their children. The frustration of the ordinary people, including the educated and the unemployed, ripened into a general revolution.

Those who hold that the only condition for a democracy is elections can learn from what happened in Gaza. Hamas exploited the rules of the democratic elections game, which were held following pressure from the Bush administration. Hamas rose to power in such elections and immediately imposed an undemocratic regime. In a society that does not value human lives, how can there be talk of human rights? Or women's rights? Obama and other Western leaders who pushed for elections in the region did not understand this. The winners of the elections were those who were the most organized. The regimes failed in repressing the Muslim Brotherhood organization. They could not close a mosque. So the mosques became branches of the movement. The political infrastructure was created by welfare projects, so-called "organizations for medical and economic assistance," which operated under the wings of Islam. The Muslim Brotherhood prepared for elections and won.

Instead of democracy, we got theocracy – a result of ignorance, naivete, wishful thinking, and Western solutions in the colonialist spirit of "We Westerners know what is good for you." This is the same mistake that created the artificial nation-states.

This complexity on the ground is not visible from the Potomac River in Washington. Many mistakes were made, including the American decision to disengage from the region. Three extreme Islamist movements rushed into the resulting vacuum, and each one aspires to regional hegemony.

The first is Iranian Shi'ite Islam. Their goal is to create revolution and convert the entire world to Shi'ite Islam so that the "Hidden Imam" (or Mahdi) will appear. To achieve this goal, they invest in developing nuclear weapons. They arm and fund Shi'ite militias in Iraq, Yemen, and Syria, and organizations such as Hezbollah, Islamic Jihad, and Hamas. They build terror infrastructures on five continents, undermine regimes in the Middle East, and call for Israel to be wiped off the map. This movement is determined to achieve hegemony in the region and beyond, and is willing to invest large sums and sacrifice many lives for this purpose.

The second movement is radical Sunni Islam, represented by ISIS and Al-Qaeda. Both aspire to an Islamic caliphate, and the only argument between them is when this will happen – now or later. ISIS wants to make it happen now. According to its theory, every territory that it occupies becomes part of the Islamic caliphate. It has occupied lands in Sinai, Syria, Iraq, and Libya. By contrast, Al-Qaeda upholds the patient route: first overthrow regimes, then establish caliphates in their stead. Instead of investing in bureaucracy and management, it invests in warfare. These organizations view Israel as representing the last stage, the icing on the cake. This is not their preference, but rather because we deter them. We are a hard nut to crack, and they prefer to leave us to the end. But in my opinion, they won't reach us. We must do everything so that they won't want to confront us. This was my policy as minister of defense.

The third organization is the Muslim Brotherhood under Turkish president Recep Erdogan. This entity is the most complex of all. Erdogan is the leader of the Muslim Brotherhood in the Middle East, but he is also a member of NATO. He accumulated power by exploiting American weakness, and for a long time he funded ISIS by purchasing oil from it. He enabled jihadists around the world to join ISIS in Syria and Iraq through the Istanbul and Ankara airports. He could have stopped them, but instead they returned as trained terrorists to their home countries, mainly to Europe.

The distance from Turkey to the European Union is five miles by rubber boat from the Turkish coast to the Greek islands in the Aegean Sea. According to Greek reports, some 40 percent of the people who have made this trip are refugees. The rest are illegal immigrants. Those who come from Morocco and Pakistan are not refugees, but immigrants. As soon as they arrive, they take a "selfie" to encourage their families and friends to follow them to Europe. Then they look for a place to charge their cellphones. All they need to get to Europe is fifty dollars – the price of the flight from Marrakesh to Istanbul, and an additional payment to Turkish smugglers. Turkish intelligence has a list of smugglers' names, but it denies its existence – just as it denies the existence of the list of Hamas activists that operate against us from Istanbul.

President Erdogan – a NATO member, let us recall – acts intentionally for the Islamization of Europe. Another American president might have levied economic and diplomatic sanctions against Turkey, but Erdogan enjoyed the vacuum left by the previous American administration in the Middle East and the weakness projected by President Obama.

The fourth factor in the regional power balance is not Islamic but exploits the vacuum in the region – Russia under Vladimir Putin. Such intervention in the Middle East has not been witnessed since the demise of the Soviet Union.

In the face of all this chaos, we have pursued a reasonable, responsible policy. First, we have been careful to avoid intervening in our neighbors' affairs. We have not declared whether we were for or against Assad, even if we did have an opinion on the matter. Even when battles have raged just across our borders in the Golan Heights, we have not intervened for the benefit of any side, unless an entity has crossed what we have defined as our red lines:

First, any entity that harms our sovereignty will feel the power of our fist, and it makes no difference if it is an intentional act or Syrian artillery fire that was aimed at the rebels but accidentally fell in our territory. In such a case, their artillery will be destroyed within minutes. This is all the more valid when the act is intentional. Until now, the units that acted intentionally were from the Iranian Revolutionary Guards (Quds Force), which operated terror infrastructures. They fired rockets into our territory and set explosive devices along the border in a dozen different attacks. None of those infrastructures exist anymore.

The second red line is assistance that strengthens entities hostile to Israel. Iranian weapons reach Syria through the airport in Damascus, and Russian arms come through the seaport in Tartus. If the weapons are designated for our enemies, particularly Hezbollah in Lebanon, that is a red line.

Our third red line is sending chemical weapons to our enemies. As of the publication of this book, this line has never been crossed.

When we realized that the Russians had arrived in the region, we reached an understanding with them that we would not disturb them, and they would not disturb us. A hotline was set up between the two sides to prevent mishaps. When we destroyed weapons that the Russians said they had sold to the Syrians, but which we knew were on the way to Hezbollah, cynically the Russians were pleased – the entity that was supposed to receive the shipment would have to purchase new weapons and thus pay twice.

But while we acted wisely, the rest of the world erred. The Americans made a mistake in leaving the Middle East, and they were forced to return to deal with ISIS. As happened when Al-Qaeda was not stopped in Afghanistan, if we do not strike at extremist Islam in its place of origin, it reaches New York and European cities and strikes there.

What's true for us is true for the West as well. The natural desire for a solution – which is unattainable – distorts our thinking to the point of blurring reality and enabling us to ignore it. It permits us to be led astray by emotion. The world must give up the idea of instant solutions. For every challenge that has no immediate solution, I propose a path instead of a solution.

To get rid of radical Islam, a historical process is needed. There must be another ideology that replaces it. The Egyptian public has already understood the error of the slogan "Islam is the solution," and it instigated the counterrevolution to overthrow the Muslim Brotherhood. This is a vital step, but it is only part of a long process. When we live in a reality of instability that can last for many years, we must find the way to manage it. We can't be searching constantly for magic solutions. The path I envision requires several steps:

First, we must defeat ISIS. This does not mean that the US has to send soldiers to fight in the field. This would only encourage the Muslims to fight even harder against the "crusaders." Rather, we must aid local elements that are fighting ISIS out of their own interest, like Kurds and non-extremist Sunnis.

The Americans did help the Kurds at one point, after a long period of conflict and after the 2015 massacre of Kurds by ISIS in Kobani. The Germans and other nations joined and gave the Kurds political, military, and financial assistance. Why not do this with the non-fundamentalist Sunnis as well? Seventy-four percent of the Syrian population is Sunni. This majority can be encouraged and aided, for example by giving intelligence to assist with air strikes, or by damaging ISIS's sources of funding, such as when an ISIS bank was attacked in Raqqa. Not all the players in the field are extremist. In the situation created, the villagers simply looked to whoever would protect and arm them. ISIS came with money and guns, while the Americans decided to retreat, and so ISIS established its influence base there.

Dismantling Islamic State by occupying Mosul and Raqqa was an important step, but it did not destroy ISIS as an ideology. The organization will continue to act from its remaining strongholds in Iraq, Syria, Sinai, Libya, the Gaza Strip, and elsewhere, and organize terror attacks and guerilla warfare from those locations. ISIS will also continue to encourage and direct terror attacks globally.

The second step is to handle rebel players such as Turkey by using the levers of political and economic sanctions. These levers should have been implemented long ago. Erdogan should not have been permitted to flood Europe with eight hundred thousand Muslim immigrants, as he did in 2015 and 2016. This is a demographic time bomb. Erdogan knew exactly what he was doing. He does not have to use an army to reach the gates of Vienna – he can simply send immigrants. The tide of immigrants in the Aegean Sea should have been stopped by deploying forces that would not permit the rubber boats to pass. We have sealed our maritime border against hostile assault activity. Why can't Europe do the same?

Of course, the humanitarian problem must not be ignored. But refugees must be aided and their needs supplied in their own villages (as Israel did) or in camps along the borders (as Jordan did), without permitting them to reach Europe. The Turks should have been forced to do so, either on the Turkish side or in a demilitarized zone on the Syrian side.

Israel prevented the arrival of Syrian refugees to its territory by providing them humanitarian aid and supplying all their needs inside Syria. The Sunni villages across Israel's border are disconnected from Damascus. They suffered from a shortage of food, fuel, clothing, shoes, winter blankets, and medical care. We decided to provide a solution, and we gave them medical assistance, first on the border and later in hospitals in Israel as well. Every day, Israeli physicians care for men, women, and children, including wounded rebels. Those who require more complex medical care are evacuated to hospitals in Israel. As a condition for providing this aid, we demanded that the Syrian rebels prevent the radicals from reaching the border fence. We also demanded that they refrain from harming the Druze on the Syrian side, despite their loyalty to the Assad regime. This was due to the special relationship between Jews and Druze in the State of Israel. We achieved these two goals.

This carrot and stick method that I espouse serves the interests of both sides. I have stopped believing in peace conferences and agreements that are written by lawyers. I believe in interests. I saw how Arafat violated the agreement that he signed. With other parties, even though we have no agreement with them, we uphold relationships of understanding and cooperation based on interests. If we follow this policy wisely, it works. We must apply the stick when necessary and effectively, so that everyone is impressed with our ability, and hand out carrots based on interests.

Iran is trying to open a front against us in the Golan Heights. If we create a policy of deterrence against Iran, ISIS sees this and is also deterred. It recognizes the IDF's strength. The same is true for ISIS in Sinai, which tried to open a front by firing rockets on Eilat and carrying out terror attacks along the border. ISIS is deterred not because it has become Zionist, but because it knows our power.

When Iran violates the resolutions of the UN Security Council on the issue of weapons and terror – and we have proof of such violations daily – sanctions must be imposed against it. When the Houthi in Yemen fired Iranian weapons on an American destroyer in the Bab-el-Mandeb Strait, the Americans responded weakly, destroying shore radar operated by the Houthis. If the reaction had been directed against Iran, they would have understood who was boss, and they would not have threatened American vessels in the Straits of Hormuz. If there is a reaction next time, the Sunnis will applaud the US president and see that finally they have someone they can trust, while the Iranians will understand that they can't continue to behave this way, because they are facing a resolute power.

The US must behave like the boss. It is the world's policeman, whether it wants this role or not. Perhaps it is not politically correct to speak of Islamic terror, because not all Muslims are terrorists. But 99.9 percent of terrorists are Muslim. Maybe closing borders is also not politically correct, but if we do not prevent the radicals from reaching Europe, we'll be meeting them in New York, Paris, London, Berlin, Barcelona, Nice, and Brazil.

One of the great challenges that the world has faced in recent years is the issue of Iran. Unfortunately, policy toward Iran has not enjoyed great success. In this case as well, the Americans made drastic errors under Obama's leadership, and Israel has added fuel to the flames.

Before I was appointed head of Military Intelligence in 1995, we discovered that Iran was working on a military nuclear project. In intelligence contacts with our American colleagues, we tried to convince them that this was Iran's goal. It took us two years to convince them. The professional entities in Europe joined us in this understanding around the year 2000. At this stage, the European Union began to place political pressure on Iran. Throughout the process, we identified lies, cover - ups, and manipulations on Tehran's part. The military nuclear project came to life. We learned that they were pursuing two avenues: plutonium and enriched uranium.

When I completed my term as chief of general staff in 2005, we were prepared for the action required to prevent Iran from military nuclear capabilities. In that year, Iran had not one centrifuge for uranium enrichment. In 2009, when I was appointed as minister of strategic affairs, the project was in a much more advanced stage, and Israel was unique in its stance on the issue.

Until 2009, our policy was to keep the issue on the back burner. Prime Ministers Rabin, Sharon, and Olmert made no overt statements on the issue. Activity took place behind the scenes, in cooperative ventures between us and our allies who viewed the Iranian threat in the same way. But Prime Minister Binyamin Netanyahu adopted a new position that transformed Israel into a global leader on the issue. He raised the issue at every opportunity – before the UN, Congress, AIPAC, the Knesset, and many other public arenas.

In parallel, the Iranians also developed their missile project. When I was head of Military Intelligence, Iran was in advanced stages of developing the Shahab missile to a range of 1,300 km. This range was hardly coincidental: it is the distance from western Iran to Israel. Iran did this using a missile that it received from a CIS state. It then developed the Shahab based on "reverse engineering" (producing a copy of an existing weapon by taking it apart and studying it). This led to harsh conflicts between us and the Russians.

One of the difficult conflicts was between myself as head of Military Intelligence and Foreign Minister Yevgeny Primakov of Russia. All our attempts failed to convince the Russians to cease their assistance to the Iranian missile project. The Russians continually denied their involvement in the project, so it was agreed that I would give him an intelligence briefing. I recognized that as a former member of the KGB, the only thing that interested him was to expose our sources. Of course, nothing came of this meeting, not for us, nor for them.

When I entered the political playing field, I again found myself at a decision-making juncture on the Iranian nuclear issue. We conducted serious discussions on the issue and examined all the options. I cannot discuss every detail, because the issue is still relevant. Iran can attain a bomb in another decade without violating the agreement that was finally achieved. If the Iranian regime decides to violate the agreement, it can achieve military nuclear capability in a shorter time span.

The underlying assumption is that Israel can't permit a situation in which an enemy country has a nuclear weapon. One way or another, we must prevent this. We have succeeded in distancing the conventional threat as a result of winning wars and acquiring deterrence capability. This has clarified to our enemies that there is no way they can defeat us. But acquiring nuclear capability will change the strategic balance against us. Even if they do not use their nuclear weapon, the very fact of the threat changes the situation and serves as an umbrella for applying force and other means against us. If Iran has nuclear capability, it will dare to activate Hezbollah and other terror organizations against Israel in a more threatening and challenging manner.

Iraq tried to achieve nuclear capability, but we stopped it when we attacked the Iraqi reactor in 1981. Bashar al-Assad tried to achieve nuclear capability, but we stopped him as well, when the Israel Air Force destroyed the North Korean reactor in Deir A-Zor.

My worldview is that a military operation should always be the last resort, even as a preventive measure. When possible, it is preferable to achieve the goal without using force. Using force always comes at a price, even if it is done partially and without injuries, because the other side must react in order to protect its status and interests. Such a process is likely to lead to conflict that will last for decades. If we attack Iran, this is likely to open a front against a regional power that has strong capabilities and that has already used terror against us. For example, Iran is likely to set Hezbollah against us, with the over one hundred thousand missiles and rockets in its possession. Therefore, we must weigh the situation seriously before deciding to use military force against Iran. As long as there is another way to achieve the goal, we must try to exploit it. We had, and we still have, other options against Iran.

I support applying pressure on the regime that will force it to decide between a bomb and its own survival. In the Iranian case, I have no doubt that they will prefer the survival of the regime. This is an achievable goal when applying pressure from three directions: international isolation, economic boycott, and the threat of military force. These three components should also create internal pressure. We witnessed this potential in the "Green Revolution" against the Iranian regime in 2009, which was unfortunately ignored by the United States. The regime succeeded in suppressing the revolution and bolstered its ability to control. In 2016, the regime executed some one thousand Iranians. The citizens of Iran did not want this regime, but the world missed the opportunity to harm it and failed to rescue the people. On December 31, 2017, another wave of riots began. Without connection to their results, these riots reflect the dissatisfaction of many Iranians with the rule of the ayatollahs.

The international system has power and means to force the Iranian regime to give up its nuclear power and its rogue behavior. Indeed, international pressure on Iran bore fruit in 2012–2013, when Supreme Leader Ali Khamenei decided to begin negotiations with the US on the nuclear issue. The expressions he used served as evidence of his intentions: he said that from his viewpoint, it was like "drinking from the cup of sorrow," and he spoke of "heroic flexibility." To him, the negotiations were like agreeing to a cease-fire when you are weak, in order to gain strength and violate it after you are strong. Still, the fact that he agreed to come to the bargaining table was in itself an achievement.

Iran came to the negotiating table after it lied to the international community for years. Iran's lies were revealed in the enrichment project at Natanz, which was exposed by intelligence, not by the inspection mechanism, and at the underground facility for uranium enrichment at Fordow. Although Iran deceived the International Atomic Energy Agency (IAEA), the US preferred to continue its policy of self-deception so as to avoid conflict. But sometimes there is no choice, and conflict is necessary.

The US did not reveal to Israel that it had begun negotiations with Iran, but we found out on our own. Khamenei entered negotiations out of despair and lack of choice, as an act of survival, because his supporters warned him that the economy in Iran would collapse within a year as a result of the international boycott. But the United States did not understand that the cards were in its hands and did not take advantage of its power, Khamenei entered the negotiations at a disadvantage, but by the time they ended, it seemed that it was the US that felt pressured to reach an agreement.

The Iranian achievement can serve as an academic case study in how to manage negotiations from a position of weakness, and how to achieve an advantageous agreement by exploiting the other side's weak points. President Obama fulfilled his promise that Iran would not obtain a bomb during his term in office. But what good did that do if he merely pushed it off to subsequent presidents? If Obama had continued the policy of political pressure, economic sanctions, and military threat without giving in, it would have been possible to achieve a much better agreement.

The weakness of the agreement between Iran and the global powers that was signed on April 2, 2015, in Lausanne was that it permitted Iran enrichment ability, which from their viewpoint was the most important thing. Within a short time, Iran could return to research, development, and production of centrifuges whose rate of enrichment is much faster. This would enable production of enriched material – the most important component of the fissionable material in a bomb. The agreement did specify that Iran would reduce the number of centrifuges in its possession by two-thirds, but Iran should not have even one centrifuge. It does not need civilian nuclear capability, because it has no energy problem. The ideal agreement should have stated clearly that Iran would have no centrifuges at all.

The agreement (JCPOA) that was signed between the P5+1 and the Iranian regime ignored the Possible Military Dimensions (PMD) of the Iranian nuclear project. After the Mossad seized the Iranian nuclear archive in April 2018, Israel exposed to the world that the Iranian regime was cheating the IAEA and the international community, led by the US. It seems that those parties preferred to keep the wool pulled over their eyes.

As if this were not enough, the agreement was limited in time. It enabled Iran to renew the race for a nuclear bomb within a decade without violating any agreement. IAEA inspectors were not permitted to enter the military facilities in Iran that contained all the important components of the nuclear project. Furthermore, the global powers did not relate to additional dangerous aspects of Iran's behavior, such as distributing arms, supporting terror, and developing missiles. The Iranians were the ones who added this issue to the agreement at the last minute, in order to obtain a commitment that within five years they would be free in this field as well.

The missile issue should also have been an inseparable part of the agreement. According to the international treaty, countries cannot produce missiles beyond a range of 185 miles (300 km). Iran was free to produce missiles of any range it wished, without paying any price for this violation. The evidence of Iran transferring weapons to Hezbollah forces in Syria was not even on the agenda. All these components should have appeared in the agreement with Iran, but the world missed its opportunity, and Khamenei came out on top.

Thus, out of dangerous American enthusiasm that stemmed from internal political considerations, many mistakes were made in the negotiations and corners were rounded, in the end leading to a disastrous agreement. Before the agreement, Iran was able to produce enough enriched uranium for a bomb within three months. Under the agreement, this time limit was put off to one year should Iran violate the agreement, or a decade if it did not violate it. In another decade, Iran could continue to produce enriched uranium in unlimited quantities.

Obama transformed the ISIS threat into the ultimate evil, and he viewed Iran as part of the solution. He wanted to present the agreement as his political achievement – in fact his only one – and thus prevent a conflict with Iran. This caused enormous frustration among the Sunni Arabs, who felt that the US had abandoned them. They had hoped for a new America, but instead they found a passive America that supported the Iranian side. From this aspect as well, the agreement was a failure.

X Mistakes were made on the Israeli side as well. Undoubtedly the Iranian issue is crucial. Iran is the only state in the world today that calls to wipe Israel off the map. From a security viewpoint, the Iranian threat to the State of Israel is primary in importance. Without Iranian support, Hezbollah would have difficulty existing, Islamic Jihad would not survive, Hamas would be hard put to finance its terror operations, and many of the sabotage activities against us would not be carried out. Without Iranian support, there would be no terror against us in Asia, Europe (for example, the terror attack in Burgas, Bulgaria), Africa, or South America.

My criticism is of Netanyahu's decision to take the lead and the public confrontation with the Americans on the Iranian issue. Israel must invest its full powers– political, diplomatic, and military – in the conflict with Iran. We can contribute a great deal in the intelligence field. But we do not have to lead the battle. Although we are the strongest military might in the Middle East, we are not a world power.

Netanyahu's decision to confront the US administration in public caused Israel damage. The height of this confrontation was his speech before Congress on March 3, 2015, in which he criticized the emerging agreement. The government of Israel must ensure American support from Republicans as well as Democrats. We must not support any one side in their internal debate. In this case, Netanyahu responded to the invitation of Republican John Boehner, then speaker of the House of Representatives. In this case, Israel's show of support for one side was understood as interference in American politics, which we cannot permit ourselves. Much of the negative atmosphere between the White House and Israel was caused by this behavior.

The damage went further. The anti-Trump atmosphere that prevails in the US today also contains anti-Israel sentiments, as Israel is considered a Trump supporter. We must recall that Jews in the US support the Democrats more than Republicans, so damage has also been done to our relationship with American Jewry. The crisis with American Jewry deepened following Netanyahu's decision to cancel plans for changes at the Western Wall and in the conversion process. The support of American Jews for the State of Israel is a strategic asset, and we must work to preserve and develop it.

We should not have reached this state. We are experiencing a deep fissure with the Democrats in the US and with American Jews, and it can and must be fixed. Israel has already paid a price for its behavior. We could have received greater defense assistance from the US. Even if the agreement with Iran was not advantageous, there is an accepted way to object to it, without interfering in a blatant, one-sided way in internal American politics.

President Trump dramatically changed the policy toward the Iranian regime, considering it as the main problem, and not part of the solution for instability in the Middle East. Following Iran's violations of the UN security council resolution on proliferation of arms and terror and because of the missiles issue, he decided to impose crippling economic sanctions on Iran. He decided also to withdraw from the nuclear agreement (the JCPOA) and created a rift between the parties that signed the agreement.

I believe that as happened in 2003 and 2012, when the Iranian leadership faces the choice between its rogue activities or survivability – and hopefully it will face this choice – it will choose the latter. This policy will bring about tension between Iran, the US, the Europeans, and the Gulf states. The Iranian regime might try to challenge Israel as well.

The Israeli policy should be very clear: Israel can't tolerate a nuclear bomb in the hands of a hostile regime. One way or another, the Iranian military project should be stopped. Of course, it would be preferable to reach this state by other means, but we cannot exclude any option. Israel should be ready to defend itself, by itself.

Ceremony for completion of officers' training course at Bahad 1 base. *From left:* Ya'alon (as defense minister), Major General Guy Zur – commander of ground forces, Lieutenant General Benny Gantz – COGS, Colonel Avi Gil – commander of Bahad 1 base.

Parting ceremony as minister of defense, with COGS Lieutenant General Gadi Eisenkot *(second from right)* and Major General (Ret.) Dan Harel – director of the Ministry of Defense *(second from left)*

With Chief Warrant Officer Yitzchak Touito, who was master sergeant of Bahad 1 base before I completed the officers' training course

With graduates of the naval officers' course, who prove that the source of our power is the quality of our people

Deputy COGS Major General Yair Golan *(far left, behind Ya'alon)*

On a tour of Samaria with COGS Lieutenant General Gadi Eisenkot *(center)* and Samaria brigade commander Colonel Shai Klapper *(right)*

Completion of officers' training course – a microcosm of diversity

On a tour of Judea

With COGS Lieutenant General Benny Gantz

Visit to an air force base, with Major General Amir Eshel, commander of the air force *(left)* and Colonel (Ret.) Haim Blumenblatt, chief of my staff *(third from right)*

Speaking to new immigrant and lone soldiers at the Alon Center for Education and Instruction

Opening of the Israel booth at the Asia Defence Expo and Conference (ADECS) in Singapore

At the Rafael Advanced Defense Systems simulator at the expo, with Major General (Ret.) Yedidya Ya'ari *(left)*

At the Israel Aerospace Industries exhibit at the expo, with then CEO Joseph Weiss

With US Secretary of Defense Chuck Hagel

With US Secretary of Defense Ashton Carter

With Senator Joe Lieberman and Representative Jane Herman

With Senator John McCain

Signing the guest book of a US Jewish community

With General Martin Dempsey, chairman of the Joint Chiefs of Staff of the US Armed Forces

On a tour of an American battleship in Haifa port with Dan Shapiro (right), US ambassador to Israel

With the prime minister of India, Narendra Modi, at the Israel booth at a defense systems expo in Bangalore

With Harjit Sajjan, Canadian defense minister

With the German defense minister, Dr. Ursula von der Leyen

With the Italian defense minister, Roberta Pinotti

With the British secretary of state for defense, Michael Fallon

One of my meetings with Henry Kissinger

With UN Secretary-General Ban Ki-moon

Lecturing at the University of Haifa, with Professor Gabi Ben-Dor, director of the National Security Studies Center, University of Haifa *(right)*

Lecturing at the Hebrew University of Jerusalem

Lecturing at Bar-Ilan University

Lecturing to members of the Israel-Switzerland Chamber of Commerce

Parlor meeting in Modi'in

Conference with supporters from the paratroopers

Visiting farmers in the Jordan Valley

Conference of Manhigut Acheret (Alternative Leadership) organization

Conference of Manhigut Acheret (Alternative Leadership)

CHAPTER 20

CRACKS IN THE ALLIANCE

At the beginning of my term as a government minister, after the 2009 elections, I began to learn the American government's policies under President Obama, who was elected that same year. I was surprised to discover its negative, and at times even hostile, attitude toward the Israeli government and its policies. I quickly realized that Obama's United States had stopped dividing the world into "good guys and bad guys," and was instead dividing it into "victims and victimizers."

During his time in office Obama viewed the Palestinians as the ultimate example of "victims." One of the first phone calls he made after he was elected was to Abu Mazen, chairman of the Palestinian Authority. Netanyahu was one of the last on the list, and when the phone call between the two was photographed from the American side, Obama's feet were seen resting on top of his desk. In the Middle East, this is a clear message: when a person shows the soles of his shoes, he is sending a message that says humiliation. Few understood the symbolism behind the photo of the conversation between the American president and the Israeli prime minister, and it didn't make headlines over here. To me, the message was obvious. I have no doubt that the message was also clear in the Arab-Muslim world. In this way, Obama apparently wanted to win over the Arab world and clarify that he was not on Israel's side – he was with the Muslims.

Obama's first visit to the region began in Ankara, the capital of Turkey, which as far as he was concerned was supposed to be the model of Islamic democracy. Afterward, he set out toward Riyadh, the capital of Saudi Arabia, and then to Cairo. On June 4, 2009, at Al-Azhar University, which represents Egyptian Islam and the Muslim Brotherhood, he delivered one of his most significant speeches, later known as the Cairo speech. In this speech, Obama aimed to express the change in US policy toward the Muslim world. His speech was designed to flatter the Muslims and it was filled with historical mistakes that ignored the facts.

The speech included three components related to relations between the United States and Islam. The Muslims viewed the US as imperialistic, so the first component was an attempt to express empathy toward the Muslims and to neutralize friction on issues of conflict between the Muslims and the United States. There are those who claim, justifiably so, that this was due to Obama's own background, as his father was a Muslim. In his speech, he shared that he grew up in Indonesia, a country with a Muslim majority, and he spoke romantically about listening to the muezzin's calls. I viewed this component as a cold and calculated consideration: Obama wanted to defuse the animosity that had developed between the Muslims and America when the civilizations collided.

The second component of Obama's speech was a message about democracy. Obama asserted that the Muslim Brotherhood was the future of the Middle East, the authentic voice of pragmatic Islam that could bring about democracy, both in Turkey and Egypt. This was why Obama first stopped in Ankara and presented Turkey as the model of a democratic Muslim country led by the Muslim Brotherhood. In hindsight, we've witnessed the kind of "democracy" that has developed there. How wrong he was.

This speech gave a big push to internal entities in Egypt that wanted to challenge President Mubarak. The Muslim Brotherhood did not lead the revolution there – it merely jumped on the bandwagon. Yet Obama's push toward democratization was wind in the sails of Mubarak's opponents. Obama essentially hinted at the fact that if the Egyptian citizens wanted internal change – via a revolution or in another manner – he would not support Mubarak.

The third component in the speech was the message that the United States did not prefer Israel, and in fact, it favored the Muslims over Israel. By putting Cairo first on his travel itinerary before Jerusalem (which he did not visit until 2013), the president sent this message loud and clear.

The speech was filled with factual imprecisions that were meant to appease the Muslim listeners. Obama claimed, for example, that there was no contradiction between Islam and human rights. He spoke of the Arab-Muslim world as reformist and progressive, blatantly ignoring the facts, such as the absence of equal rights for women in many Arab countries. The American president spoke about the commonalities between the Muslims and the United States, highlighting Islam's contribution to the world in areas such as algebra, geometry, and inventions such as the compass and the fountain pen. But he forgot to mention that all of that took place during Islam's golden age, before the Muslims underwent a process of radicalization and became an oppressed society that does not encourage thinking. Everything that Obama said is irrelevant to today's Islam, which is busy with wars and not with scientific or technological development, and which blames the great Satan (America) and the small Satan (Israel) for everything that happens to it, instead of taking responsibility for its actions. For centuries, Islam has contributed very little to the world in the fields of science and technology. Its representatives are practically nonexistent among the Nobel Prize laureates in these fields.

With that same flattering approach, Obama completely ignored the fact that more than 99 percent of the terrorists in today's world are

Muslims. He released the Muslims of all responsibility for that fact. He made no claims against Islam and demanded nothing from the Muslims.

Regarding the Israeli-Palestinian conflict, Obama mentioned the settlements as the obstacle to peace, as if they were the core of the conflict. In fact, up to the end of his term Obama never once used the term "radical Islam" or talked about "Islamic terror." As far as he saw it, it wasn't politically correct.

This speech was a bad omen. I was shocked by the sycophancy and the historical imprecisions it included. Someone who is supposed to be a world leader needs to say things as they are, and not ignore the negative contribution of Islam to the world in recent decades in encouraging radicalism and violence. I understood that an ominous era was beginning for Israel. As far as America was concerned, we had moved over to the side of the bad guys and the victimizers.

During those days, I met with a senior American figure with many years of experience under his belt, who confirmed my fears. He told me that all Israel could do was to pray that Obama would only be president for four years and not eight. If such prayers were recited, they didn't help much.

During his visit to the Middle East, Obama skipped over the State of Israel to make a statement – I am with the Muslims, not with you. Even during his visit to the Buchenwald concentration camp the day after Cairo, on June 5, 2009, he made a statement – he was with us as victims, not as victimizers. Obama only came to Israel in March 2013, during the second term of his administration.

Considering these circumstances, I was not surprised when the Obama government's policy on the Palestinian issue was against us from the start. Obama made a severe mistake when he focused the claims against us on the settlement issue with a call to freeze all construction – "not even one brick" (quoting Secretary of State Hillary Clinton). First, this was a breach of the previous administration's commitment under President George W. Bush toward then prime minister Ariel Sharon. After the roadmap was accepted, an understanding was reached between the two governments and their leaders that Israel would not build new settlements in Judea and Samaria, but the United States would not oppose construction that facilitated natural development and normal life within the outlines of the existing settlements. We, as the elected government, continued Sharon's commitment to Bush, but Obama decided to ignore Bush's commitment to Sharon, given in his letter of April 2004.

As could be expected, this unilateral behavior in favor of the Palestinian side increased the distrust between the Israeli government and the American administration. In a long telephone conversation between US Secretary of State Hillary Clinton and Prime Minister Netanyahu, the demand to freeze construction was once again raised. In its wake, the US administration sent a formal demand to freeze construction, without mentioning any corresponding Palestinian action. As we saw it, this was an erroneous unilateral step. Ever since the Oslo Accords, we had upheld our side of the agreement and ceded territory to them. But instead of "land for peace," we had received land for terror – with a toll of over a thousand casualties – or land for rockets, as occurred after the disengagement.

I also viewed the move as a tactical error in America's conduct. Anyone interested in bringing Abu Mazen to the negotiating table, despite the refusal of his predecessors and his own refusal, does not need to put pressure on the State of Israel. It's a mistake to view the settlement issue as the core of the Israeli-Palestinian conflict. This is an erroneous perspective, which unfortunately has taken over the international discourse regarding the internal Israeli-Palestinian conflict and regarding the connection between this conflict and the instability of the Middle East. In truth, the conflict between the two sides began long before the settlements were established. Essentially, it began even before the establishment of the State of Israel.

The change in American policy toward us could be felt even before the regional upheaval. Back then, I said that anyone who thinks that the Israeli-Palestinian conflict is the source of instability in the Middle East is ignorant, wrong, and guilty of misleading others. Today, this claim is heard less and less, even in Arab countries that in the past used the Palestinians as a weapon against us. But the American government exacerbated this claim with the mistaken assumption that if this conflict was solved, ISIS and Al-Qaeda would cease to exist as well, or that the Shi ’ ite-Sunni conflict would deflate.

On this issue, we were facing a confrontation with a hostile American administration. I am not claiming that Obama is anti-Semitic, but I believe that his worldview was based on empathy toward those whom he erroneously perceived as victims, and there are elements of a pacifistic worldview involved as well. I have no doubt that this outlook is also connected to Obama’s personal background. After many years of pursuing a policy toward the Arab and Muslim world that could be perceived as imperialistic, America adopted an apologetic stance, and this came at our expense.

American attempts to bring the parties to the negotiating table failed, even though we were prepared to meet in any place at any time, on condition that the discussion would include all the issues, not just the settlements, borders, and land. These were issues that the Palestinians favored, because in these areas, they were only on the receiving end. As we saw it, if the discussion addressed a permanent arrangement, then everything should be discussed, including the most substantial and important question of all: after we reached a territorial compromise based on mutually consented borders, would the Palestinians be willing to recognize it as the end of the conflict and their claims? I never heard Abu Mazen make any declaration saying that he would be willing to recognize the State of Israel as the national state of the Jewish people within any borders, however they might be defined.

This demand on Israel's part was not raised for the first time by the government elected in 2009, nor by Netanyahu. It was raised long ago as the initiative of Yitzhak Rabin, who saw this issue as one of the problems with the Oslo Accords, and demanded that Arafat change the Palestinian charter in order to express recognition of Israel. To this very day, the Palestinian charter has never been changed! This is essentially the core of the conflict – the unwillingness of the Palestinians to recognize our right to exist as the national state of the Jewish people within consented borders.

After we expressed our willingness to negotiate, together with our demand for recognition by the Palestinians, we tried to be considerate of the American government. But even when we froze construction in the settlements, and even when we were careful about construction in Judea and Samaria and in Jerusalem, the discussions did not bear fruit. After nine months of freezing construction, we refused to accept this demand any longer, because we hadn't received anything in return. Abu Mazen hadn't showed up at the negotiating table. Obama's special envoy to the Middle East, George Mitchell, apparently also understood that the direction that the American administration was pursuing was incorrect, and he resigned from his position as envoy. At this point, the Americans ceased their attempts to pressure us to come to the negotiating table.

Later, new American initiatives were raised. In July 2011, the United States proposed renewing the negotiations based on the Terms of Reference document (TOR), presented by Secretary of State Clinton. We agreed to that proposal as a basis for negotiations, making it clear that we had our objections and reservations, which we would raise at the negotiating table. But Abu Mazen rejected the proposal. The Quartet, the international body supervising the solution to the Israeli-Palestinian conflict, intervened in September 2011 and made changes to the American proposal in favor of the Palestinians that were to our detriment. We responded to this proposal in the affirmative as well, while making it clear that we had our objections and reservations, and once again, Abu Mazen refused without paying any price for doing so. The international system perceives Abu Mazen as a weak figure with no accountability, and he takes full advantage of it. Each time, Israel as the alleged strong side is blamed for the failure of the negotiations.

The American attempts halted until John Kerry took over as Secretary of State, replacing Hillary Clinton after the 2013 elections. Kerry brought a new spirit and was deeply convinced that he could orchestrate that elusive solution that no one else had been able to achieve. He was irrationally enthusiastic about bringing about the end of the conflict, based on the same erroneous assumption that the Israeli-Palestinian conflict is the source of instability in the Middle East. The Americans said that they heard this claim in the Arab capitals. The Arabs had an interest in aiming the spotlight at the conflict here, but anyone in their right mind should have understood, especially after the regional upheaval, that the Shi'ite-Sunni conflict was not because of us. Neither was the ethnic conflict in Syria and in Iraq, the tribal conflict in Libya and in Yemen, or the revolutions in Egypt.

Kerry's enthusiasm to solve the conflict became almost an obsession, and he decided to invest full state and diplomatic energy in the matter. I compared these attempts to a person who watches the same movie several times, hoping each time that the ending will be different.

In the summer of 2013, the pressure on the parties to begin negotiations increased. Netanyahu appointed Foreign Minister Tzipi Livni as Israel's representative on this matter. Abu Mazen, as usual, presented preliminary demands for arriving at the negotiating table. This has never seemed reasonable to me, since Abu Mazen has no desire to reach decisions that will bridge the huge gap between the two sides. Kerry, in turn, pressured us to accept one of Abu Mazen's preliminary demands. He proposed two alternatives – freezing all construction in the settlements or releasing prisoners. To start the process, Kerry traveled to Amman and conducted the negotiations from there.

In the end, after discussions were held between us and the Palestinians and within our own camp, we agreed to release eighty-four Palestinian prisoners, the vast majority of whom were Fatah members who had committed terror attacks prior to the Oslo Accords. I thought that it would be appropriate to release them immediately after the agreement was signed, as part of an attempt to set things straight – after all, we had signed an agreement with the person who had sent these terrorists, Arafat. Because prisoner release did not happen then, I didn't consider it as a crucial concession in 2013. Not for one moment did we agree to release Arab-Israeli prisoners, and we told Kerry this outright, because we viewed this as crossing a red line: Abu Mazen represented the Palestinian Authority, and he was not responsible for Israeli Arabs.

Netanyahu gave Kerry our answer regarding releasing the prisoners in a phone conversation, while the Secretary of State was in Amman. On Friday afternoon, Kerry arrived in Ramallah. At the end of his meeting with Abu Mazen, we discovered that Kerry had also committed to the release of Arab-Israeli prisoners, contrary to our agreement. Instead of eighty-four prisoners, he said that we'd agreed to release 104 prisoners, including some Arab-Israelis. This conduct was characteristic of Kerry throughout the entire process: he rounded corners and told each side something different. Abu Mazen agreed to begin negotiations based on Kerry's promise to release 104 prisoners – contrary to our position.

This led to an explosion between us and Kerry and a harsh conversation between him and the prime minister. On our side, we deliberated how to proceed, because we knew that if we refused to conduct the negotiations now, after Abu Mazen had given his consent, we would be viewed as the side that had caused the talks to fail. The blame game became a very important factor in the process. We had to act wisely in order to avoid having the "ball land in our court." Based on these considerations, we decided that despite everything, we would begin negotiations, and the prisoners would be released according to the pace of advancement of the negotiations. From our experience and familiarity with Abu Mazen, we knew that there would be no progress anyway, so there was no reason to start arguing now.

The first stage for releasing prisoners was in August 2013 and two additional ones were scheduled for October and December. Soon enough, we realized that Abu Mazen was continuing to insist on his position and was not willing to discuss substantial matters – only borders and settlements. Minister Tzipi Livni had always blamed Israel for intractability while sitting with the opposition side (this is one of the problems with our politics: the Palestinians blame us, and we blame ourselves). This time, she had no choice but to admit that Abu Mazen was to blame for the failure of the negotiations.

As part of his efforts to find a solution to the conflict, Kerry apparently tried to provide a response to Israel's security needs. He appointed the esteemed General John Allen to head the teams that worked with both the American and Israeli sides to prepare a security outline that would satisfy us.

The outline was never completed or presented to me, but during the team's work, Kerry presented the unfinished outline to Netanyahu and myself in the prime minister's office. Kerry focused primarily on providing a solution for the eastern border, proposing the installation of technological means on both sides of the Jordan River. It was obvious that this was not a security outline that could satisfy us, especially not me as defense minister. I was familiar with the Central Command region and fully aware that this outline did not meet our security needs. I saw it as a political move that was meant to convince us, and not a genuinely workable proposal. After Kerry and General Allen finished presenting the partial and unfinished outline, I gave my severe criticism of it and explained the many holes in its theory.

Kerry demanded that we retreat from Judea and Samaria within a short period and forfeit our freedom of operation in Area A regions, which we have held since Operation Defensive Shield. In the end, we would give up control of the Jordan River bridges as well. As far as I saw it, full Israeli control of everything that entered or exited the areas of the State of Israel and the Palestinian Authority – by land, air or sea – was a mandatory condition. If we lost control, Iran would take advantage of the situation, as it had already done in Gaza. Today, ISIS and other hostile entities know how to take advantage of breaks in the fence. For all these reasons, supervision of Israel's borders must remain in Israel's hands.

Kerry did not have answers to the questions that we raised. What would happen, for example, if the Palestinians began producing rockets or mortar shells in Nablus and then fired them at Ben-Gurion Airport or Tel Aviv? Who or what would prevent that? This was just one of the many holes in the unfinished outline that was presented to us.

The prime minister did not see a solution to our security needs in the plan either, but in a sense, his positions were softer than Rabin's positions, as the latter was not willing to talk about the Jordan Valley at all. Rabin said that even under a permanent settlement, the Jordan Valley would remain under full Israeli control. Even the king of Jordan prefers Israel at the border over the Palestinians.

After the meeting at the prime minister's office, we met for dinner at the David Citadel Hotel in Jerusalem. I had no choice but to speak very harshly in response to statements that were made there. This has been a charged issue for me for years. I have a hard time restraining myself when I hear comments about "a window of opportunity that could close," because who knows what will happen after the Abu Mazen era. It is also difficult when pressure is put on us to forfeit our best interests in favor of a political process, while there are still huge gaps between the sides. When the expression "window of opportunity" was once again mentioned, I said, "I am familiar with many types of windows, mostly shattered ones. I am also familiar with the needs of the State of Israel."

The atmosphere became more and more unpleasant with every passing moment. When Kerry left the room after asserting that Abu Mazen was moderate, this is what I said to his companions:

> About Abu Mazen's moderateness, are you familiar with the Boston Strangler and the Yorkshire Ripper? Would you agree with me that in a sense, the Boston Strangler was more moderate than the Yorkshire Ripper? Now, choose which one you prefer to murder you.... In contrast to Arafat, Abu Mazen understands that terror does not pay, but he still does not recognize our right to exist. He just operates according to a different method, which he calls "political resistance" or "popular resistance." Since the Palestinian indoctrination of terror and violence lies at the heart of the matter, as well as his unwillingness to recognize us as a nation or to recognize Israel as a Jewish state, you need to apply pressure on this issue, not on the issue of the settlements, concession of territory, and our security interests. If these issues are not solved, the conflict will be renewed with even greater energy each time that we retreat from a border.

After these events, I realized that from the American's perspective, I was an "enemy of peace." Kerry had brought a media team with him, and I discovered that he was criticizing me in his briefs, claiming that I was "a hard nut to crack" and an obstacle to peace. *Yediot Aharonot* political analyst Shimon Shiffer raised these claims to me after hearing them from the Americans. Although the conversation was supposed to be off the record, he quoted the comments I made about Kerry in a giant headline the next morning in *Yediot*: "Hallucinatory, Obsessive, and Messianic."

I was told that I had to explain myself and apologize. I refused to apologize. I knew that if I ever went to the White House, Obama would treat me as an unwanted guest. There are politicians who would compromise their opinions for the privilege of such an honor – not me! But despite this incident, I met with Kerry later and participated in many of the phone conversations that Netanyahu had with him. We continued to work together.

Between January and March 2014, as we came closer to the end of the nine-month period that Kerry had set for reaching an agreement, the Americans made another attempt to convince the parties to continue the negotiations. Kerry presented both sides with another TOR document and asked us to agree to it. This document presented the way that the United States viewed the outline of the solution to the Israeli-Palestinian conflict. We again complied and added that we had our reservations, which we would be willing to discuss at the table. In February, Abu Mazen met with Kerry in Paris and did not answer in the affirmative. On March 17, 2014, he was summoned to a meeting with Obama at the White House, during which he also preferred to delay his response. Abu Mazen returned to Ramallah and gave his negative answer from there in a militant speech.

We realized that the negotiations were stuck. We held occasional meetings between representatives of the two sides, but these were fruitless. Once again, we understood that this cow would not give us any milk. It was clear that Abu Mazen was not planning to make progress with the negotiations. He only wanted to reap the benefit of the prisoner releases. Abu Mazen didn't actually want a permanent settlement. He was interested in receiving land and prisoners, but he refused to give anything in return. Based on this reality, we gave notice that there would be no fourth round of prisoner releases.

In light of Abu Mazen's behavior and the negative response that he gave, the American side should have taken a clear stand against him. After

Arafat rejected the political initiative offered to him in 2000, President Clinton made an unequivocal statement that Arafat was to blame for the failure of the negotiations, and Bush did the same thing in 2003, when he blamed Arafat for the Palestinian terror war and the failure of the political talks. But Obama made no such statement of blame regarding Abu Mazen.

In my opinion, the international system's choice to avoid blaming Abu Mazen is critical. This choice is based on its perception of him as a weak and incapable figure who is not accountable. It is a patronizing, problematic view that sets in stone the Palestinian storyline that their problems are not their fault, but actually America and Israel's fault. This is one of the reasons for the economic, scientific, technological, political, and social demise that the Palestinians and the Arabs face, because when you don't accept responsibility for your actions and deny accountability, you cannot improve. Those who clear Abu Mazen of all responsibility and expect nothing of him are in fact playing a central, substantial part in the repeated failures to reach a settlement between the sides.

Thus, President Obama's attempts to renew the negotiations between Israel and the Palestinians reached the end of the road. Obama apparently understood, as Trump will understand over time, that there is no chance of reaching a permanent settlement with the Palestinian side, which is considered relatively moderate. Obama joined the long list of those who tried and failed. Why is that a surprise? The end of the movie never changes, even the fourth time that you watch it.

Kerry was so desperate to bring the sides to the negotiating table that at some point, I said that maybe someone should just give him a Nobel Peace Prize so that he would leave us alone... He did not have malicious intentions. Rather, he believed, contrary to all historical fact and experience, that if both sides were simply pressured, the conflict would be solved and with it, all the Middle East's problems. This conduct is based on ignorance, naivete, wishful thinking, and a patronizing attitude, in the sense of "we know what is best for you" – and these are four catastrophic components. When the process fails, another catastrophic element is added: Israel is blamed. Many times, as if all of this wasn't enough, the Jews also blame themselves.

In hindsight, I felt like I was laying myself on the line for the security of the State of Israel. While Netanyahu shared my opinion, by nature he is a leader who sometimes bends to pressure and needs someone to guard him. My feeling was that had I not been there at that time as defense minister, eventually the prime minister might have capitulated to Kerry's dangerous demands.

To the prime minister's credit, I can say that for eight years, he stood up to the pressure and acted responsibly in the face of a hostile American administration. That is, until the Amona crisis and the Regulation Law.

In September 2016, during election season in the United States, I was no longer part of the government. I was in the US on a five-week trip as a senior research fellow at the Washington Institute for Near East Policy. It was no coincidence that I chose to be there during that period. I believed that I could influence the individuals who would be formulating the documents for the next government, whatever that would be. I met with the people involved in writing the papers and tried to convince them to be accurate regarding the Palestinian issue. By the way, during those five weeks, I met many people who were preparing documents for a Democratic administration with Hillary Clinton as president. I met many professionals who were ready to serve a Republican administration under Donald Trump, but I did not meet anyone who was preparing documents for Trump's administration. At that time, people were even ashamed to admit that they supported Trump. Nevertheless, at the end of that period, my guess was that Trump would win.

As far as I know, Obama deliberated at the end of his term whether he should make a speech about the Israeli-Palestinian conflict and the failure of the talks. Apparently, this speech would have been harsh, and it would be remembered as part of his legacy. In the end, he again chose not to express a position on the issue and not to say a thing. But in December 2016, in an unusual step, Obama decided not to veto the UN Security Council resolution against the settlements. The Amona crisis, and primarily the Regulation Law, are the factors that pushed the American president to make this decision, after we "poked our fingers in his eyes."

This is an example of the irresponsible and uncalculated conduct of the Israeli government. After many years of holding fast in the face of the American government and protecting Israel's best interests, Netanyahu eventually gave in due to internal political issues. He did this so that those farther right in the coalition, especially from the Jewish Home Party, wouldn't be more right-wing than him. He capitulated, and Israel paid a heavy political price for internal politics.

When Trump won the elections, voices were heard, especially from Jewish Home and among certain elements in the Likud, saying that this was our opportunity to annex Area C regions, to settle every hilltop and expand the settlements. These irresponsible statements harm our interests. They are spoken by those who understand nothing about how discussions are held between the Israeli government and the American administration.

Certainly, some of the first reactions of the Trump administration to Israel may have stemmed from the desire to reset the system here, in the sense of "don't think that everything goes." His envoy to the Middle East, Jason Greenblatt, poured cold water on the idea of settling every hilltop. Trump's administration recognizes Israel's right to settle Jews in Judea and Samaria, but still retains the American interest in completing a political process between us and the Palestinians. If we annex Area C and settle every hill, not only will the possibility of reaching a settlement become moot, but these actions are also liable to lead us in the direction of a binational state.

As soon as Trump made his first comments and steps, we could see the change in policy toward Israel: he treats us as the good guys. He declared that Jerusalem was Israel's capital and transferred the United States embassy to the city – a landmark historical deed! The inner circle at the White House was opened to Israeli representatives after having been closed to them for years, during the Obama period. Even Michael Oren and Ron Dermer, Israel's ambassadors to the United States during Obama's presidency, were denied access to the inner circle at the White House. The positions expressed are different as well: envoy Greenblatt comes with a different attitude, as does the new American ambassador, David Friedman, who recognizes our right to settle in Judea and Samaria.

At the same time, though, Trump must look balanced and objective if he wants to reach a "deal" – as he calls it – between the sides. I presume that after his staff become familiar with the reality on the ground, he will discover the Palestinian refusal. I would recommend that he refrain from pushing for a permanent settlement as did his predecessors, as long as the conditions for it remain elusive. Instead, he should pursue a policy that supports progress based on the interests of both sides, such as economic development, the development of infrastructures, and security collaboration – a path, not a solution.

In addition, I would recommend that he focus on reforming the Palestinian education system and cancelling the funding given to Palestinian prisoners. The Palestinian Authority is the most economically supported political entity that ever existed in history relative to the size of its population, and the huge monetary assistance provided to it should have long ago been contingent upon educational reform. The Palestinians teach their children from kindergarten age to hate us and murder us. Yet the world pays no attention to this, just as they ignore the financial support that Palestinian prisoners and their families receive based on the amount of Jewish blood they have spilled.

Another way that the United States can contribute would be to work to cancel the distortion created by the very existence and operation of UNWRA, which sustains the "Palestinian problem" instead of working to solve it.

These are the cards that the United States and Europe hold to pressure the Authority to change its ways, but these things have never been done because of the claim that the Palestinians are weak. I hope that in this area, President Trump will understand the magnitude of the challenge that he is facing in dealing with an entity that encourages terror.

The most important change in the Trump administration's policy in the Middle East is in relation to Iran. The Iran speech delivered by President Trump on May 8, 2018, expresses the change in policy that matches our perception of the Iranian threat in general, particularly the nuclear threat. Defining Iran as a wayward regime that sponsors terror, exports weapons, and fans the fires of conflict in the Middle East is an extremely important change in American policy. The Trump administration understands that the Iranian regime is the greatest hazard to regional stability. While the Obama administration mistakenly saw the Iran issue as the solution, Trump views it accurately as the problem.

Trump was correct to impose immediate sanctions on the Iranian regime, in the wake of the blatant breach of the international resolutions on distributing weapons, sponsoring terror, and developing missiles. The Iranian regime cannot ignore the heavy economic pressure that those sanctions will cause.

Time will tell whether the decision to leave the Iran nuclear deal (JCPOA) was a wise move. It would have been possible to apply the same pressure of sanctions on the Iranian regime without projecting the image of someone who doesn't respect an agreement, and without losing the support of the European countries that signed it – France, Great Britain, and Germany. I hope that the European countries will join the economic sanctions and the political pressure on Iran to change the agreement.

This combination of economic and political pressure will again force the Iranian regime to choose between continuing their military nuclear project and wayward operations in the region, or survival as a regime. I have no doubt that the regime will choose its survival. The regime should know that if not, it will not survive.

The change in American policy should be credited to Israeli policy under Prime Minister Netanyahu's leadership. However, I am convinced that the same achievement might have been made without jumping in headfirst and causing a rift with the Democratic party in the United States.

PART V

My Bid for National Leadership

CHAPTER 21

MURKY WATERS

Lengthy tomes could be written about the murky relationship between Binyamin Netanyahu and Avigdor Lieberman. So when I found out that Netanyahu was meeting with Lieberman about joining the government and offered him my position of minister of defense, I understood that his interest in replacing me surpassed all other concerns. Furthermore, I discovered that previously Netanyahu had tried to bring the Zionist Union Party into the coalition, and even offered party chairman Yitzchak ("Bougie") Herzog the position of minister of defense, without Herzog requesting it. In my view, the breaking point in our relationship was on the issue of the submarines. The crisis reached in February 2016 was the heart of the matter.

Even before my term as minister of defense, my suspicions about integrity were aroused surrounding the purchase of sea vessels from Germany, specifically regarding the purchase of the sixth submarine. I heard rumors that the deal was not in line with the position of the IDF and the Navy. The IDF maintained that five submarines were enough, and if it needed a sixth, this would only be after the first submarine became obsolete and needed replacing. I had been aware of this position before I became minister of defense, and I supported it. However, it appeared that in 2019, the IDF would be receiving the sixth submarine, which would replace the first one before it became obsolete, although it was still early and unnecessary.

When I began my term as minister of defense in 2013, I brought for cabinet approval the purchase of four vessels for defending the gas platforms. The gas platforms in the Mediterranean Sea had become a strategic asset, and naturally, they were also a strategic target for attack by our enemies, primarily Hezbollah. The need for these vessels arose before I began my position, and the confirmation was delayed due to the elections. I confirmed the need and the purchase, and the cabinet confirmed it as well. When discussions began on the purchasing possibilities, the option was raised that the German government would offer to manufacture the vessels and sell them to us at a discount, as it had done in previous transactions. In the absence of a German offer, and also to avoid dependence on the Germans, the idea was discussed of issuing an international tender. This option was authorized by the cabinet.

After the cabinet gave its approval, I instructed the director general of the Defense Ministry, Major General (Ret.) Dan Harel, to issue a tender that would not obligate us to accept any of the offers. This was in case the Germans submitted a better proposal outside the tender process. I thought that from a business viewpoint, it would be good for the Germans to know that we had another option for purchasing the vessels, and that we were not their captive clients. Otherwise, I feared, they were likely to demand such a high price that even after the discount, it would be higher than the price requested by other shipbuilders.

After the tender was issued, Prime Minister Netanyahu asked me, "Why did the Defense Ministry issue a tender?" I explained my reasoning to him, but mainly I was surprised at his interference. He had no reason to get involved, because the tender did not stand in the way of any German offer. It seemed suspicious to me, but I did not suspect Netanyahu. My staff suspected that the deputy head of the National Security Council, Brigadier General (Ret.) Avriel Bar-Yosef, who was also former head of the Navy equipment division, was interfering in the developing deal and whispering into the prime minister's ears. But we had no proof of this. I learned that at the same time, Attorney David Shimron had contacted the legal advisor to the Defense Ministry, Colonel (Ret.) Ahaz Ben-Ari, in the prime minister's name. Shimron had asked Ben-Ari if we had cancelled the tender as Netanyahu had instructed. I also learned that Avriel Bar-Yosef had contacted the head of the purchasing department, Brigadier General (Ret.) Shmuel Zucker, and asked the same question. In any case, I instructed my staff to continue with the tender, unless we received an attractive offer from Germany, and they did so. Toward the conclusion of the tender, the Germans submitted their offer and my staff entered negotiations with them. Only after we were convinced that the German offer was good, even very good, did we cancel the tender.

Retroactively I learned that the seller (Germany) as well as the buyer (Israel) both had an interest in keeping the price of the vessels as high as possible!

In August 2015, a discussion was held in preparation for a cabinet meeting on the five-year national plan, known as the Gideon Plan. During the meeting, the prime minister made a specific request to enlarge the fleet of submarines to nine. Not only was this request surprising and unjustified, but no discussion or research at headquarters preceded it.

This process seemed completely astonishing to me, but at that stage I didn't yet have the overall picture. Until the end of my term as defense minister, I didn't know that David Shimron, the prime minister's confidante and personal attorney, was the attorney for the transaction. Shimron also represented Miki Ganor, the dubious agent in Israel of the German shipbuilder ThysenKrupp. According to media reports,

Shimron was involved in attempts to privatize the Israel Navy shipyard and transfer maintenance of the submarines to the German shipbuilder for which Ganor worked.

Following the heated discussion, in which I expressed my objection to nine submarines, the issue was referred to the National Security Council, which would discuss the question of how many submarines were needed and formulate a proposal. The NSC did its research. My recommendation as defense minister, which matched the recommendation of the IDF and the Israel Navy, was that we did not need more than five submarines, and this recommendation was accepted. We did not need six, and certainly not nine. With that, the discussion was over, and there was no need to contact the Germans regarding three additional submarines. But looking back, I realize that the prime minister was in another frame of mind altogether.

During the lead-up to Netanyahu's meeting with German Chancellor Angela Merkel, on February 16, 2016, I was informed by Yaakov Nagel, deputy head of the National Security Council, that Netanyahu intended to sign a memo of understanding with Merkel for the purchase of three additional submarines and two anti-submarine warships, totaling two billion euros. I was stunned by this news. The NSC had discussed the matter and agreed that we needed only five submarines. If so, why was the prime minister about to discuss with Chancellor Merkel three additional submarines (aside from the sixth submarine, for which the purchasing contract had already been signed) and two anti-submarine warships, which had not even been discussed in any forum?

The first thing I did was an extensive background check. Perhaps a discussion had been held somewhere, headquarters work that I didn't know about – in the general staff planning department of the Defense Ministry, or in the Navy. I checked all channels and discovered that no discussion had been held.

I called the prime minister. His justification was that Chancellor Merkel would be facing elections in 2017 and it was unclear if she would win. Why not get a commitment from her right now to provide us with submarines and anti-submarine warships? I answered that the commitment could be unilateral – in other words, that the German government would continue to provide us with submarines as needed in the coming years, without specifying the price, number of vessels, or timeline. We were in no rush. The earliest date that we'd need to replace a submarine would be in 2029 or 2030. Assuming that we'd need to start the purchasing process a decade in advance, we could start to handle it in 2019. By then, new technologies might be available, new submarines from new shipyards. Why commit now to a price and become Germany's captive customer in a deal that should be initiated only in 2019, if at all?

Besides, I argued, why were anti-submarine warships under discussion, when they had never been on the agenda? The assertion about upcoming elections for chancellor was irrelevant, because Israel had made weapons deals with her two predecessors, Helmut Kohl and Gerhard Schroeder.

At the end of the stormy conversation, we agreed that Nagel would send the draft of the memorandum of understanding to my office for my comments. The issue of purchasing anti-sub warships was removed from the agenda as quickly as it was raised. If those ships were so important, why did Netanyahu give them up so easily? I felt that the prime minister had been caught red-handed, although I had no proof, and at that stage, I didn't know about the involvement of his closest advisors.

The argument between Netanyahu and myself on this issue continued until his meeting with Merkel, and throughout, he voiced harsh criticism of me, including personal attacks. I felt as if I were restraining him, that something improper was going on, but I had no proof of it. Before Netanyahu began his meeting with Merkel, Nagel reported to me that the prime minister had agreed to sign a unilateral commitment, as I had suggested. Germany would commit to supplying us with submarines in the future, without specifying prices or timelines. I relaxed, and the subject did not come up again until I resigned from the government.

After my resignation, I read in the media that the cabinet had authorized a deal with the Germans to purchase three new submarines to replace three existing ones. As described, the matter should not have come up for discussion until 2019. Circumstantially, I see the clear connection between my expulsion from the government and the deal that I had tried to block.

In November 2016, journalist Raviv Drucker published an investigative report that revealed many more details. Only then did I discover that David Shimron was the legal counsel for Miki Ganor, who had acted on behalf of the German shipbuilder. One week after my resignation, Shimron had begun negotiations with Avi Nissenkorn, chairman of the Histadrut labor federation, and with the chairman of the IDF Civilian Workers' Union, about privatization of the Navy shipyard – a demand I had not been aware of as defense minister. It is legitimate to begin headquarters research on the issue from inside the system, but there is no reason for the discussion on privatization of the Navy shipyard to be held by someone who has a clear economic interest in privatizing it, without a request or recommendation by the defense establishment. Enormous sums of money are involved.

A submarine is a very expensive weapon. The price ranges between three hundred million to half a billion euros, and to this we must add the maintenance expenses. Agents are not always necessary in negotiations for purchasing such weapons. In the American system, for example, there are no agents, but rather representatives that receive salaries and a bonus from the company. The Germans manage the process in a completely different manner, which is unfortunately exploited by agents. There is no reason for us to pay exorbitant prices for weapons, and certainly not for weapons that we do not need, purely for profit.

In the end, following the media report, the issue became the subject of a police investigation. At first the attorney general declared that the affair did not require investigation, but after Avriel Bar-Yosef was interrogated by the police, further suspicions were raised. Bar-Yosef had pressured to replace the previous agent in transactions with Germany, Shaike Barkat, and to appoint Ganor in his stead. Bar-Yosef had been interrogated by the police regarding the issue of gas liquefication, and suspicions of bribery had arisen. Apparently, in that interrogation he had also been asked about the submarines. The police contacted the attorney general, prompting the AG to order a check of the submarine issue and later, the investigation.

Throughout the entire affair, I suspected that Bar-Yosef was the one pushing for the deal with the German shipbuilder and Miki Ganor. My suspicion intensified when the purchase of anti-sub warships was brought up, because only someone who understands navy subjects could make such a request. Of course, my suspicions worsened when the prime minister wanted to appoint Bar-Yosef as head of the National Security Council. I thought he did not have the appropriate skills for the position.

Slowly, layers were added to my suspicions of severe corruption, with the potential involvement of the prime minister and priority given to profit and personal favors over the good of the state. It is difficult for me to believe that the prime minister did not know what was going on around him.

I was surprised by the behavior of the attorney general and the state attorney's office, when they announced after the investigative report that there was no criminal aspect to the affair. Later on, the AG ordered a check, not an investigation – and only in February 2017 did he order an investigation. In the first stage, the check focused on Defense Ministry officials, including a search in the office of the ministry's legal advisor, even though none of them were suspects. I was surprised that the suspects in the affair, mainly members of the prime minister's office and agent Miki Ganor, were summoned for investigation only after many months. I was further surprised that no search was conducted of the offices of attorneys David Shimron and Yitzchak Molcho immediately after the investigation began. I was also surprised by the repeated declarations of the AG and the state prosecutor that the prime minister was not involved in the affair.

In December 2016, I was summoned to testify to the police on everything I knew about the affair. From the parts of the puzzle known to me, it was difficult for me to believe, and I say this with great sorrow, that the prime minister was not involved in the incident. There is no other way to explain his insistence on purchasing three unnecessary submarines, in opposition to the positions of all the professional entities; the incomplete process of purchasing two anti-submarine ships, without any professional discussion on the matter; and his surprising involvement in the attempt to cancel the tender for the defense ships for the gas platforms. If his private attorney was likely to profit from these deals, it was implausible that Netanyahu was completely in the dark.

As COGS, I had smelled corruption in various entities. When someone in Israel insists on constructing a casino in Jericho, this raises a deep suspicion that he or his associates have an economic interest in it. But whoever serves in such a position does not have the tools to investigate. In such a case, when an officeholder has suspicions of corruption, he can contact the state comptroller, the state prosecutor, or an investigative journalist. Unfortunately, even in cases when I contacted these entities, not much was done.

I had become acquainted with corruption in the days of Ariel Sharon and Ehud Olmert, but I hadn't encountered it with Netanyahu – until the submarine affair. I heard worrisome stories about his behavior, and I do not intend to get into the issues of management of the prime minister's home. But previously, I had never suspected that Netanyahu was corrupt like Olmert, that he received envelopes with money and authorized construction projects in exchange for bribes.

When the suspicion arose that our prime minister was tainted with bribery (in Case 1000 and Case 2000), I underwent a great crisis. I found it hard to believe that he had given in to the temptation of cash. This type of corruption made me lose sleep. Could it be that the person responsible for the future and security of the state preferred the personal consideration, in this case monetary, above the good of the state?

This type of rot trickles down and takes hold, and it transforms us into a corrupt nation. In certain circles, I began to hear statements like: "He's the prime minister, he deserves it. Let him enjoy it." As I write these lines, over thirty corruption cases on the municipal level are being investigated. I've heard assertions that corruption has spread throughout Israel, from individuals who are trying to promote projects, including foreign businesspeople who have told me that they've decided not to do business here. They say that Israel is a corrupt country, and I feel embarrassed and worried. This isn't why we established a Jewish national home.

I might have been able to smooth over the affair. I could have kept quiet, avoided argument, and accepted it. I also could have done so in the case of Elor Azaria (see next chapter). If so, I would probably have continued in my role as defense minister. But I would not have been able to look myself in the mirror.

Some will say that I'm not a politician. I'll take that as a compliment. Must a politician be a liar and a thief? I've known politicians who are honest and hard-working, who serve the state and the public, and not themselves. From my point of view, on the issue of ethics and honesty, the red lines are clear.

CHAPTER 22

THE FACE OF THE COUNTRY

The operational investigation of the incident in which soldier Elor Azaria shot and killed a neutralized terrorist ended around noon, just a few hours after it occurred. The conclusions were clear: this was a criminal act that contravened the rules of engagement and our ethics. The case was transferred to the Military Police Criminal Investigation Division (MPCID). A black flag flew above this act. After the operational investigation, not one piece of new information was added that might have changed it.

I could never have imagined that such a seemingly straightforward case would become a political campaign, a wrestling match between myself and the prime minister, a struggle for our values and the character of our country, and eventually the catalyst for writing my letter of resignation. The moment was approaching when I could no longer look at myself in the mirror and continue to sit in this government and stand up for it.

The incident took place on Thursday, March 24, 2016, which was also the Jewish festival of Purim. Immediately afterward, I received a short operational report: two terrorists had attempted to stab soldiers in Hebron. We had one lightly wounded soldier and two neutralized, dead terrorists. Later, I learned additional details. A soldier involved in the incident had apparently fired in a manner that did not comply with the rules of engagement, in a situation that was not life-threatening. Major General Roni Numa, GOC Central Command, ordered the commander of Kfir Brigade, Colonel Guy Chazut (later brigadier general), to investigate the incident.

I was informed of the exact details later in the day. At 8:15 a.m., two terrorists had arrived at Gilbert Checkpoint in Hebron and attacked the platoon commander and a soldier. The event was over in seconds. The platoon commander and the soldier shot at the terrorists. The soldier was slightly injured in the shoulder, and both terrorists were neutralized. A short time later, another platoon commander from the company arrived at the scene. He checked the two terrorists who were lying sprawled on the ground and turned them over to ensure that they were unarmed. One of the terrorists was still lying on a knife, and the platoon commander pushed it away from him. The platoon commander continued to examine the terrorists from head to toe. He ensured that they weren't wearing explosive belts and that they were not armed. From this aspect, the event was over.

Six minutes after the skirmish, the company commander arrived at the scene by vehicle, together with the company medic, Elor Azaria. The company commander was notified that the event had concluded. He then ordered the medic to help the Magen David Adom medics evacuate the soldier who was wounded in his shoulder. There was no urgency, as the soldier's injury was light. The company commander closed the event and reported it to the battalion commander. Eleven minutes after the skirmish had ended, and after he had finished treating the wounded soldier, Elor Azaria went with the other medics to the area where the two terrorists lay on the ground. He handed his helmet to one of his friends and asked him to "hold this for me for a second." Then he cocked his weapon and shot the twitching terrorist in the head.

The friend who was holding the helmet was the first to ask him, "What did you do?" To everyone at the scene, including civilians, clearly an unacceptable act had just occurred. Elor replied to his friend, "A person who comes to stab my friends deserves to die." He didn't speak about anyone's life being in danger. He didn't say that he felt that his life was in danger or that he thought that the terrorist was about to detonate an explosive belt or use a knife. He simply decided that the terrorist deserved to die.

Company commander Tom Na'aman had thought that the incident was over. Suddenly he heard a shot fired, so he also asked: "What did you do?" He received the same answer. The company commander reported to the battalion commander, David Shapira, who reported to the commander of Kfir Brigade. Within less than an hour, the details reached the GOC Central Command, who ordered the Kfir Brigade commander to investigate the incident quickly. The video that documented the incident had not yet been submitted – although they noticed that there was a photographer on site – but even without this video, everyone treated what had happened as an unusual event.

Elor Azaria reported to the brigade commander for his investigation and repeated his statement, "A person who comes to stab my friends deserves to die." He didn't mention anything life-threatening to the brigade commander either. At twelve thirty p.m., the brigade commander concluded the investigation: this was a severe offense that would be transferred to the Military Police Criminal Investigation Division (MPCID). The soldier would no longer serve in a combat position.

In contrast with comments made later by officers, saying that the incident should have been closed within the unit, this type of event leaves no room for judgment. It was completely clear that this was a criminal matter, like rape or manslaughter, and it had to be investigated by MPCID.

The brigade commander reported to the military attorney general, Brigadier General Sharon Afek, that this was an unusual event. The

MAG ordered the opening of an MPCID investigation. At one thirty p.m., before the investigation began, I received a report from Chief of General Staff Gadi Eizenkot, who was always in my office on Thursdays at this time for a routine situation report. At this point, we realized that a video clip of an IDF soldier executing a Palestinian was circulating on social media and causing an uproar. Such a video blends wonderfully with the Palestinian blood libel that we kill them without trial. Here was proof on film.

The chief of general staff and I halted our situation assessment to receive the full briefing on the investigation and view the video. Together, we concluded that we had to issue an unequivocal statement as soon as possible condemning the incident in order to prevent a Palestinian flare-up on the ground. This is exactly the type of event that can incite the masses, like the car accident that led to the outbreak of the First Intifada in 1987. In addition, we knew that if we didn't condemn the event quickly, the international community was also liable to use it against us. There are plenty of anti-Israel media outlets that are happy to air such a video.

I instructed my military secretary to report to the prime minister's military secretary and also recommend to him that he issue a condemnatory statement. Indeed, the three of us – the chief of general staff, Prime Minister Netanyahu, and myself, issued a statement condemning the event and saying that it was an unacceptable incident, in order to prevent a flare-up on the Palestinian stage and in the international arena. Although we did so prior to the opening of the MPCID investigation, we already had the full picture. The operational investigation was over. Its conclusions were clear, and that was not going to change.

On Thursday evening, I began to realize that the incident was becoming political. The military attorney general appointed an experienced defense attorney who was serving in the reserves, Colonel (Ret.) Avi Amiram.

Elor Azaria was immediately notified, even before he began to testify before the MPCID, of his right to consult with an attorney. But while Amiram was making his way to Hebron to meet with the soldier, he was told to turn around and head home because the Azaria family was not interested in his services.

At this point, I received a phone call from former Knesset member Sharon Gal from the Yisrael Beitenu Party. I didn't answer, and I tried to find out why he was contacting me. It turned out that he was at the Azaria home. I understood that the Yisrael Beitenu Party had taken over the event and that its members were among those advising the family not to accept the military attorney (whose services were offered to the soldier for free). I have no doubt that if the military attorney had met with Elor Azaria that day, he would have recommended to him that he confess, express remorse, and ask to be pardoned. The entire legal process would have ended differently. Instead, private attorneys were brought in and promised large sums of money in exchange for representing the soldier. Not to protect him, but to turn the incident into a political affair.

As mentioned, the event happened on the Thursday of Purim, a festival marking the victory of the Jews over the wicked Persian king Ahasuerus and his evil advisor Haman, who plotted to destroy them. On this holiday, Jews celebrate by dressing up in costume. That Friday morning, I arrived at the Kiryah and saw that the fence around it was plastered with posters depicting Chief of General Staff Eizenkot as Ahasuerus wearing a red fez, and the words: "Eizenkot, resign, and take Bibi and Bogie with you." The political campaign had begun and was gaining momentum. In the afternoon, I was notified of a Facebook post uploaded by Education Minister Naftali Bennett, in which he backed Elor Azaria and questioned why he was being abandoned. Had he genuinely been interested in answers, he could have called me and asked me what happened and heard the results of the investigation. He has my phone number. But he didn't really want to know what happened. He wanted to gain political capital from the affair.

On Saturday night, Bennett called the Azaria family. On Sunday morning, before entering the government meeting, Bennett gave an interview in front of cameras and microphones. He criticized the lack of support from the chief of general staff, defense minister, and prime minister. I was absent from that meeting due to prior commitments, but I was told that at the beginning of the meeting, he attacked Netanyahu with allegations.

Bennett started to spread lies, claiming that the army was charging a soldier with murder. The word "murder" appeared in Elor Azaria's case only once, at the beginning of the testimony collected by the MPCID. At this stage, they are obligated to notify the person under investigation, as part of the proceedings, that the case could potentially reach the point of a murder charge. When Elor was remanded in custody, before a pathological examination was completed, he was told that he was suspected of a severe offense. When the results of the pathological examination arrived and it was clear that the bullet fired by Azaria killed the terrorist, the charge was changed to manslaughter. None of this information bothered the attorney who represented Elor Azaria later on, Yoram Sheftel, when he claimed that the defense minister and the chief of general staff had charged him with murder, despite the fact that we had never used that word. But he didn't place this fabricated blame on the prime minister. Like everything related to the affair, this was also the result of political considerations.

On Monday, the "Brave Soldier" campaign was already underway. I arrived at the Knesset with no intention of speaking about the incident, but Knesset members from Yisrael Beytenu and the Jewish Home spoke about the "brave soldier who was abandoned by his commanders." Spontaneously, I approached the podium to respond. He was not a brave soldier, I said. He was a soldier who had acted incorrectly. An operational investigation had been conducted, and I could not divulge the results.

Please don't make this into a political issue, I requested. I thought that would be enough to end the story. I was wrong.

That same week, Azaria was brought before court to extend his custody, this time not in Jaffa, but in a closed military camp at Kastina. Who else showed up at court? MK Avigdor Lieberman, MK Oren Chazan, Ben-Zion Gopstein, Baruch Marzel, Moshe Feiglin and activists from the Lehava organization. Groups of supporters were bussed in. Someone was funding this campaign. In the background, cries of "He's innocent!" "Brave soldier," and similar slogans filled the air.

As defense minister, I had to respond; someone had to protect the military system from these gangs. By Tuesday, I went to visit Central Command, because a crisis was at hand and I had to back the soldiers and commanders. They were confused. On one hand, all the commanders, from the platoon commander up to the chief of general staff, as well as the soldiers who were present at the incident, were telling the same story – a soldier had fired against the rules of engagement. On the other hand, the politicians were telling a different story. I responded once again and said that the COGS was the only person who could set the orders, not gang leaders. I made no further comments on the matter until the verdict.

The COGS had to comment again five weeks after the incident, when the prime minister joined the gangs. The confusion at Central Command increased. They could handle statements by Lieberman and Bennett and a few Knesset members from the Jewish Home Party, Yisrael Beitenu, and the Likud, but it was hard to remain indifferent when the prime minister switched sides.

Netanyahu called me during the first week and wondered aloud why we had commented the way we did. He suggested that perhaps he should invite Elor's parents to his home on Balfour Street. I told him that there was no way he could do that. "You complain about Abu Mazen who goes to console the families of terrorists," I said. "If you support this act, you will confuse the soldiers." The prime minister listened to my words at that time, but he added that we shouldn't make any further comments on the matter.

A week and a half later, he nevertheless decided to call the Azaria family. I heard about it from his military secretary, and I realized that there was no longer any way to stop him. He had heard my opposition and the opposition of the chief of general staff, but he had decided to switch sides anyway. The IDF had a hard time handling the situation. Yes, the "leftist" defense minister and the "leftist" chief of general staff talk about upholding the law and about ethics. But if the prime minister, education minister, and additional Knesset members support the soldier – who is right?

While some claimed that the COGS and myself should not have gotten involved, we had no choice. In the situation that arose, we could not wait until the end of the trial. An attempt was made to twist the judge's words regarding politicians' involvement in the affair. She was not referring to the defense minister. The defense minister cannot stand on the sidelines and wait for the end of the trial while other politicians are getting involved and meanwhile, the soldiers in Hebron don't know how to operate.

Both my statements and those of the COGS were necessary at the time in light of the behavior of the politicians. Had they not become involved, we would not have said a word. Instead, we were repeatedly forced to respond to their statements in order to protect the soldiers on the ground and clarify the orders. We spoke before the legal proceeding to prevent a flare-up on the ground, and we spoke after it began in response to the politicians' intervention. Who will protect the system if not the defense minister?

The nights at the end of my term as defense minister were restless. Not because of Syria, or Iran, or Gaza, but because of these types of issues.

I started to wonder where I would be more useful – within the system or outside it? I understood that I was on a collision course with the prime minister over issues that were red lines for me. On these issues, I could not simply lower my head and duck, as political advisors sometimes recommended to me. The damage done during this affair was not only short term, as expressed by the sentiments raised in the army, but rather long term, to the country's character. As a statesman, I cannot agree that this is the way my country should look.

Another severe aspect of this affair was the ease with which the public was misled by manipulation of the facts. As early as the first week of the affair, I discovered that a PR firm with strategic advisors was managing the media campaign, using any means they saw fit. Friends from my military service, including generals, reported that they had been contacted by an investigative journalist looking for blots on my record involving the killing of captives. Of course, no such stories were found.

A post was published on Facebook blaming me for being present when a captive was killed, when I was "battalion commander 890 during the First Lebanon War." During that period, I was actually in Sayeret Matkal. One of my staff demanded that the person who published the false post remove it immediately. He did so, but then published it again after the verdict was given. In addition, a letter was published, allegedly written by Elor Azaria's mother, claiming that I had behaved like her son and had verified the killing during the elimination of Abu Jihad. It was obvious that she did not write the letter. It was part of a well-planned campaign that also funded the salaries of the attorneys, the support rally at Rabin Square, and the buses to Kastina. I had to deal with the ridiculous and unfounded claim that I, as defense minister, had recruited prosecutor Nadav Weissman and paid him $280,000 (NIS one million) to cause the indictment of Elor Azaria. I had never even spoken to the Military Attorney General about such a thing, and definitely not with the prosecutor, who performed this task as part of his reserve duty.

During the fake news era, anyone who can type can claim whatever he wants. The lies stick, and it is very difficult to disprove them. In the past, the saying was that you can fool some of the people some of the time. In this day and age, you can fool a lot of people all of the time. Politicians need to be much more responsible in times like these. But in this case, the opposite was true: politics was filled with lies, hatred, and attempts to rake in votes. The future of the country was apparently much less important.

I swore myself to silence until the verdict. Only then, after I was no longer a member of the government, did I publicly express myself. I recommended to the Azaria family that they try to understand that they were being exploited for political reasons, and that all the advisors who allegedly had helped them were not working in their service. I understand the suffering that they endured, but for Elor's good and for their own good, I suggested that he confess, express remorse, and request a pardon. His words would not have fallen on deaf ears.

I was truly surprised that the sentence was so light. Eighteen months for such an act? A British soldier who committed a similar deed in Afghanistan was sentenced to fifteen years in prison, and after an easement of his punishment, this was shortened to seven years. The sentence of eighteen months was also the result of political pressure, which reached as far as the court. What type of message are we sending to our soldiers?

Elor Azaria did not confess and did not express remorse until the end of the legal proceedings, so it is unclear why a pardon was even discussed. This soldier published a Facebook post at the end of Operation Protective Edge. He wrote: "Bibi, you fairy, why don't you wipe out Hamas?" His father and mother encouraged him on Facebook. He grew up in a home where he was taught the slogan "Death to the Arabs." Should such a home be supported?

Some claimed that Elor Azaria's case would cause soldiers to hesitate before shooting terrorists. These claims are unfounded. After the ramming attack in the Armon Hanatziv neighborhood in Jerusalem, a security guard who was at the site claimed that soldiers hesitated before acting because of the Elor Azaria affair. The video documenting the incident proved otherwise. Within twenty seconds, an officer and cadets had regained their senses and killed the terrorist. This is another example of political manipulation. At first, the soldiers ran away, because that is the natural response when a truck comes at you. They did not run because of the Elor Azaria case. After the Azaria incident, our forces killed dozens of terrorists who attacked civilians, police officers, and soldiers. But these facts did not confuse the entities with vested interests. They tried to create the impression that the soldiers' resolve was damaged as a result of the handling of the case, by both the command chain and the legal system. The soldiers' resolve was not harmed. Soldiers, as opposed to certain politicians, know their orders and their missions well. They understand exactly what needs to be done.

After the terror attack on the Temple Mount on July 14, 2017, during which two police officers were killed, Azaria's campaign managers and his attorney again manipulated the story. During the clash, a terrorist is seen sprawled on the ground and then getting up and trying to attack the police officers. The police officers obviously shot and killed him in accordance with the rules of engagement. There was an immediate attempt to compare this case to the Hebron incident, but these were two incomparable events! During the Temple Mount attack, the terrorist lay down and then got up during the skirmish. He was not checked or neutralized beforehand by our forces. But in the attack in Hebron, the shot was fired in a non-life-threatening situation, eleven minutes after the combat had ended, at a neutralized terrorist who was checked previously by an officer from head to toe. Furthermore, the soldier himself did not claim to be shooting as self-defense, but rather "because the terrorist deserves to die."

In hindsight and as time passes, I recognize that the Elor Azaria affair was a failure of leadership on Prime Minister Netanyahu's part. I had no expectations from Education Minister Bennett. I definitely had no expectations from Lieberman. But from the prime minister, I did have my expectations, and in this case, I was disappointed. I don't know if this is related to the fact that we found ourselves on opposite sides of the fence in prior events. I don't know which is the cause and which is the effect. But I do know that without the argument that had ignited between us a month earlier regarding the sea vessels affair, I presume that this affair would have ended differently. This is politics in all its ugliness. It represents a failure of leadership, and it is a very dangerous message to relay in a Jewish, democratic state.

CHAPTER 23

My Decision to Resign

Many people ask me, how can it be that when you were defense minister, everything was so good and you had no complaints about the functioning of the government, but after you resigned, everything was so bad and you became so critical of the government?

This assertion is not exact. I agree with many things that this government is doing in the political and security fields. In most cases, my position was accepted and adopted based on understanding with the prime minister. In general, our policy is correct with regard to what is happening in the region with Iran, Syria, and the Palestinian arena. The way we handled the knife terror attacks was also correct. Prime Minister Netanyahu and I had a shared language in that field.

Israel is also functioning well in the macroeconomic field and has achieved admirable successes. I do have criticism for this government's social-economic policy, and I expressed my view when I sat in the government. Back when I visited Likud branches all over the country, I argued that this was the empty portion of our cup: the cost of living, housing prices, the gap between wealthy and poor, exacerbation of the cycle of poverty, and erosion of the middle class.

The disagreements between myself and Netanyahu as well as some members of Likud and the government erupted mainly after the 2015 elections. I felt that the prime minister was treating each of us as if we owed him victory in the elections, and so he could demand things that he hadn't asked for previously. I saw that his main yardstick for evaluating people in various positions was their level of loyalty to him.

During his first term as prime minister, I became acquainted with Netanyahu's obsession on the issue of "the elites that don't allow us to rule": the media, the courts, and civil servants, mainly military personnel who voiced opinions that opposed his own. A large part of this was due to the fact that he ended his first term as prime minister in 1999 in a traumatic manner, and with the feeling that he had been ruined politically by the media, the legal authorities, and the military. He thought that the late Lieutenant General Amnon Lipkin-Shahak, then COGS, and Defense Minister Yitzchak Mordechai had taken a stand against him. Since then, he has viewed members of the defense establishment as an opposing elite. Later, he expanded the definition of this elite to civil servants, particularly those who dared to oppose him, for example on the issue of the national gas plan. They were kicked out.

I agree with the assertion that a civil servant cannot criticize the government in public while he is performing his job. But I definitely encourage voicing critical, relevant opinions during discussions in the appropriate forums. I wish to be challenged by such opinions. In all the positions I have held, I have always ensured that people avoid expressing criticism of government decisions in public and reserve such opinions for the conference or cabinet room. This is one of the lessons learned from the Yom Kippur War: we must encourage people to be critical and voice doubts.

There is no reason to worry if a civil servant thinks differently from me on issues of security, gas, or the economy. This is part of the checks and balances of a democratic society. We do not have to dismiss professionals because they hold an opposing, critical opinion, or appoint them based on their willingness to adapt themselves. In the final analysis, after the decision is made, discipline is enforced in implementation. But until the decision is made, we certainly must hear and express dissenting opinions.

A civil servant must be selected based on his skills and capabilities, and he must act out of loyalty to the state, not to a particular person. Officeholders such as the chief of general staff, head of the Mossad, head of the Shin Bet, police commissioner, attorney general, director of a government office, public ombudsman, or any other position must be loyal to the State of Israel and its laws, not personally loyal to the person who appointed them.

But during Netanyahu's time, unfortunately, I witnessed phenomena that did not fit these criteria. Personal loyalty became the main criterion. The prime minister preferred to block the democratic balances and fight the elites that he viewed as endangering his authority. He made appointments based on personal loyalty. The situation was worse for ministers and Knesset members, whom he tested for their loyalty to himself and his wife. Those who occupied center stage and made headlines that favored him became the prime minister's darlings.

The agenda that guided Netanyahu was to damage the democratic system of checks and balances, because "they do not allow him to rule." I came up against this agenda in each of my conflicts with him, on every issue. One of the first conflicts between us addressed the Locker Report and the prime minister's attempt to harm the defense budget. This also stemmed from his fear of the elites, exactly like his battle against the media and the courts.

The defense establishment must work with a multi-year plan. It cannot function when its budget is up for discussion every year, because this creates a situation that I called a "Turkish bazaar" when I was COGS.

The defense establishment asks for a certain budget that it justifies, the Finance Ministry comes back with a different number, and in the end a number is chosen without an in-depth discussion of the security issues and the budget's implications.

Against this background, the government established the Brodett Committee, which was composed of professionals in the fields of economics and security, including economists David Brodett, Dr. Karnit Flug, and Professor Manuel Trajtenberg, and defense experts, including Major General (Ret.) Ilan Biran, former director of the Defense Ministry; and Major General (Ret.) Eitan Ben-Eliyahu, former commander of the air force. They held dozens of meetings in which they examined the defense establishment in depth: challenges, needs, costs, budget structure. On this basis, they built a ten-year plan which determined that the defense establishment would need reinforcement that would cost tens of billions of shekels. They recommended that part of this sum, three billion shekels per year, would come from internal streamlining. The rest would come from budget increases.

When I began my term as defense minister in 2013, the Brodett Committee Report was in its seventh year of implementation. But during the discussion on the annual budget, I discovered that Finance Minister Yair Lapid had already decided on the budgets of the other ministries and had left the defense budget for last. Defense was given the resulting leftover budget, which did not even approach the amount determined in the Brodett Report. The gap measured NIS eight billion. It was like suggesting to someone on a diet that they cut off a leg in order to lose weight. This just wasn't done – one can't cancel a committee decision in its seventh year of implementation without any prior discussion. Here as well, I recognized unprofessional political behavior with the prime minister's backing.

When I realized the size of the problem, I asked to hold a special cabinet meeting on the shortfall in the defense budget, before the Knesset met to approve the budget. The government meeting was postponed to Monday, and on Sunday the cabinet held its discussion. The members of the cabinet agreed that an addition to the budget was necessary. Because at the moment there was no way to obtain this addition, they would hold another meeting on the issue a week later, after the budget was approved by the Knesset. At the second meeting, the cabinet decided that the Defense Ministry would be first in line to receive the anticipated budget surpluses at the end of the year.

I felt that the prime minister had not stood beside me in the fight over the defense budget. He hid behind the assertion that "this is what happens when the finance minister is not from our party." I was furious that a multi-year plan was not approved. As some of the defense establishment's developments require fifteen years to be completed, it must follow a plan that looks five years ahead and defines targets, projects, capabilities, and the budget. We cannot operate like a Turkish bazaar.

Ignorance abounds on the defense budget issue. I asked some members of the cabinet, including two who were former finance ministers: which ministry receives the largest budget from the government coffers? They all indicated the Defense Ministry. I proved to them that they were wrong. The defense budget for 2017 stood at $17 billion (NIS 60 billion), while the budget for education was $15 billion (NIS 54 billion). But as opposed to other ministries, payment for retirement and rehabilitation in the Defense Ministry are included in this sum. By contrast, the Education Ministry's retirement budget is listed under the Finance Ministry, and the Education Ministry's rehabilitation budget comes under National Insurance. These expenses total $5 billion (NIS 18 billion) of the Defense Ministry budget, which leaves it with a remaining budget of $12 billion (NIS 42 billion). An additional $2.8 billion (NIS 10 billion) comes from US aid funds, which means that the Defense Ministry actually received only $9 billion (NIS 32 billion) from the government budget, while Education receives $15 billion (NIS 54 billion).

I do not begrudge the Education Ministry's budget and I appreciate that we must allocate funds for education. However, the public, and especially members of Knesset, must be aware of these statistics.

In 2013, after the developments in our region obligated a change in the existing Defense Ministry plan, I found myself without a multiyear plan and I was forced to operate with a deficit budget. Because it's impossible to stop long-term projects, I announced that I would have to cease training exercises. This was not just an empty threat. The Defense Ministry has certain obligations that we cannot trim: projects that have already been approved and budgeted, payment of salaries to permanent armed forces personnel, subsistence payments to soldiers in mandatory service, ongoing support of an armed forces including food and travel expenses. In principle, the only expenses that the Defense Ministry can modify are current expenses such as training and noncombat operations. We can't even close units, because the closing year is more costly than usual operations. When I began my term, I ordered to close tank and artillery battalions as a result of changes in challenges, and to invest in other areas such as cyber units, active defense systems against rockets, and ways to address the tunnels problem. But even after these decisions were made, in the middle of the budget year we ran out of money for training exercises.

When the cabinet met to discuss the budget surpluses, again it operated like a Turkish bazaar. The prime minister requested from the Finance Ministry a detailed report on the budget surpluses for that year. He never received it. I asked the Finance Ministry for an additional $1.2 billion (NIS 4.5 billion), and in the end, I had to compromise for half. I asserted that it was impossible to continue to operate without a multiyear plan. It was hard for me to understand why the Brodett Report was tossed in the garbage bin at the height of its implementation and without any discussion.

Then the prime minister proposed establishing a new committee that would examine the needs of the defense establishment, to be headed by Major General (Ret.) Yochanan Locker, his former military secretary. Individuals from the prime minister's inner circle were appointed to the committee, most with backgrounds in the field of pension and finance and not in defense. One of the defense representatives on the committee, for example, was Joseph Ackerman of the defense industries, a thoroughly positive person who had served for many years as president and CEO of Elbit Systems. But his defense experience was incomparable to that of the two major generals in the reserves, Ilan Biran and Eitan Ben-Eliyahu, who had served on the Brodett Committee. The dominant members of the Locker Committee were representatives of the Finance Ministry and National Insurance. They were excellent people, but they did not understand defense. I realized that according to Netanyahu's worldview, the committee would focus mainly on the service and pension terms of regular military personnel, and that they would be harmed as a result of his battle against the military, which he considered an elite.

When the committee began its discussions, I appeared before it for two hours. Later, after I understood which way the wind was blowing, I asked to meet with Locker again, but he avoided me. I received the surprising message that the committee's conclusions would be presented at a press conference. I informed the prime minister that this was unacceptable. How could the conclusions of the committee on the Defense Ministry's needs be announced, before the COGS and defense minister had even seen a draft of the committee's report and had a chance to submit their comments? In the final analysis, the press conference was postponed, and I received the report, which was presented as a draft. Of course, I had many comments.

I discovered that the committee had adopted the multiyear plan, the Gideon Plan, which the defense establishment had begun to implement in parallel to the committee's work. But the committee had mainly focused on cutbacks to regular military personnel. For example, it decided that the improved pension conditions would apply only to battalion commanders. This was an illogical decision that deeply harmed the quality of the people who serve in the regular army and the army's ability to employ the best. It meant that a physician at the level of lieutenant colonel who served as a branch head in the medical corps and was previously a physician in combat units like Givati and Shayetet 13, but was never a battalion commander, would not have economic security. Why should he continue to serve in the army if he could earn much more in the civilian system? How could the army employ the best jurists to defend it in the international legal arena if it did not offer them attractive conditions? This also applied to the personnel in the vital field of technology.

When the Locker Committee's recommendations were leaked to *The Marker*, the army was hit by a deep crisis. People began to leave. Those who were at a decision-making juncture could not wait months until the debate over their pension conditions ended. I informed the prime minister that I could not accept the report, that I would not permit this damage to the IDF.

I also discovered that the committee wanted to transfer authorities in the field of purchasing and defense imports and exports from the Defense Ministry to the National Security Council, even though by law the Defense Ministry was responsible for purchasing. Throughout, I identified attempts by the NSC to stick its nose into matters that were not its concern. Perhaps this was related to the submarines affair that exploded afterward.

The report was published in the original version. Only the word "draft" was deleted. My comments and those of the COGS were ignored. I was presented as opposing streamlining, although COGS Benny Gantz and myself had done a great deal in this area. I warned that if the report reached the cabinet, I would fight it with all my might. In the end, the report did not reach the cabinet. Despite the prime minister's fury, I was able to reach an agreement with the new Finance Minister, Moshe Kachlon, on a budget of $17 billion (NIS 60 billion) for the Defense Ministry. When I left my position, the defense establishment had a multiyear plan that was agreed on with the Finance Ministry and a cease-fire in the discussion of service conditions for regular army personnel.

But even if the budget issue was solved, the worst problem remained: someone intended to enter the purchasing field and cause mortal harm to the IDF in general and the regular army personnel in particular. Netanyahu could speak into a microphone and declare that we had to grant an additional three billion dollars (ten billion shekels) for defense, and then make cuts based on external considerations.

Conflicts also developed on issues involving another elite that was considered an enemy: the media. I also have extensive criticism of the Israeli media. It must do its own soul-searching. But the road is long from that criticism to the minister of culture stating that the state must control the media, an MK declaring that the Likud must rule the media, and taking steps to bring public broadcasting under government control.

I witnessed an obsession, which intensified after I resigned, with the issue of the Israel Public Broadcasting Corporation and the Broadcasting Authority. Conflicts arose with channels. The media was affected by attempts at deterrence, intimidation, and control. As defense minister, I was asked to close Galei Tzahal, the official radio station of the IDF. I admit that were we at the outset of establishing the military, I would not establish an associated radio station. But because it has become part of Israeli communications and public broadcasting, it serves as an integral part of the checks and balances of democracy. After I resigned, discussions were resumed regarding the station's role and control over it.

When I began as defense minister, I summoned Yaron Dekel, then commander of Galei Tzahal, to meet with me. I told him that for years I'd heard criticisms of the station, including that it was leftist. I told him, "I won't be calling you about content, unless it's an exceptional matter. But I do want the station to represent all sectors of Israeli society. It shouldn't be a bubble. You must have representatives from the periphery and from all sectors of the Israeli society." There is a big gap between this legitimate request and the demand to interfere in content and appoint "our people," which represents a danger to democracy.

Then minister of culture Miri Regev tried to interfere in the station's affairs and to change its playlist. Regev decided to raise the issue of Mizrachi and Ashkenazi Jews. Personally, I have a bit of a problem with the ethnicity issue, because my wife is of Moroccan origin, so I wouldn't know how to define our children. At any rate, I don't see any reason to address this issue. During my childhood in the mixed neighborhood of Kiryat Haim, no one was concerned about it, nor was it an issue for my wife when she grew up in the Neve Sha'anan neighborhood of Haifa. I can understand some of the hard feelings on the issue, but there is no reason for politicians to exacerbate them.

Miri Regev asserted that Galei Tzahal did not play enough Mizrachi songs. This is an issue that should be handled by a professional committee, not by ministers. Following her interference, I responded that just as every Thursday as defense minister I approved the list of planned sorties and operations, from now on I could approve the playlist at the same opportunity. On a more serious note, if the minister thought that the playlist was not balanced, there was a way to handle the issue without breaking the boundaries of democracy. For the benefit of our state's future, we must treat the checks and balances with sacred reverence.

I observed a similar attitude toward the courts, another elite that Netanyahu and his associates disparaged for "not allowing them to rule." I also have something to say in a public debate over legal activism or the method of appointing judges, but reverently and with respect and admiration for the Supreme Court. The supremacy of the rule of law must be a given, and it is the duty of a responsible political echelon to uphold the honor and status of the Supreme Court. During Netanyahu's term, respect was not only avoided, but the honor of the Supreme Court was repeatedly trampled on. The situation reached the point where in surveys of public trust, in which the Supreme Court previously competed with the IDF over first and second place, it tumbled down almost to the level reserved for politicians.

The politicians are the ones responsible for this situation. When they need to make a decision that has a political price, such as demolishing illegal construction in Judea and Samaria, they refer the issue to the Supreme Court and then attack it for getting involved. I had intense conflicts with the prime minister and ministers on this issue as well. This behavior leads to loss of respect for young Knesset members toward the legal system.

MK Betzalel Smotrich, for example, dared to attack Miriam Naor, president of the Supreme Court, who said during the March of Living in Poland that we must learn from the lessons of the Holocaust and uphold human rights and the rule of law. He wrote: "Outposts on private land that harm the rule of law and human rights are simply a holocaust. I'm wondering whether to laugh over the idiocy or cry that this is the message that the president wants to convey. Sad." The MK distorted the president's words in an ugly manner and incited an entire sector against her. Due to politicians like him that delude it, this sector is currently undergoing a process of radicalization.

The prime minister has not fought this or tried to end it. When Ministers Ze'ev Elkin and Yariv Levin attacked the Supreme Court, he did not silence them. When MKs Oren Chazan and Smotrich entered illegal homes in Beit El and set up offices there, he was the one who should have stopped it, not the Supreme Court. I found myself on the other side of the fence from the prime minister on this issue.

The conflicts between us intensified, focused on a number of topics: Galei Tzahal, the submarines affair, the Elor Azaria affair. In the last few months of my term, I felt that Netanyahu was searching for issues on which he could confront me. I realized that we were headed for a dead end.

Then a new incident arose: the unfortunate statement (to put it mildly) of the former deputy chief of general staff, Major General Yair Golan, in his speech on the eve of Holocaust Remembrance Day 2016 at the Massuah Institute for Holocaust Studies at Tel Yitzchak. Remarking that he had witnessed youth who were exposed to processes of radicalization after entering the IDF, he called for Israeli society and its leaders to use Holocaust Remembrance Day for national introspection. He drew a terrible comparison between processes taking place in Israel and events in Europe during the Holocaust.

During his speech, he said:

> The Holocaust must lead us to deep self-examination regarding human nature, even when those humans are ourselves. It should lead to us to deep introspection regarding the responsibility of leadership and the quality of society, and it must lead us to thorough consideration of how we – in the here and now – behave toward foreigners, widows, orphans, and similar individuals. The Holocaust must lead us to think about our public life, and more than that, it must lead everyone who can to take public responsibility, and not just those who want to do so. If there is one thing that scares me about remembering the Holocaust, it is identifying shocking processes that took place throughout Europe, and particularly in Germany, seventy, eighty, and ninety years ago, and finding evidence of them here among us, today in 2016.

I demanded that Major General Golan correct his words. But before I contacted him, he realized on his own that his statement was interpreted in a problematic manner. That night, he published a correction and apology, stating that he did not mean to compare the IDF and the State of Israel with Germany seventy years ago, and that it was an absurd and unfounded comparison. But his apology did not satisfy the politicians. They demanded that I dismiss him. When I arrived at a meeting of "our ministers" (a meeting of the Likud ministers), I encountered a chorus conducted by the prime minister, who wondered loudly why the minister of defense was backing up the major general. I asserted that Golan was an excellent officer who had made a mistake and clarified his statement, and from my point of view the incident was over. I do not know if the attack by the prime minister and others was directed at Golan or myself.

Shortly thereafter, in honor of Yom Ha'atzma'ut, Israel Independence Day, I gave a routine speech to senior officers of brigadier general level and up. I said what I've been saying since I was head of Military Intelligence: "Do not hesitate to be critical of me, of your commanders, and of the political echelon. Raise doubts, be critical, and then ensure discipline in operation."

Before I concluded and descended from the podium, the prime minister issued a statement that he was summoning me the next day to admonish me and to investigate why I was encouraging the military echelon to publicly challenge the political echelon.

This assertion is ridiculous and unfounded. At my general staff headquarters as well as at those of Gantz and Eisenkot, we had never made one word of public criticism of a political decision, including during the disengagement. I was extremely careful about this. Still, I encourage criticism during discussions, even of myself. Woe to us if in meetings people say only what they think their bosses want them to hear. One can check all my speeches since I was head of Military Intelligence and see that my opinion on this issue has not changed. I have always spoken about inclusive leadership, as opposed to thought dictatorship, and I have called to encourage our subordinates to dare to be critical of us, to think, and to doubt – and in the end, to maintain discipline in operation.

I said all this to the prime minister after his summons. In the end, it did not turn out to be a reprimand. Still, we were clearly on a collision course.

After this affair, I discovered that as part of his attempt to broaden the government, the prime minister was trying to "sell" the position of defense minister to Yitzchak (Bougie) Herzog. As far as I know, Herzog's response to Netanyahu was that the current defense minister was excellent, and that he preferred to be foreign minister. I realized that the prime minister wanted to get rid of me. When the position was offered to Lieberman, I understood that it was only a matter of hours, perhaps days, until it happened. People tried to talk to me and calm me down, saying that perhaps the process wouldn't go through. But I decided to take preventive measures and announce my resignation.

I had prepared myself for the moment when I would have to resign, because I realized that I'd started on a collision course. Possibly, I'd blocked Netanyahu from benefiting from the submarines affair, and from experience I know that it's dangerous to do such a thing. I'd already observed such incidents with Sharon's Ranch Forum. From the unnecessary conflict surrounding the deputy chief of general staff's speech, I understood that the conflict that developed over the Elor Azaria affair wasn't coincidental, nor was the entire atmosphere. There was an obvious trend to cause friction with me and try to present me as a "leftist purist."

On Friday, May 20, 2016, I called the prime minister and said that I intended to resign, as I'd reached a dead end and come to the conclusion that he wanted to get rid of me. Netanyahu asked me to reconsider my decision and offered me the position of foreign minister. I told him that I didn't know how to explain the policy that he was pursuing and therefore I'd decided to resign from all my positions.

That same day, I held a press conference, at which I announced my resignation from the government and my intention to run for national leadership. Some pressured me to continue to serve as a member of Knesset, but I had to continue looking at myself in the mirror every day. If I was elected to represent the Likud but I didn't support the path that the Likud was following, I couldn't remain in the Knesset as a Likud representative. After I had decided to establish my own party, I announced that I was cancelling my membership in the Likud.

It wasn't the same Likud that I'd joined in 2009, nor the Likud for which I'd voted for the first time in 1996, after undergoing a process of transforming my views. At that time, the Likud worldview was right-wing on politics and security, as I am, but also liberal democratic in viewing the rule of law as a given. Over the years, the party underwent a process of radicalization. Good people were pushed out, and those who were elected in their stead led a rhetoric that was brash and disrespectful.

Not only does Netanyahu fail to set limits, but he also swims with the current. During elections, he called for people to rush to vote, because "Arab voters are going to the voting booths in droves." I can't lie to myself and remain a member of a party that encourages discourse that highlights Arabs, Ashkenazi Jews, or leftists. This is not the discourse of a leadership that is supposed to unify; rather, this is divisive politics.

The situation became even more extreme after I left. After attacking the media, the courts and public servants, Knesset members dared to attack bereaved parents during a discussion over the state comptroller's report on Operation Protective Edge. This incident broke all norms and fundamental values. Two Knesset members, behaving like Dobermans, attacked bereaved parents, but the prime minister did nothing to shut their mouths, and no Likud member dared to speak out against this phenomenon.

Some prefer to speak in extremes, others prefer to remain silent. This generation's behavior can be compared to that of a dog. A dog looks back, sees where his master wants to go, and leads in that direction. Instead of leading, the master navigates in the direction that the evil wind blows and provides an answer to the needs of the rabble.

I am built of different stuff. I don't think about politics and political maneuvers, or about how I'll retain my seat. Yet the State of Israel is important to me. That's why I resigned. I announced that I intended to start out on the long road of running for leadership of the state.

CHAPTER 24

The Race for National Leadership

I don't know many people who have experienced what I have in their lifetime. I could say that I've been privileged – but the privilege comes with obligation. I've been privileged to observe the young generation in Israel, ever since I was eighteen during my first days in the army as an ordinary soldier, as a parachutist, and up to the position of chief of general staff. When I was appointed parachute brigade commander, I set myself the habit of speaking with our youth before they were drafted into the IDF. I've kept up this habit till today – it's how I get to know our weaknesses as well as our strengths.

I educated successive generations to take responsibility, just as I grew up with this value. I looked in the eyes of young people deliberating before they began their military service and at major junctions throughout it, and I influenced their decisions – including some who are no longer with us today.

I was the one who convinced the late Captain Yossi Chaim and the late Captain Eran Alkawi, both company commanders in Battalion 890, to continue their military service and sign on for the regular army. Both were killed in Lebanon. The late Captain Muki Kenishbach, who was my deputy in the Paratroopers Brigade Reconnaissance Company, deliberated over his next step. We met for a talk one Friday after a week of training exercises, and I recommended that he take command of a company in the brigade. He did so, and he was serving as a company commander in Battalion 202 when he fell in Operation Leader in Ramat Arnon in Lebanon. The late Colonel Dror Weinberg was a squad commander in Sayeret Matkal when he discussed his future with me. He wondered whether to continue in the Unit or leave it for the "big army." When I understood his intentions, I recommended that he serve as deputy company commander in Battalion 890, and I recommended him for the position. He became company commander and battalion commander in the Paratroopers Brigade. He was killed while serving as commander of Judea Brigade, in a terror attack in Worshipers' Alley in Hebron. I was chief of general staff at the time, and I had already decided to appoint Weinberg to be the next commander of the Paratroopers Brigade. I also spoke with twin brothers Tzur and Hadar Goldin before they were drafted, and they both chose combat service and joined the officers' training program.

I've been privileged to occupy a position from which I can observe the young generation as it develops, and I have a special vantage point for comparison between periods. Some of the trends that worry me arise from this awareness: the process of radicalization and the loss of values. Today's youth are ethical but also sometimes confused, and they face a serious problem of leadership. Instead of outlining a path and providing a personal example, the leaders that the youth observe act out of the desire to survive in government. They make decisions only because they are popular, and not because they are right, and they exacerbate negative tendencies.

Considering this situation, after acquiring such a large store of knowledge and experience, can I go home and permit inexperienced, irresponsible people to try their hand at governing, at the expense of the State of Israel?

When I decided to resign from my position as minister, and later from the Knesset, I realized from the start that I would make every attempt to return to national leadership, and even to play a leading role. The decision to resign was accompanied by a difficult feeling due to the negative trends that I witnessed from up close. But I do not forget the extensive experience I accumulated in my senior positions in the military; my involvement in the State Security Cabinet since 1995, and my work with five prime ministers. From my viewpoint, the negative trends that I identified presented a challenge, and I had the necessary knowledge and experience to face it. I could not be true to myself if I didn't try to reach a position of taking responsibility.

Since I completed my position as COGS, I have received attractive offers from many companies that were interested in an individual of my experience and good reputation in handling security challenges. Many firms were willing to pay me sizeable sums for my advice on fighting terror, developing weapons, and facing the challenges of the cyber age. I chose to ignore the financial temptation and continue to invest in issues that I felt were important to the State of Israel, and not to other countries.

I can reasonably assume that my family would have preferred that I make a different choice, considering the many years in which I was far from home due to my military service, and after they had gained a close acquaintance with the political world. As my wife defines it, "I married a sergeant in the reserves, and in the end, I got a COGS, a politician, and a minister." Military service comes at a price. Without a full-time father, the burden of running the home falls on the wife and children. I also paid the price of distance from my family, but today I find compensation in enjoying my grandchildren.

In our home, we've always made a clear distinction between public activity and family life. My wife guards her privacy closely, and our children do as well. The family has paid a price, even though they have tried to develop a thick skin. It's hard to get used to the nasty sides of the political system, but we learn to lower our threshold of sensitivity. We understand that the system is manipulative and guided by self-interest, and that it does not always pursue truth.

What I have seen in the world of politics has not discouraged me – on the contrary. What I have seen has awakened within me a sense of emergency and the desire to lead. Despite all the slaps in the face, my sense of obligation and responsibility overcome all else. The bug I caught since I was eighteen isn't political, but rather the bug of responsibility. I absorbed and implemented this sense of responsibility in my parents' home; in the youth movement as a member and leader; in the decision to go to a young kibbutz in the Arava Valley, out of the desire to fulfill Ben-Gurion's vision by settling the Negev Desert; in the decision to return to the army following the Yom Kippur War, after I'd been elected as kibbutz secretary; in the command track I followed in the IDF up to the position of chief of general staff; and in political life.

I have no political bug – and what's more, I'd be glad to leave the political culture behind, as I've never liked it. But in the end, that is where the important decisions on our lives are made, in all fields: war and peace, education, the economy, health, welfare, society. When I look at what I bring to the job, I can't say that the time has now come for someone else to do it. This is all the more true when I observe the severe crisis of leadership that we are experiencing.

The current leadership makes decisions based on surveys and "likes" on Facebook. More than any other example, the case of Elor Azaria cries out to the heavens. The leadership was carried away by the fundamental, understandable feelings of the public, which preferred an Israeli soldier over a terrorist. But the role of leadership is to understand and explain that this is not the case of a soldier against a terrorist, but rather a soldier acting against the values of the IDF, against the rule of law, and against commanders' orders. It's easier to speak to the public's gut feelings in order to get a "like" than to uphold more complex ethical positions, but that's not leadership.

In the face of such leadership, I can't remain true to myself unless I run for public election. I am full of motivation. I am dedicated and experienced. If the public decides that it won't support me, I'll be sorry on the public level, because I know the important tasks that we must accomplish. But on the personal level, I'll have other projects to pursue.

Looking ahead after my resignation, I decided to continue public activity through the Manhigut Acheret ("Alternative Leadership") nonprofit organization. This organization was established by friends, and it served as a platform that enabled me to continue reaching people all over Israel – from youth before military or national service to senior citizens, who will also be casting a vote in the ballot box. The goal of the organization, as its name indicates, was to promote a responsible, ethical leadership that would protect the security of the State of Israel while preserving our shared values and ensuring the rule of law. It called for correcting the issues that require correction, as I saw them.

The organization also enabled me to perform important work on social media. Ministers are not permitted to use their office budget to sponsor a political Facebook page. Only after I resigned from the government did I discover the depth of the damage caused me because as a minister, I had been absent from this media. An individual who is interested in harming you politically can act against you on social media and erode your status, and you can't fight back. I experienced this illegitimate and libelous culture in person. People who ran against me for "leadership of the right" presented me as a destroyer of settlements, and they invested large sums in this campaign: in videos, color brochures distributed before the Likud primary elections, activity to erode my security status, attempts to present Operation Protective Edge as a failure, creating spin on the tunnels issue and on the Elor Azaria affair. This period has been defined as the "post-truth era" – and for good reason. I met entire communities that were swayed by false information. The direct encounter with them permitted me to present who I am and what I really think. Through the means at its disposal, the nonprofit organization enabled me to be more active in the field – in encounters with as many Israelis as possible, and on social media. I acted to rehabilitate my status on these two fronts.

Despite everything I have experienced, I have never resorted to using the kind of weapons that have been used against me. I have often been told that one can't survive in politics with my kind of ethics. When I was commander of the Judea and Samaria division, people hinted to me that with my honesty, I would not go far. So far, I have proved them wrong.

I say to the youth I meet today that in this period of overwhelming information, they must know how to choose the people they can trust. I advise them to develop tools they can use to judge whether what they read is true or false. It's not easy. I've seen with my own eyes how someone can be destroyed by false accusations and spreading lies. In this jungle, they must find the path defined by Maimonides and in which I believe: "Truth will carve its own path."

Within this jungle, I know from my experience how to define the right path in many fields, including state and security, economy, society, education, health, and welfare.

Undoubtedly, many challenges still face us in the state security field. In 2002, during Operation Defensive Shield, we switched from retreat and defense to offense. Even before we shot the first bullet, Israel underwent a transformation from a state in retreat that portrayed weakness to a state on the offense that demonstrated power. Our enemies realized that we were not a "spider web" state. They saw how Israeli society supported the offense into the midst of Jenin and the Shechem casbah. They heard that the rate of reporting for duty by reserve forces was 130 percent – in

addition to those who were called up, even people who were
came to volunteer on their own initiative. So, they understood
of our own leaders did not: we are a nation that desires pea , but we are not tired of war, and if we are called to defend our country, then we will fight. The Americans created this transformation on September 11, 2001, when they switched from defense to offense against radical Islam. We did the same in Operation Defensive Shield.

But undoubtedly, with the disengagement we returned to retreat and the spider web strategy, which led us to the kidnapping of Gilad Schalit, the Second Lebanon War, the rise of Hamas and its takeover of the Gaza Strip, and the strengthening of Iran and extremist Islam in the region. When radical Islam shows its public that the Zionist entity is in retreat, it gains strength, which is expressed in elections.

I saw for myself how corruption led a leader to make political decisions that he did not intend to make. Media entities were willing to wrap Prime Minister Ariel Sharon in cotton wool, as long as he carried out the disengagement. In this manner, following a decision made out of distress and the desire for political survival, we created a precedent. Just as we left the Gaza Strip to the last inch, now we are expected to retreat from Judea and Samaria. We opened the Philadelphi Corridor and enabled Iran to enter Gaza and create a launch base there. Since then, the rounds of warfare against Hamas do not end in Gush Katif or Sderot – they reach Tel Aviv and Ben-Gurion Airport. Concern over what I saw then continues to accompany me today. I don't know what decisions will be made by a prime minister under investigation, for his political survival.

My worldview in the security field is consolidated and complex, which means that in certain circles I'm considered an extreme rightist, and in others – a leftist. I've always valued human life above land, but as head of Military Intelligence I discovered the big holes in the Swiss cheese that was the Oslo agreement. I reached the understanding that the gaps between us and the Palestinians are enormous, and that neither Arafat nor Abu Mazen could serve as partners in a permanent arrangement. I do not see an agreement in the visible future, but I also do not want to rule the Palestinians and I do not want a binational state. I am in favor of strengthening the separation, creating a modus vivendi using sticks and carrots, and a process that takes place from the bottom up.

We must transmit a very clear message to the number one threat to us, Iran: we cannot permit it to achieve military nuclear capability. International pressure almost achieved this, but unfortunately the Obama administration missed the historic opportunity. Now we must continue handling the situation by creating opportunities for cooperation based on shared interests. I've learned from experience that when two sides have shared interests, there is no need for a signed contract, and that a contract without interests is not worth the paper it's printed on. In the security field, we have before us a broad arena for action, and I believe my experience will prove invaluable.

I have my eyes on social and economic issues as well. As a military man, I was able to feel the pulse of Israel's educational system. When I visited schools throughout the country, I came equipped with data about their situation: the percentage of draftees, percentage of those who become officers, and the percentage that drop out of military service. These statistics are a true mirror, rendering the standard tests unnecessary. I use them to identify strengths as well as weaknesses. Some of the youth do not understand the great privilege of living in a young, independent state after two thousand years of exile. Beyond the need to defend the state, they do not understand the meaning of the need to develop it and take responsibility for its future.

Some of the youth I've met are well acquainted with Israel. They have visited every corner of the country, as I did in my youth, mainly on youth movement trips. On the other hand, I've met other youth who never visited Jerusalem before they began their military service. They never participated in the "Sea to Sea" hike from the Mediterranean to the Sea of Galilee, they've never been to the Galilee region or the Negev, nor Mount Carmel or the Sharon Valley. I've met youth who are aware of the issue of Jewish ethical identity, because they have studied it in a youth movement, school, yeshiva, or pre-military program. But I've also met youth who have no knowledge of Jewish history or Zionism, and who never considered their ethical identity before induction.

One of the first times I encountered ignorance and lack of awareness on the question of Jewish roots was in the 1980s. When I was commander of Battalion 890, then stationed in Lebanon, I responded to a query from commander of the unit known as "Raful Youth" (Center for Promoting Special Populations) to check the request of ten young men to volunteer for the paratroopers. I realized that due to their disadvantaged socioeconomic and educational background, these youth had no chance of being accepted into the unit through the regular placement process. During one of my breaks on the way out of Lebanon, I passed by the Raful Youth unit in Givat Olga and met these youth. The motivation they demonstrated in our conversation convinced me to accept them into the battalion without the usual placement tests.

I instructed the company commander to watch them and help them, considering their low starting scores in comparison to the other soldiers. In case of a crisis that led to a request to leave, I told him not to permit them to do so before speaking with the platoon commander, the company commander, and myself.

Six of the ten volunteers completed full, successful service as combat soldiers in the battalion, while four left. The first of these four came to see me three weeks after the beginning of basic training. When I asked him why he had decided to leave the paratroopers, he quipped, "It's hard, sir!" I asked him what was hard. He said it was hard for him to get up early and leave his warm sleeping bag for the cold morning air, and hard to complete the five-mile (8 km) march for completion of basic training. I asked him if he'd been unaware that the paratroopers would be difficult, and why he had volunteered for it in the first place. His answer surprised me: "I volunteered for the paratroopers because my girlfriend said I'd look great in a red beret."

That conversation made me think of the expression "hydroponic." Before me sat a young Israeli who was "hydroponic" – rootless. He didn't know where he'd come from, he had no sense of identity. He lacked deep roots in the ground, and so he was blown off course by the slightest breeze – in this case the morning chill instead of the storm of battle, or a five-mile march instead of the true physical and emotional effort he'd have to face during service. This soldier was not at fault for his condition. He grew up in an environment that did not give him the roots that come from knowledge of Jewish heritage and history, and from exploring Jewish values and identity. He did not have the awareness or sense of obligation to defend the Jewish national home – an obligation that sometimes means sacrificing one's life.

I grew up with the values of David Ben-Gurion, Berl Katznelson, A. D. Gordon and later, Ze'ev Jabotinsky and Menachem Begin. Their Jewish ethical worldview upheld the sanctity of life and the principles of "love your neighbor as yourself," "do unto others," and "all Jews are responsible for one another." If our youth reach the military service without these values, they do not have the answer to the question of why they are sacrificing their lives on behalf of the State of Israel. For the red beret? To avoid embarrassment in front of their friends? The answer must come from a much deeper place.

I know where the strengths and weaknesses of the educational system lay, demographically as well. For example, I met the principal of a Bnei Akiva-style national religious school who told me what he has witnessed in the past decade. His educational staff has fought a process of radicalization among the students, but the battle has become impossible to win. If the students hear expressions of hatred from above – from Knesset members, ministers, and a prime minister who warns that the Arabs are flocking in droves to the voting booths – nothing will help. When politicians blame the Supreme Court and the "leftist media," how can we raise youth who respect the rule of law? When the youth hear that the government, the IDF, and the law enforcement system cannot be trusted, some decide to take the law into their own hands: they cut down olive trees, burn mosques, and even burn a family. I know it's hard to hear this, but I am aware that if there is no respect for the rule of law, "one person would eat the other alive," as written in Ethics of the Fathers (3:2).

The problem also lies with the curriculum. I am aware of all the reforms and changes, including the decision to give up history studies to tempt students in 150 attractive subjects for the matriculation exams. I received all the tools needed for life in the college prep program I completed in Kiryat Haim. At age forty when I attended Haifa University to complete my BA degree, the professor who helped me construct my program told me that as a graduate of Kiryat Haim in 1968, my background was equivalent to a BA degree from the university. I am confident we must focus on fundamentals. Good research has been conducted in this field, and the Dovrat Committee presented excellent recommendations, but to make this change we need a full-time education minister, not someone who pretends to address security but mainly deals in politics.

One of the main challenges in the education field is to raise the level of education among Arabs and ultra-Orthodox (*charedi*) Jews. Particularly in these sectors, we must bring people into the employment market. I believe that we cannot do anything by force. "Bearing an equal burden" is a nice slogan, but in the current Israeli reality it's difficult to ask the Arabs to join the IDF, and there is no certainty that the IDF will accept all of them. Instead, we must create an alternative of civil national service, like the system that was established in 2007. Today the demand for this track is greater than the number of positions.

The situation is more complex among the ultra-Orthodox, where the system is a closed circle. We have encouraged young ultra-Orthodox Jews to remain in yeshivas by giving them incentives. If every student enrolled in yeshiva means more budget allocations, of course the goal will be to increase the number of yeshiva students. Further, until recently, anyone who studied in a yeshiva and did not serve in the military was prohibited from working until age thirty-six, when he becomes exempt from military service. In fact, through legislation we have encouraged fictive enrollment in yeshiva and undeclared employment without paying taxes.

When the subject came up before the government, I said what I had said previously while in uniform: we cannot force a solution and solve the issue in one day through legislation and enforcement. If we attack the ultra-Orthodox with laws and punishment, none of them will serve. We must build tracks that will enable them to serve, like the Nahal Haredi Battalion, which was established in 1998 and which I accepted into service as GOC Central Command. These tracks must have appropriate conditions, without female soldiers, but without harming the opportunities for women to serve. Today, there are combat tracks in the Givati and Paratroopers Brigades, as well as tracks in technological units, and all view these as a positive development. The numbers speak for themselves: in the conscription year that ended in July 2016, over twenty-five hundred ultra-Orthodox men joined, compared to a mere eighty-nine that joined the first Nahal Haredi company. Some fifteen thousand ultra-Orthodox serve in the reserves.

During military service, these ultra-Orthodox acquire a profession – in the technological track or in appropriate training in the last year of combat service. As a result, some 90 percent of the ultra-Orthodox soldiers join the workforce following their release. All sides profit – they serve in the IDF, and they also earn a living, pay taxes, and do not need government assistance. The vicious cycle that keeps them in poverty is broken. This process can no longer be stopped. It proves that we don't need to be right, we need to be wise.

In academia as well, over twelve thousand ultra-Orthodox women and men are studying under special conditions. Still, more remains to be done. For example, we must ensure that the ultra-Orthodox community studies basic secular subjects. It is impossible to live in this world without knowledge of these subjects, which are the keys to life. If we do not work to integrate this group into the employment market by giving them tools in education, this could lead to the collapse of the economy, because when birth rates go up but the cycle of poverty stays in place, this creates a dangerous situation. On the other hand, an ultra-Orthodox Jew with secular knowledge who works will no longer be poor. He can live in a comfortable four-room apartment instead of two rooms, and even own a car. I hope that the trend of integrating the ultra-Orthodox into Israeli society will continue. We won't achieve this with political slogans, but rather by finding wise and sensitive solutions.

We must also work to integrate Arabs into Israeli society, without separation, in contrast to the position of the politicians who are supposed to represent them. There is a deep process of Israelization taking place within Arab Israeli society, which has minimized the power of the Islamic movement even before it was made illegal. This is a result of everyday life, or because they compare their situation to that of Arabs in Syria, Egypt, Iraq, Yemen, and Libya. Arab Israelis know that they have been lucky, and we must enable them to integrate. The solution is education, integration into employment, and service – whether military or civil-national. But instead of working toward solutions, politicians are busy with a discourse of hatred.

We must also speak in clear language about the State of Israel as the national home of the Jewish people, in which minorities enjoy equal rights. The minorities do not have to identify with the state, but they must respect it and its institutions, the national hymn and the flag. I do not expect Druze officers and soldiers to sing "the Jewish soul yearns" as part of the *national anthem, "Hatikvah,"* but they must respect it by standing at attention and saluting the flag, as they in fact do. Recently, Arab Israeli Knesset members have adopted disturbing practices, such as advising our enemies or waving flags of enemy entities. Ignoring these trends has created confusion in a large portion of the Arab Israeli population.

As chief of general staff, I paid consolation visits to the houses of three Arab Muslim families whose sons served in the IDF and were killed in the war against Hamas in Gaza. In the latest wave of terror attacks, individual terrorists from the Arab Israeli population participated. Most were from families mixed with Palestinians, but the discourse of hatred that has developed here has turned all of them into terrorists. How can we respond to the words of a Knesset member who declares that his wife won't give birth if there's an Arab woman in the room? From my point of view, this person is not a Jew, even if he wears a kippah. Judaism is not measured by the size of the kippah or observance of certain mitzvot. This principle follows the proscription of the ancient Sage, Rabbi Akiva: love your neighbor as yourself.

Prime Minister Netanyahu did not respond to the racist statement by the Knesset member, but when I lecture abroad, I must address it – because I don't know how to explain it. When I speak to Jewish communities abroad, I must criticize the radicalism that has spread in Israel. This process trickles down to the youth, and here leadership is required. But even in these cases, as in the Elor Azaria incident, the person who is supposed to lead is swayed by the "likes," the surveys, and base reflexes. He reinforces negative processes that endanger us as a society, even more than the external dangers posed by Iran, ISIS, Hamas, or Hezbollah.

In the economic arena as well, we have much work ahead of us. To the government's credit, in the macroeconomic field it can be proud of a correct stance on challenges and targets. Meeting targets for the deficit, inflation, and debt is an important achievement, but the positive effect does not trickle down. Instead, the gaps only increase. The number of poor people in Israel has increased and the middle class is being eroded. In the years when I was in government, each year ended with surpluses of billions in the budget. But instead of ensuring that this money reaches those in need – persons with disabilities, for example, who must make do with an allocation of $650 (2300 NIS) per month – the prime minister suggests a tax cut. This is a benefit for the "haves." Only after the disabled demonstrated and blocked roads was an agreement obtained to raise their allocations.

In the State of Israel, there are some 870,000 persons with disabilities. One of the national challenges is to fully integrate them into society without exclusion, discrimination, or segregation. As COGS and defense minister, I viewed their integration into the IDF as a national challenge. In the period between my departure from the IDF and entrance into politics, I volunteered to head Shekel (Community Services for People with Special Needs) a modest nonprofit organization that made full integration its goal.

During my military service, I became closely acquainted with the issue of the income gap between wealthy and poor. I observed soldiers who received the keys to a brand-new car as a gift to celebrate their induction, while others came from homes with empty refrigerators. How can a soldier who must help support his family serve in the Golani Brigade? These gaps also harm our national resilience. Chances are nil that a soldier who comes from a needy home will identify with Israeli society and feel a sense of obligation toward it. The IDF is involved in various social projects to extract these youth out of the vicious circle – such as the Magshimim program, which I initiated to bring cyber studies to the periphery.

I went into politics with the understanding that there are several classes within Israeli society and that the gaps between rich and poor are untenable, as well as the knowledge of how to handle these challenges. One of the main problems we must face is the erosion of the middle class. Income in the last decade has remained steady, but expenses per family have gone up: a young couple that spends $1400 (5000 NIS) per month on rent or a mortgage and another $1400 (5000 NIS) per month for two children in daycare cannot make it through the month and has no chance of saving. Many young couples cannot manage without their parents' help.

The solutions offered on the housing issue – no VAT and a tax on the third apartment – will not solve the problem. Everything is a matter of supply and demand, and if there is no supply but demand continues, then housing prices go up. Today there is a shortage of one hundred thousand housing units. Olmert pursued a policy of limiting development in the center of the state, so that people would move to the periphery. But employment opportunities on the periphery are limited. Development of workplaces in peripheral areas is an important part of the solution, but in the meantime, most of the workplaces are in the center, not in the Golan Heights. Youth are willing to pay more for housing in the center to be near their parents, who often give them the childcare help they need so they can go to work. The shortage of building in the center is a sure recipe for rising prices.

As defense minister, I said that until we increase the number of apartments, prices won't go down, and no other solutions would help. I suggested freeing up military bases in areas of high demand between Haifa and Ashdod: Tzrifin, Sde Dov, Ramat Gan, part of Tel Hashomer, Sirkin, and Givatayim. Construction could be carried out in these areas. I presented a plan stating that in exchange for $280 million (NIS one billion), I would begin to evacuate the bases and move them to new locations in the periphery. The IDF would gain a new base instead of an old one that has been around since British Mandate times, the periphery would profit, and the state would gain land that it could put on the market. This would enable construction in demanded areas and earn about $23 billion (NIS 80 billion) for the national coffers. The plan was given the green light after a two-year delay for various reasons, including politics, bureaucracy, and involvement of interest holders who wanted the prices to keep going up.

I suggested to the cabinet that we privatize Israel Military Industries and move the factories from Ramat Hasharon to Ramat Beka in the Negev. Between twenty to forty thousand housing units can be constructed in the area to be freed up, which will bring over $8.5 billion (NIS 30 billion) into the state's coffers. After privatization was concluded, the Finance Ministry asked that the Defense Ministry take responsibility for the planning and authorization process for the residential project. I agreed at once, but a minister in the cabinet objected. She stated, "Why on earth should the Defense Ministry be in charge of that? It's not an issue of security." I answered, "It most certainly is a security issue – to secure the option that it will be carried out." Indeed, this is the only part of the plan that has been carried out since then. Under Defense Ministry leadership, tens of thousands of housing units were authorized for construction, but since then the project has been stalled. Apparently, the Defense Ministry is the only entity that's serious about implementation. Whenever there's a plan that requires cooperation among ministries, it gets stuck.

The same happened with the "IDF Moves South" project for moving the training base center to southern Israel. I expected this project to be given national priority, but it also got stuck due to bureaucracy, politics, and corruption. I laid the cornerstone for the new city in the Negev in December 2004, when I was COGS, but I inaugurated it only when I became defense minister. The project could have been completed four years earlier. Such a complex project requires preparation in the fields of housing, education, transportation, and health, and cooperation among several government ministries. It must be led by the director of the prime minister's office. This was the case under Rabin and Sharon. Whenever there was a regional plan that required interministerial cooperation, the PMO director took all the ministry directors on a bus to the region, to verify proper implementation of the plan and to check what else had to be done. Today this doesn't happen. The current government does not have implementational ability, and the person in charge doesn't have his predecessor's ability to push the system around him into action – to go out to the field, supervise, and implement.

A plan designed to solve the problem of the Bedouins in the Negev also stalled due to various objections. This plan was headed by Minister Benny Begin in 2011, with the support of myself and Ehud Prawer from the prime minister's office. The plan proposed to regularize some of the settlements, and to move the Bedouins living in illegal dispersion to existing settlements. It would have provided them with housing, education, and employment. Some thought it wasn't right to give the Bedouins land, but we can't evacuate people from their homes without offering alternatives, even when their construction is illegal. This is true for the Arab sector as well: we cannot only carry out enforcement without offering an alternative. If there is no policy that directs from above, no solution, then people break the law out of distress.

But like many other plans, the government failed to implement this plan as well. When I feel that I have the knowledge, the solutions and the ability to lead – how can I go back home at this juncture?

In December 2018, Netanyahu announced the dissolving of the Knesset and called for elections. Elections were originally planned for November 2019, but they were moved up to April 9, 2019. To me, it was clear that advancing the election date was a result of the attorney general's decision to indict Netanyahu, pending a hearing, for cases 1000, 2000, and 4000, for bribery, fraud, and breach of trust. In this case, as in other incidents,

Netanyahu's attempt to avoid justice came at the expense of many other national interests.

The decision to hold early elections led me to declare the formation of a new party, Telem (acronym for "National Statesmanship Movement"). I realized that in order to become an alternative to the regime, I had to develop relationships with other political elements. Within a short time, I was able to connect to the new party of former chief of general staff Lieutenant General (Ret.) Benny Gantz, and soon we connected to the Yesh Atid Party under Yair Lapid. Former chief of general staff Lieutenant General (Ret.) Gabi Ashkenazi also joined, and together we created Blue and White Party, with Gantz as our leader.

The three former chiefs of general staff and former finance minister (and I was also a former defense minister) shared a sense of emergency, based on what we saw taking place before our very eyes in Israeli society. The four of us had worked with Netanyahu as prime minister. We shared a deep concern of the political and public discourse of hatred that Netanyahu was leading against entire sectors of Israeli society. This discourse divided between Jews and Arabs, right and left, Ashkenazi and Mizrachi, and religious and nonreligious. Each of us viewed the divisive discourse as an existential danger to the State of Israel.

In addition, we worried about the unbridled attack on the checks and balances of Israeli democracy. These include a free press; the rule of law with equality for all citizens; the status of law enforcement entities, particularly the Supreme Court; and the repression of government officials, who should be able to express their professional opinion without fear.

We established Blue and White after overcoming differences of opinion on many issues. We agreed that due to the state of emergency that endangered the future of the State of Israel, we would prioritize the issues and challenges that we would address. We agreed on a shared platform that reflects agreement on the majority issues (90 percent). For a minority (10 percent) of these issues, we agreed to disagree and to leave these for future handling, if and when they became relevant.

The success of the Blue and White Party in the April 2019 elections reflected the Israeli public's thirst for leadership that would "put Israel back on track." Ours would be an ethical leadership that led according to the compass of Jewish and democratic values, leadership that would serve the citizens and not itself.

Blue and White received an unprecedented vote of confidence from the Israeli public – thirty-five mandates. But despite this astounding achievement, Netanyahu had apparently made pre-election alliances with the ultra-Orthodox parties and with the radical religious Zionist party led by Betzalel Smotrich (who allied with Otzma Yehudit, another extremist party that followed the late Meir Kahane). Once again, Netanyahu proved that he was prepared to sacrifice Israel's future to ensure his political survival and to avoid legal proceedings.

Still, Netanyahu proved unable to form a coalition. Instead of returning his mandate to form a coalition to the president, he preferred to legally disperse the twenty-first Knesset, which had not yet begun to act. In this process as well, Netanyahu revealed his willingness to sacrifice the interests of the state to save himself from the court process. Within a very short time, we were facing yet another election.

The sense of emergency and responsibility for the future of the State of Israel continues to connect the members of the Blue and White list. We intend to reach a position of leadership, so that we can put Israel back on track and ensure its future.

My vision, which I have not abandoned and will not do so, is to construct an exemplary society based on three fundamental values. First is the sanctity of life – every human being is created in the divine image. Second is to love your neighbor as yourself – especially with regard to people different from you, without a discourse of hatred, without invalidation or delegitimization. Third is that all Jews are responsible for one another – mutual responsibility. This is the ethical basis. These are the values of a Jewish state in which the government is based on democratic values: the rule of law, checks and balances among authorities, freedom of expression, and so forth.

In the economic and social realm, we must continue a responsible policy with regard to microeconomics, but we must enable our achievements to trickle down. Socialism and communism have collapsed. Even the kibbutz movement understands that without competition, we do not have the ability to drive an economy in a serious manner. But capitalism cannot be greedy. The correct policy of competition and free market must be combined with compassion and welfare, so that at the end of the day, people who work can support themselves in a respectful manner, stay out of the red, and put some money in savings. The government must enable this to happen.

In the field of education, we must continue to nurture knowledge and excellence. But educating the spirit is no less essential. Education must include teaching Jewish values, recognizing the importance of defending the Jewish national home, and cultivating it so that it will truly be an exemplary society. By exemplary society, I mean one that is not only measured by material achievements but also by the values according to which it lives. This aspiration should be taught from a young age.

Part of the answer to the problem is material. The educational system will not be excellent if most of the people who choose to work in this field, aside from those few individuals who choose do so out of a sense of mission, do so mainly out of convenience or because they were not accepted into other areas of study. We must encourage people to choose the teaching profession out of a feeling of mission and excellence, and we must offer fair pay as a sign of society's appreciation.

I have faced this issue with regard to members of the regular army as well. If society does not think that a person who serves in the regular army must earn a decent living, it states that the defense issue is not important.

Similarly, if society does not think that a teacher must earn a decent salary, it essentially states that education is not important. Of course, if a teacher's salary goes up, the value of the profession will go up and it will no longer be considered a default. As I have explained, today the Education Ministry receives the largest budget. The question is whether the money remains at headquarters offices or reaches the teachers in the schools.

In parallel, we must encourage the activity of youth movements. Some assert humorously that today's largest youth movement is the movement of the hand on the cellphone, where everything is accessible and unfiltered. I spent my formative years in the youth movement, mainly as a counselor. I had to conduct value-based activities, and I took responsibility as part of the movement leadership. There are other channels for teaching values aside from the youth movements – it can be done at community centers with educational content, or in nonprofit organizations for military preparation. We must invest money in these activities and encourage them.

As stated above, I am in favor of a free market competitive economy, but the state must take responsibility for its citizens in the fields of internal and external security, education, health, welfare, and infrastructure. Today, the only field in which the state fulfills its responsibility toward its citizens is external security. In all other areas, part of the answer to the citizens' needs is given by private entities or third-sector entities (nonprofits and volunteers). The fact that a large portion of these services has been privatized causes the gap between rich and poor to increase. Those who have the ability to pay purchase better education for their children, shorten the line for an operation through private medical care, and even purchase security services when the state doesn't provide them. In this reality, the gap between wealthy and poor continues to grow. Equality of opportunity is critically harmed, and the sense of alienation from the state felt by the underprivileged expands.

To meet these tasks and obligations, the government must broaden civil expenditure. In our economic state, we can do this by allotting some $42 billion (NIS 150 billion) for ten years, even if it means changing the deficit target by 1 percent per year. In addition, it is imperative to prepare a multi-year plan for ten years, in each field. The fact that most of the government ministries do not have a long-term plan is untenable! In the field of health, for example, if we do not have a plan for the next decade that defines the target for the number of beds based on the population, and the number of physicians, nurses, and other professionals per the population, the level of service to the citizen will go down, as it has in past years while the population has grown. The same is true in every field.

In the field of education, we must aspire to free education from daycare age through the first degree, so that the child's education level will not be dependent on the parents' economic status.

But nothing will work without worthy leadership. The proper combination is education that pushes from the bottom up and leadership that leads from the top down. Leadership that sets a personal example will result in a different scale of values, stop the ethical decline and radicalization, and change the order of priorities. Leadership that believes in the vision of the State of Israel as a democratic Jewish state that is secure, flourishing, and just.

I am encouraged by the youth that I meet. In the pre-military academies, I discover youth that cares and is thirsty to take responsibility. But it is also frustrated and disappointed by what it sees in politics. When the youth read in the media about politicians who were elected to lead, but whose priorities and value scale got mixed up, then they ask probing questions.

People often ask me whether I'm too pessimistic. They ask whether my concept of reality is too cold, or whether I'm dreaming of something that is impossible to achieve. The answer is definitely not! I am optimistic and I see a chance for a better society. I have no doubt that we can rehabilitate. A different composition of people in national leadership will lead to change. I saw this in the IDF. When a new, worthy commander was brought to a failing unit, it was able to stand on its feet. When I was brought to Battalion 890 after the previous commander was dismissed, the battalion became the outstanding one in the brigade. I was called from abroad to lead Sayeret Matkal after operational failures, and I led it to a period of thriving and victory that is still considered one of its peak periods. In my view, the human component is the determining factor. The question is, who is the leader and who are the people that he appoints? Do they lack backbone and remain loyal only to him, or are they loyal to their profession, to the values of society and state? If they are loyal to a politician, this is the process of corruption that harms every area of the state.

I am a Jew, an Israeli, and a Zionist. I believe in the hidden powers of this people and this state. I think that the Zionist project is a just historical project that has succeeded and has a rosy future. But I refuse to bury my head in the sand and to remain blind to the dangers facing us. I believe that only if we see the true reality, can we find within us the strengths we need to face the challenges that it poses us. Only then will we be able to navigate our path in "bravery, wisdom, and purity," as Ben-Gurion said.

In over one hundred years of Zionism and seventy years of independence, we have proven the hidden strengths of the Jewish people. These strengths are based on human spirit and knowledge, not on natural resources or other physical advantages. These strengths still exist today, but they need nurturing through education and leadership.

The coming years will not be easy. As opposed to the false promises that we've heard, the comprehensive peace that we hoped for in the 1990s will not arrive anytime soon. On the other hand, we need not fear an imminent holocaust. To meet the challenges facing us, we must start to tell the truth. With full understanding for the need for hope, we must not feed the public with false hopes. True hope must be based on true words. I believe that if we do not delude ourselves, if we do not lead our citizens astray and frighten ourselves for no reason, we will be able to meet the challenges that we are facing. We did this during the pre-state period, during the War of Independence and in the early decades of the state. There is no reason we shouldn't be able to do so now, when our physical state is immeasurably better.

But to do so, we must put the various golden calves behind us. We must detach ourselves from the culture of spin and lies. We must make difficult decisions in an educated, practical manner. We must return to our basic values as Jews, as Israelis and as Zionists. We must recognize our strengths as well as our weaknesses. We must be proud of the achievements of the Jewish people, of Zionism, and its realization in the State of Israel. But we must prepare and act to face the challenges of the present and the future.

We need a new strategy for the State of Israel and Zionism, based on clarity instead of obfuscation, on decisiveness instead of hesitation, clear understanding of challenges instead of illusions, and on ethical clarity instead of corruption. We need a vision and path that will inspire the citizens of Israel and Jews around the world, particularly the younger generation, to want to participate in the Zionist project and its realization in the State of Israel.

To a large degree, Israel has gone off track. We must put it back on track. In summary, the key is leadership that presents a vision and a path, and ethical education that strengthens the belief in that path and its justness. The key is leadership that pulls from the top downward, and education that pushes from the bottom upward.

It's a long path. But in the end, the longer path is the shorter one.

Index